and Modern Cultu

THE

MAKING

OF A

LEGEND

OSCAR WILDE

and Modern Culture

EDITED BY JOSEPH BRISTOW

OHIO UNIVERSITY PRESS

Athens, Ohio

Ohio University Press, Athens, Ohio 45701

www.ohioswallow.com

© 2008 by Ohio University Press

All rights reserved

To obtain permission to quote, reprint, or otherwise reproduce or
distribute material from Ohio University Press publications, please contact our
rights and permissions department at (740) 593-1154 or (740) 593-4536 (fax).

Printed in the United States of America

Ohio University Press books are printed on acid-free paper ⊗ ™

15 14 13 12 11 10 09 08   5 4 3 2 1

Library of Congress Cataloging-in-Publication Data

Oscar Wilde and modern culture : the making of a legend / edited by Joseph Bristow.

   p. cm.

Includes bibliographical references and index.

ISBN 978-0-8214-1837-6 (alk. paper) — ISBN 978-0-8214-1838-3 (pbk. : alk. paper)

1. Wilde, Oscar, 1854–1900—Influence. 2. Wilde, Oscar, 1854–1900—Criticism and interpretation.

3. Homosexuality and literature—Great Britain—History—19th century. I. Bristow, Joseph.

PR5824O85 2008

828'.809—dc22

2008039566

Contents

Illustrations

Preface

THE CHAPTERS IN *Oscar Wilde and Modern Culture* share one aim: they seek to reveal how and why a gifted Irish author who experienced varying kinds of fame, notoriety, and shame across the course of his twenty-five-year career would claim greater and greater attention from successive generations of writers, critics, composers, dancers, filmmakers, and performers throughout the late nineteenth, twentieth, and early twenty-first centuries. As I point out in the introduction, the depressing circumstances surrounding Oscar Wilde's early death at the age of forty-six hardly suggested that within a matter of decades he would become one of the most valued literary influences on the modern world. After his reputation collapsed on 25 May 1895, when he was sent to jail for two years in solitary confinement with hard labor for committing acts of "gross indecency" with other men, he seemed fated to be consigned to perpetual obscurity.

On Wilde's release from his brutalizing sentence in 1897, his character was so besmirched and his spirit so demoralized that he deserted Britain, moving around France and Italy under a carefully chosen incognito, "Sebastian Melmoth," the two parts of which allude to the early Christian martyr murdered by Diocletian, on the one hand, and the nomadic protagonist of his great-uncle's gothic romance, *Melmoth the Wanderer* (1820), on the other hand. The silence that muffled the remaining three and a half years of his existence was so deafening that he decided to publish his final work, *The Ballad of Reading Gaol* (1898), initially not under his name but using the number of his prison cell, "C.3.3." Only when thousands of readers had bought copies of this poem, whose protests against an unjust prison system proved an instant runaway success, could Wilde recover some dignity by disclosing his authorial identity in the seventh edition, which came out a year before his death. Despite his disappearance into exile, and thus into anonymity, there nonetheless remained a substantial audience that still wanted to read him, albeit more for the punishment he had suffered than for the pleasure they derived from the sparkling comedies that had wowed the London stage during the years before his downfall. The *Ballad* kept the widely reviled author very much in the public's consciousness in the months leading up to his demise from meningitis on 30 November 1900.

The complicated rehabilitation of Wilde—a figure whose experiences of fame were seldom distant from perilous infamy—arguably began with the stir created by the *Ballad*. But other developments, including Richard Strauss's 1905 opera based on Wilde's play *Salomé,* also ensured that neither his legacy nor his memory would be lost. Even though Wilde was laid to rest after a modest funeral at the suburban Bagneux Cemetery on the outskirts of Paris, some eight years later the talented American sculptor Jacob Epstein took up the challenging commission of designing a tomb in honor of a man to whom the world was belatedly paying its respects. Epstein's monument (erected at Père Lachaise, Paris, in September 1912) is a fine example of early modernist sculpture, but like many other phenomena linked with Wilde's reputation, it would remain a source of controversy. The sculptor's striking male sphinx, inspired by Wilde's 1894 poem dedicated to that mythical being, featured noticeably protruding genitals. At an early stage, the offending organs of this exuberant creature—which looks as if it is about to rush headlong through the air—were covered by a bronze *cache-sexe* that Wilde's literary executor, Robert Ross, arranged at the request of the cemetery managers after the police had insisted that the tomb should be covered in tarpaulin. (The monument was not unveiled for another two years.) The metallic decoration was soon vandalized. Much later, in 1961, the genitals suffered the same fate, as Michael Pennington points out in his history of the tomb (*An Angel for a Martyr: Jacob Epstein's Tomb for Oscar Wilde* [Reading: Whiteknights Press, 1987]). The sculpture remained castrated until 2000, when artist Leon Johnson commissioned silversmith Rebecca Scheer to create the prosthesis that he duly affixed that year in a ceremony titled, appropriately enough, "Re-Membering Wilde." Epstein's visually arresting monument has attracted thousands of homosexual tourists, some of whom have declared their love by entwining their names in graffiti carved into the tombstone.

The desire to memorialize Wilde—to pay one's proper respects to him, especially by acknowledging the wrongfulness of his prison sentence—began some time before Epstein's tomb became accessible to the public. Between 1902 and 1912, at least five biographical studies (all uneven in quality) reached a growing audience, and in 1908 Ross arranged with leading publisher Methuen the issue of an excellent, reliable fourteen-volume *édition de luxe* of Wilde's collected works. A steady stream of memoirs containing tributes to Wilde continued to flow into the 1930s (as did some hostile retrospectives by his enemies), by which time comparatively more reliable full-length studies of his career—particularly Léon Lemonnier's 1931 biography—had come into circulation. In 1936, Lloyd Lewis and Henry Justin Smith published their exceptionally well documented *Oscar Wilde Discovers America,* an engaging study that has enjoyed far-reaching influence on many later works, including Brian Gilbert's film *Wilde* (1997). By the late 1940s, H. Montgomery Hyde had edited the derivative but first popular study of the three trials that Wilde endured in 1895. In 1949, Wilde's surviving son, Vyvyan Holland, published a full-length version of the lengthy autobiographical document that Ross in 1905 had edited in a much-truncated form (and had taken the liberty of calling, on the advice of his publishers, *De Profundis*). Wilde completed this 55,000-word masterpiece of prose in jail with a different title in mind (he wished to call this substantial document "Epistola: In Carcere et Vinculis" [Letter: In Prison and in Chains]). This complete edition of the "Epistola," which Wilde addressed to his lover, Alfred Douglas, for the first time revealed the extent of Wilde's irritation with the young aristocrat's reckless behavior in the lead-up to the trials. The fact that Douglas (who went to great lengths, often in court, to protect his reputation after Wilde's demise) passed away in 1945 created an atmosphere in which the more sensitive aspects of the Irish writer's life could be discussed more freely.

In 1954, the centenary of Wilde's birth, Vyvyan Holland issued a touching memoir titled *Son of Oscar Wilde* that presents an inspiring picture of a father who remained devoted to the children he was barred from seeing after his prison sentence began. In the early 1960s, the appearance of Rupert Hart-Davis's magnificent *Letters of Oscar Wilde* provided insights that gave a comprehensive picture of a writer whose literary achievements ranged well beyond his dazzling society comedies and his writings urging penal reform. Hart-Davis's volume, more than any other study that had previously been dedicated to Wilde, divulged a substantial amount of information that created much of the backbone of what remains the definitive biography: Richard Ellmann's *Oscar Wilde,* which first appeared in Britain in 1987. Ellmann's findings, despite including many smaller and larger inaccuracies, constitute a biography that is warmly humanist in tone, unembarrassed when discussing sexual matters, and filled with materials gleaned from archives. An indubitably major work, Ellmann's book inspired a fresh generation of literary historians and cultural practitioners to write in an informed manner on a man whom Ellmann believed was "one of us"—modern to the core (*Oscar Wilde* [New York: Knopf, 1988], xvii).

Even if some critics contend that Wilde's seemingly avant-garde tendencies exhibit more of their late-Victorian cast than we might care to imagine, it is fair to state that as the new century unfolded, the modern world began to advance the view that Wilde's unique creative powers were in many ways ahead of their time. Although he expired a month before the beginning of the century that eagerly embraced his controversial legacy, Wilde's achievements—ones that regularly unsettled some of his more conservative-minded contemporaries—would prove to be sources of inspiration for such diverse developments as franker depictions of marital discord on the English stage, campaigns for homosexual rights, the emergence of the culture of celebrity, critical methodologies that champion "the birth of the reader," and modern obsessions with the figure of the beautiful, though fatal, young man.

Everywhere we look in Wilde's writings—especially in light of the life he led as a dazzling talker who learned at an early stage how to embody a memorably iconic style—we can detect the fin-de-siècle origins of post-1900 fascinations with dissident sexuality, critiques of the patriarchal family, the creative spirit of criticism, and the callous mindlessness of the British prison system. Over time, Wilde has become a figure upheld for his distinctly oppositional qualities—as an Irishman who at times felt decidedly at odds with an English literary culture to which he never fully belonged, as a man martyred for his sexual intimacy with other men, and as a maverick who refined his unrivaled wit through epigrams that turn received wisdom on its head. (At times, however, scholars have paid welcome attention to some of his far-from-radical activities, such as his betrayal of the Dreyfusards in 1898 and his support for the jingoistic Anglo-Boer War the following year.) There is no question that in the academic universe, Wilde has recently been viewed as the late-nineteenth-century progenitor of styles of materialist, postmodern, and queer criticism, each of which has made him stand, in Linda Dowling's words, "perhaps more than any other Victorian . . . in symbolic relation at least to our own age" (Oscar Wilde, *The Soul of Man under Socialism and Selected Critical Prose*, ed. Linda Dowling [Harmondsworth, UK: Penguin, 2002], viii). In her introduction to the 2002 Penguin edition of Wilde's critical essays (a fine volume that testifies to Wilde's assured place in the literary canon), Dowling points somewhat skeptically to how "[h]e has been portrayed as a critic of commodity capitalism, as a professional writer struggling to overcome the gritty material conditions imposed by Grub Street, and as an early postmodern exponent of irony, plagiarism and pastiche" (viii). Her intention,

Preface

she says, is to reclaim Wilde as a "philosophical spokesman for the autonomy of art" (viii–ix): a thinker, in other words, who had a highly developed sense of why the guiding aestheticist principle of *l'art pour l'art* commanded such influence during the fin de siècle.

While it is difficult to dissent from Dowling's view that Wilde remains a serious thinker in his own right, there is no doubt that the ever-amassing adaptations, appropriations, and depictions of Wilde's life and works raise pressing questions about why he has come to matter so much to the "us" that for Ellmann characterizes modernity. In a sense, the various versions of Wilde that we find, say, in Ellmann's biography, recent stage representations of Wilde, and the advent of queer theory converge on one point: the insubordinately witty, eminently stylish Irishman was a harbinger of what "we" have apparently become. At present, there seems to be no end in sight to Wilde's enduring attractiveness to our contemporary world. Duncan Roy's 2006 independent film that locates *The Picture of Dorian Gray* in our own historical setting is a case in point, and the impending production of Bruce Beresford's *A Woman of No Importance*, which reveals Hollywood's ongoing interest in Wilde, is another. In early 2008 Gyles Brandreth published *Oscar Wilde and a Death of No Importance*, a celebrity murder mystery in which the protagonist leads the reader through the homosexual underworld of 1890s London. Meanwhile, at auction houses, Wilde's manuscripts fetch higher prices than do those of any modern author. At the same time, the amount of scholarly activity devoted to Wilde has intensified as never before. The very fact that the present volume exists bears witness to the academic fascination with the seemingly mesmerizing power that Wilde holds, and most probably will continue to hold, over modern—if not postmodern—culture.

Many of the chapters contained in *Oscar Wilde and Modern Culture* examine the ways in which radical writers, political campaigners, experimental artists, and risk-taking dramatists addressed aspects of Wilde's legacy not long after his turn-of-the-century death. The first three chapters, however, focus attention on Wilde's astute engagement with several modern developments in fin-de-siècle society. In chapter 1, Lucy McDiarmid addresses Wilde's intimate knowledge of the ways in which late-Victorian political life was increasingly shaped by the semipublic, partly private realm of upper-class table-talk of the 1880s and 1890s: a period in which, as Lord Illingworth declares in *A Woman of No Importance* (1893), one can survive only if one knows what it means to be "modern." This dastardly dandy makes plain to the young man named Gerald (who has no inkling that he is Illingworth's illegitimate son) that to be modern scarcely entails following the example of a mother who is "always going to church" (*Collected Works*, ed. Robert Ross, 14 vols. [London: Methuen, 1908], 4:109; cited as *CW* throughout the present volume). "You want to be modern, don't you, Gerald?" Illingworth asks this ingénue. "You want to know what life really is?" "Well," Illingworth continues, "what you have to do at present is simply to fit yourself for the best society" (*CW*, 4:109).

As McDiarmid shows, Wilde sought to thrive in the eminent dinner-party set in which Illingworth believed modern power circulated, though Wilde did so at his peril. The son of a knighted Irishman (one of the greatest eye surgeons of his day), Wilde moved among members of English Society (as the "upper ten thousand" was frequently known in the 1890s), including aristocrats such as Wilfrid Scawen Blunt, Lady Archibald Campbell, the Honorable George Curzon, Lord Ronald Sutherland-Gower, and Lord Alfred Douglas, who became intimate with Wilde in the summer of 1892. Wilde knew this upper-crust milieu very well, and several of his society comedies cleverly depict its double standards and its political inveigling. But as McDiarmid reveals, this new type of power brokering, which took place in the chitchat exchanged between the pudding and the port, could rebound on those individuals, such as Wilde, who entranced many of their listeners with spirited table-talk.

Blunt, an English aristocrat and agitator for Irish Home Rule, wrote a volume of poems on his political imprisonment titled *In Vinculis* (1889) that influenced parts of *The Ballad of Reading Gaol.* As McDiarmid shows, Blunt could never forget the hideous irony of what occurred some ten months after July 1894 when Wilde—a brilliant raconteur—had been gently mocking his dinner-party host, Herbert Asquith: a man whose political career was in the ascendant. By the spring of 1895, Asquith had become home secretary; while holding this high-ranking post, Asquith laid the criminal charge against Wilde that resulted in the callous two-year prison sentence. One might add that Wilde's precarious relations with Society are also borne out by the fact that the person to whom he dedicated his short story "The Star-Child" (1891), Margot Tennant, would long after Wilde's death dishonor his memory. Two months before Wilde attended the dinner at Asquith's home, Margot Tennant married the politician who would in 1908 become prime minister. In 1933, when she and her husband looked back on their long, much-publicized careers, she went into print recalling her earliest encounter with Wilde in 1888, when she met him through the fashionable aristocrat Lady Campbell. From the outset, she says, "the artificiality of his nature was . . . alien to my own," and she adds that this factitiousness was so extreme that, when all was said and done, there "was *no* Oscar Wilde—he was not a human being" (Margot Asquith, *More Memories* [London: Cassell, 1930], 117, 120). Perhaps the only grace that saves the Asquiths' attitude toward Wilde came nineteen years later in the much-appreciated form of their son Anthony's 1952 film adaptation of *The Importance of Being Earnest* (1895), which features some of the finest performances of Wilde's works ever witnessed, including Edith Evans's cherished rendition of Lady Bracknell's horrified reaction to the idea that Jack Worthing was born in a handbag.

In chapter 2, Daniel A. Novak directs our attention to Wilde's connections with the eminently modern technology of photography. Not long after he graduated with a Double First in *literæ humaniores* from Oxford and moved to a fashionable part of London, Wilde modeled himself as a "professor of aesthetics": a self-appointed role that soon made him the best candidate to undertake the year-long lecture-tour that would help Richard D'Oyly Carte promote the North American production of W. S. Gilbert and Arthur Sullivan's satire on the aesthetic movement, entitled *Patience,* which enjoyed a long run in London for much of 1881. Some of the most cherished pictures of Wilde date from the time when he posed in carefully stylized aesthetic garb (which he modeled in part on Freemasons' ceremonial dress) at the studio of Napoleon Sarony in New York at the start of 1882. Sarony's photographs—there were twenty-seven poses in all—were available for sale, in three different sizes, at venues where Wilde instructed American and Canadian audiences on the finer points of such topics as the English renaissance of art and the house beautiful. Sarony's celebrity photographs, which capture Wilde's embodied aestheticism more fully than any other images of the time, remain familiar to us even to this day, as they turn up on book jackets, on posters, and on greeting cards that celebrate Wilde's legendary wit.

Novak's contention is that this well-known feature of Wilde's much-discussed entrance into American culture has seldom been linked with aspects of photographic posing that have many telling implications for Wilde's aesthetics. For a distinctly modern studio photographer such as Sarony, the sitter had no rights over how he or she was posed. As a consequence, when Sarony sued a lithographic company for reproducing one of his images of Wilde without permission, it became clear that the question of who owned the image had no relevance to the young Irishman, who devised the outfits, as well as the hairstyle, in which he had been shot. Instead, Sarony's manipulation of the photographic negative provided the ground that established the belief that he, not Wilde, had authored the image at the center of this legal dispute. Novak shows that this debate about the ownership of the modern photographic pose elucidates a noticeable pattern in Wilde's thinking on the ways in which art, in an era increasingly dominated by this newfangled technology, represents bodily likeness.

Erin Williams Hyman, in the third chapter, addresses an area of Wilde's engagement with fin-de-siècle politics that modern scholarship has seldom researched in depth. Although several critical studies dating back as far as George Woodcock's *Paradox of Oscar Wilde* (1949) have associated the author's political inclinations with types of anarchism, comparatively few inquiries have explored in detail the connections that Wilde made in the early 1890s with important symbolist writers based in Paris, such as Stuart Merrill and Marcel Schwob, who were closely linked with the *Mercure de France:* the journal that featured defenses of anarchist insurgency in France. (It was in the *Mercure de France* that Douglas intended to protest his lover's incarceration in an article that included some of Wilde's letters to him. Once the imprisoned Wilde learned of Douglas's plan, he put a stop to it.) Likewise, as Hyman discloses, other well-known journals associated with anarchist politics, such as the *Revue blanche* (in which, in 1896, Douglas remonstrated against Wilde's imprisonment), were prompt to condemn Wilde's two-year jail sentence. Moreover, French author Octave Mirbeau, who never ceased to voice his support for the anarchist cause, remained outraged at the injustice of Wilde's solitary confinement. Yet the most powerful, if rarely acknowledged, tie that binds Parisian anarchist circles and Wilde relates to the first stage production of the biblical revenge tragedy *Salomé*. This work, which Wilde wrote in French in 1892, was originally intended for performance in London with the famed French tragedienne Sarah Bernhardt in the leading role. (The British state censor banned the London production, partly on the grounds that the law regulating the theater had since the time of the Tudors forbidden depictions of biblical characters on stage.) In February 1896, almost halfway through Wilde's prison sentence, François-Aurélian Lugné-Poe's avant-garde Théâtre de l'Œuvre opened its production of Wilde's drama in an act of solidarity with the prisoner. But as Lugné-Poe recognized, the decision to stage *Salomé* had to steal upon the theatergoing audience as a surprise, since he knew that his theater company might experience reprisals if this implicitly defiant production had too much advance publicity. Noticeably, the Parisian revolutionaries who sought to champion Wilde did so in the face of considerable opposition, and Merrill's efforts to raise a petition for Wilde's release failed—just as George Bernard Shaw's similar attempts in Britain foundered.

Richard A. Kaye, in a critical assessment of how and why homophile commentators during the early 1900s depicted Wilde as a modern saint, pays close attention to the links that the Irish writer established at an early stage of his career between male same-sex desire and martyrdom. As Kaye reminds us in chapter 4, Wilde's first published essay, which appeared in the *Irish Review* in 1877, is titled "The Tomb of Keats," and it contains a sonnet in which the speaker eroticizes the young Romantic poet by comparing his graceful body to Renaissance painter Guido Reni's St. Sebastian: the early Christian martyr whose exquisite flesh is pierced in two places by arrows—ones that appear miraculously to draw no blood. By referencing St. Sebastian as a homoerotic icon in the 1870s, Wilde was in part following a trend begun a little earlier by John Addington Symonds, whose prose writings often furnished Wilde with a rich supply of information for his homoerotically inflected works, including "The Portrait of Mr. W.H." and *The Picture of Dorian Gray* (both of which stirred up controversy in their time). To be sure, some of Wilde's writings, such as "The Grave of Keats," invest homosexual desire in protagonists whose youthful masculinity is closely connected with tragedy. But as Kaye discloses, there is considerable irony in the idea—one developed almost immediately after Wilde's demise—that the Irish author deliberately expressed errant desires that necessarily sealed his fate. Even Hugo von Hofmannsthal, who in 1902 recognized how misled his contemporaries were when they sought to uphold Wilde as a modern saint, could not let go of the belief that through the trials of 1895 the Irishman underwent what amounted to the type of ritualized death that anthropologists had witnessed among island peoples.

Kaye reveals that for French writers such as Mirbeau (whose 1890s fictions appear to be in dialogue with *The Picture of Dorian Gray*), the image of Wilde as the haloed apostle of aestheticism informs the character of Sir Harry Kimberly in Mirbeau's 1900 *Le journal d'une femme de chambre* (Diary of a Chambermaid). In Mirbeau's novel, it is Kimberly, "whose look and gestures, and even the orchid that adorned the buttonhole of his coat," who "expressed the most ardent ecstasy," and it is he whose dinner-party "stories of transgression and of extraordinary sensations . . . filled women with mad enthusiasm" (*Diary of a Chambermaid,* trans. Anon. [New York: Harper Perennial, 2006], 199, 200). Kaye proceeds to show how the belief that the entrancing Wilde commanded disciples, this time of a whole community of sexual dissidents, is central to the extravagant sentence that Marcel Proust devised in *Sodom et Gomorrhe* (1921–22). This image underwent many permutations as the decades rolled by. By the time we reach Terry Eagleton's play *Saint Oscar* (1989), Wilde has been transformed into a sexually obsessed queer martyr. Had he adhered to his radical politics, Eagleton suggests, Wilde would have become a saint for an Ireland—one struggling for Home Rule—whose nationalist ideals the homosexual aesthete appears to have betrayed. In Kaye's view, if modern readers continue to view Wilde as a sexual outcast who could not control his destructive desires, then his legacy will remain mystified by the belief that he was—albeit in purely secular terms—a homosexual martyr.

In the fifth chapter, Yvonne Ivory shows that the European country that arguably took up Wilde's cause more emphatically than any other was Germany: a nation that for Wilde held few attractions. Through Max Meyerfeld's translations and editorial work, Germany had the good fortune to see the first edition of *De Profundis* appear in print. Likewise, Meyerfeld's labors inspired Richard Strauss to devise his opera based on *Salomé*. As Ivory points out, however, *De Profundis* and *Salomé* were not the only works by Wilde that excited German-language audiences in the first decade of the twentieth century. Practically everything he had published in single volumes promptly appeared in German-language editions, including the comparatively little-known revenge drama *A Florentine Tragedy,* which remained unfinished at the time of his death. (The play, which was completed by T. Sturge Moore, had its first stage performance in London in 1906. The work inspired Austrian composer Alexander von Zemlinsky's *Eine florentinische Tragödie* [1914–16], with a libretto by Meyerfeld. In the early 1920s, Zemlinsky completed another opera, *Der Zwerg,* based on Wilde's short story "The Birthday of the Infanta" [1889]. Much earlier, in 1908, Zemlinsky's compatriot Franz Schreker had premiered an orchestral piece that adapts the same narrative.) One of the key German translators of Wilde's writings was Hermann Freiherr von Teschenberg, a prominent homophile campaigner who was active in Magnus Hirschfeld's Scientific-Humanitarian Committee, which lobbied for the repeal of Paragraph 175 (the law that prohibited homosexual relations in Imperial Germany). As one might expect, Wilde's writings became crucial points of reference for subscribers to the committee's *Jahrbuch,* as well as to the readers of Adolf Brand's *Der Eigene* (a journal dedicated to championing chaste homosexual love), who used Wildean names when making donations to these organizations or placing advertisements for lodgings. But as Ivory makes clear, the contributors to Brand's periodical were more often than not hostile to what they saw as Wilde's narcissistic individualism. In other words, in early twentieth-century Germany, Wilde's legacy accentuated a flashpoint between the competing politics of the libertarian sexuality propounded by Hirschfeld's followers, on the one hand, and the romantically inclined chastity espoused by the group that adhered to Brand, on the other hand.

In chapter 6, Julie Townsend examines both the nineteenth-century literary ancestry and the twentieth-century choreographic legacy of *Salomé:* the highly stylized French-language play that established Wilde's reputation in continental Europe. As Townsend points out, the project of Wilde's biblical tragedy owes much to a distinguished genealogy of nondramatic French writings that include Gustave Flaubert's *Salammbô* (1862), Stéphane Mallarmé's "Hérodiade" (1864, revised 1867), and J.-K. Huysmans's *À rebours* (1884). Townsend maintains, however, that while scholarship dedicated to Wilde's one-act tragedy readily acknowledges Wilde's debts to these influences, the fact that Wilde's drama obviously draws plentifully on these sources—ones linked with the French avant-garde—should not give the impression that his depiction of the daughter of Herodias, who tries to dominate over her stepfather Herod's desires (only to be murdered by him), is a wholly derivative work. Neither does it make sense to try to champion the creative originality of Wilde's drama by detaching the play from this all-too-evident literary lineage. Instead, Wilde's dramatic representation of Salomé forms a critical dialogue with those French antecedents that seek to make this biblical character into an inscrutable, if highly eroticized, aesthetic icon—one whose dancing body is increasingly abstracted from narrative structures and historical contexts that would lend intelligibility to this young woman's outlandish actions. Whereas Flaubert, Mallarmé, and Huysmans concentrated in turn on Salomé as a figure who confounds conventional assumptions about literary interpretation, Wilde placed Salomé at the center of a cast of characters attending Herod's court, where they articulate frequently disconnected and strikingly figurative dialogues that reiterate their difficulties in reading the world around them. It would be left to Loïe Fuller—the Paris-based American choreographer credited with inventing modern dance in the early 1890s—to recast Salomé as an erotically powerful protagonist who need not die at the hands of the stepfather whose sexual desires she frustrates. In Fuller's 1907 *Tragédie de Salomé,* her tumultuous performance, celebrated for its immensely innovative use of lighting, triggers nothing less than an earthquake that results in the heroine's death.

Filmmaker Lizzie Thynne, in chapter 7, travels further into French cultural history of the twentieth century by focusing on the work of lesbian surrealist Claude Cahun (born Lucy Schwob). Cahun's long-lasting engagement with Wilde's legacy owed much to his association with her uncle, Marcel Schwob; in the 1890s, Cahun's relative, like Pierre Louÿs, assisted Wilde in drafting the French script of *Salomé*. To some degree, Cahun followed in her uncle's footsteps by publishing some of her earliest writings in *Mercure de France* and by engaging with the impact that Wilde's *Salomé* had on European culture. Thynne's interest lies in the ways in which both Wilde's antirealist works and his dandyish style became noteworthy points of reference in Cahun's journalism, fiction, and photographic autoportraiture (which Cahun developed with her partner, Suzanne Malherbe—who produced art under the name of Marcel Moore). At least one of the self-portraits that Cahun devised with Moore in the early 1920s was modeled on the famous shots of Wilde taken by Sarony in 1882. In 1918, Cahun reported on the widely publicized libel suit that Canadian dancer Maud Allan brought against Independent MP Noel Pemberton Billing after he published an offensive article, titled "The Cult of the Clitoris," in which he declared that the audience members who attended Allan's private dramatic performance of the English-language version of *Salome* in London were among the "47,000 perverts" whose names were kept in the "black book" held by the German enemy. Allan's suit, which occupied many column inches in the press, took place during the final year of World War I, and it served as an occasion to reactivate much of the hostility that had surrounded the Wilde trials twenty-three years before.

In the 1920s and 1930s, Cahun returned to Wilde's *Salomé* on two further occasions. In her 1925 novella "Salomé the Skeptic," she looks satirically at how the long line of male writers figured this character as an aesthetic embodiment of uncontrollable lust. In some ways comparable to Loïe Fuller's 1907 performance, Cahun's narrative revises nineteenth-century renditions of the biblical story by indicating that Salomé's desires are not aimed at John the Baptist. Instead, her story in part explores how the decapitation of the prophet evokes psychoanalytic understandings of the castration complex. In her autobiographical work *Cancelled Confessions* (1930), Cahun once again invokes Salomé's voice, this time seeking corporeal alternatives to the Freudian belief that the phallus is the primary marker around which concepts of sexual difference are organized.

Back in Britain in the early decades of the twentieth century, as Laurel Brake discusses in chapter 8, Wilde's legacy became particularly visible in noteworthy dramatic works by W. Somerset Maugham. Seldom have scholars recognized that Maugham's *Penelope* (1909) and, more important, *The Constant Wife* (1926)—a play that has recently enjoyed revivals on both sides of the Atlantic—comprise sexual-political dialogues with two of Wilde's dramas: *An Ideal Husband* (1895) and the less well known *Mr. and Mrs. Daventry* (1900), for which Wilde wrote the scenario that his close associate Frank Harris turned into a full-fledged play. (*Mr. and Mrs. Daventry*, which opened shortly before Wilde's demise, had a fairly successful run.) Brake's powerful thesis reveals that Maugham's dramas modernize a debate about the need for sexual equality in marriage that Wilde elaborated in all of his society comedies, especially *An Ideal Husband*. In his 1895 drama, Wilde explores, among other things, the corrupt political past of the outwardly blameless Sir Robert Chiltern, whose spouse, Gertrude, has long believed him to be the ideal husband of the title. But when the drama exposes the fact that in his youth Sir Robert sold state secrets to the late Baron Arnheim, the perfect marriage appears to be in jeopardy. When Sir Robert is threatened with blackmail, the situation proves especially testing for his spouse, who slowly but surely has to relinquish her puritanical high-mindedness and instead express willingness to accept the fact that she must forgive her husband's treachery. Meanwhile, Lady Chiltern has been placed in a predicament in which her spouse might be led to believe that she is conducting an affair with his close friend, the dandyish Lord Goring. In the circumstances, this righteous aristocrat has to acknowledge that she is not well placed to pass harsh moral judgment on her husband's indiscretions. The upshot of this clever drama is to show that a strong marriage necessitates compromises, ones made in the name of greater—though far from fully achieved—sexual equality.

As Maugham's 1909 and 1926 plays imply, the freedom that a woman character such as Gertrude Chiltern might enjoy in modern marriage remained severely limited, and even the idea that Lady Chiltern might benefit from an extramarital affair was inconceivable in 1895. To be sure, in Wilde's scenario for *Mr. and Mrs. Daventry*, the woman protagonist decides to take a lover and travel with him to the Continent. But it remained for Harris, and subsequently for Maugham, to envision the dramatic consequences of such adulterous behavior. In *The Constant Wife*, the main character—who is perhaps by no accident called Constance (the name of Wilde's spouse)—maintains rational control over her decision to have a short-term affair, develop her career as an interior designer, and stay in a marriage to a surgeon whom she discovers has been unfaithful. In many respects, in 1926 Maugham represented dramatically the modern womanhood that in 1895 Wilde was attempting to disconnect from the kind of social-purity feminism that he believed hampered progress toward sexual equality. It would be left to Noel Coward to take this aspect of Wilde's approach to modern marriage much further. In Coward's *Private Lives* (1930), we see the rekindled passion of two former lovers, both of whom have married other people; the episode in act 2 in which the exes reunite perturbed the British censor, and it is to Coward's credit that he persuaded the authorities that the scene should stay because it was played with dignity. Even more risk-taking was Coward's *Design for Living* (1933), which comically explores a bohemian ménage à trois.

Not long after *Design for Living* broke fresh sexual ground when it premiered on the New York stage, the time was ripe for Wilde to become a dramatic character in his own right. Leslie Stokes and Sewell Stokes's *Oscar Wilde,* which followed several European and American theatrical portrayals of the Irishman, opened at the Gate Theatre, London, in September 1936, with Robert Morley in the leading role. Although the reviewer in the London *Times* acknowledged that the play depicted a man whose "name" is "famous in literature," the Stokeses' drama still was judged to touch upon a career whose "swift passage from opulence to wretchedness" was deemed "best forgotten" (30 September 1936, 10). This innovative drama, which for its time takes many risks in pointing to Wilde's history of sexual intimacy with men, derived in part from the transcripts of the 1895 court proceedings that his bibliographer, Christopher Sclater Millard, published as *Oscar Wilde: Three Times Tried* in 1912. (Millard's title is somewhat misleading, because the first trial proceeded from Wilde's libel suit against Alfred Douglas's aggressive father, the Marquess of Queensberry.) As legal scholar Leslie J. Moran reminds us in chapter 9, screenwriter Jo Eisinger—whose distinguished career included the film noir classic *Gilda* (1946) and the 1960s ITV series *Danger Man*—first came into contact with the story of Wilde's trials through the 1938 New York City production of the Stokeses' drama. Not until 1960 did Eisinger see his screenplay about the Wilde trials go into production, however, largely because he had run into problems with the prohibitions laid down by the Hays Code (adopted by the Motion Picture Association of America in the early 1930s), which barred "morally unacceptable" material from appearing on screen. For some time, he worked with Warwick Films, which bought the film rights to H. Montgomery Hyde's *Trials of Oscar Wilde* (1948): a rehash of much of the material that Millard had compiled in 1912 from an earlier source. In the end, Eisinger parted company with Warwick Films, and producer Irving Allen and director Ken Hughes took on the task of developing a screenplay about the trials. Meanwhile, Eisinger's *Oscar Wilde,* under the direction of Gregory Ratoff, with Morley in the starring role, went into production with Vantage Films. Both Eisinger's *Oscar Wilde* and Allen and Hughes's *Trials of Oscar Wilde* (distributed in the United States as *The Man with the Green Carnation*) were ready for release in 1960.

Film historians concur that these two British films about the Wilde trials count among the more notable early 1960s challenges to the Hays Code. Similarly controversial films dating from this time include American director Alfred Hitchcock's *Psycho* (1960), with its unforgettable scenes of violence, and British director Basil Dearden's *Victim* (1961), in which homosexual blackmail is the central topic. Less widely noted is the fact that the competition between the two trial films sparked yet another lawsuit in which Wilde's name was enmeshed. On this occasion, as Moran shows, the struggle that took place in court focused specifically on who held the rights to the transcripts of the 1895 proceedings at the Old Bailey. In *Warwick Film Productions Ltd. v. Eisinger,* the defendant claimed that he had not infringed copyright, because the various sources that he consulted about the Wilde trials (Millard's compilation, the Stokeses' play, and Hyde's volume) contained pretty much the same factual information. The court, however, reasoned otherwise by concluding that Hyde's 1948 volume, with its ample editorial commentary, comprised a literary work, and thus the screenplay of *Oscar Wilde* violated the law. Moran shows that this case accentuates the substantial problems involved in establishing whether Hyde's volume is more correctly characterized as the result of literary inventiveness or as a derivative record of transcripts that were first pieced together in a publication dating from 1906. What emerges from this intriguing legal dispute is that the so-called transcripts used in turn by the 1906 edition, the 1912 one by Millard, and the 1948 one by Hyde appear to have been based on edited newspaper reports—rather than the work of courtroom secretaries—that tactfully withheld some of the more sensitive aspects of the cross-examination. Moran contends that Merlin Holland's more recent attempt to reproduce a trustworthy transcript of the "real trial" that Wilde endured when he took Queensberry to court also underwent a fairly comprehensive editorial process. Such editing raises questions about the degree to which the document presents an authentic representation of the proceedings.

In chapter 10, Francesca Coppa returns to the dramatic representation of Wilde on stage by observing that the Stokeses' 1936 play is remarkable not only for its unapologetic depiction of Wilde's homosexuality but also for its positive characterization of Alfred Douglas, who furnished a preface for the published edition. Coppa's study of Wilde on stage reveals that, as with film history, it took until the second half of the twentieth century before Micheál MacLiammóir's one-man show *The Importance of Being Oscar* (which opened in Dublin in 1960) began the revisionary work of viewing Wilde as a distinctly Irish individual who was not tragically at the mercy of degrading sexual desires. Later dramas, such as Eric Bentley's *Lord Alfred's Lover* (1981), would follow MacLiammóir's lead, informed as they were by the political climate fostered by the Gay Liberation Front. Once Ellmann's 1987 biography appeared—advancing the influential view that "[h]omosexuality fired" Wilde's "mind" because it was "the major stage in his discovery of himself" (*Oscar Wilde,* 281)—the scene was set for a further batch of plays about the homosexual risks that Wilde took. On this occasion, however, the plays suggest that the exceptional Irishman would not have suffered had he not been seduced by the manipulative Douglas. (Recent biographies of Douglas give a different impression.) Both Tom Stoppard's *Invention of Love* (1997) and David Hare's *Judas Kiss* (1998) adhere to this interpretation. Only in gay playwright Neil Bartlett's *In Extremis* (2000) do we find a welcome alternative to the overfamiliar narrative that blames Douglas for spurring Wilde into such a perilous legal action. Bartlett's drama focuses on Wilde's visit to a palm reader one week before the first trial; in a speech delivered from beyond the grave, the fortuneteller reveals that she told Wilde that his future beheld a "very great triumph" (*In Extremis* [London: Oberon, 2000], 50). Such a vision attests to the assured authority that Wilde's life and works, despite his downfall in 1895, maintain over theatergoers one hundred years after his death.

In chapter 11, Matt Cook—author of an influential study of male homosexual subculture in London during the fin de siècle and the Edwardian era—begins by looking at Bartlett's powerful meditation on his own and Wilde's queer London lives: *Who Was That Man? A Present for Mr. Oscar Wilde* (1988). Bartlett takes Wilde as an important reference point for making sense of gay liberation and oppression in Britain during the 1980s. Perhaps it is no coincidence that in 1986 (the year before Ellmann's humanist biography of Wilde was published), British independent filmmaker Derek Jarman caused a furor among the moral Right when two of his works from the 1970s—including his homoerotic film about St. Sebastian —were broadcast on Britain's Channel 4. Not long after Ellmann's research produced one of the most unembarrassed accounts of Wilde's sexuality ever to have appeared, the Thatcher government added Clause 28 to the 1988 Local Government Act in the name of banning the "promotion" of homosexuality by local authorities.

During this politically oppressive period, as Cook shows, Jarman was not only fighting HIV but also struggling to continue his filmmaking, writing, and gardening at the newly acquired Prospect Cottage, set on the windswept sands of Dungeness, Kent. In all of these activities, Jarman's work bears comparison with Wilde's. Cook reveals several striking points of similarity between Jarman's and Wilde's respective choices of subject matter. Not only does Jarman's *Sebastiane* continue a tradition inaugurated in the previous century by Symonds and Wilde, but his later film, *The Angelic Conversation* (1985), explores the homoeroticism of Shakespeare's sonnets that Wilde identified in "The Portrait of Mr. W.H." Furthermore, the full text of *De Profundis,* which Jarman obtained in the 1980s, contains episodes of homosexual oppression that bear plausible comparison with the rabid homophobia that gay men such as Jarman, who were living with AIDS, frequently endured before the pandemic came under some measure of control through combination therapy. In Cook's view, the links between Wilde and Jarman emerge most powerfully when one sees how both men—the one languishing in solitary confinement, the other battling a perilous illness—developed parallel responses to the pressures of the immediate present in a style that infuses extraordinary resonance (if not timelessness) into painful experiences that are at once inspiring and agonizing. It is perhaps no accident that when faced with such extreme hardship, both Jarman and Wilde developed an aesthetics—one that Cook characterizes as part of a distinctly gay tradition—in which lavish gardens, with the most ebullient of blooms, become sensually rich spaces in which queer desire can imaginatively flourish.

Chapter 12, by Oliver S. Buckton, marks a shift from Jarman's independent filmmaking to the slightly later revival of Wilde's life and works in Hollywood, in the form of Brian Gilbert's *Wilde* (1997) and Oliver Parker's *The Importance of Being Earnest* (2001). Both of these films belong to a resurgence of cinematic interest in Wilde that burgeoned in the mid- and late 1990s. Buckton discloses that Gilbert's *Wilde,* inspired by Ellmann's sympathetic biography, presents a version of the author's life that appears uncertain about the best way of accounting for what it takes to be the defining component of Wilde's identity: his homosexuality. On the one hand, *Wilde* follows a trajectory that suggests that Wilde's same-sex eroticism was visibly evident when he lectured half-naked Colorado miners on the finer points of Benvenuto Cellini's art during his North American tour of 1882. On the other hand, Gilbert's directing focuses attention on the event that was supposed to instantiate Wilde's sexual activity with other men: his seduction by the young Robert Ross, several years into Wilde's marriage, in 1887. Meanwhile, Gilbert's film follows Vyvyan Holland's *Son of Oscar Wilde* (1954) by portraying the Irish writer as a loving husband and father. The result is a tellingly incoherent account that keeps forcing attention on the belief that Wilde's sexual entanglements tragically defined his very being. Even if, as Buckton suggests, *Wilde* wishes to present its subject's eros in a reasonably complex light (that is, Wilde as a man whose intimacies involved his wife, young men such as Ross and Douglas, and male prostitutes), the film accumulates scenes that keep returning to the view that for Wilde, in a prejudiced world, his same-sex desires were what precipitated his tragedy.

Whereas Gilbert's 1997 film goes out of its way to portray Wilde as an individual for whom homosexuality was his perilous destiny, Parker's 2001 version of *The Importance of Being Earnest* goes to the opposite extreme by taking every step imaginable to eradicate the homosexual coding that lies not far beneath the surface of this epigrammatically charged society comedy. One can only speculate on why Parker chose to exclude from his film the queerness that informs Wilde's fast-paced plot, in which two young bachelors discover that both of them have constructed elaborate fictions to escape from their families. Exactly what goes on in their hidden lives remains a tantalizing mystery to the audience, to their family members, and to each other. But as the drama rapidly unfolds, we learn that Jack Worthing and Algernon Moncrieff—for all their attempts to enjoy secret lives of unnamed pleasures—remain under obligations to become affianced to suitable young women. The episodes that hurtle them toward this conclusion are filled with so many farcical coincidences that the very idea of the prospect of marriage looks ridiculously artificial. And the fact that Jack and Algy at the very last moment learn that they are brothers makes their kinship appear as contrived as the overwrought plot. Parker's film does away with these unsettling aspects of the play by including scenes in which Jack and Algy spend time at nightclubs consorting with showgirls. Perhaps this straightening out of Wilde's comedy intends to run deliberately against the grain of the kind of narrative that Ellmann's biography has made all too familiar. Whatever the reasons motivating Parker's heterosexualization of *Earnest*, it results in a rather conservative film that blunts the edge of Wilde's rebellious wit.

Taken together, Gilbert's and Parker's very different films bear out the point that Wilde remains an intractable figure whose life and works continue to intrigue us because they lend themselves readily to ever-transforming adaptations and appropriations. The chapters in the present volume certainly give support to Bartlett's assertion that "[a] hundred years after his death, we find other truths in Wilde's life and work other than those found when he swore to tell the truth, the whole truth and nothing but the truth in the dock at the Old Bailey" (*In Extremis*, 9–10). Yet it would be a mistake, as Bartlett suggests, for us to think that in the twenty-first century we can adequately account for his achievements:

> We flatter ourselves that we read his story very differently to the jury who found him guilty, or to the newspaper editors who boosted their circulation on the back of lurid, moralising editorials, or to all those who approved of or revelled in his humiliation. We've put up a statue, given him a plaque in Westminster Abbey, adopted him as an icon, claimed him as a pioneer, studied him to death, republished him endlessly and made him one [of] the very few above-the-title box office guarantee names of our entertainment industry. But I do not think we have understood him yet, or what was done to him. I don't think we realise how much he is with us, rather than behind us. (*In Extremis*, 10)

For the sake of consistency and reliability throughout the present volume, I have taken references to most of Wilde's works (bar *De Profundis* and the English-language translation of *Salomé*) from the fourteen-volume *Collected Works of Oscar Wilde*, edited by Robert Ross, which Routledge/Thoemmes Press reprinted in 1993. This excellent edition remains unsurpassed even today. Certainly, numerous recent editions of Wilde's specific and selected works contain reliable texts and notes, including the Oxford English Texts edition of *The Complete Works of Oscar Wilde*. (At the time of writing, four volumes of the OET edition have been published.) But the 1908 edition, which Wilde's literary executor oversaw, is the only collected one that currently provides the reader with accurate texts of nearly all of Wilde's oeuvre. By way of reference to this enduringly important edition, the abbreviation *CW*, together with volume and page numbers, appears in parentheses after the quotations from Wilde's writings.

References to the complete text of *De Profundis* are taken from *The Complete Letters of Oscar Wilde*, edited by Merlin Holland and Rupert Hart-Davis (London:

Fourth Estate, 2000). In Holland and Hart-Davis's definitive edition of Wilde's letters, the document known as *De Profundis* is not presented with that title; instead, this work is presented as an item of Wilde's correspondence. In principle, their decision makes sense because this document, which Wilde composed in prison probably from late 1896 to March 1897, is a work addressed to "Dear Bosie" (Douglas's nickname) and signed "Your affectionate friend, Oscar Wilde." Holland and Hart-Davis based their text on the manuscript of this document, which Wilde handed to Ross for safekeeping after his release from jail. As I point out in the introduction, one may logically contend that this long epistle, which Wilde wished to preserve for posterity, is something more than a letter addressed to a specific person.

Wilde's *Salomé* presents a much smaller but nonetheless significant editorial matter. The author composed this experimental drama in French, and its earliest French edition was published jointly in 1893 by the Librairie de l'Art Indépendant in Paris and Elkin Mathews and John Lane in London. Throughout Wilde's French text, he gives the name of the eponymous protagonist as Salomé—with an accent on the final syllable. In the English translation produced by Alfred Douglas, published by Elkin Mathews and John Lane in 1894, the accent does not appear. Thus, the *e* is accented throughout the present volume whenever the contributors discuss Wilde's French text; the accent has been omitted when they refer to the 1894 English translation. Quotations from the first English edition are taken from the Dover 1967 facsimile reprint of the 1894 edition, which contains Aubrey Beardsley's startling illustrations; references to this volume are presented parenthetically with the abbreviation "*S*," followed by the page number.

Readers will notice that the same documentation reappears in the notes at the end of the chapters. Such documentation includes, for example, providing sources for works such as Alfred Douglas's "Two Loves." To minimize page flipping, full documentation has been provided for references of this kind that recur in several chapters.

To enable readers to gain an immediate sense of both the shape of Wilde's career and his legacy to modern culture, I have compiled a reasonably detailed chronology that lists his major achievements during his lifetime, followed by the most noteworthy and influential biographical works, critical studies, dance productions, films, music, and stage adaptations that relate to his life and writings. Moreover, I have included many literary representations of Wilde. This chronology should clarify that although Wilde's name remained a source of prurient interest for many years after his death, a growing number of supporters during the earlier parts of the twentieth century publicly recognized his significance as a critical thinker, playwright, and novelist of the Victorian fin de siècle. For a fully comprehensive listing of the main events that occurred during Wilde's career, readers may wish to consult Norman Page, *An Oscar Wilde Chronology* (Basingstoke: Macmillan, 1991).

The select bibliography that appears at the end of the present volume includes important articles, monographs, and collections of essays that focus on Wilde's position as a distinctly modern writer, as well as celebrity icon, anarchist and socialist, character in drama, fiction, and film, homosexual, Irishman, aesthete, dandy, and wit.

Acknowledgments

Oscar Wilde and Modern Culture: The Making of a Legend has its origins in a two-day conference, "Wilde at 150," which was held at the William Andrews Clark Memorial Library, University of California, Los Angeles, on 22–23 October 2004. My thanks go to the staff of the Clark Library—especially Scott Jacobs, Jennifer Schaffner, Carol Sommer, Suzanne Tatian, and Bruce Whiteman—for the help they gave in ensuring the success of this event. Moreover, my colleagues at UCLA's Center for Seventeenth- and Eighteenth-Century Studies (which oversees all of the scholarly activities held at the Clark Library) provided characteristically unstinting help with arranging the program of this symposium. In particular, Peter Reill, Candis Snoddy, and Elizabeth Krown Spellman offered much-appreciated advice on the administrative arrangements for the conference. The center kindly supplied me with research support during the spring quarters of 2006 and 2007. I remain grateful to my research assistants, Nicole Horejsi and Celine Dauverd, for tracking down numerous sources. UCLA's Center for Digital Humanities assisted me with technical questions about electronic files. At UCLA, Michelle Clayton offered help with a reference.

At Ohio University Press, David Sanders, who commissioned this collection, and Nancy Basmajian, who saw the manuscript through the production process, kept an unwavering eye on crucial details. All of the contributors responded promptly to my numerous queries about their drafts, and I remain particularly grateful to Oliver S. Buckton, Yvonne Ivory, Daniel Novak, Julie Townsend, Lizzie Thynne, and Erin Williams Hyman for devoting precious time to clearing permissions. Marysa Demoor of the University of Ghent provided the identifications of two of the *Athenæum* reviewers whose comments Laurel Brake discusses in her chapter. Merlin Holland helped clarify a point of information.

Toward the end of editing this volume, I had the privilege of directing a National Endowment for the Humanities seminar on the extensive Wilde archive held at the Clark Library. I wish to extend my thanks to the enthusiastic and vigorous discussions generated by the participants: Rachel Ablow, James Campbell, Gregory Castle, Loretta Clayton, William A. Cohen, Ellen M. Crowell, Lois

Cucullu, Christofer C. Foss, Neil Hultgren, Casey A. Jarrin, Dejan Kuzmanovic, Elizabeth C. Miller, John Paul Riquelme, Felicia J. Ruff, and Molly C. Youngkin. I owe particular thanks to Ellen M. Crowell for alerting me to a range of materials that I discuss in the introduction, including the reception of *De Profundis* in 1905 and the colorful lives of several followers of Wilde: Arthur Cravan (Fabian Lloyd), Mrs. Chan Toon (Mabel Wodehouse Pearse, née Cosgrove), and George Sylvester Viereck. Both Noah Comet and Adam Seth Lowenstein, who provided research assistance during the seminar, located various items that were needed for the present volume.

The editor and the contributors would like to thank all of the collectors, copyright holders, librarians, and publishers who have granted permission to reproduce materials in this volume. Parts of chapter 1, in a slightly different form, appeared in Lucy McDiarmid, "Lady Gregory, Wilfrid Blunt, and London Table Talk," *Irish University Review* (special issue on Lady Gregory, ed. Anne Fogarty, Spring/Summer 2004), 67–80. We are grateful to Anne Fogarty for permission to reprint sections of this essay. In this chapter, quotations from Lady Gregory's correspondence are reprinted with the permission of the Henry W. and Albert A. Berg Collection of English and American Literature, The New York Public Library, Astor, Lenox and Tilden Foundations; Anne de Winton; and the heirs of Catherine Kennedy. Thanks to Isaac Gewirtz, curator of the Berg Collection, Philip Milito of the Berg, and Colin Smythe. In chapter 1, quotations from Wilfrid Scawen Blunt's letters are printed with the permission of the Henry W. and Albert A. Berg Collection of the New York Public Library and the Fitzwilliam Museum, Cambridge. Thanks are given to Isaac Gewirtz of the Berg and Stella Panayotova of the Fitzwilliam for making these resources available. Significant portions of chapter 2 are from *Realism, Photography and Nineteenth-Century Fiction* by Daniel A. Novak. Copyright © Daniel A. Novak 2008. Reprinted with the permission of Cambridge University Press.

Figures 1, 10, 11, 13, 14, 15, and 16 are reproduced by kind permission of the William Andrews Clark Memorial Library, University of California, Los Angeles. Figures 2, 4, and 6 are reproduced by permission of the National Media Museum, Bradford, UK / Science and Society Picture Library, London. Figure 3 is reproduced by permission of the Metropolitan Museum of Art, New York. Figure 5 is reproduced by permission of the Getty Research Institute, Los Angeles. Figures 7, 8, and 9 are reproduced courtesy of the Galton Collection, University College, London. Figure 12 is reproduced by permission of Arnold Roth, Andy Borowitz, and Condé Nast for the *New Yorker*. Figure 17 is reproduced by permission of the Musée d'Orsay, Paris, and Erich Lessing/Art Resource, New York. Figures 18, 19, and 20 are reproduced courtesy of Schwules Archiv, Berlin. The photograph in figure 21 was taken by Yvan Leclerc. Figure 22 is reproduced by permission of Réunion des Musées Nationaux/Art Resource, New York. Figures 23 and 24 appear by permission of Soizic Audouard. Figures 25 and 26 appear by permission of the Jersey Heritage Trust. Figure 27 appears courtesy of the Young Research Library, University of California, Los Angeles. Figure 28 is reproduced by permission of the National Portrait Gallery, London, and Art Resource, New York. Figures 29, 30, 31, and 32 are reproduced by permission of Sony Pictures Classics. Figures 33, 34, and 35 are reproduced by permission of Miramax Films.

In chapter 4, the long quotation from Marcel Proust, *Sodom and Gomorrah*, translated by John Sturrock, is reproduced by permission of Penguin Books. Bernard Horrocks, copyright officer at the National Portrait Gallery, offered helpful advice on the reproduction of images, as did Tricia Smith at Art Resource, New York. The contributors, editor, and publisher have taken every step to ensure that all copyright holders have been contacted for permission to reproduce images.

During the concluding stages of editing, I have been grateful for the rewarding company of both my partner, Blaine Ashton Noblett, and my dachshund, Leo Lascelles.

Chronology

1854 (16 October) · Oscar Fingal O'Flahertie Willis Wilde born to a Protestant family in Dublin. His father, Sir William Wilde (1815–1876), was a leading eye surgeon; his mother, Jane Francesca Wilde, née Elgee (c. 1821–1896), firmly established her reputation as a nationalist poet writing under the name of "Speranza" (Hope) in the 1840s.

1864 · Attends Portora Royal School, Enniskillen.

1871 · Attends Trinity College, Dublin, where he becomes closely acquainted with Rev. J. P. Mahaffy (1839–1919), professor of ancient history.

1874 (June) · Sits examination at the University of Oxford, where he wins Demyship in Classics at Magdalen College. Some of his earliest poems date from this period. (October) Enters Oxford.

1875 (June–July) · Travels in Italy with Mahaffy, visiting Florence, Bologna, Venice, and Milan.

1877 (March–April) · Travels to Italy and Greece; his visit includes an audience with Pope Pius IX. (Late April) Attends private view at the fashionable Grosvenor Gallery, London. (May) Attends fancy-dress ball dressed as Prince Rupert.

1878 (April) · Visits Rev. Sebastian Bowden at the Brompton Oratory, London, to discuss his interest in converting to Roman Catholicism, which both Sir William and Mahaffy had discouraged. (June) Sits his final examinations in *literæ humaniores* ("Greats"); is awarded a Double First the following month. Wins prestigious Newdigate Prize for his poem "Ravenna." (Late November) Moves to London, where he will soon share rooms with painter Frank Miles (1852–1891).

1879 · Establishes himself as a fashionable literary man-about-town, publishing a poem on revered French actress Sarah Bernhardt (1844–1923) in the *World*. His dress, manner, and style of conversation soon capture the interest of the press. He is quickly thought to embody many of the affectations associated with the loosely defined aesthetic movement.

1880 (October) · Aspects of his fashionable style treated satirically in a cartoon lampooning the aesthetic movement by George Du Maurier (1834–1896) in the popular magazine *Punch*.

1881 (April) · Gilbert and Sullivan's opera *Patience* opens at the Opera Comique, London; it partly satirizes the aesthetic style associated with Wilde. (September) Theater impresario Richard D'Oyly Carte (1844–1901) invites Wilde to undertake a tour lecturing on aesthetic topics throughout North America; the tour supports the American production of *Patience*. (December) London production of his play *Vera*, on Russian nihilism, cancelled. Sets sail for New York City on the S.S. *Arizona*.

1881 (May) · *Poems* published at his own expense; reviews mostly unfavorable, leading to more satirical jibes against him in *Punch*.

1882 (January) · Arrives in New York City. The following month he begins a ten-month, highly profitable lecture tour. (December) Signs a contract for the production of his play *The Duchess of Padua*. Sails from New York City to London.

1883 (January) · Agrees to terms for an American production of *Vera*. (Late January–May) Visits Paris, where he makes the acquaintance of his earliest biographer, Robert Harborough Sherard (1861–1943), and leading French literary figures such as Edmond de Goncourt (1822–1896). (June–July) Lectures on personal impressions of America in England. (August) Travels to New York City to see opening of *Vera*; production closes after a week. (September) Returns to England, where he delivers lectures on a regular basis until late 1885.

1884 (May) · Marries Constance Lloyd (1858–1898). (November) Begins reviewing for the *Pall Mall Gazette*, an influential London afternoon newspaper.

1885 (April) · His poem "The Harlot's House" appears in the *Dramatic Review*. (May) His first major essay, "Shakespeare and Stage Costume," published in *Nineteenth Century*, later revised and reprinted as "The Truth of Masks" (1891). (June) Birth of his first son, Cyril.

1886 (November) · Birth of his second son, Vyvyan. American painter James Abbott McNeill Whistler (1834–1903) attacks Wilde's opinions on art in the *World*.

1887 (April) · Takes up editorship of *Lady's World*, a journal published by Cassell and Co., London. He renames it *Woman's World*, making it a progressive, largely feminist journal covering a wide variety of cultural, literary, and political topics. Contributes several important reviews to this periodical. Editorship lasts until sometime in 1889.

1888 (May) · Publishes *The Happy Prince and Other Tales*, a collection of fairy tales, with David Nutt.

1889 (January) · Publishes two long, intellectually ambitious essays: "Pen, Pencil, and Poison," in the *Fortnightly Review*, and "The Decay of Lying," in *Nineteenth Century*. (July) Publishes novella, "The Picture of Mr. W.H." (on the story behind Shakespeare's sonnets), in *Blackwood's Edinburgh Magazine*. (August) J. M. Stoddart, editor for the J. B. Lippincott Co. of Philadelphia, invites Wilde to contribute a work of fiction to *Lippincott's Monthly Magazine*.

1890 (June) · British edition of the July issue of *Lippincott's Monthly Magazine* is published, featuring the thirteen-chapter text of *The Picture of Dorian Gray*. Immediate hostility from influential quarters of the London press. (July–September) The first and second parts of his major essay, "The True Function and Value of Criticism: With Some Remarks on the Value of Doing Absolutely Nothing" (later retitled "The Critic as Artist"), appear in *Nineteenth Century.*

1891 (January) · *The Duchess of Padua* produced on Broadway, New York City. (February) "The Soul of Man under Socialism" appears in the *Fortnightly Review.* (March) The contentious preface to *The Picture of Dorian Gray* published in the *Fortnightly Review.* (April–May) The twenty-chapter, single-volume edition of *The Picture of Dorian Gray* issued by Ward, Lock, and Co. in London; this edition of 1,000 copies features design on the boards and spine by Charles Ricketts (1866–1931). (July) The foolscap quarto edition of the novel, 250 copies on hand-laid paper, issued by Ward, Lock and Co. *Intentions,* which collects revised versions of his major essays, published. Around this time, Wilde meets Alfred Douglas (1870–1945), who will later become his lover and companion. (November) *A House of Pomegranates,* his second book of fairy stories, appears.

1892 (February) · His first society comedy, *Lady Windermere's Fan,* opens at the fashionable St. James's Theatre; production runs until the end of July. (May) Re-bound edition of *Poems* (1882), with a new title page, boards, and spine designed by Ricketts, issued by Elkin Mathews and John Lane. (June) Proposed production of his French-language play, *Salomé,* starring Sarah Bernhardt at the Palace Theatre, London, cancelled because the Lord Chamberlain censors it.

1893 (February) · French-language edition of *Salomé* published in Paris and London. (April) His second society comedy, *A Woman of No Importance,* opens at the Theatre Royal, Haymarket; production runs until August.

1894 (February) · Mathews and Lane issue English-language version of *Salome,* translated from the French by Douglas, with controversial illustrations by Aubrey Beardsley (1872–1898). (June) *The Sphinx,* designed and illustrated by Ricketts, issued by Elkin Mathews and John Lane in an edition of 250 copies. (July) Six prose-poems appear in the *Fortnightly Review.* (September) Mathews and Lane decline to publish revised version of "The Portrait of Mr. W.H." (November) Nineteen of his aphorisms, titled "A Few Maxims for the Instruction of the Over-Educated," appear in the *Saturday Review.* (December) Thirty-five aphorisms, titled "Phrases and Philosophies for the Use of the Young," published in the *Chameleon,* an Oxford undergraduate magazine.

1895 (January) · His third society comedy, *An Ideal Husband,* opens at the Theatre Royal, Haymarket. (February) His fourth society comedy, *The Importance of Being Earnest,* premieres at the St. James's Theatre. (March) Begins libel suit against Douglas's father, John Sholto Douglas (1844–1900), 8th Marquess of Queensberry, who has accused Wilde of sodomy. (Early April) Wilde's libel suit fails. (Late April) Bankruptcy sale of Wilde's belongings to meet costs of failed libel suit. Evidence produced by the defense in court results in trial of *Regina v. Wilde.* Production of *An Ideal Husband* closes. (Early May) Jury cannot agree on questions put to them by the judge. Fresh trial ordered. Production of *The Importance of Being Earnest* closes. (Late May) Wilde sentenced under the provisions of the Criminal Law Amendment Act (1885) to two years of solitary confinement with hard labor for committing acts of "gross indecency" with other men in private. Enters Pentonville Prison, London. (July) Transfers to Wandsworth Prison, London. (October) Ward, Lock and Co. issues another crown octavo edition of *The Picture of Dorian Gray*. (November) Moves to Reading Gaol, west of London. Wilde's name removed from Honours Board at Portora Royal School.

1896 (February) · First production of *Salomé* at Théâtre de l'Œuvre, Paris. Death of Jane Francesca Wilde.

1897 (January–March) · Probably during these months he completes the 55,000-word prison letter addressed to Douglas; in 1905, his literary executor, Robert Ross (1869–1918), at the suggestion of his publisher, will title this document *De Profundis*, publishing part of it in that year. (May) Leaves Reading Gaol and proceeds to Dieppe, France, where he settles at the nearby village of Berneval.

1898 (January) · Based in Naples, Italy. (February) Publishes, as "C.3.3." (the number of his prison cell), *The Ballad of Reading Gaol* with Leonard Smithers; by 1899, the seventh edition of this highly popular work will bear Wilde's name. (April) Constance Wilde dies after surgery to correct spinal injury.

1899 (January) · Smithers issues first edition of *The Importance of Being Earnest*; Wilde's name is not mentioned. (April) Wilde signs agreement with American producer Charles Frohman for a play based on the scenario that Harris turns into *Mr. and Mrs. Daventry*. (May) Based in Paris. (July) Smithers issues first edition of *An Ideal Husband*; Wilde's name is not mentioned. (September) Laurence Housman meets Wilde and Ross at Paris.

1900 (January) · Marquess of Queensberry dies; Douglas inherits nearly £20,000. (February) Wilde sells performance rights to Ada Rehan for play based on the scenario that Harris turns into *Mr. and Mrs. Daventry*. (March) Cora Brown-Potter asks Wilde to turn over the play based on the scenario that Harris turns into *Mr. and Mrs. Daventry*. (September) Smithers goes bankrupt. (October) *Mr. and Mr. Daventry*, which Frank Harris (1856–1931) has developed from an outline by Wilde, opens at the Royalty Theatre, London; production runs until February 1901. (30 November) On his deathbed, under Ross's supervision, Wilde converts to Roman Catholicism. Dies of meningitis at the Hôtel d'Alsace in the Latin Quarter of Paris. (2 December) Buried at Bagneux Cemetery; Douglas is chief mourner.

1901 · George Alexander's productions of *The Importance of Being Earnest* and *Lady Windermere's Fan*, Coronet Theatre, Notting Hill, London (Wilde's name does not appear on program).

1902 · Publication of first biography of Wilde: Robert Harborough Sherard, *Oscar Wilde: The Story of an Unhappy Friendship*. George Alexander's production of *The Impor-*

tance of Being Earnest, St. James's Theatre, London. (February) André Gide, "Oscar Wilde," *L'ermitage,* Paris. (November) *Salome,* directed by Max Reinhardt, opens at the Kleines Theater, Berlin.

1903 · *A Woman of No Importance,* Empire Theatre, Balham, London.

1905 · British premiere (private performance) of *Salome,* Bijou Theatre, London. (January–February) Max Meyerfeld publishes German translation of *De Profundis* in *Die neue Rundschau.* (February) In London, Methuen issues Robert Ross's edition of *De Profundis.* (May) J. M. Stuart-Young, *Osrac the Self-Sufficient.* (December) Richard Strauss's *Salomé,* opens at Royal Opera House, Dresden, Germany.

1906 · Maud Allan, *The Vision of Salome,* Vienna (dance). (February) Wilde's bankruptcy annulled. (June) Wilde's *Florentine Tragedy* (completed by T. Sturge Moore) staged in London.

1907 (September) · Alfred Douglas, "The Dead Poet," *Academy.*

1908 · Stuart Mason [Christopher Sclater Millard], *Oscar Wilde: Art and Morality—A Defence of* The Picture of Dorian Gray. *The Collected Works of Oscar Wilde,* ed. Robert Ross, 14 vols. Franz Schreker, *Der Geburtstag der Infantin* (The Birthday of the Infanta) (orchestral work). Maud Allan tours England with *The Vision of Salome* (250 performances).

1909 · W. Somerset Maugham, *Penelope* (play). Max Meyerfeld's new German edition of *De Profundis* reveals that the complete document takes the form of a letter to Douglas. (November) Ross bequeaths manuscript of *De Profundis* to British Museum; the document is sealed for fifty years.

1912 · Arthur Ransome, *Oscar Wilde: A Critical Study* (reprinted with emendations in 1913).

1913 · G. Constant Lounsbery, *The Picture of Dorian Gray: A Play,* Vaudeville Theatre, London.

1914 · *An Ideal Husband,* St. James's Theatre, London (dir. George Alexander). Stuart Mason [Christopher Sclater Millard], *Bibliography of Oscar Wilde.* (August) Jacob Epstein's tomb for Wilde unveiled at Père Lachaise.

1913 (April) · Douglas's libel suit against Ransome, his publisher, the printer, and the Times Book Club.

1915 · Alexander von Zemlinsky, *Eine florentinische Tragödie* (opera). (May) Death of Cyril Holland.

1916 · Frank Harris, *Oscar Wilde: His Life and Confessions* (biography). *The Picture of Dorian Gray* (film) (dir. Fred W. Durrant).

1918 (May–June) · "The Cult of the Clitoris" case, Old Bailey, London: Maud Allan and J. T. Grein's libel suit against Noel Pemberton Billing for attacking their involvement in a private production of *Salome.* (October) Death of Robert Ross.

1919 · Nicola Guerra (choreography) and Florent Schmitt (music), *La Tragédie de Salomé* (dance starring Ida Rubinstein).

1920 · Jacques Ibert, *La ballade de la geôle de Reading* (symphonic poem). (April) Sale of John B. Stetson Jr.'s collection of Wilde materials, Anderson Galleries, New York City.

1921 · *The Portrait of Mr. W. H. as Written by Oscar Wilde Sometime after the Publication of His Essay, of the Same Title, and Now First Printed from the Original Enlarged Manuscript which for Twenty-Six Years Has Been Lost to the World.* (October) Mabel Wodehouse Pearse publishes forgery, *For Love of the King,* as one of Wilde's works, in *Hutchinson's Magazine,* London.

1922 · Alexander von Zemlinsky, *Der Zwerg* (based on Wilde's "Birth of the Infanta") (opera). Methuen adds forgery, *For Love of the King,* to its edition of Wilde's *Collected Works.*

1923 · *Salomé* (dir. Charles Bryant), starring Nazimova.

1924 · Hester Travers Smith, *Psychic Messages from Oscar Wilde.* Carl Sternheim, *Oskar Wilde: Sein Drama* (play). Wilde's name restored to the Honours Board, Portora Royal School.

1925 · Millard campaigns against Methuen for publishing *For Love of the King.*

1926 · W. Somerset Maugham, *The Constant Wife* (play). (November) Methuen wins £100 libel damages against Millard.

1927 · Death of Christopher Sclater Millard.

1928 · Sale of Wilde materials by Dulau and Company, London; William Andrews Clark buys sixty-five of the lots to form the largest collection in private hands. Lester Cohen, *Oscar Wilde* (play).

1931 · Léon Lemmonier, *La vie d'Oscar Wilde* (biography). (October) Lord Chamberlain's ban on *Salome* lifted; first public production in Britain at Savoy Theatre, London.

1934 · Maurice Rostand, *Le procès d'Oscar Wilde* (play). William Andrews Clark's library bequeathed to the University of California.

1936 · Leslie Stokes and Sewell Stokes, *Oscar Wilde* (play). Lloyd Lewis and Henry Justin Smith, *Oscar Wilde Discovers America.*

1937 · John Betjeman, "The Arrest of Oscar Wilde at the Cadogan Hotel."

1939 · *The Importance of Being Earnest* (dir. John Gielgud), Globe Theatre, London.

1944 · *The Canterville Ghost* (film) (dir. Jules Dassin).

1945 · *La Sainte Courtesane, or the Woman Covered in Jewels* (performed as *Myrrhina* on French radio). *The Picture of Dorian Gray* (film) (dir. Albert Lewin).

1946 · Hesketh Pearson, *The Life of Oscar Wilde.*

1950 (30 November) · Ross's ashes placed in special chamber alongside Wilde's in Epstein's tomb at Père Lachaise. Dinner held in Wilde's honor at the Hôtel d'Alsace.

1952 · *The Importance of Being Earnest* (film) (dir. Anthony Asquith).

1953 · *Salome* (film) (dir. William Dieterle), starring Rita Hayworth.

1954 · Noel Coward, *After the Ball* (musical). (October) Dinner held in honor of the 100th anniversary of Wilde's birth at Savoy Hotel, London. Plaque in Wilde's memory erected by London County Council at his home at 34 (formerly 16) Tite Street, Chelsea. Vyvyan Holland, *Son of Oscar Wilde* (memoir).

1960 · Micheál MacLiammóir, *The Importance of Being Oscar* (play). *Oscar Wilde* (film) (dir. Gregory Ratoff). *The Trials of Oscar Wilde* (film) (dir. Ken Hughes). *Ernest in Love* (musical), Gramercy Arts Theatre, New York.

1962 · Oscar Wilde, *Letters*, ed. Rupert Hart-Davis.

1972 · Joe Layton, *O.W.* (ballet), Sadler's Wells, London.

1974 · Tom Stoppard, *Travesties* (play), Aldwych Theatre, London.

1977 · John Gay, *Diversions and Delights* (play). *Salome* (dir. Lindsay Kemp), Round House, London, starring Kemp as Salome.

1981 · Eric Bentley, *Lord Alfred's Lover* (play).

1983 · Peter Ackroyd, *The Last Testament of Oscar Wilde* (fiction).

1985 · John Hawksworth, *Oscar* (British miniseries).

1987 · Richard Ellmann, *Oscar Wilde* (biography). *Salomé's Last Dance* (film) (dir. Ken Russell).

1988 · Neil Bartlett, *Who Was That Man? A Present for Mr. Oscar Wilde.* Charles Marowitz, *Wilde West* (play).

1989 · Terry Eagleton, *Saint Oscar* (play). *Salome* (dir. Steven Berkoff), Royal National Theatre, London.

1992 · Walter Satterthwaite, *Wilde West* (novel).

1995 · *A Man of No Importance* (film) (dir. Suri Krishnamma).

1997 · Moisés Kaufman, *Gross Indecency: The Three Trials of Oscar Wilde* (play). Jeremy Reed, *Dorian* (novel). Tom Stoppard, *The Invention of Love* (play), Royal National Theatre, London. *Wilde* (film) (dir. Brian Gilbert). Derek Mahon, *The Yellow Book* (poetry). Danny Osborne, *Oscar Wilde,* Merrion Square, Dublin (statue).

1998 · David Hare, *The Judas Kiss* (play), Almeida Theatre, London. Mark Ravenhill, *Handbag* (play), Lyric Studio Theatre, Hammersmith. *Velvet Goldmine* (film) (dir. Todd Haynes). Maggi Hambling, *A Conversation with Oscar Wilde,* Adelaide Street, London (sculpture). Oscar Wilde Centre for Irish Writing, School of English, Trinity College, Dublin.

1999 · *An Ideal Husband* (film) (dir. Oliver Parker).

2000 · Neil Bartlett, *In Extremis* (play).

2002 · *The Importance of Being Earnest* (film) (dir. Oliver Parker). Will Self, *Dorian: An Imitation* (novel).

2003 · Louis Edwards, *Oscar Wilde Discovers America* (novel). Merlin Holland, ed., *Irish Peacock and Scarlet Marquess* (transcript of first trial).

2005 · *A Good Woman* (film based on *Lady Windermere's Fan*) (dir. Mike Barker).

2006 · *The Picture of Dorian Gray* (film) (dir. Duncan Roy).

2007 · Gyles Brandreth, *Oscar Wilde and the Candlelight Murders* (novel).

2008 · Gyles Brandreth, *Oscar Wilde and a Death of No Importance: A Mystery* (novel). Matthew Bourne, *Dorian Gray* (dance), Edinburgh International Festival.

OSCAR WILDE

and Modern Culture

Introduction

JOSEPH BRISTOW

> A Reuter telegram from Paris states that Oscar Wilde died there yester-
> day afternoon from meningitis. The melancholy end to a career which
> once promised so well is stated to have come in an obscure hotel of the
> Latin Quarter. Here the once brilliant man of letters was living, exiled
> from his country and from the society of his countrymen. The verdict
> that a jury passed upon his conduct at the Old Bailey in May 1895, de-
> stroyed for ever his reputation, and condemned him to ignoble obscu-
> rity for the remainder of his days. When he had served his sentence of
> two years' imprisonment, he was broken in health as well as bankrupt
> in fame and fortune. Death has soon ended what must have been a life
> of wretchedness and unavailing regret.
>
> —Unsigned obituary, London *Times*, 1 December 1900

JUST BEFORE the end of the nineteenth century, Oscar Wilde died in trying
circumstances, as unsympathetic obituaries in the British press were prompt
to note. To the London *Times*, Wilde's demise from an infection of brain tissue
at age forty-six did not come soon enough. How could a man who suffered such
degradation continue a life that was anything other than shameful and remorse-
ful? How could this once-fêted author ever have stood again before the public
with any measure of dignity? From this perspective, the attack of meningitis is
portrayed as a blessing that put Wilde, once and for all, out of his misery. Yet if

this notice of Wilde's death seems at best dismissive, it appears more favorable than the brief commentary that appeared a week later in another well-regarded publication, the *Academy,* which could not bring itself to mention Wilde's identity. Here he figures only as "the unhappy man who died in Paris the other day."[1] To be sure, the *Academy* concedes that, regardless of what we think of Wilde as an individual, it is "what he did in literature" that "remains in witness for or against him." Such wording suggests that even when critics recognize that they must separate the quality of Wilde's writings from his scandalous disgrace, his achievements will never escape the judgmental attitude that makes naming him impossible.

At the time of Wilde's decease, on 30 November 1900, the idea that he would soon become a legendary figure was for most commentators inconceivable. But the urgency with which a group of devotees salvaged his reputation quickly turned public attention on the injustice that had led to the incarceration, exile, and premature demise of an immensely talented writer. The restoration of Wilde's standing, however, hardly went uncontested, even among the friends who were closely attached to him. The contending efforts among his loyal companions, ardent followers, and estranged acquaintances to recount the story of Wilde's career were often hampered by bouts of infighting, which led in turn to plenty of mythmaking about the kind of man Wilde actually had been. On several awkward occasions in the 1910s, the closest of Wilde's associates developed such animosity toward each other that they rushed into court praising and blaming a genius with whom all of them—whether emotionally or professionally—had been involved. Such squabbles ensured that modern audiences would never forget the scandal attached to Wilde's much-maligned person and concentrate instead on the high quality of his work.

Such publicity fascinated the public at a moment when Wilde's writings had been translated into many languages. In 1905, even Wilde's symbolist play *Salomé* —which the British censor had banned from public performance in June 1892— reemerged in Richard Strauss's opera, which premiered to acclaim in the Dresden production and was transferred to Covent Garden, London, a year later. John Lane, who had issued several of Wilde's volumes in the 1890s, promptly released a guide to Strauss's opera, which alludes to the still-censored drama as "a remarkable *tour de force*."[2] Try as it might, the British press, no matter how embarrassed by the thought of Wilde's homosexuality, could not hush up his legacy. As numerous editions of his works began to circulate, Wilde's stock rose so sharply that his manuscripts began to fetch high prices on both sides of the

Joseph Bristow

Atlantic. By the 1920s, the Wilde legend, elaborated in biographies of varying quality, had become so alluring that various eccentrics managed to pass off convincing forgeries to unsuspecting experts. Even though Wilde died next-to-penniless in Paris at the end of the nineteenth century, he was transformed into one of the most lucrative modern authors of the twentieth. Wilde, who observed in late 1900 that he was "dying above his means," would have been appalled by the idea that his much-needed rise from rags to riches was a posthumous one.[3]

Wilde not only died above his means but also passed before his time and in near isolation. When he lay on his deathbed at the shabby Hôtel d'Alsace in the Latin Quarter of Paris, he had few friends and no family members to take care of him. During his brutal sentence, his devoted mother, Irish poet Jane Francesca Wilde, passed away. Two years later, in April 1898, his estranged wife, Constance, died from complications arising from a spinal injury. The following year, his elder brother Willie was sent to his grave through alcoholism. Meanwhile, from the time of his entry into prison on 25 May 1895 until his death, Wilde remained incommunicado with his two teenage sons, who, like their mother, changed their name to Holland. (His children, Cyril and Vyvyan, learned of their father's death through the press.)

The other person who remained absent was the one whose intimacy with Wilde complicated his legacy more than anybody else. Wilde met his beloved "Bosie," the young aristocrat Alfred Douglas, at Oxford in 1891, and it was Douglas's father—the hot-tempered Marquess of Queensberry—who left the offending visiting-card that attacked Wilde for posing as a "sodomite": an insult that precipitated, with much encouragement from Douglas, the perilous libel suit that exposed Wilde's homosexuality and landed him in jail for two years. During Wilde's imprisonment, Douglas—who fled England when the Crown subsequently prosecuted Wilde—followed advice not to make any visits to his lover, though in the French press he tried to protest Wilde's incarceration as unapologetically as possible.[4] Even though Wilde and Douglas were reconciled in September 1897, four months after Wilde's release, news of their renewed attachment so inflamed Constance Holland (the name she had taken) that she threatened to withdraw her modest allowance from her disgraced husband. At the end of that year, for practical reasons, Wilde and Douglas bade each other farewell once more. After Constance's death, the two met on many occasions around Paris until the summer of 1900. There is no record that Bosie visited Wilde during his decline.

In late 1900, Reggie Turner and Robert Ross were the two remaining people who ministered to their dying friend. Both were anxious about meeting the fees of the doctor and the surgeon who made frequent visits to the patient during September, October, and November that year. Moreover, they made certain that Wilde did not go without any material comfort. The steadfast Ross pointed out that he and Turner ensured that "Wilde wanted for NOTHING during the last weeks of his life."[5] In Ross's view, although Wilde's death was "melancholy and dreadful . . . in many ways," rumors about the late writer's "poverty" were "exaggerated" (65). Fortunately, the hotelkeeper, M. Jean Dupoirier, turned a blind eye to bills that had been owed to him for months. Receipts show that Wilde was still able to obtain a supply of reading matter from a local bookseller, which added to his personal library of three hundred books.[6]

In these final weeks, Wilde understood that not only his health but also his finances were worsening, and his mind focused on how he might settle the mounting debts. In the last of his letters, he fixates on why a recent business transaction should alleviate the financial pressure. He tells Frank Harris (who published some of Wilde's more insubordinate writings) that the expense of his illness is "close on £200"; the surgeon's fee, he says, amounts to "1500 francs."[7] To defray these substantial sums, Wilde insists that the time has come for Harris to fulfill an agreement that they made earlier that year. Even Harris, an ally who had given Wilde two new suits on his release from prison, apparently did not treat the author respectfully during this grueling time. Wilde needed cash, and Harris was obliged to help—or so Wilde wished to suggest.

Wilde's reason for seeking money from Harris relates to the fact that on 25 October that year, a play titled *Mr. and Mrs. Daventry* opened at the Royalty Theatre, London, with the well-known Stella Campbell ("Mrs. Pat") in the leading role. This drama, which received mixed reviews but ran for 116 performances, was the result of a problematic collaboration (if one can call it that) between the two men. The play, which Wilde sketched out in a scenario in August 1894, had come to hold a troublesome position in his career. Before he finished *The Importance of Being Earnest* (1895), Wilde had opened discussions with actor-manager George Alexander—the director of this brilliant society comedy—about the prospect of a drama focusing on marital discord, an adulterous husband's suicide, and a wronged wife's desire to elope with her lover.[8] "*I want the sheer passion of love to dominate everything*," he emphatically informed Alexander.[9] "No morbid self-sacrifice," he added. "No renunciation." In no respect was the woman protagonist to subscribe to the Victorian moralizing that Wilde did everything he could to resist in his work. Clearly, the subject matter, for its time, was risk-taking, as Laurel Brake explains in chapter 8 of the present volume.

In all likelihood, Wilde would have developed the scenario into a full-fledged drama had the trials of April–May 1895 not taken place. His sketch of this ambitious play counts among the small number of dramatic works that Wilde left unfinished at the time of his death.[10] In February 1895, just after the opening of *Earnest,* Wilde tried to interest Alexander in "the vital parts" of *A Florentine Tragedy,* the fragment of which would appear in the fourteen-volume *Collected Works* (1908), edited by Ross.[11] Wilde appears to have continued working on this revenge drama, which follows the style of a Jacobean tragedy, until his hazardous libel suit interrupted his career. Besides resulting in his imprisonment, Wilde's failed case against Queensberry incurred massive damages. On 24 April 1895, his belongings went up for sale outside his beautifully furnished home at 16 Tite Street, Chelsea. Wilde therefore entered jail a bankrupt man, and at the end of his life, more than £1,000 was still owed to the official receiver. After his release from prison, when he moved around France and Italy incognito as "Sebastian Melmoth," Wilde never recovered pecuniary stability, even though friends were at times generous to him.

Once Wilde left England for the Continent, he realized that the scenario he had shared with Alexander in 1894 could reap much-needed rewards. In the summer of 1897, while he resided near Dieppe, Normandy, he sold the performance rights to American actress Cora Brown-Potter. The following year, when his expenses outstripped his income, he did the same thing to English theatrical manager Horace Sedger, who promptly sold on the rights to another agent. At the end of 1898, Leonard Smithers—a dubious figure who was the only publisher to accept Wilde's *Ballad of Reading Gaol* (1898)—relieved the other agent (his name was Roberts) of the deal and quickly took steps to ensure that Wilde would settle at Paris, where he could work on the script. But even Smithers's support did not inspire Wilde to finish the drama. Laurence Housman, who enjoyed Wilde's company in September 1899, reports Wilde's demoralization at the prospect that there was no further market for his literary works: "If I could write what I have been saying to you, if I could hope to interest others, as I seem to have interested you, I would; but the world will not listen to me—now."[12]

Around this time, Wilde was so hard-pressed for cash that the proprietor of the Hotel Marsollier (where he had been staying during the early summer of 1899) was withholding his clothes until bills were paid. In these straits, Wilde sold the copyrights for the publication of two of his plays—*Lady Windermere's Fan* (1892) and *A Woman of No Importance* (1893)—to Smithers for a paltry £20 apiece. But as James G. Nelson reminds us, with the completion of this deal Smithers's business began to fail, and therefore "the relationship between Smithers and Wilde as publisher and author appears to have ended for all practical purposes."[13] Twelve months later, on 18 September 1900, Smithers went bankrupt, leaving Wilde without any publisher. By the time Smithers's business collapsed, Harris had become deeply involved in what Wilde in June 1900 called "our collaboration."[14] The plan was for the two of them to work together on drafting the play based on the scenario, with Wilde composing the first act and Harris the remaining three. At this point, Harris knew that Wilde had already sold an option on the drama to Cora Brown-Potter, who had some months earlier petitioned Wilde to turn over to her what she called "my play."[15] Toward the end of September, however, when Wilde's inability to complete his part of the bargain became clear, the situation with Harris grew more complicated. Although Harris had no previous experience of writing for the stage, he was eager to gain the best financial return. He steamed ahead and finished the drama without Wilde "seeing a line of it."[16] Moreover, Harris sent Stella Campbell his script, and she quickly agreed to take the lead role at the Royalty, whose management she had just taken over. At this juncture, Wilde agreed that Harris should buy the plot and scenario for the following terms: £200 as down payment, £500 worth of "shares in the Reserve," and 25 percent of the profits of the play.[17]

This was, by any account, an advantageous deal, and the promised down payment was substantially larger than the sums that George Alexander had advanced Wilde during his heyday on the London stage from 1892 to 1895.[18] Although Wilde admitted to Harris that he had already taken money from Cora Brown-Potter and her performance partner, English actor Kyrle Bellew, he was not explicit about other options that he had sold. As Harris soon learned, Wilde had in addition received handsome payments for various publishing and performance rights not only from Smithers but also from Australian theater manager Louis Nethersole (December 1899) and American actress Ada Rehan (February 1900).[19] Once the forthcoming performance of *Mr. and Mrs. Daventry* was announced in the press, each of these individuals made a claim (rightfully or not) on Harris.[20] Ross, for one, took a negative view of Wilde's behavior. In a letter written two weeks after Wilde's death, he explains to his roommate More Adey that "Oscar,

Joseph Bristow

of course, deceived Harris about the whole matter," having used the scenario to raise sums of £100 on repeated occasions.[21] To make matters worse, the aggrieved parties "threatened Harris with proceedings." Such information troubled Ross because he had been doing his best to support Wilde by administering an allowance of £150 a year from Constance Holland's estate.

In any case, Harris had his own reasons for not fulfilling his side of the bargain. Like Wilde, Harris—a habitually extravagant man—was hard up. Pressed for funds, in 1898 Harris sold the *Saturday Review,* in which he had made space for some of the most gifted authors of the day. During his four-year editorship, Harris had brought George Bernard Shaw, H. G. Wells, and Max Beerbohm into the public eye; there, too, he had published Wilde's "A Few Maxims for the Instruction of the Over-Educated" (1894). Meanwhile, among Harris's riskier business ventures was the recent acquisition of a costly hotel in Monte Carlo, which ended up emptying his pockets. With his finances at a breaking point, Harris sensed that he had been swindled, and he "wrote rather sharply to Oscar for having led [him] into this hornets' nest."[22] He had little faith in how Wilde might dispose of any monies he might send to the Hôtel d'Alsace, where Wilde had been staying since August. In his memoir about Wilde's last days, Harris's secretary, T. H. Bell, recalls that the only solution to Wilde's writer's block was to have had a "combination nurse, guardian, and amanuensis" to ensure that Wilde completed his part of the collaboration.[23] Above all, in Bell's view, Wilde should "have been kept encouraged and from getting drunk too early in the day" and "kept in good humor" (143). (During his exile in France, Wilde indulged his taste for absinthe and cognac.)[24] Whether fairly or unfairly, all that Harris would part with before Wilde's death was £25, a fact that Wilde repeats in letters that enumerate his surgeon's fee (£50), the bill for his consulting physician (£35), and his bill at the chemists (£35) (*Complete Letters,* 1201, 1204). Ross records that in November 1900, Wilde's hotel expenses stood at £190 (*Complete Letters,* 1223).

After *Mr. and Mrs. Daventry* enjoyed the best part of a month's performances, Harris capitulated to the demands that Wilde made in an urgent letter dated 21 November 1900. Harris dispatched Bell to travel from London to Paris with the sum that was owing to Wilde. Even at this stage, Harris suspected that Wilde was feigning illness. (The truth of the situation became known to Harris at the eleventh hour, for on 27 November Ross wired him about Wilde's perilous condition.) Bell recalls the instructions that his employer wanted him to follow once he reached the Hôtel d'Alsace:

If I found Oscar's illness humbug, I was to talk things over with him, show him the documents in regard to Bellew and Smithers. If I found him drunk I was to hold the money till I saw him sober. Get his signature for it. Yes, surely, I was to use my own judgment a bit. But I must be aware of the people around him, parasites and blackmailers. I should be sure to go directly to Oscar's room (Harris somehow had the number of it) so as not to give him any chance to stage a sickness.

These warnings disheartened me not a little. Harris knew Wilde certainly much better than I did; and, alas, I knew enough myself to realize that these suspicions were not unreasonable. But I was being disillusioned about Harris, too. I felt that poor Oscar had been treated very badly. (149)

After entering the Alsace by a side entrance, Bell made his way to Wilde's room, only to find a "white-coiffed nun . . . sitting at one side with candles burning before her" (149). "And there before me," Bell adds, "lay Oscar—dead" (149). If ever there was a parable of too little arriving too late, this must surely be it. After speaking with Ross and Turner, as well as with Wilde's friend Henry-D. Davray, Bell headed back to London, and the money appears to have returned with him as well.[25] Everyone whom Harris needed to reimburse from the takings of *Mr. and Mrs. Daventry* was paid off, including the bankrupt Smithers, who received his £100 after the fiftieth performance. (According to Ross, Harris said he would settle the bills owing to Dupoirier.[26] But this promise appears to have gone unfulfilled because the debts were still owed to the hotelkeeper in 1902.[27]) This ending to Wilde's life is as poignant as it is pitiful.

In his letter to Adey, Ross records Wilde's painful dying hours. He mentions that after he returned to the Hôtel d'Alsace after a two-week absence, he learned from two doctors that "Oscar could not live for more than two days" (*Complete Letters*, 1201). Furthermore, Ross, a faithful Catholic since 1894, recalls how he quickly arranged, with the Protestant Wilde's consent, a deathbed conversion to the Church of Rome, in which Father Cuthbert Dunne performed the first and last sacraments (1223–24). Ross's most vivid memory concentrates on the "death rattle" that began during the early morning of 30 November: "[I]t sounded like the turning of a crank, and it never ceased until the end" (1220). After Wilde expired, Ross writes, "the appalling *débris* . . . had to be burnt" (1220). There was, however, another mess that he had to clear up, because French officialdom made "[d]ying in Paris . . . a very difficult and expensive luxury for a foreigner" (1221). Particularly problematic was the signing of Wilde's death certificate. He had registered at Dupoirier's hotel as "Sebastian Melmoth"—a violation of French law, which forbade taking rooms under an assumed name. Technically, then, Wilde died a criminal, and Ross feared that his friend's body might be carried off to Paris's most lurid tourist destination, the morgue.

Fortunately, with help from an undertaker connected with the British embassy, Ross managed to cajole the district doctor, appease another official, and arrange the funeral as a matter of necessity (doctors advised him "to have the remains placed in the coffin at once, as decomposition would begin very rapidly" [*Complete Letters*, 1221]). Two days later, Wilde was buried in a modest grave at Bagneux Cemetery, four miles from Paris, in a coffin on which the inscribed plate misspelled his first name. As Ross informed Adey, the ceremony was a muted affair, with fifty-six people in attendance (Douglas was chief mourner) and twenty-four wreaths. There is no question that Ross's dedication to Wilde had turned into a labor of love. In the end, as he admits in a letter to painter William Rothenstein, Ross "had begun to feel, rather foolishly, a sort of responsibility for Oscar."[28] "[H]e had become for me," Ross adds, "a sort of adopted prodigal baby." At the time, Ross also sensed that his friend's prodigality would involve far more than defraying debts. Certainly, Ross knew that he could not tackle writing a memoir, which publisher Arthur Humphreys encouraged him to produce. "I am not alas a Boswell," Ross confides in his correspondence with Adela Schuster (who had generously put up £1,000 for Wilde's defense at the Old Bailey).[29] He also believed that it might prove inadvisable to embark on telling Wilde's life story, since that could appeal unhealthily to "morbid curiosity" (1230). In making this observation, Ross was mindful of Wilde's chilling foresight in a line that reverberates in "The Critic as Artist" (1890, revised 1891): "Every great man nowadays has his disciples, and it is always Judas who writes the biography" (*CW*, 8:102).[30] Such devotion could well lead to betrayal. Ultimately, the only succor Ross took from the "silence in the press" that met Wilde's death was the prospect that at some later point "everyone will recognise his achievements; his plays and essays will endure" (1229).

From every angle, Wilde's demise could not appear more wretched. Yet what is obscured in the depressing accounts of his death is that at the time, Wilde was in part responsible for a money-making play, starring a leading actress, which attracted audiences because it was rumored to have originated with him. To be sure, the idea that he could keep raising cash on the scenario of *Mr. and Mrs. Daventry* may well point to his unscrupulousness when he was in need of funds.

But evidence suggests that the repeated selling of his outline occurred when Wilde was trying to restore his professional standing after the success of *The Ballad of Reading Gaol,* which Smithers issued in seven successful editions between 1898 and 1899. After his release from prison, Wilde expressed his intention to complete a libretto for *Daphnis and Chloë,* a play, and an essay for the *North American Review.*[31] To be sure, no drafts or sketches of these works have survived —a fact that may indicate that Wilde was prepared to make false promises at a time when he frequently lost hope in his literary prospects. Yet it is worth bearing in mind Josephine M. Guy and Ian Small's observation that "[i]n the light of his attempts to restart his career as a dramatist, and the number of managers still interested in his work, we should perhaps be cautious about writing off the post-1897 years as straightforward failure."[32] Nor did Wilde's works die with him. No matter how dismissively the *Times* and the *Academy* treated Wilde in their obituaries, such dismissiveness hardly prevented George Alexander—who obtained performance rights to two of Wilde's plays—from arranging productions of both *Lady Windermere's Fan* and *Earnest* at the Coronet Theatre, London, in 1901.[33]

Alexander stated on 11 December 1900 that he wished Ross to accept "10 per cent of the sums" that came from a new edition of these society comedies.[34] In making this gesture, Alexander wanted to ensure that Ross did not remain out-of-pocket when trying to settle Wilde's debts. Moreover, Alexander wrote in his will that on his death the copyright of the two dramas would return to Wilde's estate. When Alexander first revived Wilde's society comedies, the author's identity was omitted from the program, yet everyone attending Alexander's productions more than likely knew who had written the plays. In other words, even if publicizing Wilde's name in the months following his death was problematic, his writings plainly survived journalistic condescension. Even more to Wilde's credit, his works eventually managed to rise above the noisy public frays that would follow—in which, as Ross suspected, several Judases would betray not only the great man but also the other disciples.

"The Truth of What I Prophesied When Wilde Died in 1900"—Robert Ross (1914)

Not all quarters of the London press treated Wilde's passing with disdain. On 8 December 1900, one of his closer acquaintances, the young satirist Max Beer-

Joseph Bristow

bohm, provided an unapologetic defense of Wilde's achievements. Beerbohm courageously devoted the second half of his theater review in the *Saturday Review* to a thoughtful assessment of a man whose death "extinguishes the hope that the broken series of his play might be resumed."[35] (Beerbohm cleared these remarks with his editor in advance, lest there be any objection to mentioning Wilde's name.)[36] Even if, in Beerbohm's judgment, Wilde was not "what one calls a born writer," this was not a hindrance to Wilde's art. Wilde, Beerbohm observes, came to creating drama "when he was no longer a young man," and the playwright correspondingly brought to the form not only his skills "as a thinker and a weaver of ideas" but also his established prowess "as the master of a literary style" (230, 231). No matter how much Wilde might be faulted for writing in a manner that bore "too close a likeness to the flow of speech," Beerbohm judged that "this very likeness . . . gave him in dramatic dialogue as great an advantage over more careful and finer literary stylists as he had over ordinary playwrights with no pretence to style" (231). In other words, for Beerbohm it is unquestionable that "now Wilde is dead" the public "will realise . . . fully, what was for them involved in his downfall"—namely, "how lamentable the loss to dramatic literature" (232).

Three days after this supportive notice appeared, a one-act play by Beerbohm opened as a forty-minute curtain-raiser for *Mr. and Mrs. Daventry*. In November of that year, Stella Campbell had approached Beerbohm to provide a dramatic adaptation of his story "The Happy Hypocrite" (1896), which was first published in the *Yellow Book*—the initially controversial quarterly magazine that, in its earliest issues, helped focus attention on an emergent body of Decadent writing in Britain. Beerbohm's witty narrative amounts to a playful inversion of Wilde's *Picture of Dorian Gray* (1890, revised 1891). Whereas Wilde's Dorian Gray remains youthfully unblemished as he commits increasingly heinous crimes, Beerbohm's Sir George Hell dons the mask of a saint to conceal that he is no longer an infamous Regency libertine but a man who lives instead in marital bliss under the hypocritical pseudonym "George Heaven." At the end of Wilde's story, Dorian Gray comes face to face with the portrait hidden away in his home, where it has grown hideous through acts of violence and betrayal. By comparison, when a former lover threatens to destroy the saintly-looking George Hell's happiness, the demand that he remove his mask leads to a surprising outcome: his face beneath has become as impeccable as the flawless waxen device affixed to it. Instead of hiding under the mask, Sir George therefore has come to embody it, in a style that strikingly runs against the grain of the moral that sends Dorian Gray to his grave. Even though Wilde's downfall had made him an unspeakable figure in polite society, Beerbohm had no hesitation in going into print with what amounts to a homage to a writer whom he generally held in esteem. Beerbohm's career, after all, began in 1893 with a respectfully amusing piece that asserts that "a more complete figure than Oscar Wilde has not been known since the days of Byron."[37] That the one-act version of "The Happy Hypocrite" introduced *Mr. and Mrs. Daventry,* a play that impressed Beerbohm, reveals his enduring commitment to Wilde.[38]

Beerbohm belonged to a fairly tight-knit group of Wilde's disciples, which included Ross, Turner, Adey, and Rothenstein, all of whom moved in similar circles. On hearing of Wilde's demise, Beerbohm commiserated with his friend Turner: "You must have had an awful time in Paris. Poor Oscar! I wish he were here, alive and superb—the Oscar before the fall."[39] Similarly, in 1901, Rothenstein wrote to Ross to say that he had "read a most interesting letter . . . about poor Oscar's death, and felt deeply how good you and Reggie had been."[40] During this period, Ross and Adey took over the fashionable Carfax Gallery at Ryder Street, St. James's, London, where they mounted Beerbohm's well-received 1901 exhibition of one hundred caricatures. In 1902, they showed a range of Rothenstein's works. This turn of events marked the beginning of Ross's rise in the art world, which in 1906 led to his regular reviews in the *Academy,* the journal that at one time could not mention Wilde's name.

Meanwhile, as Ross began to establish a successful career as a critic, he informed Adela Schuster that he had "for some time been in communication with the Official Receiver in regard to Oscar Wilde's copyrights of his books and plays."[41] Even in early 1902, Ross already had interest from two publishers who wanted to buy the copyrights "*en bloc.*" These companies promised to purchase all of them so long as the official receiver did not make unreasonable demands. By pursuing these deals, Ross was fulfilling a duty that Wilde had assigned to him shortly before leaving jail, in a detailed letter dated 1 April 1897: "I want you to be my literary executor in case of my death, and to have complete control over my plays, books and papers."[42] In particular, Wilde had wanted Ross to "be in possession of the only document that really gives any explanation of my extraordinary behaviour with regard to Queensberry and Alfred Douglas" (*Complete Letters,* 780). The document in question is the 55,000-word prose work written on twenty folio sheets of blue prison notepaper. Wilde explained that this was his precious gift to posterity, a means of unveiling the truth someday, though not in his or Douglas's lifetime. To ensure the preservation of this work, Wilde gave Ross specific instructions on how it should be copied on that "thoroughly modern" machine, the typewriter (781). The typed copy, he insisted, should contain "a wide rubricated margin" in which one could insert all corrections; this directive suggests that Wilde probably wished to make emendations to the work at some point in the future (781). Thereafter, as Wilde states in this letter, Ross should dispatch the original manuscript to Douglas. "There is no need," Wilde adds, "to tell A.D. that a copy has been taken" (782). Once this was done, a further typewritten copy was to be kept in Ross's hands for safekeeping, while shorter typewritten sections were to be sent to two cherished friends. Wilde had given a title to his work: "[I]t may be spoken of as the *Epistola: In Carcere et Vinculis*" (Letter: In Prison and In Chains) (782). The title certainly accords with the fact that the document is a letter addressed to "Dear Bosie." At the same time, the choice of title shows that this work, in a more general sense, comprises a self-standing epistle (one that Wilde believed should be conserved in typewritten form). Consequently, the careful naming of this lengthy manuscript implies that its meaning exceeds that of a regular item of correspondence.

In 1897, Ross followed all of Wilde's directives bar one. In what may or may not have been an act of disobedience—one that, at any rate, had serious consequences —Ross held onto the original manuscript; he also may have failed, deliberately or otherwise, to send a copy to Douglas.[43] Although he was not officially recognized as Wilde's executor until 1906, Ross assumed responsibility for the maintenance of the literary estate upon Wilde's death, and he kept in his hands papers belonging to Wilde, including several personal letters written by Douglas. Probably because German culture expressed the greatest interest in Wilde's work (Max Reinhardt's 1902 production of *Salomé*, which inspired Strauss's opera, is one example), Ross released to Max Meyerfeld—who translated several of Wilde's writings—a typewritten copy of the prison letter to Bosie. As Horst Schroeder has explained in detail, Meyerfeld's tactful selection of excerpts from this work appeared in *Die neue Rundschau* in January–February 1905.[44] Presumably in compliance with Ross's wishes, Meyerfeld's translation makes no mention that the entire work is addressed to Douglas. Ross later informed Meyerfeld that, after he first submitted his transcription of the prison document to respected publisher Algernon Methuen, he "anticipated refusal, as though the work were my own."[45] Methuen's reader, E. V. Lucas, however, had faith in the manuscript and recommended publication, as well as suggesting that it should be called *De*

Profundis. (Taken from Psalm 130, the Latin phrase means "out of the depths.") Both Meyerfeld's and Methuen's respective editions, which appeared within weeks of each other, bear this title.

Methuen, who knew that he was testing the water, hoped that the volume would "take an enduring place in the literature of misfortune."[46] Unexpectedly strong sales proved him right. By the end of the year, the sixth edition was in print. The immense commercial success of *De Profundis* marks the first decisive step toward Wilde's rehabilitation in modern British culture. In the next few years, the work was translated into numerous languages, including Dutch, French, Italian, Russian, Spanish, and Yiddish. Its wide circulation, however, involved no small measure of risk. Even though in his 1905 text Ross carefully omits any allusion to Douglas, he nonetheless quotes from correspondence by Wilde that shows that the work had its origins in a letter. Ross's preface, though, avoids any suggestion that the epistle in question largely amounts to the indictment of a specific individual. Instead, he states that this document "renders so vividly, and so painfully, the effect of social *débâcle* and imprisonment on a highly artificial and intellectual nature" as Wilde's.[47] As the biblical title indicates, Ross aimed to show that Wilde's reflections on his solitary confinement emerged from a deeply Christian anguish, which contrasts sharply with the image of Wilde as an exclusively "witty and delightful writer" (ix). Not surprisingly, the line that opens Ross's edition runs as follows: "Suffering is one very long moment" (11). In the eloquent passages that follow, Wilde proceeds to expose both the reprehensible manner in which the legal system treated him and the recklessness with which he had brought about his ruin: "Terrible as was what the world did to me, what I did to myself was far more terrible still" (21). Such finely balanced phrasing presents a gifted stylist in full command of a self-reproachful, almost penitent mood in which he accepts much of the onus for his downfall.

When *De Profundis* appeared from Methuen, most reviewers revealed an eagerness to reclaim Wilde in ways that might appear to have fulfilled Beerbohm's wish that the author who died in 1900 would arise again "alive and superb." Even those commentators who acknowledged the "evil associations" attached to Wilde's name felt obliged to speak of the book as a "work, tragically written, of a genius whose ruin was one of the saddest tragedies in" one's "lifetime."[48] In similarly cautious vein, Lucas observes in his review that Wilde's manifest genius lay "in his lawlessness."[49] What appear to redeem the writer for Lucas are those passages that show that "everything which Wilde says of Christ in this little book" is

Joseph Bristow

"worth reading and considering and reading again" (247). To radical politician R. B. Cunninghame Graham in the *Saturday Review*, the religious resonance of Wilde's prose is instructive, if for different reasons. In Graham's eyes, one of the most appealing aspects of the volume is that any individual, if charitably disposed, can study the suffering that Wilde records and find in it "his martyrdom, and read it as a thing that might have happened to himself."[50]

Beerbohm was not slow to catch the irony of Wilde's reinstatement in British culture through *De Profundis*. In the popular weekly *Vanity Fair*, in which some of his famous caricatures appeared, Beerbohm observes that the 1905 volume has ensured "that all the critics are writing, and gossips gossiping, very glibly . . . about the greatness of Wilde."[51] Beerbohm's wording suggests his serious doubts about this frenzied "magnifying" of a man "whom we so lately belittled" (249). He refuses to join the consensus that Ross's welcome edition of *De Profundis* expresses what Wilde "really and truly felt" (249). Astutely, Beerbohm concludes instead that even in a state of supposed humility Wilde remained admirably conceited: "Even 'from the depths' he condescended. Nor merely to mankind was he condescending. He enjoyed the greater luxury of condescending to himself" (250). Beerbohm sees this hyperbolical self-humbling evident in remarks that emphasize Wilde's continuing rhetorical authority despite his harsh sentence: "I, once a lord of language, have no words in which to express my anguish and my shame" (*De Profundis*, 13–14). As Beerbohm could see, *De Profundis* hardly presented Wilde as a crushed man: "It is a joy to find in this last prose work of his the old power, all unmarred by the physical torments that he had suffered" (251). Moreover, the punitive system that left Wilde "broken, and powerless, and aimless" could not eradicate "the invincible artist in him" (251). If the 1905 edition of *De Profundis* proved one thing for Beerbohm, it was that even in the face of hardship Wilde remained "immutable" (251).

Responsibility for the widespread reception of *De Profundis* lay mostly with Ross. He launched a campaign to put this work into the hands of a broad circle of friends and editors, as well as influential people with whom he was not acquainted. The positive responses that he promptly received bears out George Bernard Shaw's canny observation, made on 13 March 1905, that the "British press is as completely beaten by" Wilde "*de profundis* as it was *in excelsis*."[52] "The unquenchable spirit of the man," Shaw enthuses, "is magnificent." Within fifteen months, handsome royalties discharged Wilde's debts. At this time, however, Ross's edition of *De Profundis* and Strauss's *Salome* were not all that helped restore

Wilde's reputation. Altogether more quietly, though with far-reaching consequences, two dedicated researchers were beginning to piece together the immense
scope of Wilde's bibliography. The labors of these two men, Christopher Sclater
Millard and Walter Ledger, made a decisive contribution to the next phase of Ross's
initiative to do justice to his "prodigal baby." By 2 February 1906, when Ross's tire-
less work resulted in the annulment of Wilde's bankruptcy, the path had been
cleared for him to begin editing the fourteen-volume *Collected Works,* which
Methuen agreed to issue in an *édition de luxe,* with designs by Charles Ricketts,
whose distinctive motifs appeared in several of Wilde's first editions in the 1890s.[53]
The *Collected Works,* which remains fairly authoritative to this day, would become
one of the lasting tributes to Wilde's memory.

Millard, who published under the pseudonym Stuart Mason, came to notice
with his 1905 English edition of André Gide's "Oscar Wilde," an essay that had appeared three years earlier in the French review *L'ermitage.* Gide's reminiscences,
which date back to his first meeting with Wilde in 1891, scarcely present an admiring picture ("Wilde was not a great writer," Gide insists).[54] Gide's emphasis falls instead on tracing the downward transformation of a onetime "wonderful creature"
(22) into an individual who eventually grew "reckless, hardened, and conceited"
(45). When he recalls his unexpected meeting with Wilde at Blidah, Algeria, in
January 1895, Gide dares not be too explicit about what instilled his horror at a
man whose "lyrical adoration was fast becoming frenzied madness" (46). For
those early-twentieth-century readers acquainted with homosexual tourism,
Gide's meaning would have been clear enough. Pursued in Algiers, as Gide remembers, "by quite an extraordinary mob of young ruffians," Wilde shocked the
French author by making the following scandalous declaration: "I hope to have
thoroughly demoralized this town" (47). Gide recollects that several years later,
when he enjoyed cocktails with Wilde at a Parisian café, "[n]othing remained in"
Wilde's "shattered life but a mouldy ruin" (83). It is almost as if Gide predicted
that Wilde's presumed dissipation could only result in this piteous spectacle.
Therefore it may appear strange that Millard chose to disseminate Gide's largely
negative account. Millard, however, no doubt recognized that Gide's memoir is
valuable because it stands among the earliest documents that flesh out what had
already become, by 1905, a contested biographical record. More to the point, Gide's
comments touch upon sexual intimacy between men, which in the early 1900s
was undeniably the most sensitive aspect of Wilde's troubled life story. In the closing pages of his edition, Millard balances Gide's candid remarks by including a

Joseph Bristow

fairly comprehensive bibliography of Wilde's works, which showed for the first time the striking extent and diversity of the Irish writer's oeuvre.

In other ways, too, Millard's efforts provided a scholarly alternative to the emerging body of biographical writing on Wilde, which began with Robert Harborough Sherard's unreliable 1902 memoir. Sherard, who had become closely acquainted with Wilde in Paris in 1883, remained loyal to his friend throughout the two-year prison sentence. Sherard recalls, however, that their long-standing association deteriorated when Wilde made "a great and unfortunate mistake" by reuniting with Douglas at Posilippo, near Naples.[55] After Sherard voiced stern disapproval, Wilde responded with a searing letter denouncing him as a "Tartuffe": the kind of petty-minded moralist whose prissiness is clear at the start of Sherard's high-minded biography (259).[56] "Of his aberration which brought this fine life to shipwreck so pitiful," Sherard intones, "I have nothing to say" (10). Such "cruel and devilish madness," he declares, belongs to "the domains of pathology" (10). Instead, he depicts a man whose "supreme delicacy of tongue" always enchanted him (12). Regardless of his straitlaced attitude, Sherard—who did his utmost to become the leading authority on Wilde—was an important contact for Millard.[57] Together, in the summer of 1904, the two men visited the Hôtel d'Alsace, where Dupoirier showed them the room in which Wilde had died, which had become, in Millard's words, "a place of pilgrimage from all parts of the world for those who admire his genius or pity his sorrows" (in Gide, Oscar Wilde, 10).

By the time Gide's essay appeared in English, Millard had been in touch with Ross, though their initial meeting was stymied by Millard's arrest on the charge of "gross indecency" at Iffley, near Oxford. Ross, who was probably Wilde's earliest male lover, remained only too aware of the hazards facing homosexual men; upon receiving Millard's wire for help, he rushed to Oxford to see whether this thirty-four-year-old Wilde scholar would be sent down for "10 years' penal servitude."[58] Millard was jailed for three months with hard labor. On his release, he followed in Wilde's footsteps by exiling himself in Dieppe. The following year, however, he returned to London, found employment at a bookstore, and soon began researching the publication history of The Picture of Dorian Gray for Ross's Collected Works. The upshot of his inquiries was the noteworthy volume Oscar Wilde: Art and Morality—A Defence of The Picture of Dorian Gray (1908). In this remarkable book, which was issued again in 1912, Millard brings together the handful of hostile reviews that encouraged newsagent W. H. Smith to remove the 1890 edition of Wilde's story from its shelves. Moreover, Millard reprints the lengthy exchanges about immorality and modern fiction that stemmed from the furor that exploded around *The Picture of Dorian Gray* in W. E. Henley's *Scots Observer*. His study reveals that the violence Wilde suffered at the hands of the state in 1895 was in some ways anticipated by the notorious shot that one of Henley's journalists had fired at Wilde's novel five years earlier: "The story— which deals with matters only fitted for the Criminal Investigation department or a hearing *in camera* is discreditable alike to author and editor. Mr. Wilde has brains, and art, and style; but if he can write for none but outlawed noblemen and perverted telegraph boys, the sooner he takes to tailoring (or some other decent trade) the better for his own reputation and the public morals."[59] Numerous commentators have pointed out that these sentences allude to the Cleveland Street Affair of 1888–89, in which at least one well-known aristocrat fled the country because he was suspected of having sex in a brothel with young men from the nearby post office.[60] By reminding readers of the *Scots Observer*'s sexual enmity, Millard, a man who experienced further persecution for his homosexuality, became an outspoken apologist for Wilde.

Ross, who later employed Millard as his secretary, was the first to acknowledge the significance of this scholar's contribution to the edition that reestablished Wilde's literary standing. The *Collected Works* provided influential reviewers with the chance to draw an informed overall picture of Wilde's diverse canon. Given the uneven quality of some of Wilde's earlier works, it is no surprise that the most engaged assessments were keenly critical. As dramatist St. John Hankin observes in the *Fortnightly Review*, these volumes show that "Wilde as a playwright was always an imitator rather than an original artist"—though Hankin admits that the "nearest approach to absolute originality" occurs in *The Importance of Being Earnest*.[61] Arthur Symons, who had written sympathetic reviews of Wilde's work in the past, furnished a lengthy notice in the respected *Athenæum*, in which he states that only now is the "artificial world Wilde created" beginning to "settle down in any sort of known order."[62] Symons appears to have been taken aback by what he saw as the patchy quality of Wilde's canon, and he was quick to remark on the "bad epigram" that too often mars the work of a "prodigious entertainer" (294). Less impressed, Harold Child in the *Times Literary Supplement* states that even in "the most thoughtful, the most illuminating things" that we might find in an essay such as "The Soul of Man under Socialism" (1891), Wilde seems superficial; from Child's perspective, Wilde lacks "that conviction,

Joseph Bristow

that deeper personality, without which a man must be content to go on saying what other people have said before him."[63]

No matter how many deficiencies these commentators identified in Wilde's oeuvre, the fact that they expended so much energy on the *Collected Works* served Wilde's legacy well. Just after the final two volumes of this major edition appeared in late 1908, Ross delivered a speech at a large dinner held in his honor. His audience comprised more than 160 guests—among them Wilde's sons (then in their twenties), Frank Harris, W. Somerset Maugham, William Rothenstein, and H. G. Wells. This was distinguished company. Once he gave his thanks, Ross disclosed that he had received a large anonymous gift of £2,000 "to place a suitable monument to Oscar Wilde at Père Lachaise" in Paris.[64] This generous donor stipulated that the commission should go to the young American sculptor Jacob Epstein. In the course of disclosing this good news, Ross stressed that there were three people in particular "to whom this dinner should really have been given— Mr. Methuen, Mr. Stuart Mason, and [Ross's] solicitor, Mr. Holman" (156). None of these men, as Ross observed, had had any personal contact with Wilde.

Noticeably, Ross made no tribute to Douglas. As it turned out, Douglas chose to stay away from an "absurd dinner" that, as he informed Ross, brought together people who either had no connection with Wilde or were "not on speaking terms with him" when he died.[65] But at the time, Douglas's relations with Ross were under strain, not least because this literary executor, as soon became clear, had not treated Wilde's former lover with sufficient respect. Certainly, as Ross said in his after-dinner speech, he had fulfilled the promise he made to himself "at the deathbed of Oscar Wilde" (154). Eight years after his friend's impecunious passing, Ross made sure that both Wilde's estate and his reputation were in good order. This was more than Douglas ever did. Certainly, Douglas helped reverse the *Academy*'s former antipathy toward Wilde by using his recent editorship of that journal to print his fine sonnet "The Dead Poet," which honors his former lover's memory.[66] Moreover, in the *Academy* he went out of his way to expose the recently deceased Henley as a man whose repeated attacks on Wilde's works had not "the smallest nobility of soul."[67] Yet Douglas soon held an extremely vexed, if on occasion misunderstood, place in Wilde's legacy. Ross had knowingly taken risks in publishing *De Profundis,* and in the *Collected Works* he included a slightly expanded version of this text, which once again made no mention of Douglas's name.

There were other reasons why Ross's relations with Douglas were deteriorating after several years of reasonably friendly, if intermittent, contact between them. Even though Douglas invited Ross to his secret marriage to poet Olive Custance in 1902 (her father disapproved of the match because of Bosie's former attachment to Wilde), five years later a breach opened up. The rift occurred, somewhat ironically, after Ross suggested that Douglas should assist Harold Child in editing the *Academy*. (Ross also suggested that Douglas's cousin by marriage, Edward Tennant, should take over proprietorship of the journal, which he did.) When Child joined the London *Times* later that year, Douglas took his place and needed an assistant. Douglas's choice was seasoned polemicist T.W.H. Crosland, a moral crusader who was determined to make the journal—in the words of his admiring biographer—an organ for "conducting a campaign against all sorts of evil and wickedness."[68]

Ross appears to have been among the first contributors to succumb to Crosland's blue pencil, on the grounds that his submission did not maintain "sound morality" (*Genius of T.W.H. Crosland*, 218). Unhesitatingly, in the *Academy*, Crosland embarked on a series of attacks against all forms of supposed immorality. Ross's second book, *Masques and Phases* (1909), was just the kind of study that would have met with his disapproval. (It was a sign of Ross's growing prominence that his first monograph, on the sexually controversial fin-de-siècle artist Aubrey Beardsley, appeared earlier that year.) *Masques and Phases,* which Beerbohm found a "joy from first to last," comprises twenty-five essays and reviews that Ross had contributed to various journals over the years, including one edited by Douglas, *The Spirit Lamp* (1893), a homoerotically oriented journal whose contents include three of Wilde's short works.[69] Although none of Ross's succinct pieces was aimed at generating scandal, one does touch upon homosexuality, which Crosland abominated. The essay in question, which dates from 1905, outlines the life of London artist Simeon Solomon, whose career was cut short when he was arrested for sexual contact with another man in a public restroom in 1873. To be sure, Ross does not spell out the events that led to Solomon's imprisonment. Nonetheless, he comments that for "poor Solomon there was no place in life," not least because this artist—who once enjoyed the company of Walter Pater and Algernon Charles Swinburne—was "an inverted Watts."[70] The description is apt because much of Solomon's greatest art explores patterns of same-sex desire in mythological scenes that share elements of G. F. Watts's eminently heterosexual representations of Classical legend.

By the time Harold Child favorably reviewed *Masques and Phases* in the *Times Literary Supplement*, Ross had begun to enjoy some prominence as an expert on modern art.[71] Margot Asquith, spouse of the recently elected prime minister, invited Ross into her influential circle, which in turn led to his acquaintance with high-ranking officials whose clout ultimately resulted in Ross's appointment as a trustee of the Tate Gallery in 1917. Since Crosland and Douglas, as they put it, could not stand "the tee-total, socialistic, and wild-cat Premier," the battle lines with Ross became sharply defined.[72] In these hostile circumstances, Ross decided to bequeath the complete manuscript of *De Profundis* to the British Museum; the director, Sir Frederic Kenyon, accepted Ross's gift on 15 November 1909. Under the terms of this bequest, the museum agreed to keep the document sealed for fifty years. Moreover, as Maureen Borland discloses, the director and his colleagues acknowledged that in parting with this manuscript Ross was making considerable financial sacrifice. Furthermore, the trustees understood that Ross wished to ensure that no members of Douglas's family would be hurt by the contents.[73] In the manuscript, after all, Wilde mercilessly attacks Douglas for supposed negligence: "Why did you not write to me? Was it cowardice? Was it callousness? What was it?" (*Complete Letters*, 725). Nowhere does Wilde appear to have understood that Douglas might have been legally compromised had this aristocrat sent any mail to the prison authorities, who as a matter of course vetted incoming and outgoing correspondence with inmates.[74] In the process of berating Douglas for his incomprehensible silence, Wilde heaps praise upon Ross for writing at twelve-weekly intervals "real letters"—ones that "have the quality of a French *causerie intime*" (something greater, it seems, than any of Douglas's literary efforts) (726). Yet no matter how flattering Wilde's comments are toward Ross, it is strange to think that Ross assumed authority over a manuscript that ostensibly takes the form of a personal letter that begins "Dear Bosie." To the end of his days, Douglas protested (perhaps rightly) that the document initially placed in Ross's hands, and then handed over to the museum, was his.[75]

In any case, Ross, in his role as Wilde's literary executor, had been entrusted with a manuscript that he seems not to have handled with due caution. In 1909, a German translation edited by Meyerfeld presented an extensively annotated text of a larger portion of the document than had previously appeared. This edition opens with a long, complimentary letter from Ross to Meyerfeld, dated 31 August 1907, in which Ross discloses who has been privy to the complete manuscript: "With the exception of Major Nelson [governor of Reading Gaol], myself, and a confidential typewriter, no one has read the whole of it" ("To Max Meyerfeld," xi). "Contrary to a general impression," he adds, disingenuously, "it contains nothing scandalous" (xi). Ross proceeds to characterize the work as "desultory": "a large portion of it is taken up with business and private matters of no interest whatever" (xi). But when we learn that Max Meyerfeld, along with Algernon Methuen and Hamilton Fyfe (editor of the popular *Daily Mirror*), had also seen the manuscript, it becomes clear that word may well have begun to spread about the truly consequential nature of this document. Meyerfeld was the first to reveal that *De Profundis* was "ein Brief Oscar Wildes aus dem Zuchthaus in Reading an seinen Freund Lord Alfred Douglas" ("a letter written by Oscar Wilde at Reading Gaol to his friend Lord Alfred Douglas") (xvii). Moreover, Meyerfeld reveals that the work was originally called "Epistola: In Carcere et Vinculis," and he places this title at the head of his translation. So that readers can comprehend the autobiographical import of this work, Meyerfeld introduces his notes by filling in the background to Wilde's involvement with Douglas, from their earliest meeting in 1891 to the events that resulted in the failed libel trial of 3 April 1895. Since this edition was quickly translated into English and became available in New York, though not in London, its appearance doubtless spurred Ross to put the manuscript out of public reach until 1959.

Matters came to a head in 1912 with the first serious critical inquiry into Wilde's achievements, which quietly disclosed to the British audience what Meyerfeld had explicitly revealed to the German-speaking world three years earlier. In *Oscar Wilde: A Critical Study,* by Arthur Ransome (the author who later earned fame for his children's classic, *Swallows and Amazons* [1930]), readers learned that the "book called *De Profundis* . . . is not printed as it was written, but is composed of passages from a long letter whose complete publication would be impossible in this generation."[76] In preparing this book, Ransome drew on Ross's comprehensive knowledge of Wilde's career, as well as important documents such as the letter that Ross sent to Adey two weeks after their friend's death. In a document that relates to his dealings with Ransome, Ross asserts, "I did not show Ransome the typewritten copy of the unpublished portions of *De Profundis.*"[77] Caspar Wintermans is probably right to say that Ross's statement sounds dishonest, especially when we compare Ransome's recollections of what happened (Wintermans, *Alfred Douglas,* 123).[78] On the evidence that exists, Ross seems to have given Ransome a free hand, since *Oscar Wilde:*

A *Critical Study* contains the following indiscreet assertions: "The letter, a man-uscript of 'eighty close-written pages on twenty folio sheets,' was not addressed to Mr. Ross but to a man whom Wilde felt he owed some, at least, of the circum-stances of the public disgrace. It was begun as a rebuke of this friend, whose actions, even subsequent to the trials, had been such as to cause Wilde consid-erable pain. It was not delivered to him, but given to Mr. Ross by Wilde, who also gave instructions as to its partial publication" (157). Once he learned of Ransome's insinuations, Douglas was indignant. He launched a libel suit against the publisher, the printer, the Times Book Club of London (which distributed copies), and the author. In 1913, when he stood before the court, Douglas con-fronted the fact that much of the work from which Ross had taken extracts was exactly as Ransome characterized it—a wholehearted rebuke of himself. As lengthy transcripts in the *Times* show, the defense read out large sections from those parts of *De Profundis* that Ross had suppressed in his edition. Under cross-examination, Douglas withstood a further barrage in the form of letters that he had sent to Wilde, which Ross had appropriated at the time of their friend's death. With such questionable evidence held against him, Douglas had no chance of a verdict in his favor, even when he revealed from his passbooks that during the last ten months of Wilde's life he had generously given his friend "£390 in cheques (in addition to a lot of ready money)."[79] Years later, in 1925, Douglas informed Harris that at the start of the Ransome trial he had "not the slightest idea that it was a letter addressed by Wilde" to him—though this is a claim open to some question.[80] Douglas, it is worth noting, reviewed the 1905 volume in *Motorist and Traveller*. There he shrewdly remarks, "If Oscar Wilde's spirit, returning to this world in a malicious mood, had wished to devise a pleasant and insinuating trap for some of his old enemies of the press, he could scarcely have hit on a better one than this book."[81] He adds, almost as if the point hardly mattered at all, that "this interesting post-humous book . . . takes the form of a letter to an unnamed friend."

Although Douglas lost his case in 1913 (the judge took delight in humiliating him, and the costs were a hefty £1,500), Methuen tried to settle matters by emend-ing the offending paragraphs in a second imprint of *Oscar Wilde: A Critical Study*.[82] But there was no smoothing over the conflict. In 1912, in preparation for the trial, Crosland had access to the manuscript of *De Profundis,* and he quickly issued an invective in verse, titled *The First Stone: On Reading the Unpublished*

Parts of "De Profundis." In his foreword, Crosland (who does not mention Douglas as the recipient of the prison document) states that the "parts cut out of" Ross's 1905 edition "are sufficiently discreditable to render the whole ignominious."[83] "Wilde is dead," Crosland adds. "[L]et his crowning devilry die with him—yes, Mr. Robert Ross, I say, devilry!" (6). Given that this agent provocateur seldom left Douglas's side, no one could appease the impulsive aristocrat. As a precautionary step against Douglas making any attempt to issue his own edition of the prison document (he had already approached an American publisher), Ross brought out in New York an edition of fifteen copies of the "suppressed portion of *De Profundis,*" which satisfied the Library of Congress's guidelines on copyright.[84] Matters worsened because Douglas was declared bankrupt not long before the court proceedings began. Soon enough, to defend his blemished reputation and to raise urgently needed funds, Douglas went into print with a book, largely written by Crosland, lambasting Wilde in general and denouncing in particular "the disgraceful document which Mr. Ross has so generously bestowed upon the nation."[85] Consequently, the hostility between Douglas and Ross intensified, leading them into further bruising legal battles—as well as several poetic tirades—until Ross died in 1918.[86]

As we can see, the Ransome trial vented in public the animosity between Ross and Douglas that had intensified during the previous four years. The tumult in the courtroom extended the vendetta that Douglas had already spearheaded against the increasingly successful Ross, who in 1912 was appointed valuer of pictures for the Board of the Inland Revenue. Even before Ross's defense began quoting at length the unpublished parts of *De Profundis,* Douglas employed a private detective to monitor Ross's movements. The purpose was to find incriminating evidence of improprieties between Ross and his young lover, Freddie Smith. Douglas's campaign, in which Crosland was involved, included the attempted blackmail of a male prostitute to confess that he had been sexually intimate with Ross. In March 1914, Ross—who counted "litigation" among his interests in *Who's Who*—decided to sue Douglas for criminal libel; he also issued writs for criminal conspiracy and perjury against Crosland and Douglas together. Jonathan Fryer points out that while Douglas escaped the proceedings by staying in France, Crosland in court "portrayed himself as a decent, upright man who was fighting a moral crusade against those who were trying to whitewash Wilde and legitimize his filthy practices."[87] Accordingly, Crosland's counsel focused the jury's attention on the questionable morality of Wilde's work, which

Millard, among others, was asked to defend. It must have been somewhat eerie for Millard to find himself in a courtroom situation similar to the one in April 1895, when Wilde was asked to explain whether sections of *The Picture of Dorian Gray* were "sodomitical."[88] The fact that the jury acquitted Crosland came as a terrible shock to Ross and his supporters.

Toward the end of the year, however, a noteworthy event gave Ross cause for celebration. Millard's magnificent bibliography, which he had compiled over the years with Ledger's help, appeared from independent publisher T. Werner Laurie.[89] The *Library Association Record* extolled it as "the most comprehensive bibliography that exists in English."[90] Meanwhile, in the scholarly world, Ernst Bendz— who produced some of the most informed early research on Wilde's oeuvre —celebrated the manner in which this great work gives "one anew a sense of Wilde's amazing versatility and the wide scope of his talents, of his increasing importance as an intellectual and literary power, and of the immense vogue his works have had during the past decade," which led in turn to individuals being willing "to pay large sums for signed copies of first editions."[91] It thus comes as no surprise to learn that for Ross, as he remarks in his introductory note to that fine bibliography, Millard's labors afforded him "peculiar pleasure": "They emphasise the truth of what I prophesied when Wilde died in 1900—that his writings would in a few years' time excite wider interest than those of almost any of his contemporaries. Indeed, with the possible exception of Dickens and Byron, I doubt if any British author of the nineteenth century is better known over a more extensive geographical area."[92] Ross does not overstate matters when he says that by 1914 Wilde's reputation had few rivals on a global scale. Were it not for Ross's extraordinary efforts together with those of Millard, which occurred in the face of attacks against their sexual preference, Wilde's literary standing could not have resurged so triumphantly.

Just at the point when World War I would wreak havoc across Europe (the subsequent bloodbath would take the life of Cyril Holland), one further event completed Ross's important efforts to commemorate Wilde. After months of wrangling with French authorities (first, customs officers wished to levy a heavy customs duty, then cemetery officials objected to the sexual aspects of the design), Ross witnessed at long last the unveiling of Jacob Epstein's imposing memorial to Wilde. At Père Lachaise, Epstein's distinctly modernist sphinx—an icon derived from Wilde's 1894 poem—finally paid a monumental tribute to Wilde's legendary reputation.

"Being Dead Is the Most Boring Experience in Life"—Oscar Wilde's Spirit Channeled by Hester Travers Smith (1925)

By 1914, some of the legends about Wilde had come to prove untrustworthy, and during the war many (and much more disreputable) tall tales would come into circulation, sometimes courtesy of close friends such as Ross. Among the earliest myths were those that claimed that Wilde had escaped an early death. Soon after Ross's edition of *De Profundis* appeared, George Sylvester Viereck—later notorious as an American supporter of Nazism—explored the question "Is Oscar Wilde Living or Dead?" In light of the success of *De Profundis,* Viereck speculates, "[I]f now, crowned with the world's admiration, he should come back, would it not pardon the re-arisen poet who had died at least one death for his sin?"[93] It is almost as if Viereck were trying to will the Christ-like Wilde back to life to make the world repent for its wrongdoing. Viereck's essay counts among numerous accounts featuring Wilde's wished-for resurrection. In 1908, for example, the *Los Angeles Times* devoted a full-page spread to apparent sightings of Wilde on the West Coast.[94] Stranger by far than these tales of Wilde *redivivus* are those involving the various oddballs who believed that they could forge a living connection with a man whom they did not know. Their insurgence into what became the increasingly fictitious memory of Wilde does not merely make plain the degree to which his extraordinary legacy activated almost delusional, cultish fantasies. This colorful cast of characters—which includes a practiced forger who traded palm oil in West Africa, a surrealist boxer who disappeared into the Pacific, and a perfidious, parrot-loving English widow who sported a Thai name—also throws light on the escalating material value attached to Wilde's legacy.

In the same year that Viereck claimed Wilde had become "famous all over the world" (87), a young poet called J. M. Stuart-Young published the first of several editions of a peculiarly named book: *Osrac the Self-Sufficient.* In his introductory memoir (dated 1 May 1905 from Conakry, West Africa), Stuart-Young records his earliest meeting with Wilde—or "Osrac," as he specially names his hero: "We went to the Haymarket after dinner [supposedly in June 1894 to see *A Woman of No Importance*], and he had my hand clasped within his all evening, when a more than usually happy aphorism had been uttered by the players he would turn to me for approval, and I recall his manifest pleasure when I repeated a few lines between the acts. 'The book of life begins with a man and a woman and ends—with Revelation.'"[95] Later, Stuart-Young claims to have been in Wilde's company at the Hôtel d'Alsace in 1898, when he glimpsed the manuscript of *The Ballad of Reading Gaol* on a table. To prove his intimacy with this much-loved friend, Stuart-Young included facsimile plates that supposedly reproduce Wilde's handwritten letters to him.

To anyone closely acquainted with Wilde, some of this account would look absurd. The first run of Wilde's play finished at the Haymarket in August 1893, and his fine Greek hand scarcely resembles the scrawl that Stuart-Young attributes to him. Yet as Stephanie Newell observes, through *Osrac* Stuart-Young—who was thirteen in 1894—managed to hoodwink Hesketh Pearson, whose respected biography of Wilde appeared in 1946.[96] Pearson, who believed these fabrications, draws harsh conclusions about Wilde's decision, as we are told in *Osrac,* to escort Stuart-Young to the rooms of male prostitute Alfred Taylor (with whom Wilde was tried in May 1895). "Wilde," Pearson observes, "must be regarded . . . as . . . one whose innocence approaches imbecility."[97] To be sure, Pearson assumed that Stuart-Young, whose poetry on "Osrac" accompanies his memoir, must have been middle class. Little did he understand, as Newell reveals, that Stuart-Young—a working-class youth from Manchester—began his extraordinary career as a lowly clerk and exiled himself from England in 1901 after a period in jail. The local magistrate had found him guilty of theft by forgery; he had used the monies to buy luxurious books and furnishings for his modest rooms. Once settled in West Africa, Stuart-Young elaborated fantasies about the aesthetic life in the imperial homeland that he had already tried, through criminal activity, to make real. The eccentric story of Stuart-Young, who by 1919 had reinvented himself as the wealthiest palm producer in Nigeria, presents an extreme but telling example of the lengths to which individuals could go to make Wilde the object of their obsessive wish fulfillments.

Stuart-Young's strenuous tale telling, however, pales by comparison with the legends that two of Wilde's closest acquaintances enlarged upon. Harris's *Oscar Wilde: His Life and Confessions,* a truly unreliable work, became a best seller in 1916. When Douglas heard that Harris planned to publish a biography of Wilde that drew on materials held by Ross, he sought to prevent it. For this reason, Harris's *Oscar Wilde* appeared in New York instead of London, and—if we are to believe Harris—it sold 40,000 copies (Douglas and Harris, *New Preface,* 6). As Wintermans reminds us, there is plenty of "bad taste . . . unreliability, and venom" in Harris's sensational two volumes, and "most of the nonsense written about Bosie over the years" can be traced back to this influential source (*Alfred*

Douglas, 161). Harris asserts, for example, that Douglas—who in 1894 became Lord Cromer's honorary attaché in Egypt—returned to London because there had been some implicitly homosexual "disagreement" between them (*Oscar Wilde*, 1:159). More to the point, Harris paints a negative picture of Douglas's supposedly fatal influence when he reunited with and then parted from Wilde at Posilippo in 1897: "[T]he forbidden fruit," Harris writes, "quickly turned to ashes" in Wilde's "mouth" (2:406). Harris is least trustworthy when expounding his intimate acquaintance with Wilde. He claims, for instance, that he witnessed the sickening scenes that took place outside the courtroom on 25 May 1895 when Wilde was sentenced: "We had not left the court when cheering broke out in the streets, and when we came outside there were troops of the lowest women of the town dancing together and kicking up their legs in hideous abandonment, while the surrounding crowd of policemen and spectators grinned with delight" (1:319–20). Unfortunately, as Sherard points out, at the time Harris was nowhere near this grisly spectacle at the Old Bailey.⁹⁸

The most untruthful parts of *Oscar Wilde: His Life and Confessions* relate to the circumstances of Wilde's painful death, which Harris learned about from Ross. In his letter to Adey, Ross reports that "[f]oam and blood came from [Wilde's] mouth," and the "painful noise became louder and louder" (Wilde, *Complete Letters*, 1220). "[H]e passed," Ross states, at "10 minutes to 2 p.m. exactly" (1220). To Harris, this gruesome episode could not have made for a "more degrading" episode: "Suddenly, as the two friends sat by the bedside in sorrowful anxiety, there was a loud explosion: mucus poured out of Oscar's mouth and nose, and—Even the bedding had to be burned" (*Oscar Wilde*, 2:539). No sooner has he amplified the "death rattle" into an explosion than Harris turns to another remarkable legend that Ross circulated about Wilde's corpse. Harris claims that at the Alsace the doctors told Ross "to put Wilde's body in quicklime, like the body of the man in 'The Ballad of Reading Gaol' [1898]" "The quicklime, they said, would consume the flesh and leave the white bones—the skeleton—in tact, which could then be moved easily" when the time came to take Wilde's remains to Père Lachaise (2:540). Harris states that in 1914 Ross discovered that "the quicklime, instead of destroying the flesh, had preserved it." "Oscar's face," he declares, "was recognisable, only his hair and beard had grown long" (2:540). Ross seems to have not been far from believing that Wilde might arise and walk forth from the tomb.

Such an anecdote beggars belief, and even Harris—who made capital from exaggerating the story of Wilde's life—would later take pains to correct this extravagant tale. In the mid-1920s, Harris decided to approach Wilde's former lover, Alfred Douglas, with the intention of toning down the unflattering picture of the aristocrat. In 1925, Harris hoped that Douglas could be persuaded that the time had come for a fresh edition of *Oscar Wilde*—one furnished with a preface that made appropriate apologies for defaming Douglas—to be published in Britain. Harris duly supplied Douglas with the text of his preface. But Douglas, after their meeting at Nice in April that year, stated that he would capitulate to Harris's demands only if the new edition of *Oscar Wilde* included "marginal notes and the modification of the worst passages" that would counter the "mass of malicious lies and misrepresentations" of him (*New Preface*, 8).

According to Douglas, Harris responded by stating that such changes "would involve the destruction of a great many of the stereotyped plates," and thus the expense of such revisions would be well in excess of what he could afford (*New Preface*, 8). In the circumstances, Douglas refused Harris permission to print a new edition of the biography in Britain. As a consequence, Harris's *Oscar Wilde* was not issued in the United Kingdom until 1938. Douglas, however, took the publication of Harris's recantation into his own hands, and the resulting short volume comprises Douglas's foreword, Harris's new preface, and Douglas's letter to Harris dated 30 April 1925, which aims to set the record straight. One event that particularly irked Douglas puts Ross in a very poor light. Douglas explains in some detail to Harris what happened before he turned up at the Hôtel d'Alsace on 2 December 1900:

> While Wilde lay dead, and before I arrived in Paris, Ross went through the papers and manuscripts he found in Wilde's rooms. Among them he found a quantity of my letters to Wilde. These letters he appropriated without a word to me. I naturally had not the slightest idea that he had found and stolen letters written by me to Wilde, and I suppose that even those queerly misguided persons who profess to admire Ross as a model of "faithful friendship" . . . will admit that to steal or appropriate letters written by one of one's friends to another friend, and to keep them secretly and finally use them against their writer in a law court, is a wicked, disgraceful, and dishonourable action. The facts as to this business cannot be denied. Ross took my letters, and his executors or heirs have got them to this day. How many letters he found and kept

I have no idea. When the Ransome case ... came on, some of these letters were produced in Court during my cross-examination by Sir James Campbell, Ransome's counsel. (*New Preface*, 31–32)

Douglas adds that this unexpected development in the courtroom agitated him even more because the pilfered letters were ones that by 1913 he felt "ashamed" of (32)—since he had, for more than a decade, repudiated his homosexual past.

Harris, when he caught up with Douglas in April 1925, was willing to admit that Ross was not as reliable as he had thought, particularly in connection with certain facts about Wilde's last hours. In his self-congratulatory new preface, Harris states that during a meeting two months earlier, Reggie Turner—who regarded *Oscar Wilde* as "one of the best biographies in the language" (*New Preface*, 12)—had asked him to "cut down the death scene of Wilde by omitting a few lines" about the "explosion" that allegedly took place when Wilde expired (13). "This," Harris said, "was an elaboration of Robert Ross['s]: he told me that all Oscar's bowels came away in the bed, and the smell was so disgusting that it made him violently sick, and he had to cleanse the place and burn the bedding" (14). In Turner's view, "the whole scene" was "an invention of Robbie's," the kind of episode that was characteristic of a man "afflicted with a dramatic imagination" (14). As Turner remarked, the truth was that "Oscar's end was as quiet and peaceful as that of an innocent child" (15). Similarly, Turner put Harris to rights on the transfer of Wilde's remains to the coffin that was interred at Père Lachaise. If, Turner suggested, Harris contacted Coleridge Kennard, who had been present during these proceedings, then he would learn that this too was "an invention of Ross['s]" (14). When Harris spoke to Kennard, he learned that "Ross's story was mere fiction" because Ross "did not go into the grave or move the body with his own hands: he left all that to professional grave-diggers" (16–17). Yet such correctives to Ross's mythmaking did not deter Richard Ellmann, in the most substantial biography of Wilde to date, from expressing considerable sympathy with Harris's reckless account of Wilde. No doubt this is why Ellmann perpetuates Harris's unreliable tale of Wilde's exploding corpse and depicts Douglas as a wholly treacherous figure.[99]

Douglas did serious disservice to Wilde by dragging the deceased's name back into several libel suits. He also made himself appear altogether undependable by reacting to the Ransome trial with a book in which he claims that Wilde possessed a "shallow and comparative feeble mind, incapable of grappling unaided with even moderately profound things, and disposed to fribble and antic with old thoughts for lack of power to evolve new ones" (*Oscar Wilde and Myself*, 62–63). Douglas confused matters further in his 1929 *Autobiography* by stating that in 1914 he did "not tell the whole truth" about his relations with Wilde (25); he thus began what amounts to a partial recantation in two further autobiographical works. In 1940, five years before his death, Douglas's volte-face became complete when he went into print declaring that the "assurance that Wilde died a Catholic . . . enabled" Douglas "to undertake the task" of defending Wilde, since Douglas had been a convert to Rome since 1909. "When I speak of defending Wilde," Douglas writes, "I do not mean defending his vices. . . . I mean defending his character apart from his vices."[100] Even though in this later work Douglas disavows that he had any homosexual involvement with Wilde, he goes out of his way to claim that when reading the critical essays gathered in *Intentions*, "all the time one is conscious of an alert and well-informed intelligence which is not exploiting merely personal prejudices but is unobtrusively testifying to profound intellectual and artistic principles" (108). Understandably, the fact that Douglas engaged in tedious squabbles with other biographers has often discredited him as a reliable source in the study of Wilde.

Yet Douglas, for all his tempestuousness, was more honest than the two (or, depending on how we count them, three) individuals who in the 1920s were responsible for committing serious frauds in Wilde's legendary name. One of them, Arthur Cravan, happened to be a relative. Born Fabian Avenarius Lloyd, he was the second son of Constance Wilde's brother, Otho Holland Lloyd, and he was raised in Switzerland. Even though Cravan had no contact with Wilde (he was thirteen when his uncle by marriage died), he brought Wilde's spirit alive in a posthumous interview published in his Surrealist magazine, *Maintenant: Revue littéraire*, in 1913.[101] A performance artist, he delivered lectures, which involved bizarre displays of dancing and boxing. By all accounts, he cut an imposing figure; Blaise Cendrars recalled the amazing spectacle of Cravan doing the tango at a Paris nightclub "in a black shirt with the front cut away to reveal 'bleeding tattoos and obscene inscriptions on his skin.'"[102] After traveling to New York in 1917, Cravan fell in love with and subsequently married American poet Mina Loy. They moved to Mexico City, where he became a competition boxer, and in 1918 he set sail to meet his spouse, who awaited him in Buenos Aires. It appears that he was lost at sea; at least, Loy, who recalled her marriage as the happiest period of her life, thought so.

Yet in 1921 Cravan may have done something far more surreal than anything found in his art. If commentators are right, he managed to resurrect himself in the guise of Dorian Hope: a mysterious forger, exposed in New York, whom Vyvyan Holland, for one, assumed was his first cousin. At the time, two well-known antiquarian book dealers—Hodges, Figgis and Co. of Dublin and Maggs Brothers of London—received communications from a gentleman trying to pass himself off as André Gide. The senior partner of the firm, William F. Figgis, learned from this masquerader that certain manuscripts of Wilde's were available for purchase. Noticeably, all of the documents on offer were not ones that had gone up for sale in April 1920 at Mitchell Kennerley's Anderson Galleries in New York City, when John B. Stetson Jr.—son of the Philadelphia hat-making magnate—parted with what was the largest collection of Wilde materials in the world, much of which had been acquired from the Wilde estate through Ross. Matthew J. Bruccoli points out that all 423 lots brought the astonishing sum of $46,686: "The top item, twenty-five letters to Lord Alfred Douglas . . . went to Dr. R [Abraham Simon Wolfe Rosenbach] for $7,900."[103] Over the years, the value of some of these items would go sky-high, with the corrected typescript of *The Importance of Being Earnest*—which Dr. Rosenbach acquired for $500— fetching the equivalent of $99,000 at Christie's of London in 1981. In 1921, then, the market for Wilde materials was more buoyant than ever before, and it is perhaps no accident that this was the year that Kennerley—who as a teenager worked for John Lane—issued the thoroughly revised manuscript of Wilde's "Portrait of Mr. W.H.," which had remained in Lane's office at the time of the trials.[104]

In the early 1920s, the time was only too clearly ripe for opportunists to capitalize on what they knew of Wilde's life, his extant manuscripts, and his contacts. The fact that readers had since 1902 learned of Gide's acquaintance with Wilde provided the pretext for the scam that duped Figgis. In his letters, the pretender to Gide's identity declared that he had acquired the earliest manuscript of *The Importance of Being Earnest* through a mutual contact, the French author Octave Mirbeau. Figgis bought up everything that was offered to him, and he subsequently sold on the manuscripts of two works—"The Tomb of Keats" (*CW,* 14:1–4) and "The Disciple" (*CW,* 7:206–7)—to a London dealer. Dudley Edwards observes that once the London booksellers, Davis and Orioli, concluded that these documents were forgeries, further information arose about this fraudster.[105] Earlier that year, the charlatan had made overtures to Maggs Brothers, asking for checks to be made out either to "Monsieur Sebastian Hope" or "Monsieur Dorian Hope"—pseudonyms likely to arouse suspicions among Wilde's followers.[106] Figgis, as we can see from the large file of materials containing these forgeries held at the Clark Library, contacted a colleague at Brentano's in Paris to establish whether the real André Gide knew anything of this matter. Since Figgis wanted to track down the forger, he expressed interest in further offers of manuscripts, including ones supposedly in the possession of Octave Mirbeau's widow. After telling the so-called M. Gide that he needed to see the manuscripts before agreeing to the sum of 8,000 francs, Figgis traveled to Paris. After dinner at his hotel, Figgis was greeted by a gentleman going by the name of Dorian Hope: "He was dressed like a Russian count with a magnificent fur-lined overcoat; a plausible and well turned-out youth of about 25."[107] This individual purported to be Gide's secretary. Once the real Gide learned that someone was exploiting his good name, he took legal advice. Meanwhile, as matters were turned over to the police, Figgis sought to entrap the forger—who was at the time based at Amsterdam—by trying to persuade him to notarize an affidavit, which would of course disclose the man's true identity. It comes as no surprise to learn that Figgis never heard again from Dorian Hope, whoever this imposing young man was. Elsewhere, in 1920, someone using this pseudonym had managed to fool G. P. Putnam's of New York into publishing a volume of poems, *Pearls and Pomegranates,* which the publisher withdrew from sale just before Figgis received the impostor's letters. This small volume contains poems that other writers, notably Miriam Vedder, had previously published in journals such as the *Wellesley Review.* The fraud, according to the *New York Times,* had been committed by one of their overseas salesmen, Bret Holland, who put up $500 for an edition of 700 copies.[108] Was this Bret Holland any relation to Fabian Lloyd? Was this the same Hope who had joined Figgis after dinner? Were all of these impersonations the elaborate prank of a surrealist who had faked his death at sea?

While resolving these tantalizing questions remains impossible, one thing is for sure. Some of the forgeries look so convincing that Millard, a recognized authority on Wilde's bibliography, was at first eager to believe they were authentic. Although unable to muster funds to purchase all of these documents, Millard (who at the time ran his own antiquarian business) acquired the manuscripts of "The Tomb of Keats" and "The Disciple," which he then sold to American customers, and he convinced the Paris branch of Brentano's that other documents of this kind were genuine. In July 1921, however, Millard abruptly went back on his word. After a discouraging meeting during which Maggs Brothers informed him of their dealings with "M. Hope," Millard finally conceded that all of the manuscripts that had passed through the Dublin and London book dealers' hands were fakes. As Vyvyan Holland observes, many of these documents, which at first seduce a practiced eye, could never have come from Wilde's pen because his father did not write in the purple ink that covers many of their pages.[109] Yet while one can see that Millard's initial enthusiasm may have been the result of a bibliographic fantasy that spun out of control, the forger could very well have laid his hands on some genuine manuscripts. In other words, if we choose to imagine that Dorian Hope was the reinvented persona of Arthur Cravan, then we might be led to believe that this surrealist litterateur had sufficient contacts in Paris, such as publisher Charles Carrington (who at one time had held rights over the authorized edition of *The Picture of Dorian Gray*), to acquire some authentic manuscripts upon which he could develop impressive forgeries. These frauds, as Edwards suggests, are so good that they maintain "a place among the immortals in the ranks of forgers" (*Wilde Goose Chase*, 14). Even to this day, forgeries of similarly high quality come onto the market with sellers hoping—as they were in the summer of 2007—to command prices as high as £200,000.[110]

Millard, however, was quick to spot another forgery, which appeared in *Hutchinson's Magazine* in 1921. This is the "Burmese masque" titled *For Love of the King,* which he discovered came from the hand of "Mrs. Chan Toon," who purported to be the widow of a nephew to the Thai king. (This individual's legal name was Mabel Wodehouse Pearse; her second husband died in the war.) Among the ludicrous claims made by the person who, in 1873, was born Mabel Cosgrove were that the masque had been received in Burma as a Christmas play in 1894 and that she had at one time been engaged to Willie Wilde. Few reviewers could believe that this appalling piece was by an author who in the 1920s commanded considerable respect. Ever intent to press her case, in 1925 Wodehouse Pearse tried to sell Millard six letters supposedly from Wilde to herself. No sooner had she turned up at Millard's home with her constant companion, the parrot Co-Co, on her shoulder than he realized that everything about her was bogus. At this point, Millard decided to launch a campaign against Methuen, who in 1922 issued an edition of the masque in a binding that complemented the 1908 *Collected Works.* Millard's letters appeared in the daily press, and he circulated a provocative pamphlet and poster exposing the fraud.

The moment that Millard accused the publisher, with whom Ross worked so closely, of "foisting" this book on the public, Lucas at Methuen responded with

Figure 1. Press clipping on Mrs. Mabel Wodehouse Pearse, from *Daily Sketch,* 6 January 1926. Courtesy of William Clark Andrews Memorial Library, M645Z W6286 [1908–26], Boxed.

a libel suit. The company won in November 1926, with damages of £100. Since Millard was not a wealthy man, several supporters—including Figgis, Symons, Turner, and Wells—set up a fund for him. Meanwhile, Methuen's victory took place ten months after Wodehouse Pearse had been charged with stealing £240 from underneath the mattress of her neighbor, Mrs. Bridget Wood, at Aldwych Buildings, London (fig. 1). Millard plainly suffered rough justice, and after 1927, when he died of heart failure, "Mrs. Chan Toon" was released from jail and traveled around England under several aliases, including the fanciful "Princess Arakan." George Sims, in his study of this controversy, remarks that the only contact that "Mrs. Chan Toon" had with Wilde came when his spirit was channeled by Hester Travers Smith, whose "psychic messages" from the long-deceased writer were pieced together from scraps of information about him that had come into circulation.[111] "Tell us about Mrs. Chan Toon," the medium was asked. "I want you," Wilde is supposed to have said, "to make enquiries about that lady."[112] But on the basis of these psychic encounters, by 1922 Wilde's ghost seems to have become exhausted by a hereafter that had begun to look much more bizarre than his mortal existence: "Being dead," he informed Smith, "is the most boring experience in life" (9).

The following contributions to this volume show that Wilde's reemergence in modern culture has not always taken the eccentric forms that I have outlined here. But as this introduction indicates, the more that disciples such as Ledger, Millard, and Ross tried to establish a firm bibliographical basis on which to appreciate Wilde's career, the more readily this legendary author became the object of peculiar fantasies, including their own. In the discussions that follow, twelve scholars explore the ways in which Wilde's relations with the modern world often proved precarious both during and after his lifetime. There is no question that at times readers have frequently wanted him to return from the past to answer present needs. But there is much to be said in favor of Ellmann's claim that Wilde is "not one of those writers who as the centuries change lose their relevance" (*Oscar Wilde*, xvii). Unquestionably, Oscar Wilde is with us still, and he will remain so into the foreseeable future. His epigrams, his iconic presence, his rise and fall—all cast their spell on our times, just as they did in his own. Even if, as he admitted on his deathbed, it was painful to think that he "would never outlive" the nineteenth century, little could Wilde have guessed the extraordinary ways in which his spirit would live on in modern culture (*Complete Letters*, 1212).

Notes

1. [Anon.], "Bibliographical," *Academy*, 8 December 1900, 542; later quotations also appear on this page. I discuss this and other materials mentioned in this introduction in "Memorialising Wilde: An Explosive History," *Journal of Victorian Culture* 5 (2000): 311–22.

2. Lawrence Gilman, *Strauss's "Salome": A Guide to the Opera with Musical Illustrations* (London: John Lane, 1907), 26.

3. Robert Ross to More Adey, 14 December 1900, in *The Complete Letters of Oscar Wilde*, ed. Merlin Holland and Rupert Hart-Davis (London: Fourth Estate, 2000), 1212; further page references appear in parentheses. Ross claims that Wilde made this remark when he received two visitors, Aleck Ross (Robert Ross's brother) and Wilde's recently remarried sister-in-law, Lily, and her second husband, Texeiria de Mattos, on 25 October 1900.

4. Wilde, through Robert Harborough Sherard, put a stop to Douglas's attempts at publishing a polemical article in French on Wilde's sentence in *Mercure de France*. The typescript of this remarkable document, held at the Clark Library, contains Douglas's impenitent comments on his intimacy with Wilde: "I say, frankly (let my enemies interpret it as they will!) that our friendship was love, real love, love, it is true, completely pure but extremely passionate" ("Oscar Wilde," trans. Christopher Sclater Millard, Clark Library, D733M3 091 1895, f. 2). In two letters to politician Henry Labouchère, editor of *Truth*, Douglas expresses his contempt for the dismissive manner in which he was represented in this journal. In the first letter, dated 31 May 1895, he attacks

Labouchère for adding the clause to the 1885 Criminal Law Amendment Act, under which Wilde was given the maximum sentence. In the second letter, dated 9 June 1895, Douglas comments on male homosexuality: "[T]hese tastes are perfectly natural congenital tendencies in certain people (a very large minority) and ... the law has no right to interfere with these people provided they do not harm other people" (quoted in Robert Ross's "Statements of Evidence" for the Ransome trial, typescript, Clark Library, MS Wilde Uncataloged Box No. 2, folder 22 [there are two documents of this kind in the folder]). Douglas published "Une introduction à mes poèmes, avec quelques considérations sur l'affaire Oscar Wilde," *Revue blanche*, 1 June 1896, 484–90.

5. Robert Ross to Adela Schuster, 23 December 1900, in *Robert Ross, Friend of Friends: Letters to Robert Ross, Art Critic and Writer, together with Extracts from His Published Articles*, ed. Margery Ross (London: Jonathan Cape, 1952), 64; further page references appear in parentheses hereafter cited as *Robert Ross, Friend of Friends*.

6. An invoice from Brentano's, Paris, dated 3 December 1900, shows that Wilde wished to keep in touch with recently published works of literature: John Oliver Hobbes, *The Ambassador;* Beatrice Harraden, *Hilda Strafford;* Arthur Morrison, *A Child of the Jago;* E. W. Hornung, *The Amateur Cracksman;* Alfred Lord Tennyson, *Works* (four-volume edition); Bret Harte, *Colonel Starbottle's Client* and *A Protégé of Jack Hamlin's*. The amount owing was 22.50 francs, which Ross duly paid (Clark Library, Wilde B8392 W6721). Wilde's earliest biographer, Robert Harborough Sherard, who visited the Hôtel d'Alsace in 1904, claims that Dupoirier stowed some "three hundred odd volumes in two trunks" that "showed little sign of usage." Robert Harborough Sherard, *Twenty Years in Paris* (London: Hutchinson, 1905), 456–57.

7. Oscar Wilde to Frank Harris, 21 November 1900, *Complete Letters*, 1206.

8. The text of the play that Harris developed, adhering closely to Wilde's scenario, was first published as Frank Harris, *Mr. and Mrs. Daventry: A Play in Four Acts, Based on a Scenario by Oscar Wilde* (London: Richards Press, 1956); this edition contains an introduction by H. Montgomery Hyde.

9. Wilde to George Alexander, [August 1894,] *Complete Letters*, 600; further quotations also appear on this page. The editors' dating of this and other letters appears in square brackets.

10. Wilde's plays that remained unfinished at the time of his death include the scenario that Harris transformed into *Mr. and Mrs. Daventry, A Florentine Tragedy, La Sainte Courtesane; or the Woman Covered with Jewels,* and *The Cardinal of Avignon*. In 1922, Methuen, the publisher of the 1908 fourteen-volume *Collected Works,* added a fifteenth volume containing a play titled *For Love of the King: A Burmese Masque*. This work was eventually exposed as a forgery.

11. Wilde to George Alexander, [February 1895,] *Complete Letters*, 633.

12. Laurence Housman, *Echo de Paris: A Study from Life* (London: Jonathan Cape, 1923), 34. Housman's book comprises a dialogue that derived in part from his memories of his second meeting with Wilde, which took place at a café near the Place de l'Opéra, Paris, in late September 1899; he claims that the dialogue "has a solid basis in fact" but is recorded in a manner that amounts to "free rendering of what was then actually said" (9). In a lengthy "Footnote" to this dialogue with Wilde, Housman provides a defense of the nonpathological nature of homosexuality (55–60).

13. James G. Nelson, *Publisher to the Decadents: Leonard Smithers in the Careers of Beardsley, Wilde, Dowson* (University Park: Pennsylvania State University Press, 2000), 222. Nelson's study provides the most complete account of Wilde's dealings with Smithers.

14. Wilde to Frank Harris, 20 June 1900, *Complete Letters*, 1189. At the time, the working title of the play was *Love Is Law*.

15. *Complete Letters,* 1190n1.

16. Wilde to Frank Harris, [c. 20 September 1900,] *Complete Letters,* 1198; the later quotation also appears on this page.

17. The "Reserve" was the Cesari Réserve, Monte Carlo, which Harris's secretary, T. H. Bell, describes as a "high class restaurant with several apartments attached; and with a tank cut into the side of the rock, where, with the sea washing, a supply, a réserve, of live fish was retained." This restaurant was part of a costly tourist venture, including the Cesari Palace Hotel, in which Harris had invested money with Jules Cesari, whom Bell calls "a splendid *maître d'hôtel*... but ... no businessman." Bell, "Oscar Wilde without Whitewash," quoted in Philippa Pullar, *Frank Harris* (London: Hamish Hamilton, 1975), 195. Bell's study was published as *Oscar Wilde: Sus amigos, sus adversarios, sus ideas,* trans. S. Schijman (Buenos Aires: Editorial Americalee, 1946).

18. George Alexander commissioned *Lady Windermere's Fan* with an advance of £50 and *The Importance of Being Earnest* with an advance of £150. See Josephine M. Guy and Ian Small, *Oscar Wilde's Profession: Writing and the Culture Industry in the Late Nineteenth Century* (Oxford: Oxford University Press, 2000), 102, 127.

19. The most complete accounts of Wilde's dealings with Louis Nethersole and Ada Rehan can be found in Russell Jackson, "Oscar Wilde's Contract for a New Play," *Theatre Notebook* 50 (1996): 113–14; and Guy and Small, *Oscar Wilde's Profession,* 205–9.

20. The question of which individuals had rights to specific options—whether for publication or performance—on Wilde's scenario are not entirely clear, and by September 1900, Smithers may have had no rights to the scenario because of sums that were to be refunded from the deal that Wilde had struck with Brown-Potter and Bellew. The degree to which Wilde was involved in "double-dealing" or deliberately "deceiving and misleading" the various interested parties such as Nethersole and Rehan is open to question. Guy and Small take a counterintuitive view of the situation, stating that throughout his negotiations with these literary and theatrical figures, Wilde may have imagined that "the same scenario could be worked up to produce quite different plays" (*Oscar Wilde's Profession,* 208).

21. Robert Ross to More Adey, 14 December 1900, in Wilde, *Complete Letters,* 1211; further page references appear in parentheses.

22. Frank Harris, *Oscar Wilde: His Life and Confessions,* 2 vols. (New York: privately published, 1916), 2:534; further volume and page numbers appear in parentheses. For Harris's detailed account of his version of these events, see "The Story of 'Mr. and Mrs. Daventry,'" in *Oscar Wilde,* 2:589–94.

23. T. H. Bell, "Oscar Wilde's Unwritten Play," *Bookman* 61 (1930): 143; further page references appear in parentheses.

24. Dupoirier mentions that "[t]owards the end it became very difficult for [Wilde] to write, and he used to whip himself with cognac. A *litre* bottle would hardly see him through the night" (quoted in Robert Harborough Sherard, *The Real Oscar Wilde* [London: T. Werner Laurie, 1915], 415). Dupoirier's memories of Wilde appear in a number of places, including an interview with Michelle de Royer, *L'intransigeant,* 30 November 1930, 1–2, reprinted (in English translation) in *Oscar Wilde: Interviews and Recollections,* ed. E. H. Mikhail, 2 vols. (Basingstoke: Macmillan, 1979), 2:453–54.

25. Bell, however, did forward Ross "the tenner [£10] that Mr. Harris spoke of... to pay restaurant, nurse, or whatever you find immediately necessary" (Bell to Robert Ross, Clark Library, Wilde B435L R825). In a 1938 letter to Reggie Turner, Bell says he cannot recall whether Harris gave him a check or cash when he was dispatched to Paris to meet Wilde (Clark Library,

Wilde B435L T951). Davray produced many important translations of Wilde's works: *The Ballad of Reading Gaol* (*Mercure de France,* May 1898), five prose poems (*Revue blanche,* 1 May 1899), and *De Profundis* (1905). His co-translation (with Madeleine Vernon) of Frank Harris's *Oscar Wilde: His Life and Confessions* appeared in 1928.

26. Ross makes this observation in his 23 December 1900 letter to Adela Schuster (Ross, *Robert Ross, Friend of Friends,* 64). Dupoirier's final bill is reproduced in Robert Harborough Sherard, *The Life of Oscar Wilde* (London: T. Werner Laurie, 1906), facing 421.

27. In a letter dated 3 January 1902, Ross informs Adela Schuster that "Dupoirier is still owed £56[,] half of his original bill." He adds that Dupoirier will be "cheered by the smallest contribution" and asks Schuster to address any check she might wish to send him "in favour of Jean Dupoirier." Ross, *Robert Ross, Friend of Friends,* 74.

28. Robert Ross to William Rothenstein, 11 December 1900, quoted in Jonathan Fryer, *Robbie Ross: Oscar Wilde's Devoted Friend* (New York: Carroll and Graf, 2000), 169; the later quotation also appears on this page.

29. Robert Ross to Adela Schuster, 23 December 1900, in Wilde, *Complete Letters,* 1229; further page references appear in parentheses.

30. Wilde's remark originally appeared in his review of Walter Dowdeswell's comments on the life of James Whistler: "Every great man nowadays had his disciples, and it is usually Judas who writes the biography" (*Court and Society Review,* 20 April 1887, 378).

31. During the years following his release, in letters to Dalhousie Young and to Robert Ross, Wilde (in collaboration with Douglas) appears to have made some progress on the libretto for *Daphnis and Chloë* (Wilde, *Complete Letters,* 936, 946, 949, and 1049); he told Reggie Turner that he had begun a play and informed Leonard Smithers that he wished to secure a contract for a drama with American director Augustin Daly (976, 998); and he informed the editor of *North American Review,* William B. Fitts, from whom he accepted £75, that he planned to contribute an essay (1147).

32. Guy and Small, *Oscar Wilde's Profession,* 209.

33. Details of these productions can be found in Robert Tainitch's invaluable *Oscar Wilde on Stage and Screen* (London: Methuen, 1999), 103, 261. In 1902, *Earnest* reopened at the St. James's Theatre, London (where it had debuted on 14 February 1895), with Alexander in the role of Jack Worthing. Alexander promised Ross that he would pay the remaining debts owing to Dupoirier from the proceeds of this production (Ross, *Robert Ross, Friend of Friends,* 74). Alexander obtained performance rights for the two plays from the official receiver.

34. George Alexander to Robert Ross, 11 December 1900, in Ross, *Robert Ross, Friend of Friends,* 61.

35. "Max" [Max Beerbohm], review of *The Swashbuckler,* by Louis N. Parker, *Saturday Review,* 8 December 1900, 720, in *Oscar Wilde: The Critical Heritage,* ed. Karl Beckson (London: Routledge and Kegan Paul, 1970), 231; further page references to this volume appear in parentheses.

36. Max Beerbohm to Reggie Turner, 1 December 1900, in Beerbohm, *Letters to Reggie Turner,* ed. Rupert Hart-Davis (London: Rupert Hart-Davis, 1964), 137.

37. Max Beerbohm, "Oscar Wilde," *Anglo-American Times,* 25 March 1893, in Beerbohm, *Letters to Reggie Turner,* 291.

38. "Mr. Harris is to be congratulated on a perfect essay in psychology"; Beerbohm, review of *Mr. and Mrs. Daventry,* by Frank Harris, *Saturday Review,* 3 November 1900, quoted in Harris, *Mr. and Mrs. Daventry,* 29. As Hyde points out, Beerbohm's counted among the most favorable reviews that Harris received. Hyde claims that part of the success of Harris's play derived from

the fact that "the rumour persisted that Wilde was its real author" (30). Beerbohm's dramatic version of "The Happy Hypocrite" had a successful run until 23 February 1901 (excluding the fortnight between 22 January and 5 February that year, when the theaters closed in honor of Queen Victoria's death).

39. Max Beerbohm to Reggie Turner, 11 December 1900, in *Letters to Reggie Turner,* 139.

40. William Rothenstein to Robert Ross, 14 February 1901, in Ross, *Robert Ross, Friend of Friends,* 69. Rothenstein read the letter from Ross to Adey at the lodgings that the two men shared in Kensington, London.

41. Ross to Adela Schuster, 3 January 1902, in Ross, *Robert Ross, Friend of Friends,* 74; the later quotation also appears on this page.

42. Wilde to Robert Ross, 1 April 1897, *Complete Letters,* 780; further page references appear in parentheses.

43. In one of the typewritten statements he prepared for the 1913 Ransome case (which I discuss below), Ross makes the following claim about what happened during a meeting with Wilde in Normandy in 1897: "I pointed out to Wilde that Douglas would be sure to destroy the MS and that it would be better to send him a copy. This was done by Wilde's instructions and I retained the MS" (Clark Library, Wilde MS Uncataloged Box No. 2, folder 22, f. 25).

44. Horst Schroeder, "The 'Definitive' Edition of Oscar Wilde's *De Profundis,*" http://horst .schroeder.com/DeProfundis.htm (accessed 24 July 2007). Schroeder's essay amounts to a critique of the editorial principles that Ian Small adopts in *De Profundis: "Epistola: In Carcere et Vinculis,"* in *The Complete Works of Oscar Wilde* (Oxford: Oxford University Press, 2005).

45. Robert Ross to Max Meyerfeld, 31 August 1907, in Oscar Wilde, *De Profundis—Neue deutsche Ausgabe von Max Meyerfeld* (Berlin: S. Fischer, 1909), ix; further page references appear in parentheses. I discuss aspects of Meyerfeld's 1909 edition below.

46. Methuen's comments appear in a publisher's announcement, quoted in Maureen Duffy, *A Thousand Capricious Chances: A History of the Methuen List, 1889–1989* (London: Methuen, 1989), 36.

47. Oscar Wilde, *De Profundis,* ed. Robert Ross (London: Methuen, 1905), ix; further page references appear in parentheses. By *artificial,* Ross does not mean "superficial" or "inauthentic" but "interested in artifice."

48. G. S. Street, "Out of the Depths," *Outlook,* 4 March 1905, 294–95, in Beckson, *Oscar Wilde,* 255.

49. [E. V. Lucas,] review of *De Profundis,* by Oscar Wilde, *Times Literary Supplement,* 25 February 1905, 64–65, in Beckson, *Oscar Wilde,* 246; further page references appear in parentheses.

50. R. B. Cunninghame Graham, "Vox Clamantis," *Saturday Review,* 4 March 1905, 266–67, in Beckson, *Oscar Wilde,* 256. Graham, who served time as a prisoner for defending workers' rights during the riot at Trafalgar Square in 1887, wrote a supportive letter to Wilde in which he praised *The Ballad of Reading Gaol* (see *Complete Letters,* 1021).

51. Max Beerbohm, "A Lord of Language," *Vanity Fair,* 2 March 1905, 309, in Beckson, *Oscar Wilde,* 248; further page references appear in parentheses. Beerbohm begins his review by discussing the ways in which both Oscar Wilde and James Whistler were given the same treatment in the press at this time. The retrospective exhibition of Whistler's paintings opened at the New Gallery early that year. Ross's edition of *De Profundis* appeared on 23 February 1905.

52. George Bernard Shaw to Robert Ross, 13 March 1905, in Ross, *Robert Ross, Friend of Friends,* 111; the later quotation also appears on this page. In this letter, Shaw mentions the young American sculptor Jacob Epstein, who was eager to exhibit his work at Ross's Carfax Gallery,

London. As I mention below, at the celebratory dinner in honor of Ross's editing of *The Collected Works of Oscar Wilde*, held at the Ritz Hotel in London on 1 December 1908, he would announce Epstein's commission to design Wilde's tomb at Père Lachaise.

53. Ricketts designed the title page and binding of the single-volume edition of *The Picture of Dorian Gray* (London: Ward, Lock, 1891), *Poems* (London: Elkin Mathews and John Lane, 1892), and *The Sphinx* (London: Elkin Mathews and John Lane, 1894), as well as the binding of *Intentions* (London: Osgood, McIlvaine, 1891) and *Lord Arthur Savile's Crime and Other Stories* (London: Osgood, McIlvaine, 1891). Later, Ricketts designed the sets for the 1906 productions of *A Florentine Tragedy* and *Salome*. He published (with his pseudonymous alter ego John Paul Raymond) *Oscar Wilde: Recollections* (London: Nonesuch Press, 1932).

54. André Gide, *Oscar Wilde: A Study*, trans. Stuart Mason [Christopher Sclater Millard] (Oxford: Holywell Press, 1905), 16; further page references appear in parentheses. Gide subsequently discussed his memories of Wilde in *Oscar Wilde: In memoriam (souvenirs)* (Paris: Mercure de France, 1910) and in the final chapter of his autobiography, *Si le grain ne meurt* (Paris: Éditions de la Nouvelle Revue Française, 1924). The relations between Gide and Wilde are explored in Jonathan Fryer, *André and Oscar: Gide, Wilde, and the Gay Art of Living* (London: Constable, 1997).

55. Robert Harborough Sherard, *Oscar Wilde: The Story of an Unhappy Friendship* (London: Hermes, 1902), 258; further page references appear in parentheses.

56. Wilde came across Sherard some months after Constance Holland forced her husband to part from Douglas in late 1897; in May 1898, Sherard indulged in an anti-Semitic outburst at Campbell's Bar, Paris, in the company of both Wilde and Douglas (who reunited once more a month after Constance Holland's death). See Wilde, *Complete Letters*, 1076.

57. There is not space here to address in detail Sherard's numerous forays into debates about the record of Wilde's life. Sherard's contributions to these disputes include *The Life of Oscar Wilde* (1906); *The Real Oscar Wilde: To Be Used as a Supplement to, and in Illustration of "The Life of Oscar Wilde"* (London: T. Werner Laurie, 1916); *André Gide's Wicked Lies about the Late Oscar Wilde in Algiers in January 1895* (Corsica: Vindex, 1933); and *Bernard Shaw, Frank Harris, and Oscar Wilde* (London: T. Werner Laurie, 1937). Sherard's mission, which culminated in his 1937 volume, was to condemn Harris, defend Douglas, and uphold Wilde's reputation. In the last of these works, Sherard exposes many of Harris's fabrications while also, quite unfairly, taking Bell to task for publishing a memoir of Wilde's last days that was "pure fake" (306).

58. Robert Ross to Walter Ledger, 29 April 1906, quoted in Maureen Borland, *Wilde's Devoted Friend: A Life of Robert Ross, 1869–1918* (Oxford: Lennard, 1990), 105.

59. Unsigned notice, *Scots Observer*, 5 July 1890, 181, in Beckson, *Oscar Wilde*, 75. This notice was likely written by Henley's deputy, Charles Whibley.

60. For a reliable and detailed account of the Cleveland Street Affair, which encouraged Lord Arthur Somerset to flee the country, see Morris B. Kaplan, *Sodom by the Thames: Sex, Love, and Scandal in Wilde Times* (Ithaca, NY: Cornell University Press, 2005), 186–213.

61. St. John Hankin, "The Collected Plays of Oscar Wilde," *Fortnightly Review*, n.s. 83 (1908): 791–802, in Beckson, *Oscar Wilde*, 284.

62. [Arthur Symons,] review of *Collected Works*, by Oscar Wilde, *Athenæum*, 16 May 1908, 598–600, in Beckson, *Oscar Wilde*, 294. Symons's thoughtful reviews of *Intentions* (1891) and *The Ballad of Reading Gaol* (1898) are reprinted in Beckson's volume (94–96 and 218–21).

63. [Harold Child,] review of *Collected Works*, by Oscar Wilde, *Times Literary Supplement*, 18 June 1908, 193, in Beckson, *Oscar Wilde*, 304.

64. "The Speech of Robert Ross," in Ross, *Robert Ross, Friend of Friends,* 157; further page references appear in parentheses. This generous sum came from Helen Carew, mother of Vyvyan Holland's close friend Coleridge Kennard.

65. Quoted in Fryer, *Robbie Ross,* 200. Fryer does not date this correspondence.

66. "A.D." [Alfred Douglas], "The Dead Poet," *Academy,* 21 September 1907, 917.

67. "A.D." [Alfred Douglas], "The Genius of Oscar Wilde," *Academy,* 21 July 1908, 35, in Beckson, *Oscar Wilde,* 309. In this notice, Douglas echoes Beerbohm's 1893 essay when he states, "We unhesitatingly say that his influence on the literature of Europe has been greater than that of any man since Byron died" (310). Ross's 1909 edition of Wilde's poetry also elicited Douglas's staunch support. Douglas observed that "at his best," Wilde "was a great poet whose immortality is assured as long as the English language exists." Douglas, *Academy,* 23 January 1909, 703.

68. W. Sorley Brown, *The Life and Genius of T.W.H. Crosland* (London: Cecil Palmer, 1928), 216; further page reference appears in parentheses. Douglas's and Crosland's antipathy toward Asquith was not in Tennant's interests; as Caspar Wintermans points out, Tennant soon sold the journal to Douglas for £500. Wintermans, *Alfred Douglas: A Poet's Life and His Finest Work* (London: Peter Owen, 2007), 110; further page references appear in parentheses.

69. Beerbohm to Robert Ross, 17 October 1909, in Ross, *Robert Ross, Friend of Friends,* 168. Wilde published the following works in the Oxford undergraduate periodical *The Spirit Lamp:* "The New Remorse" (6 December 1892, 97), "The House of Judgment" (17 February 1893, 52–53), and "The Disciple" (6 June 1893, 49–50). The moralistic Crosland, who had at times had to confront Douglas's history of close involvement with the homosexual literati of the 1890s, commented that it was not possible to assert that "the whole of the verses Lord Alfred Douglas published in *The Spirit Lamp* were impeccable, faultless and distinguished verses"—though this remark served as a preface to his view that the literary contents of Douglas's journal were superior to two current undergraduate periodicals: *Granta* (Cambridge) and *Isis* (Oxford). T.W.H. Crosland, "Poppycock and Sniggs," *Academy,* 6 March 1909, 848.

70. Robert Ross, *Masques and Phases* (London: Arthur L. Humphreys, 1909), 147; Ross's essay on Solomon originally appeared in the *Westminster Gazette* in 1905.

71. [Harold Child,] review of *Masques and Phases,* by Robert Ross, *Times Literary Supplement,* 28 October 1909, 398. Child observed that Ross's "style . . . belongs to yesterday rather than to the present," and he linked Ross's name with the *Yellow Book,* Beardsley, and Wilde.

72. "Asquith and Anarchy," *Academy,* 20 February 1909, 798.

73. Borland, *Wilde's Devoted Friend,* 147.

74. Douglas had good reason to be cautious about any correspondence he might mail to Wilde. Letters that blackmailers had stolen from Douglas's coat at the Café Royal were quoted by the defense in Wilde's libel suit against the Marquess of Queensberry; the letters were, of course, used as incriminating evidence of Wilde's "sodomitical" desires. See, in particular, Merlin Holland, ed., *Irish Peacock and Scarlet Marquess: The Real Trial of Oscar Wilde* (London: Fourth Estate, 2003), 268–70.

75. "[T]he MS. now residing in the British Museum quite plainly belongs to me." Douglas, *Autobiography,* 325.

76. Arthur Ransome, *Oscar Wilde: A Critical Study* (London: Martin Secker, 1912), 157.

77. Ross, "Statement of Evidence," ff. 37–38.

78. Ransome's recollections of Ross are very favorable ("He seemed sure that mine would be a good book"); Ross introduced Ransome to a broad range of contacts, including Wilde's sons, Ada Leverson, Robert Harborough Sherard, and Walter Ledger. "Later," Ransome recalled, "he

entrusted me with the complete typescript of *De Profundis* and let me take it away to Wiltshire, where we had taken at a very low rent an old farmhouse." Arthur Ransome, *The Autobiography of Arthur Ransome*, ed. Rupert Hart-Davis (London: Jonathan Cape, 1976), 142, 143.

79. The *Times* reports of the court proceedings (18 April 1913, 4; 19 April 1913, 3–4) reveal that Douglas claimed to have given Wilde substantial sums during Wilde's exile in Italy and France. Douglas inherited a substantial fortune of almost £20,000 on the Marquess of Queensberry's death in January 1900. Douglas makes the claim about the monies he gave to Wilde in 1900 in Alfred Douglas and Frank Harris, *New Preface to "The Life and Confessions of Oscar Wilde"* (London: Fortune Press, 1925), 33; further page references appear in parentheses. Douglas itemizes the payments he made to Wilde in 1900 in his *Autobiography* (London: Martin Secker, 1931), 323.

80. Alfred Douglas to Frank Harris, 30 April 1925, in Douglas and Harris, *New Preface*, 34. During the Ransome trial, Douglas stated that Ross had handed him a copy of the prison document, which he had subsequently destroyed (*Times*, 18 April 1913, 4d). Later in the trial, Douglas declared, "I got one long letter from Wilde, enclosed from Ross; but it was not that document, it was not one-fifth so long. I read about the first three lines of it and then threw it in the fire, writing at the same time to Ross that I resented very much his having interfered, and if Wilde wanted write to me he could do it direct. I always thought *De Profundis* was written to Ross, not to me" (*Times*, 19 April 1913, 4f). Whether Douglas knew about Meyerfeld's 1909 edition is unclear.

81. "A." [Alfred Douglas], review of *De Profundis*, by Oscar Wilde, *Motorist and Traveller*, 1 March 1905, in H. Montgomery Hyde, *Oscar Wilde: The Aftermath* (London: Methuen, 1963), 208; the later quotation also appears on this page.

82. In the second edition of Ransome's book, the sentence that declares that *De Profundis* is a "rebuke of this friend" is omitted. Ransome, *Oscar Wilde: A Critical Study*, 2nd ed. (London: Methuen, 1913), 171.

83. T.H.W. Crosland, *The First Stone: On Reading the Unpublished Parts of "De Profundis"* (London: privately published, 1912), 5–6; further page reference appears in parentheses.

84. Wilde, *The Suppressed Portion of "De Profundis" by Oscar Wilde, Now for the First Time Published by His Literary Executor, Robert Ross* (New York: P. R. Reynolds, 1913). Two copies were placed at the Library of Congress; Ross kept the remaining thirteen.

85. Alfred Douglas, *Oscar Wilde and Myself* (London: John Long, 1914), 179; further page reference appears in parentheses. Douglas discloses Crosland's coauthorship in his much later *Autobiography*, 25; further page reference appears in parentheses. The publisher John Long offered Douglas an advance of £500 for the book.

86. Douglas's privately published poetic satire, *The Rossiad*, first appeared in 1916; three further editions appeared through 1921. This insulting poem charts Douglas's and Crosland's conflicts with Ross. Douglas sought to wage warfare against Ross once more during a highly publicized libel trial of 1918, in which dancer Maud Allan and director J. T. Grein issued a writ for obscene libel against Independent MP Noel Pemberton Billing for describing a private performance of Wilde's *Salome* in London as representing "The Cult of the Clitoris." The case is recorded in Michael Kettle, *Salome's Last Veil: The Libel Case of the Century* (London: Hart-Davis, MacGibbon, and Granada, 1977); see also chapter 7 of the present volume.

87. Fryer, *Robbie Ross*, 235.

88. See, for example, Holland, *Irish Peacock and Scarlet Marquess*, 93.

89. Ledger's name does not appear on the title page of the volume. Ransome recalls that Ledger was an "eccentric individual"—an "efficient seaman" dressed in a sailor's outfit—whom

Ross claimed suffered from "homicidal mania and was accustomed to having himself shut up." Ransome, *Autobiography,* 142.

90. Quoted in H. Montgomery Hyde, *Christopher Sclater Millard: Bibliographer and Antiquarian Book Dealer* (New York: Global Academic Publishers, 1990), 40.

91. Ernst Bendz, review of *Bibliography of Oscar Wilde,* by Stuart Mason, *Englische Studien* 49 (1915–16): 318. Bendz's important contributions to scholarship on Wilde are brought together in *Oscar Wilde: A Retrospect* (Vienna: Alfred Hölder, 1921).

92. Stuart Mason [Christopher Sclater Millard], *Bibliography of Oscar Wilde* (London: T. Werner Laurie, 1914), v–vi. Millard acknowledges the considerable help that Ledger gave him in preparing this volume (viii).

93. George Sylvester Viereck, "Is Oscar Wilde Living or Dead?" *Critic* 47 (1905): 87; further page reference appears in parentheses.

94. "Oscar Wilde Alive?" *Los Angeles Times,* 22 November 1908, in uncataloged press clippings collection, William Andrews Clark Memorial Library.

95. J. M. Stuart-Young, *Osrac the Self-Sufficient and Other Poems, with a Memoir of the Late Oscar Wilde* (London: Hermes Press; Paris: Charles Carrington, 1905), 12. Stuart-Young corresponded with both Ross and Millard in 1905 and 1907, respectively. In his letter to Ross, he claims that he enjoyed a friendship with Wilde (Clark Library, Wilde S9321L R825).

96. Stephanie Newell, *The Forger's Tale: The Search for Odeziaku* (Athens: Ohio University Press, 2006), 63.

97. Hesketh Pearson, *Oscar Wilde* (Harmondsworth: Penguin Books, 1960), 263. This edition is a reprint of the 1954 revised edition of Pearson's original 1946 biography.

98. Robert Harborough Sherard, *Bernard Shaw, Frank Harris, and Oscar Wilde,* 23. Sherard's depiction of the scene of the dancing prostitutes appears in *Oscar Wilde: The Story of an Unhappy Friendship,* 200.

99. Richard Ellmann, *Oscar Wilde* (New York: Knopf, 1988), 584. Ellmann insists that the underlying cause of Wilde's death was syphilis; in this regard, he follows the views of Harris, Ross, and Ransome (92). Ellmann's negative portrayal of Douglas is evident on pages 384–96.

100. Alfred Douglas, *Oscar Wilde: A Summing-Up* (London: Duckworth, 1940), 12, 13; further page reference appears in parentheses.

101. Arthur Cravan, "Oscar Wilde est vivant!" *Maintenant: Revue littéraire* (October–November 1913): 1–26.

102. Charles Nicholl, "The Wind Comes Up out of Nowhere," *London Review of Books,* 9 March 2006.

103. Matthew J. Bruccoli, *The Fortunes of Mitchell Kennerley, Bookman* (San Diego: Harcourt Brace Jovanovich, 1986), 135. Full details of the sale are given in *The Oscar Wilde Collection of John B. Stetson, Jr., Elkins Park, PA* (New York: Anderson Galleries, 1920). The copy held at the University of California Southern Regional Facility (Z8975 S8) contains notes on the prices that the 423 lots fetched. Some of Stetson's collection had been acquired in 1913 through Bernard Quaritch, who disposed of many letters and books that Douglas had sold him.

104. Wilde ran into conflicts with Elkin Mathews, who, with John Lane, formed the partnership that published under the Bodley Head imprint. In November 1894, the partners declined to publish Wilde's revised manuscript. Later that year, however, when the partners decided to go their separate ways, Wilde informed them that he wished Lane to publish *The Sphinx, Salome,* and the revised "Portrait of Mr. W.H." and Mathews to issue his plays (*Complete Letters,* 613). On this matter, see James G. Nelson, *The Early Nineties: A View from the Bodley Head* (Cambridge,

MA: Harvard University Press, 1971), 274–75. The manuscript of "The Portrait of Mr. W.H." was waiting to go into production when news broke about Wilde's failed libel suit in April 1895. Bruccoli states that Kennerley knew that the revised version had been in the hands of Lane's office manager, Frederic Chapman, and he sold it for Chapman's sister to Dr. Rosenbach for $3,000. Bruccoli, *Fortunes of Mitchell Kennerley*, 141–42.

105. Dudley Edwards, "The Wilde Goose Chase," *American Book Collector* 7, no. 5 (1957): 3–14. Edwards's commentary relates to the stack of forgeries held at the Clark Library (Wilde 6271 C687).

106. These pseudonyms suggest an insider's knowledge of Wilde's circle. "Sebastian" is, of course, taken from Wilde's own incognito, "Sebastian Melmoth"; "Dorian" comes from Wilde's novel *The Picture of Dorian Gray;* and "Hope" is a name belonging to Constance Wilde's family through marriage (Adrian Hope [1858–1904] became the guardian of Cyril Holland and Vyvyan Holland after their mother's death).

107. Quoted in Edwards, "Wilde Goose Chase," 5. Cravan would have been about thirty-three years of age at the time of this meeting.

108. "'Dorian Hope' Verses Filched by Clerk," *New York Times*, 5 April 1921. The previous owner of my copy of Hope's volume identified the author of each work that Hope plagiarized.

109. Vyvyan Holland made this observation in a letter to William Figgis, 23 Sept 1955 (Clark Library, Wilde 6271 C687).

110. Anthony Gardner, "The Oscar Sinners," *Sunday Times* [London], 8 July 2007. Gardner reports that at the New York Antiquarian Book Fair, a manuscript of Wilde's "Happy Prince" was expected to command this figure until Ed Maggs of the famous book dealers exposed it as a fake.

111. George Sims, "Who Wrote *For Love of the King?* Oscar Wilde or Mrs. Chan Toon," *Book Collector* (Autumn 1958): 276–77. Wilde's translator, Henry-D. Davray, inquires into the activities of "Mrs. Chan Toon" in *Oscar Wilde: La tragédie finale—suivi de épisodes et souvenirs et des apocryphes* (Paris: Mercure de France, 1928), 173–237.

112. Hester Travers Smith, *Psychic Messages from Oscar Wilde* (London: T. Werner Laurie, 1924), 13; further page reference appears in parentheses. For further commentary on Smith's book, see John Stokes, *Oscar Wilde: Myths, Miracles, and Imitations* (Cambridge: Cambridge University Press, 1996), 5–8.

Oscar Wilde, Lady Gregory, and Late-Victorian Table-Talk

LUCY McDIARMID

Since the wealth elite was also the power elite, high society was an essential adjunct to political life, where dinner parties might be as important as cabinet meetings.

—David Cannadine, *The Decline and Fall of the British Aristocracy* (1990)

[D]oors were open to the successful Victorian intellectual as much on account of the social standing of the roles he and his peers characteristically occupied as for his individual achievement in some department of "serious work." Some of these doors opened on to dinners and receptions at the houses of the wealthy and the powerful.

—Stefan Collini, *Public Moralists* (1991)

"A MAN WHO can dominate a London dinner-table can dominate the world": Lord Illingworth's epigram from Oscar Wilde's third society comedy, *A Woman of No Importance* (1893), is a bit ambiguous (*CW*, 4:109). Does it mean that the London dinner table is a stepping-stone to "the world," a rung on a career ladder? Or does it simply mean that skills in dominating the one and the other are comparable? In any case, the word *dominate* suggests that one should perhaps be uneasy about the idea. Or is the statement merely glib, self-referential praise of table-talk? All of these suggestions are present. Underlying them are the notions that dominating a London dinner table is an art or power that everyone would recognize immediately and that the dinner table is an important site, worldly and political in its nature, as the quotations from David Cannadine and Stefan Collini indicate.[1] Without analyzing closely the precise nature and kind of comments uttered over dinner, both Cannadine and Collini acknowledge that such comments may constitute high politics in another form. Lord Illingworth's epigram is witty, sinister—and true.

Table-talk was both practiced and described by Oscar Wilde and by Lady Gregory. Anglo-Irish Protestants living in London during the 1880s, these writers were coevals who were also acquaintances. Wilde and Gregory dined with many of the same people: the overlap in their circles, according to letters, journals, and other records, includes such politicians and diplomats as W. E. Gladstone, Willie Grenfell, and James Russell Lowell, U.S. ambassador to England; aristocrats such as Lord Curzon and Wilfrid Blunt; writers such as W. B. Yeats, Bernard Shaw, and Henry James; and artsy Society types such as Marc-André Raffalovich, John Gray, and Aubrey Beardsley.[2] John Gray, frequently said to be the original of Wilde's protagonist Dorian Gray, was a close friend of Lady Gregory's and gave her copies of his privately circulated devotional poems (*Diaries*, 46).[3] Gregory and Wilde were admirers of one another's work. They most likely met sometime in 1888 or 1889, probably at a dinner or salon at the Gregorys' London home, though Sir William Gregory may have met Wilde at one of the gentleman's clubs somewhat earlier.[4] In a letter dated September 1887, Wilde asked Gregory to contribute to the journal *Woman's World*, which he began editing for the publishing house of Cassell that year. In a journal entry from 1928, Gregory remarks that she believes Wilde's last major poem, *The Ballad of Reading Gaol* (1898), "will outlive all Wilde's other work and a great deal of the work of his contemporaries."[5] In an entry for July 1930, Gregory at the age of seventy-eight describes herself "resting on the sofa" and reading "again the Ballad of Reading Gaol" (*Journals*, 2:535). (Although not relevant to the topic of table-talk, it is worth mentioning—if merely to indicate their generational alignment—that both Wilde and Gregory had sons who were killed in World War I.)

As a field of scholarly inquiry, table-talk exists in the overlap of cultural anthropology, cultural history, and sociolinguistics. The meal as a cultural phenomenon has been theorized by Mary Douglas in "Deciphering a Meal," which looks at "the message encoded by food," considering such issues as "the line between intimacy and distance," the "hot meal" as a "threshold of intimacy," and the hierarchical scale of importance and grandeur of meals throughout the week and the year.[6] Placing the meal in historical context, Robert Jameson in "Purity and Power at the Victorian Dinner Party" examines "the active social uses of eating rituals by individuals and the use of dining to legitimate whole social groups," especially the way in which the dinner is "structured by an increasingly complex code [that] separates the diner from foods of different character."[7] Historians such as Roy Strong have commented on the "bourgeois display" of the dinner party and have noted the importance of the centerpiece, the table setting, and all the material indications of opulence.[8] In the most comprehensive recent approach to dinner parties, Natalie Kapetanios Meir analyzes what she calls "Victorian dining taxonomies."[9] Meir touches only obliquely on table-talk as an item in the taxonomy in one of the citations from *Everybody's Book of Correct Conduct, Being the Etiquette of Every-day Life* (1893):

> *It is not correct*
> To ignore your partner at dinner, however little he or she may be to your taste. Join in the general conversation if you prefer, but address yourself from time to time to your neighbour. This is a duty you owe to your hostess. (144)

In *Feast*, Strong suggests a more Wildean take on dinner conversation, noting that the "cult of the dinner party . . . opened a whole new arena of social competition, in which success depended on recruiting the best talkers" (307).

Table-talk, though not named as such, is considered as part of the taxonomy of "conversation" in *The Principles of the Art of Conversation* by J. P. Mahaffy, Wilde's Trinity College tutor and close friend. The book's date of publication, 1888, places it at the same time as Wilde and Gregory were talking at the highest London dinner parties. Although Mahaffy never considers table-talk under its own heading, a dinner party is the implicit setting of many of his examples:

> In a country house where I was staying, the host had invited the colonel commanding a neighbouring depot and his wife to dinner, and the conversation was flagging seriously. Some mention of New Zealand in that day's papers suggested it as a topic, upon which a couple of us brought out all we knew about New Zealand, discussed the natives, then savages generally, and so restored the fortunes of the evening. The colonel and his wife still sat silent.

Lucy McDiarmid

When they were gone, we said to the host that we thought it very hard work to entertain people who would not say anything to anybody. He replied that they *had* said something as they got into their carriage. What was it? The colonel observed that it was very impertinent of people to talk about countries they had never seen, especially in presence of a man like himself, who had not only lived for years in New Zealand, but had written a book about it! This was the thanks we got.[10]

The politics of this example deserve their own analysis in some other context. But here, as in the rest of the book, Mahaffy's focus is on the social and theatrical skill of the talkers. Not only does he never consider the kind of London dinner party that Cannadine and Collini refer to; he privileges Irish talkers, of whom Wilde and Gregory are prime examples, on almost every page (for example, "in Irish society, where wit is less uncommon than elsewhere, and where it is no less highly prized" [84]).

Most students of the Victorian dinner party refer to its context as a domestic site. Strong says that in post-Napoleonic Europe, "the arts of the table became finally separated from politics and the state," and the "archetypal meal of the nineteenth century was to be the private family dinner party," an expression "not only of domestic bliss but also social status" (*Feast*, 288–89). A chapter titled "Bourgeois Rituals" in Philippe Ariès and Georges Duby's multivolume *History of Private Life* discusses dinner parties as a relationship of households to one another, a means of "proclaiming" and maintaining social position in a community.[11] In addition, the chapter "Private Spaces" in the same book talks about the dining room as the place where "the family put itself on display for its guests."[12] The concept of "display" raises the issue of the extradomestic circle: Who are the guests? And when they are assembled together with the host family in the dining room, what kind of "circle" do they form? Like the "display" of silver, servants, and food, the category of table-talk implies performance and audience; it suggests that the dinner party—particularly the kind of dinner party that Wilde and Gregory attended—is a crossover zone, with characteristics of both an intimate domestic sphere and a public, often official, one.

Discussing seventeenth-century architectural developments that extended, under the same roof, both private space for individual family members and salon space for guests, Jürgen Habermas observes, "The line between private and public sphere extended right through the house. The privatized individuals stepped out of the intimacy of their living rooms into the public sphere of the *salon*."[13] But the late-Victorian London dinner party, as I see it, was different. This kind of dinner party typically moved across several rooms, from front hall to library to dining room to drawing room (where the men joined the women after coffee was served to them separately). In this respect, it is the *talk,* not the *room,* that created a zone with a certain elasticity, making the occasion a flexible one. Such socializing was public enough to have an aura of power—to be, potentially, a significant event, to command attention. The dinner parties that Wilde and Gregory went to included guests who were powerful, well-known figures in art and politics, the kind of people mentioned regularly in the press. Such individuals comprised London's elite: the "leading minds" that Stefan Collini analyzes in *Public Moralists.* They were the political and cultural celebrities, the diplomats, journalists, historians, and "public intellectuals" of the time (13–59). In this context, table-talk was secular, worldly, and contemporary in its orientation. Within an atmosphere created by the licensed informality of famous or powerful people who were slightly off duty and by the heightened formality of a meal where such people were present in a private dining room, table-talk constructed a zone in which the activities of the empire's ruling classes, artists, and intellectuals could be circulated, critiqued, and reimagined. The Victorian dinner party therefore was private enough to allow for risk-taking, permitting guests to broach subjects or opinions not possible in a more open space. Because these dinner parties took place within a domestic setting, there was an assumed safety about anything that was said there. Comments were made without necessarily being considered official to guests who understood the implicit confidentiality of the talk.

Two brief examples help to illuminate the social elasticity that I identify with late-Victorian table-talk. Both instances help to frame the points that Wilde and Gregory raise about table-talk in their writings. My first example comes from the diaries of a contemporary of Lady Gregory and Wilde, the Fabian activist Beatrice Webb (1858–1943). The dinner party was the ur-unit of Fabian "permeation," the technical term for the means by which—precisely because of its flexibly private and public nature—the Fabians sought to influence government policy by getting to know important policy makers socially. Webb's diaries record hundreds of such dinners, given and attended by herself and her husband. These events were always planned with much care to bring together people who could be useful to one another. On one such occasion, on 22 November 1905, Webb was dining at the house of Lord Lucas, a Liberal peer who, she said, "cultivated our friendship."[14] Sitting after dinner with the wives, Webb (writing about Mrs. Willie Grenfell), begins to doubt the value of dinner parties and their talk altogether: "But when I sat with her and the other smart little woman in that palatial room I felt a wee bit ashamed of myself. Why was I dissipating my energy in this smart but futile world in late hours and small talk? Exactly at the moment this feeling was disconcerting me, the door opened and Mr. Balfour was announced. I confess that the appearance of the P.M. dissipated my regrets. It is always worth while, I thought, to meet those who really have power to alter things" (*Diary*, 3:12). The nature of this social zone thus changes as the prime minister walks in—or, more precisely, as Webb sees him enter and rejoices in her proximity to power. The after-dinner "small talk" of women changes to a more significant conversation, not strictly table-talk but nevertheless the kind of semiprivate conversation among public figures that makes dinner parties politically valuable.

In the second example, another prime minister, Herbert Asquith, took advantage of the unofficial space of the dinner party to enlist support for his government's policy. This episode occurred much later, on 1 August 1916, and one book refers to it as a dinner party, but in his memoirs Walter Page, the U.S. ambassador to whom Asquith was speaking, calls it a luncheon.[15] Whatever the meal, its date was the eve of the execution of Roger Casement, the Irish rebel convicted of High Treason for his attempt to run guns in aid of the Easter Rising. After a trial in June, Casement had been found guilty and was sentenced to hang, but the government had also circulated *sub rosa* pages from homosexual diaries said to be Casement's. Typed transcripts of these inculpating documents had been shown to people who would talk about them, as a means of destroying popular support—especially Irish and American support—for Casement. On this occasion, Page mentioned that he had seen the transcript, and Asquith said to him, "Excellent. And you need not be particular about keeping it to yourself."[16] Although one cannot know for certain whether Asquith would have said something like that in his office, clearly the context of a meal created a zone that felt less-than-official and granted license for the encouragement to gossip. Page's memoirs do not mention that comment, and its origin is difficult to find. All Page's account says is that Asquith remarked of Casement's imminent execution, "In all good conscience to my country and to my responsibilities I cannot interfere."[17] Either way, the meal provided a semiprivate arena in which political issues could be discussed while remaining off the record. Of course, with the presence of Page's *Life and Letters* on the World Wide Web, the conversation is on the record now.

Lady Gregory and "London Table Talk"

A paradigmatic Irish conversationalist of the type privileged by Mahaffy, Lady Gregory understood intuitively, as Cannadine puts it, that "dinner parties might be as important as cabinet meetings" (*Decline*, 344). An entire chapter of Lady Gregory's autobiography is titled "London Table Talk," and it seems on first glance to be merely anecdotal, a loose assemblage of *bons mots* uttered at London dinner parties.[18] Sentences such as "A dinner last night was pleasant to me because I sat next Sir Hercules Robinson, whom I like very much" do not seem to promise much in the way of insights into the powerful exchanges that could and did occur at such semiprivate events (*Seventy Years*, 116). But Lady Gregory's chapter makes clear that, like Oscar Wilde, she understood the importance of dominating a London dinner table: it was a necessary worldly skill in which she shows her growing competence. Gregory recalls her first dinner party at Lough Cutra, when she was so shy that "[t]he salt being out of reach I dared not ask my neighbour at the table to bring it within my reach" (*Seventy Years*, 96). Much later, in the winter of 1881–82, when she was living in Cairo, Gregory could converse confidently with the distinguished company: "[O]ne evening, coming from a small dinner at Sir Edward Malet's, where I had held my own, my husband made me very happy by saying he was Content" (*Seventy Years*, 101). Moreover, Gregory indicates a clear understanding of the dinner party as a crossover zone. "I used to dine often in later years with the Childerses, who lived almost next door to us in St. George's Place," she writes. "He was Chancellor of the Exchequer, and it was at one of their small round-table dinners that Gladstone had first met Parnell in private life, and had made a compact with him, giving some concession, I forget what, to the Irish party, while Parnell agreed not to oppose an extra allowance to the Prince of Wales (the late King Edward) for his children. I used to propose putting an inscription: 'At this round-table Parnell was squared'" (*Seventy Years*, 118). Meeting in the house of a member of the government, a domestic space in which public figures were off duty, the prime minister and the leader of the Irish Party could make a "compact" unofficially, one they both honored. No doubt the atmosphere of the dinner party enabled both men to concede something to the other.

Gregory's proposed inscription shows off not only a minor witticism but also her sense of what could be accomplished around a table. High politics and high culture alike, as she saw them, were grounded in conversational exchanges over meals in the houses of the powerful. The primacy of London table-talk for

Gregory, especially its determining role in her view of the literary profession, can be seen not only in her chapter of that title but also in the correspondence with her friend and former lover Wilfrid Blunt, an exchange that lasted from 1882 until his death in 1922. The dinner party does not appear in any of Gregory's plays or literary works, but the material in her letters shows how it functioned in her life, and those are the sources on which I draw here. The letters, along with her autobiography, reveal how for Gregory a published work may be understood as an intervention in a conversation, its significance arising from the way in which it will be talked about. The trajectory of a published work, as the paradigm implied in the letters indicates, is from *talk* to *print* to *talk*.

One episode from 1882 (when Lady Gregory's first publication, "Arabi and His Household," was printed in the London *Times*) shows how for her writing was embedded in table-talk. During the winter of 1881–82, the Gregorys traveled to Egypt, where, as she writes, they "tumbled into a revolution" (*Seventy Years,* 34). Her interest in the nationalist army colonel Ahmed Urabi originated over the meals that constituted the heart of British colonial social life in Cairo. Sir William Gregory had met Urabi and was sympathetic to his political goals—a restored legislative assembly and reform of the army, in which the careers open to native Egyptians had recently been limited by the Dual Control, France and England, which determined Egypt's finances. Sir William and Lady Gregory discussed Urabi on many occasions and heard varying opinions of him: he was the subject of conversation when they "dined with Sir E. Malet," the British consul-general in Cairo, and when they went "with Lord Houghton and Mrs. Fitzgerald" to lunch with the Blunts in their tent at Heliopolis (*Seventy Years,* 37). Dining at the Van der Nests, they "heard the account of Arabi's reception at the Feast of the Sacred Carpet in the morning" (*Seventy Years,* 37–38). When Lord Cawdor, the Duliers, and the Goldsmids came to tea, stories were told of Urabi (*Seventy Years,* 40, 41). Lady Gregory's friendship with Wilfrid Blunt also began over table-talk at that time: "It was one day at lunch at the Fitzgeralds, we had met Wilfrid and Lady Anne Blunt, the beginning to me of a long friendship" (*Seventy Years,* 35). The Blunts had no official diplomatic position: they were living in Egypt because they loved all things Arabic. Gregory's first visit to Urabi's house was undertaken in the company of Lady Anne Blunt, who spoke Arabic and could interpret what Urabi's wife and mother were saying.

The following summer, back in Ireland, Lady Gregory began writing her essay on Urabi while staying at her childhood home, Roxborough (in County Galway).

Blunt was the inspiration of this essay; he and Gregory became lovers during the summer of 1882, but of course she could not write about Blunt openly. Blunt, however, was so identified in her mind with Urabi—whose cause he supported absolutely—that writing about the Arab nationalist was a satisfactory displaced way of writing about Blunt.[19] In late July she corresponded with him: "I am not unhappy about Egypt but only about Arabi, and I am afraid what you prophesied has come true and Sir William has gone over to the enemy. However, it does not much matter now. I am writing from memory an account of Arabi and his household and will publish it someday." She asked Blunt, "Do you think any of the magazines would take it?" Blunt wrote back two days later saying the account was "excellent," and he suggested that she submit her piece to either the well-respected *Contemporary Review* or *Fortnightly Review*.

Whereas Blunt served as Gregory's muse, Sir William acted as gatekeeper, patrolling the boundary between talk and print. Sir William, a popular clubman and diner-out, had a highly developed sense of appropriate and inappropriate behavior relative to what his wife would later call "spreading the news."[20] During the summer of 1882, the state of things in Egypt changed, and Urabi's situation became more desperate: the British (with the help of the French) sent a military force "in support of the authority of His Highness the Khedive" to suppress an alleged military revolt by the Urabist army officers.[21] Blunt passed along to Lady Gregory his own article on Urabi, and she passed it along to Sir William. In a letter to Blunt, Lady Gregory conveyed her husband's response: "Sir Wm. thinks it exceedingly good and says there is not a sentence he would wish left out. He would not like his name to be mentioned . . . as the conversations he had with members of the Cabinet were mentioned to you for your information and not to be made public" (Gregory to Blunt, 29 August 1882).

Initially, Sir William authorized publication of his wife's article, which had already been vetted by Blunt. "Rather to my surprise," Gregory writes Blunt on 29 August 1882, "Sir Wm. said he saw no objection to my publishing my article in my own name if one of the magazines will take it. I shall be glad to say a word for Egypt and Arabi when there are so few to do so." Blunt submitted Lady Gregory's essay to John Morley's liberal *Fortnightly Review*, prefixing "a few opening sentences" of his own "as the beginning seems hardly to explain itself" (Gregory to Blunt, 29 August 1882). The piece was about to be published when British forces invaded Tel El Kebir and accepted Urabi's surrender on 14 September 1882. Writing to Blunt on 15 September 1882, Lady Gregory made the following announcement: "I am very sorry but Sir Wm. now says he does not wish my article to appear as he thinks it too late to do any good. . . . I cannot tell you how sorry I am." When Blunt agreed that at this point, with Urabi a British prisoner, there was no point in publishing the essay, Lady Gregory was palpably relieved: "I am very glad . . . to know that you approve of my paper being suppressed. It could not do any good now and Sir Wm. was quite decided about it" (Gregory to Blunt, 17 September 1882).

By the middle of October, however, the possibility of Urabi's getting a fair trial seemed unlikely, and the queen's counsel hired (and partly funded) by Blunt to represent him risked arriving too late to help. Sir William, who was genuinely sympathetic toward Urabi and wished the colonial authorities to be fair to him, changed his mind. Believing in his wife's "power of writing well and piquantly," he encouraged her to publish the article so that the British public would understand the true nature of Urabi's position.[22] As cautious in her old age as her husband was in his, Gregory omits all of these complicated negotiations from her autobiography, where she casually remarks, "I don't remember if it was at Hayward's suggestion that I wrote an account of *Arabi and His Household*" (*Seventy Years,* 46).[23] Submission and publication, as she reconstructs the situation, came about as an easy, natural function of social life: Hayward (man of letters, Sir William's friend, and fellow member of the Athenæum) suggests and Chenery (editor of the London *Times*) accepts. Lady Gregory is one of the guys: "I took it to friendly Chenery," she writes, "and on the 23rd it was printed in *The Times*" (*Seventy Years,* 46).

The story of the article ends as it began, in the conversation of her husband's friends. The printed work finds its significance, its ultimate review, in speech:

> It really was a success. Sir William was pleased when he went to the Athenæum because so many of his friends, Dicey and Chenery among them, paid him compliments about it; and especially because when someone had said it was so good that people would think it was written by him, W. E. Forster had growled, "I know you didn't write it because I know you couldn't." And Hayward came on Sunday saying he had dined at Downing Street the night before to meet the Granvilles, and they were all talking about it, and Gladstone had said it was very touching. (*Seventy Years,* 46)[24]

Lady Gregory's wifely pride in Sir William's husbandly pride ("Sir William was pleased") did not prevent her from including Forster's compliment that she wrote better than her husband did (Forster was a Liberal party politician). But the highest compliment of all is that at the prime minister's dinner party, "they were all talking about it." Gregory's first publication, which arose from dinner-party conversation, became in turn table-talk at the premier table in London.

Oscar Wilde: Dominating the Dinner Table

In "London Table Talk," Lady Gregory includes many of her own little witticisms as well as compliments people gave her on them. Wilde was in a different league altogether: he was a star of table-talk. As his contemporary W. B. Yeats said, "The dinner table was Wilde's event and made him the greatest talker of his time."[25] André Gide, hearing Wilde talk in Paris in 1891, said of him, "*Il rayonnait*" ("he shines" as well as "he holds sway").[26] As late as 1953, Wilde's table-talk remained a powerful presence in living memory. In a letter to Wilde's son, Vyvyan Holland, Max Beerbohm wrote,

> I suppose there are now few survivors among the people who had the delight of hearing Oscar Wilde talk. Of these I am one. I have had the privilege of listening also to many other masters of table-talk—Meredith and Swinburne, Edmund Gosse and Henry James, Augustine Birrell and Arthur Balfour, Gilbert Chesterton and Desmond MacCarthy and Hilaire Belloc—all of them splendid in their own way. But assuredly Oscar in *his* own way was the greatest of them all—the most spontaneous and yet the most polished, the most soothing and yet the most surprising. That his talk was mostly a monologue was not his own fault. His manners were very good; he was careful to give his guests or his fellow guests many a conversational opening; but seldom did anyone respond with more than a few words. Nobody was willing to interrupt the music of so magnificent a virtuoso. To have heard him consoles me for not having heard Dr. Johnson or Edmund Burke, Lord Brougham or Sydney Smith.[27]

But when Wilde described his own talking, it was almost apologetically. Of his novel *The Picture of Dorian Gray* (1890, revised 1891), he said, "I am afraid it is rather like my own life—all conversation and no action."[28] According to Yeats, Wilde said to him of the Irish, "We are a nation of brilliant failures, but we are the greatest talkers since the Greeks" (*Autobiography*, 90). Blunt took a similar tack: he wrote in his diary that "looking always for immediate applause" was "the snare of all brilliant talkers and facile writers . . . witness, as an extreme example, Oscar Wilde."[29]

For Wilde—unlike for Lady Gregory—table-talk therefore did not have ontological primacy. It did not supply the grounding for high politics (as it did also for Beatrice Webb) and high culture. In other words, for Wilde, table-talk is contingent and secondary, an alternative to serious worldly business. In fact, it offered an alternative politics: what might be called a shadow public realm. The power of table-talk was thus its power to charm, and its charm was oppositional. In this regard, table-talk was deliberately and usefully trivial. If we look closely at the passages (there are not very many of them) where Wilde writes explicitly about table-talk, we can see that the nature of this triviality changes. Table-talk as Wilde writes about it in "The Decay of Lying" (1889, revised 1891) and *The Picture of Dorian Gray* is not a collective phenomenon, like Gregory's. Instead, it is an individual one, the charismatic utterance of a single performer before a reverential audience. Its value is dependent on his value, and as he comes increasingly to "dominate" the table, table-talk becomes a corrupting force.

At first, the talker is a hero, leader, and savior, the potential source of a new society. The audience for whom he performs is given a vision of what an improved society could be like. Perhaps that is why, on the same occasion in Paris when Gide said of Wilde, "*Il rayonnait*," the hostess, Princess Ouroussoff, claimed to see a halo around his head. His talk emanated from a spiritually superior zone, and he turned the dinner party, however briefly, into such a space. The semipublic nature of this social arena made the power to charm its guests a significant one: witticisms spoken in such a site were emergent public speech.

Through the character Vivian, Wilde theorizes this idea of table-talk in "The Decay of Lying," where it becomes the founding energy of a new society:

> Bored by the tedious and improving conversation of those who have neither the wit to exaggerate nor the genius to romance, tired of the intelligent person whose reminiscences are always based upon memory, whose statements are invariably limited by probability, and who is at any time liable to be corroborated by the merest Philistine who happens to be present, Society sooner or later must return to its lost leader, the cultured and fascinating liar. Who he was who first, without ever having gone out to the rude chase, told the wandering cavemen at sunset how he had dragged the Megatherium from the purple darkness of its jasper cave, or slain the Mammoth in single combat and brought back its gilded tusks, we cannot tell, and not one of our modern

anthropologists, for all their much-boasted science, has had the ordinary courage to tell us. Whatever was his name or race, he certainly was the true founder of social intercourse. For the aim of the liar is simply to charm, to delight, to give pleasure. He is the very basis of civilized society, and without him a dinner-party, even at the mansions of the great, is as dull as a lecture at the Royal Society, or a debate at the Incorporated Authors. (*CW,* 8:29)

The "cultured and fascinating liar" is the "lost leader" of society; his place has been taken by those who speak "tedious and improving conversation," but his day will come—"before this century has drawn to its close," Vivian predicts (*CW,* 8:28–29). This is the manuscript that at proof stage Wilde was reading to Yeats on Christmas Day 1888, on the same occasion when he said the Irish were "brilliant failures" but "the greatest talkers since the Greeks." Simultaneously, Wilde was imagining the great site of important talk, the dinner party, as the place from which the talkers would emerge to become brilliant successes. The dinner-party talker is the "very basis of civilized society," and soon he will return to power. His every *bon mot,* his every epigram, is speech that is in the process of becoming public; the dinner party is only his beginning.

The kind of talking praised in "The Decay of Lying"—narrative talking, not epigrammatic wit—is reminiscent of at least two examples from Wilde's own life. A friend from Portora Royal School, Edward Sullivan, tells of the time when the sixteen-year-old Wilde, running through the town of Enniskillen with several friends, "collided with an aged cripple and knocked him down."[30] Back at school, this event was revised: "[A]n angry giant had barred his path, he had had to fight him through round after round and eventually, after prodigies of valour to leave him for dead."[31] It also sounds like a story told by Mrs. Claude Beddington about a dinner when someone asked Wilde, "Where have you been this past week?" and he replied that he had been at "an exquisite Elizabethan country house, with emerald lawns, stately yew hedges, scented rose-gardens, cool lily ponds, gay herbaceous borders, ancestral oaks, and strutting peacocks. 'And did she act well, Oscar?' asked Constance. . . . He had gone to a play."[32] The "cultured and fascinating liar" was gathering his forces, practicing at the level of the dinner party, surviving assaults from "the intelligent person whose reminiscences are . . . based upon memory."

However charming and various Wilde's actual performances were judged to be by others, table-talk in his writing came gradually to be associated exclusively with the speech of the dandy. In the dinner party at Lady Narborough's that occurs near the end of the 1891 edition of *The Picture of Dorian Gray*, Lord Henry Wotton is the "cultured and fascinating liar" whose charming talk creates a witty, beautiful alternative reality for the hostess, the widow "of one of our most tedious ambassadors" (*CW*, 12:283). Having "buried her husband," she is no longer interested in what "The Decay of Lying" calls "tedious and improving conversation"; she wants only the "pleasures of French fiction, French cookery, and French *esprit*" (*CW*, 12:283). Lord Henry's table-talk replaces the presumably public-spirited talk of the late husband; his is anti-public, but its very definition in contrast to Lord Narborough's suggests an implicit critique. To the extent that Lady Narborough's dinner party gives Lord Henry an audience, his flow of epigrams (most of which Wilde uses again in his plays) begins to constitute a kind of social policy: "Nowadays all the married men live like bachelors, and all the bachelors like married men" or "A man can be happy with any woman as long as he does not lover her," to which Lady Narborough responds enthusiastically, "What a cynic you are! You must come and dine with me soon again. . . . You must tell me what people you would like to meet, though. I want it to be a delightful gathering" (*CW*, 12:289, 290). His power will grow with his audience; his public is increasing; he is launching his alternative view at dinner parties. The problem is that all this table-talk comes from the sinister Lord Henry, under whose influence Dorian's amorality has become immorality. The narrative suggests, implicitly, that table-talk may be consequential and even destructive.

With Lord Illingworth in *A Woman of No Importance*, this dangerous type of table-talk is seen expanding into a more public discourse, and the "fascinating liar" becomes a threat to society. Lord Illingworth, who repeats some of Lord Henry's epigrams, is a quasi-governmental figure, though what kind remains unclear. "I fancy . . . that Diplomacy is what Lord Illingworth is aiming at," Lady Hunstanton suggests. "I heard that he was offered Vienna" (*CW*, 4:8). A vaguely public personage, Lord Illingworth speaks with authority, presenting his witticisms as career advice for Gerald Arbuthnot, his as-yet-unrecognized illegitimate son: "You want to be modern, don't you, Gerald? You want to know life as it really is. Not to be put off with any old-fashioned theories about life. . . . Well, what you have to do at present is simply to fit yourself for the best society. A man who can dominate a London dinner-table can dominate the world. The future belongs to the dandy. It is the exquisites who are going to rule" (*CW*, 4:109).

Understood in this context, Lord Illingworth's famous epigram can be seen to make the case of the dinner party as crossover zone and to suggest how easily power exerted in the flexibly public-private realm of the dinner party may extend into a purely public sphere. The dandy, like the "cultured and fascinating liar," is society's "lost leader." But the play has condemned, before he appears, the site from which he launches his campaign. When the sexy, amoral Mrs. Allonby says to the idealistic American Hester Worsley, "Don't you find yourself longing for a London dinner-party?" Hester says, "I dislike London dinner parties" (*CW*, 4:36). Lady Caroline's brother, Lord Henry Weston—who may be seen as a combination of Lord Henry Wotton and Dorian Gray—is mentioned exclusively, it seems, to be condemned for his table talk. Hester exclaims, "Lord Henry Weston! I remember him, Lady Hunstanton. A man with a hideous smile and a hideous past. He is asked everywhere. No dinner-party is complete without him. . . . What of those whose ruin is due to him? They are outcasts. They are nameless. If you met them in the street you would turn your head away" (*CW*, 4:71). Table-talk therefore is the talk of the corrupt, its alternative vision becoming, in Lord Illingworth, more systematic in its philosophy, more public in its aspirations, and more shamelessly destructive. Like *The Picture of Dorian Gray*, however, *A Woman of No Importance* thwarts the power of its witty talker: given the insistence with which the play links table-talk and corruption, its young couple, Gerald and Hester, will go forth, it seems, to a loving, moral life without dinner parties.

THE KIND OF table-talk that took place when writers dined regularly with cabinet ministers, and those cabinet ministers were running an empire, represents a brief moment in the history of dinner parties. London in the late nineteenth and early twentieth centuries was a political, financial, and cultural capital, an imperial center, able to concentrate with its own residents alone more power around a table than any other city before or since. In his *Diaries*, Wilfrid Blunt describes such a table, a dinner party at the Asquiths in July 1894 where Wilde was also a guest ("the last occasion on which I found myself in his company" [1:146]). Blunt writes, "Of all those present, and they were most of them brilliant talkers, he was without comparison the most brilliant, and in a perverse mood he chose to cross swords with one after the other of them, overpowering each in turn with his wit, and making special fun of Asquith, his host that day, who only a few months later, as Home Secretary, was prosecuting him on the notorious criminal charge which sent him to hard labour in prison" (*My Diaries*, 1:145–46). Certainly, there was no causal connection between Wilde's behavior at a dinner party in July 1894 and the trials in which he was a defendant, which began in late April 1895; Blunt's syntax is somewhat misleading. What this passage suggests, however, is the consequentiality of table-talk and its connection, however oblique, with high politics, especially when the host is home secretary.

Notes

1. David Cannadine, *The Decline and Fall of the British Aristocracy* (New Haven, CT: Yale University Press, 1990), 344; Stefan Collini, *Public Moralists: Political Thought and Intellectual Life in Britain, 1850–1930* (Oxford: Clarendon Press, 1991), 33.

2. See *The Complete Letters of Oscar Wilde*, ed. Merlin Holland and Rupert Hart-Davis (London: Fourth Estate, 2000); and *Lady Gregory's Diaries, 1892–1902*, ed. James Pethica (Gerrards Cross: Colin Smythe, 1996), the latter cited in the text as Gregory's *Diaries*.

3. In his study of John Gray, G. A. Cevasco remarks, "Shortly before Christmas 1894, Gray distributed the first of the *Blue Calendars* to close friends. A small blue-covered booklet measuring 4-⅝ by 3-⅜ inches, it contained twelve devotional poems assigned to the months of the forthcoming year. On the page following that of the title appear the words 'A Book of Carols Invented and Writ by John Gray.' Since the booklet was such a private affair, Gray noted the work was 'Not for General Distribution,' and also included his London address, 'Forty-three Park Lane'.... A second *Blue Calendar* appeared in 1895, a third in 1896, and a fourth in 1897." The calendars contained poems on the models of Richard Crashaw, George Herbert, and Thomas Traherne. The third and fourth calendars comprised sonnets addressed to various saints. These were the devotional poems read by Lady Gregory: "Lady Gregory did not comment on the sonnets as sonnets, but apparently she was so pleased with each of the *Calendar*s that she had them bound together in a dark green calfskin cover. The work, exquisitely bound, has the appearance of a small prayer book, and its well-thumbed appearance allows the inference that it was so used." Cevasco, *John Gray* (Boston: Twayne, 1982), 77, 81.

4. I am grateful to James Pethica for this information.

5. Oscar Wilde to Lady Gregory, [September 1887,] *Complete Letters*, 319; Lady Gregory, *The Journals*, ed. Daniel J. Murphy, 2 vols. (New York: Oxford University Press, 1987), 2:327, cited in the text as *Journals*.

6. Mary Douglas, "Deciphering a Meal," in Douglas, *Implicit Meanings* (London: Routledge and Kegan Paul, 1975), 249, 256–57.

7. Robert Jameson, "Purity and Power at the Victorian Dinner Party," in *The Archaeology of Contextual Meanings*, ed. Ian Hodder (Cambridge: Cambridge University Press, 1987), 55.

8. Roy Strong, *Feast: A History of Grand Eating* (London: Jonathan Cape, 2002), 292–95; hereafter cited in text.

9. Natalie Kapetanios Meir, "'A Fashionable Dinner Is Arranged as Follows': Victorian Dining Taxonomies," *Victorian Literature and Culture* (2005): 33, 133–48.

10. J. P. Mahaffy, *The Principles of the Art of Conversation* (New York: G. P. Putnam's Sons, 1888), 58–59; further page reference appears in parentheses.

11. Michelle Perrot and Anne Martin-Fugier, "Bourgeois Rituals," in *A History of Private Life*, ed. Phillipe Ariès and Georges Duby, trans. Arthur Goldhammer, 5 vols. (Cambridge, MA: Harvard University Press, 1987–91), 4:278.

12. Michelle Perrot and Roger-Henri Guerrand, "Private Spaces," in Ariès and Duby, *History of Private Life*, 4:367.

13. Jürgen Habermas, *The Structural Transformation of the Public Sphere*, trans. Peter Burger (Cambridge, MA: MIT Press, 1981), 45.

14. Beatrice Webb, *The Diary of Beatrice Webb*, ed. Norman MacKenzie and Jeanne MacKenzie, 4 vols. (Cambridge, MA: Harvard University Press, 1982–85), 3:11; further page reference appears in parentheses.

15. http://net.lib.byu.edu/~rdh7/wwi/memoir/Page/Page12.htm.

16. Lucy McDiarmid, *The Irish Art of Controversy* (Ithaca, NY: Cornell University Press, 2005), 182, 252n34.

17. http://net.lib.byu.edu/~rdh7/wwi/memoir/Page/Page12.htm.

18. Augusta Gregory, *Seventy Years: 1853–1922* (New York: Macmillan, 1976), 96–125; further page references appear in parentheses.

19. For a discussion of Blunt as Gregory's muse, see Lucy McDiarmid, "The Demotic Lady Gregory," in *High and Low Moderns: Literature and Culture, 1889–1939,* ed. Maria DiBattista and Lucy McDiarmid (Oxford: Oxford University Press, 1996), 212–34. For a detailed analysis of the entire context—personal, political, and historical—of Gregory's essay on Urabi, see Maureen Lees, "Secret Histories: Lady Gregory's Egyptian Intrigues," unpublished MA dissertation, Villanova University, 1996.

20. Lady Gregory's play, *Spreading the News,* was written in 1905.

21. Letter from Hugh C. E. Childers, secretary of state, War Office, to General G. J. Wolseley, G.C.B., B.C.M.G. See "Five British Battles, 1805–1951," in *Pathways to the Past,* Public Records Office, Kew, formerly at http://www.pro.gov.uk/pathways/battles/egypt/ego8t.htm.

22. Quoted in Brian Jenkins, *Sir William Gregory of Coole: The Biography of an Anglo-Irishman* (Gerrards Cross, UK: Colin Smythe, 1986), 271.

23. Abraham Hayward (1801–1884) was a man of letters and, like Sir William and many of his friends, a member of the Athenæum Club. Collini discusses his hostile obituary of J. S. Mill in *Public Moralists* (312–14, 320, 321–22).

24. Granville George Leveson-Gower, 2nd Earl Granville (1815–1891), was a Liberal politician and foreign secretary in the years 1870–74 and 1880–85.

25. W. B. Yeats, *Autobiography* (1916; repr., New York: Macmillan, 1963), 93.

26. Quoted in Richard Ellmann, *Oscar Wilde* (London: Hamish Hamilton, 1987), 334.

27. Max Beerbohm to Vyvyan Holland, 14 September 1953, *Letters of Max Beerbohm, 1892–1956,* ed. Rupert Hart-Davis (New York: W. W. Norton, 1989), 223n1.

28. Oscar Wilde to Beatrice Allhusen, [undated, early 1890], *Complete Letters,* 425; Ellmann, *Oscar Wilde,* 296.

29. W. S. Blunt, *My Diaries, Being a Personal Narrative of Events, 1888–1914,* 2 vols. (New York: Knopf, 1921), 2:223. Elsewhere in his diaries, Blunt praises Wilde's table-talk. Hearing the news of Wilde's death, Blunt wrote, "He was without exception the most brilliant talker I have ever come across, the most ready, the most witty, the most audacious. Nobody could pretend to outshine him, or even to shine at all in his company." Blunt, *My Diaries,* 1:375; further page references appear in parentheses.

30. Ellmann, *Oscar Wilde,* 22.

31. Ellmann, *Oscar Wilde,* 22.

32. Mrs. Claude Beddington, *All That I Have Met* (London: Cassell, 1929), 41; see also Ellmann, *Oscar Wilde,* 251.

Sexuality in the Age of
Technological Reproducibility

Oscar Wilde, Photography, and Identity

DANIEL A. NOVAK

> No investigation of the work of art in the age of its technological re-
> producibility can overlook these connections.... To an ever increasing
> degree, the work reproduced becomes the work designed for repro-
> ducibility. From a photographic plate, for example, one can make any
> number of prints; to ask for the "authentic" print makes no sense.
>
> —Walter Benjamin, "The Work of Art in the Age
> of Its Technological Reproducibility"

A T THE HEART of this chapter is a simple question: For the late Victorians, what does the photograph capture? Does the photograph capture body, soul, identity, and/or sexuality? If so, then what should we learn from Victorian photographs and, more specifically, from photographs of Oscar Wilde? If not, then how does the camera redefine sexuality, along with identity and the body? In other words, to borrow from Walter Benjamin's formulation, what happens to sexuality in the age of technological reproducibility?[1] This question is perhaps most appropriate for Wilde because photographs of Oscar Wilde are often used as a shorthand or as an icon for the modern concept of "sexuality" if not modern culture itself—the very culture of modernity that Benjamin associates with me-chanical reproduction.

Yet while we most often think of photography in terms of the particular and the immediate, the technology of realism in the Victorian and fin-de-siècle imagination presents its subjects as disembodied and indeterminate. The Victorians consistently figured photography as a process that turned concrete individuals into anonymous abstractions—in short, for the Victorians, realism *produced* abstraction. Here, in an attempt to historicize how we read photographs of Wilde, his writings on the artistic body, and his theories of legibility, I locate Wilde's critical essays and his only novel, *The Picture of Dorian Gray* (1890, revised 1891), in the context of perhaps unfamiliar Victorian photographic techniques, theories, and discourses.

In the fin de siècle, Wilde emerges as the nexus of these questions in the spheres of literature, photography, and the law. My discussion centers on two moments in which all of these domains converge. The first is a trial that occurred in 1883, in which Napoleon Sarony, the photographer of the most widely circulated photographs of Wilde, argued before the U.S. Supreme Court that his photographs of Wilde (more specifically, Wilde's "pose") were "original" creations —essentially works of fiction. When Sarony sued a lithographic company in 1883 for copyright infringement after the company used an image of Wilde without Sarony's permission and without payment, Sarony's lawyer argued that his photograph of Wilde was an original work of fictional composition. Ruling in Sarony's favor, the Supreme Court ruled not only that photography could be an art of fiction but also that Wilde's famous "pose" was not his own property.[2]

This trial over the authorship and proprietary rights of a "pose" points to a later trial about posing: Wilde's first trial in 1895, in which he sued the Marquess of Queensberry for libel. Like copyright infringement, libel is an accusation that aims to halt an unwanted, unauthorized, and injurious circulation. But whereas Sarony had argued that his photographs were works of fiction, the prosecution in the Wilde trials looked to Wilde's fiction for a form of photographic evidence against him. The counsel for the prosecution, Sir Edward Carson, read a passage from *The Picture of Dorian Gray* in which the painter Basil Hallward confesses his secret idolatry of Dorian: "[E]very flake and film of colour seemed to reveal my secret" (*CW,* 12:184). What followed became an argument between the prosecutor and Wilde over a delicate semantic distinction that strictly discriminates between acts and subjects, criminality and art, and reality and fiction:

> "Do you mean to say that that passage describes the natural feeling of one
> man towards another?" "It would be the influence produced by a beautiful

Daniel A. Novak

personality." "A beautiful person?" "I said 'a beautiful personality.' You can describe it as you like. Dorian Gray's was a most remarkable personality." "May I take it that you, as an artist, have never known the feeling described here?" "I have never allowed any personality to dominate my art." "Then you have never known the feeling you described?" "No. It is a work of fiction."[3]

Turning a disembodied fictional subject (a "beautiful personality") into an embodied and criminal subject (a "beautiful person"), Carson ultimately turned fiction into a form of "photography." If Wilde's defense was that his novel was only "a work of fiction," then Carson attempted to turn Wilde's fictional body into a photographic body that can be caught in the act.

My reading of *The Picture of Dorian Gray* picks up on both this argument over the definition of fiction and acts and the distinction between "person" and "personality." For many cultural and literary critics, this linguistic quibble signifies a turning point in the history of sexuality. For critics such as Ed Cohen and Alan Sinfield, the Wilde trials act as the key moment in which (to quote the famous passage from Michel Foucault) the "homosexual became a personage, a past, a case history, a childhood, and in addition to being a type of life, a life form, and a morphology, with an indiscreet anatomy and possibly a mysterious physiology. . . . The sodomite had been a temporary aberration; the homosexual was now a species."[4] Seemingly inverting Foucault's theory of a discursive shift from the sodomite as a perpetrator of forbidden acts into the "species" or personality of the homosexual, the exchange I just quoted and *The Picture of Dorian Gray* as a whole mark the point at which Foucault's history breaks down and the moment at which this very transformation becomes the subject of debate and conflict.[5] Thus, while Cohen reads the trials and their popular representation as producing "a new constellation of sexual meanings predicated upon 'personality' and not practices," I argue that, rather than turning the act into a subject, Carson attempted both to turn the subject into an act and to transform the fictional subject into a juridical body.[6] In a sense, *The Picture of Dorian Gray* uncannily allegorizes the issues addressed by both trials: specifically, the problem of reproduction, reproducibility, and authorship. Focusing on the problematic distinction that Carson failed to make and that Wilde insisted upon, the novel literally draws a fatal distinction between "personality" and "person," a subject and its body, a person and his portrait. But in drawing this distinction, Wilde also problematizes both terms. Making both portrait and body the creation of another artist, Wilde makes Dorian Gray's sexuality and subjectivity, "person" and "personality," both already a reproduction and eminently reproducible. Wilde makes Dorian Gray's identity and body at one and the same time both a work of fiction and a photographic reproduction.

Moreover, as Jeff Nunokawa contends, the novel defines homosexual desire as the disembodiment of a desiring subject; it offers a model of "homosexual desire whose subject is finally nowhere and thus everywhere at once"—simultaneously nobody and everybody, anything and nothing.[7] This disembodiment of the subject, both in Wilde's essays on the artist's model and in *The Picture of Dorian Gray*, can be seen within a different and wider context of literary and photographic abstraction. As a negative body and a photographic body, Dorian Gray therefore is a model subject both for fiction and for photography. In other words, Wilde's representation of the homosexual body is photographic precisely in its abstraction and spectrality.

The link I draw between photography and fiction, mechanical reproduction, and disembodiment may seem counterintuitive, but my reading of Victorian photographic culture is historically based both in a specific nineteenth-century photographic practice called "composition-photography" (fig. 2) and in the tropes used to describe photography in Victorian journalism. Victorian art-photographers such as Oscar Rejlander and Henry Peach Robinson created large tableaux by transposing independently photographed figures into a single scene —sometimes using more than thirty negatives (figs. 3 and 4). They even produced a single body from different models. By using different body parts to produce new photographic subjects and by transposing figures from scene to scene, art-photographers used the medium of realism to produce a fictional body that can appear in new photographic fictions. In both the theory and the practice of these photographers, the bodies of photographic models are not only endlessly divisible but also abstract, anonymous, and endlessly exchangeable. One nineteenth-century photographic critic argued that the photographic body and its parts take on the qualities of a language. The "value" of composition photography, he argued, is "in the thought it embodies. . . . All else is no more to the picture than words—regarded simply as words—are to the poem or essay."[8] That is to say, photographic bodies provided an evacuated and abstract raw material that could be used for any arrangement, inscription, and "embodiment."

Significantly, this body and these tropes reappear in Victorian literary journalism. While the Victorians famously trusted the objectivity of photography, they also figured it in terms of bodily disfigurement, violation, defacement, and

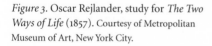

Figure 2. Henry Peach Robinson, study for
Bringing Home the May (1862). Courtesy of
National Media Museum, Bradford, UK / Science
and Society Picture Library, London.

Figure 3. Oscar Rejlander, study for *The Two
Ways of Life* (1857). Courtesy of Metropolitan
Museum of Art, New York City.

Figure 4. Oscar Rejlander, *The Two Ways of Life* (1857). Courtesy of National
Media Museum, Bradford, UK / Science and Society Picture Library, London.

Figure 5. Marcelin, "Le fauteuil mécanique," *Le journal amusant,* 21 February 1857. Courtesy of the Getty Research Institute, Los Angeles.

even decapitation (fig. 5). This trope appeared throughout the 1890s as well. In many articles, photographic subjects come out of the process either without their heads or without their identities (fig. 6). In an article from Charles Dickens's journal *Household Words* by John Hollingshead entitled "A Counterfeit Present-ment," a photographer threatens a literary celebrity who is reluctant to have his picture taken by arguing that a picture of another person can be substituted under his name: "[Y]ou are aware . . . that, when a demand reaches a certain height it must be supplied. . . . I don't want to do anything offensive but, knowing your objection to sit for a photograph, I have been compelled to look amongst my stock for something like you."[9] Hardly a "likeness," the photograph offers "the linea-

Figure 6. Oscar Rejlander, *The Head of John the Baptist on a Charger* (1857–58). Courtesy of the Royal Photographic Society, Bath, UK / National Media Museum, Bradford, UK / Science and Society Picture Library.

ments of a church warden mixed with those of the professional burglar, but whether the church warden turned burglar or the burglar turned church warden, it was impossible to determine." Bringing together literary, photographic, and economic circulation, this Hollingshead article situates the production of the author in a photographic economy of interchangeable bodies and subjects.

As if to literalize this literary and cultural trope of photographic abstraction and anonymity, Francis Galton (the scientist, photographer, and father of eugenics) combined these abstract photographic pieces in the 1880s to make photographic types of criminals, Jews, and generally "unfit" types in Britain. Galton's method consisted of exposing several portraits on the same negative, each one only for a fraction of the time necessary to produce an ordinary portrait (fig. 7). This process differs from composition photography, which entails cutting and pasting figures or parts of figures from one scene to another (fig. 8). Instead, this double exposure produced a single face from several "component portraits" superimposed on each other, and these composite faces were combined with other composites as well. Describing his purpose, Galton wrote that he intended

Figure 7. Francis Galton, *Composites of Three Sisters.* Courtesy of the Galton Collection, University College London.

Figure 8. Francis Galton, *Composites of Violent Criminals.* Courtesy of the Galton Collection, University College London.

Figure 9. Francis Galton, *Composites of the Jewish Type.* Courtesy of the Galton Collection, University College London.

to "obtain with mechanical precision a generalised picture: one that represents no man in particular, but portrays an imaginary figure possessing the average features of any given group of men."[10] Galton made photographic fiction into photographic science; he made a nonexistent body into a type derived with scientific accuracy, a photographic science fiction (fig. 9).[11] Despite some distortion, Galton and others noted that the composite types passed for portraits of existing individuals. Yet the type also appeared spectral and abstract to nineteenth-century observers, one of whom described it as "a shadow of a thing unseen."[12]

Although, as far as I know, Galton did not make any composites of the "homosexual type," one of his main concerns was the identification of eugenically "unfit" types within Britain. Late-nineteenth- and early-twentieth-century sexology, however, used Wilde's photographs with this sexual typology in mind (figs. 10–11). For example, Edgar Beall's *The Life Sexual* (1905) offers the following captions for photographs of Wilde in a chapter on how to read the signs of "born or typical" sexual perverts who desire the same sex: "note the femininity in all the features" and "note the femininity in the pose."[13] Moreover, the critical and popular discourse around Wilde deploys these figures of typology, abstraction, and composition. For example, when Alan Sinfield describes Wilde's typicality, he argues that Wilde becomes the "brilliantly precise image" of a "disconcerting" and fragmented nexus of sexual practices (*Wilde Century,* 3). Yet at the same time, he argues that though the "parts were there already, and were being combined by various people," they came together fully in Wilde to form the "queer" (3). Wilde, like Galton's photographic type, is thus simultaneously a composite and spectral body of queer identity and a "precise image" of homosexual practices (3). A more humorous example from popular culture can be found in a recent edition of the *New Yorker,* in which there is a cartoon of John Ashcroft claiming to be a "gay American" to help the Republican cause (fig. 12).[14] He is, as you can see, in the pose of the classic parody of Wilde, sunflower, limp wrist, and all. If Wilde is thus figured as a type, as the embodiment of homosexuality as such, then sexuality becomes legible as a specific and individual image and pose but, paradoxically, as a reproducible one. At the same time, sexuality and identity take the form of a type: an abstract composite from abstract parts. To put this perhaps too baldly, the homosexual type as defined photographically is at once Wilde and not Wilde—both a concrete individual and a spectral type.

In a way, this spectral and unstable photographic and literary body-in-pieces should be familiar to scholars of aestheticism. While theorizing and redefining the body of aestheticism, both Wilde and his Oxford tutor and mentor Walter Pater offer a body whose parts can be arranged according to the dictates of style. Pater's *Studies in the History of the Renaissance* (1873) had an enormous influence on Wilde's life and thought. Wilde, as Richard Ellmann observes, "never ceased to speak of it as 'my golden book,' and in *De Profundis* he described Pater's work as the 'book which has had such a strange influence over my life'"[15] In his conclusion to *The Renaissance* (as Pater renamed it in 1877), Pater famously calls for an attitude of perpetual and passionate receptivity to a world of continually shifting forms of beauty: "Every moment some form grows perfect in hand or face . . . some mood of passion or insight or intellectual excitement is irresistibly real or attractive to us,—for that moment only. . . . To burn always with this hard, gem-like flame, to maintain this ecstasy is success in life."[16] That such sentiments sound more likely to come from the mouth of Wilde's Lord Henry Wotton as he seductively describes the duties and pleasures of youth and beauty to Dorian Gray than from the mouth of an Oxford professor testifies to the strength of Pater's influence on Wilde and the aesthetic movement as a whole. It also explains why Pater omitted the conclusion in the second edition of *The Renaissance,* on the grounds that "it might possibly mislead some of those young men

Daniel A. Novak

OSCAR WILDE—Note Femininity in All the Features

Figure 10. Reproduction of photograph of
Wilde by Napoleon Sarony in Edgar C.
Beall, *The Life Sexual: A Study of the
Philosophy, Physiology, Science, Art, and
Hygiene of Love* (New York: Vim, 1905).
Courtesy of William Andrews Clark Memorial
Library, University of California, Los Angeles.

OSCAR WILDE—Note the Femininity in the Pose

Figure 11. Reproduction of photograph of Wilde
by Napoleon Sarony in Edgar C. Beall, *The Life
Sexual: A Study of the Philosophy, Physiology,
Science, Art, and Hygiene of Love* (New York:
Vim, 1905). Courtesy of William Andrews Clark
Memorial Library, University of California,
Los Angeles.

*Campaigning in San Francisco, John Ashcroft
declares, "I am a gay American."*

Figure 12. Arnold Roth (cartoon) and Andy
Borowitz (caption), *New Yorker,* 27 September
2004, 160. Courtesy of Arnold Roth, Andy Borowitz,
and Condé Nast for the *New Yorker.*

into whose hands it might fall" (it was restored in the 1888 edition; see *The Renaissance*, ed. Hill, 186).

This life of aesthetic spectatorship, however, is made possible by the instability of any and all boundaries—especially that of self and other: "Like the elements of which we are composed, the action of these forces extends beyond us. . . . [B]irth and gesture and death . . . are but a few of ten thousand resultant combinations. That clear, perpetual outline of face and limb is but an image of ours, under which we group them—a design in a web, the actual threads of which pass beyond it . . . but the concurrence renewed from moment to moment, of forces parting sooner or later on their ways" (Pater, *Renaissance*, 186–87). Only a temporary "combination" of elements, the body of aestheticism forms the abstract raw material for "ten thousand" possible combinations. Capable of a productive dissolution and recomposition, the malleable "face and limb" of Pater's subject bears a family resemblance to the subject of art-photography.

However, Pater's body-in-pieces has a longer literary history. For the purposes of the present discussion, we need to go back only as far as the Victorians. For example, in an 1850 satire by Dickens entitled "The Ghost of Art," the speaker meets with an artist's model who explains, by tracing the dispersal of his dismembered body, why he looks familiar to the speaker: "Do you know what my points are? . . . My throat and my legs. . . . When I don't set for a head, I mostly sets for a throat and a pair of legs. . . . Then, take and stick my legs and throat on to another man's body, and you'll make a reg'lar monster."[17] A body that is not *one*, the model offers the raw material for the production of an infinite number of new subjects. Just as the photographic model in Rejlander's and Robinson's theory and technique was divisible into reproducible and abstract parts, so too does Dickens's Victorian cut and paste erase the traces of identity in order to produce new and improved artistic bodies. In other words, this new body of aestheticism and of the fin de siècle was, in many ways, a reproduction of a quintessentially Victorian photographic and literary body.[18]

Of course, not only those who celebrated aestheticism and decadence turned to the figure of the body-in-pieces. For example, the fin-de-siècle cultural critic Max Nordau turned his attention to the figure of the dandy and diagnosed the dandy's fragmented body as a symptom of pathological degeneracy in his controversial 1892 book *Degeneration*. As early as 1881, Wilde became the embodiment of the new dandyism with the staging of W. S. Gilbert and Arthur Sullivan's parody of aestheticism, *Patience*. As Ellen Moers points out, "*Patience* fixed

Daniel A. Novak

Wilde's position as the most affected man in London."[19] But Nordau's book was tied to Wilde not only by its subject matter (a savage critique of fin-de-siècle art and artists) but also by its publication history. *Degeneration* appeared in its English translation almost simultaneously with Wilde's trials (1895), and writers including Bernard Shaw and Vernon Lee responded to his book with Wilde's fate explicitly in mind.[20] Nordau deploys tropes of bodily composition similar to Pater's but uses them to critique rather than celebrate aestheticism. Citing the fragmented body of the dandy as a symptom of pathological degeneracy, Nordau writes,

> The common feature in all these male specimens is that they do not express their real idiosyncrasies, but try to present something that they are not. They are not content to show their natural figure, nor even to supplement it by legitimate accessories . . . but seek to model themselves after some artistic pattern which has no affinity with their own nature, or is even antithetical to it. Nor do they for the most part limit themselves to one pattern, but copy several at once, which jar with one another. Thus we get heads set on shoulders not belonging to them. . . . [O]ne seems to be moving amongst dummies patched together at haphazard, in a mythical mortuary, from fragments of bodies, heads, trunks, [and] limbs, just as they came to hand.[21]

While one might read Nordau's anxiety about the unnatural combination and disposition of bodies as an anxiety about "unnatural" sexual dispositions and positions, his "mythical mortuary" presupposes both an endlessly divisible body and a store of abstract parts—a store of "heads, trunks, limbs" and hands "ready to hand." The dandy, then, is photographic in two senses. First, like Dickens's artist models and the products of art-photographers, the dandy is a body "patched together . . . from fragments of bodies"—from miscellaneous and abstract parts. Second, the dandy's perversity consists of an unnatural and "illegitimate" form of reproduction, "copy[ing] several" artistic patterns at once. The dandy therefore is defined by monstrous reproduction and monstrous combination—by photographic reproducibility and photographic composition.[22]

But like Dickens's model and the photographic model, Nordau's dandies also "try to present something that they are not." The dandy poses or models both a composite and fictional identity and an abstract body that can be anything or nothing.[23] When Wilde theorizes the artist's model, he resorts to many of the figures that Dickens offers in "Ghost of Art."[24] In an 1889 essay entitled "London

Models," Wilde mocks both the model's negative capability and the model's coarseness—the perfect acting and absurd posing:

> Now and then some old veteran knocks at a studio door, and proposes to sit as Ajax defying the lightning, or as King Lear upon the blasted heath. . . . [A] popular painter . . . told him to begin by kneeling down in the attitude of prayer. "Shall I be Biblical or Shakespearean, sir?" asked the veteran. "Well— Shakespearean," answered the artist, wondering by what subtle *nuance* of expression the model would convey the difference. "All right, sir," said the professor of posing, and he solemnly knelt down and began to wink with his left eye! (*CW,* 14:122)

But Wilde's models, like Dickens's and like the photographers', can also embody any character, regardless of class or gender:[25]

> As a rule the model, nowadays, is a pretty girl from about twelve to twenty-five years of age, who knows nothing about art, cares less, and is merely anxious to earn seven or eight shillings a day without much trouble. . . .
>   As to what they are asked to do they are equally indifferent. . . . They . . . are only interesting when they are not themselves. . . . "What do you sit for?" said a young artist to a model. . . . "Oh, for anything you like sir," said the girl; "landscape if necessary." (*CW,* 14:122–23)

Wilde's "indifferent" models are both valuable and "interesting" only to the extent to which they embody no visible difference. Never "themselves," models can form the raw material for new subjects. Wilde's model takes the technological abstraction of art-photography to its perfectly logical and simultaneously perfectly absurd conclusion. In the context of the techniques used by art-photographers and Dickens's theorization of the artist's model, the model can, in fact, sit for "landscape."

But, as in the passages I quote above from Pater's and Nordau's works, Wilde also figures the model as a product of montage and pastiche: "[I]t is impossible to look through any collection of modern pictures in London . . . without feeling that the professional model is ruining painting, and reducing it to a condition of mere pose and *pastiche*. . . . For all costumes are caricatures. The basis of Art is not the Fancy Ball."[26] Reproducing the technique that he mocks, Wilde's phrase "pose and *pastiche*" performs a logical and syntactical montage, through which "pose" *is* "pastiche" and composition. While Fredric Jameson associates "pastiche" with a form of postmodern parody and camp, I am placing the art of "pastiche" in the context of a technology of Victorian literary and photographic realism.[27] As Roland Barthes points out, "realism cannot be designated a 'copier' but rather a 'pasticheur.'"[28] Moreover, by juxtaposing bodily composition and posing, Wilde reproduces Pater's composite picture of the subject of aestheticism. In other words, realism and aestheticism depend on the same technology and aesthetic. Wilde's model, then, embodies a photographic logic in two ways. First, the model's reproducible and divisible body makes possible the pictorial "pastiche" that offends Wilde's artistic sensibility. Wilde's "professional model," who sells the reproduction of his or her parts for a wage, carries with him or her the aesthetic of fragmentation and recomposition that I argue is central to photographic production. Second, whether posing successfully or successfully posed by an artist, the model offers an anonymous and negative body.[29]

If photography evacuated rather than recorded identity, the controversy over a particular set of Wilde photographs dramatizes the problems and possibilities that the medium represented both for Wilde's theories of identity in particular and for questions of subjectivity and agency in the age of technological reproducibility in general. The most famous of the photographs of Wilde are those from a series taken of Wilde during his trip to America in 1882 (fig. 13).[30] Wilde's photographer in America, Napoleon Sarony, was the best-known practitioner of his art in America and the top celebrity and theatrical photographer.[31] Sarony boasted of having photographed two hundred thousand people, thirty thousand of whom were famous and a thousand of whom were "world renowned." Although Sarony prided himself on his ability to pose his sitter before the photograph was taken, he was not above manipulating the image after the photographic fact. For example, in his portrait of General Hancock, Sarony drew a goatee on the negative because he felt that Hancock needed one: "After I had taken his picture I placed my hand over the lower portion of his face. . . . 'You need a goatee,' I said. He assented. So I drew a tuft of hair over his chin on the negative."[32] Although in their book *Oscar Wilde Discovers America* Lloyd Lewis and Henry Smith insist that Wilde had to be instructed in the value and art of photographic advertisement, Wilde was already well practiced in the art of self-promotion in all forms.[33] After all, Wilde was following Gilbert and Sullivan's *Patience* to America precisely because of the value of parody as a form of advertising. Wilde was aware that Sarony's photographs often created as much as they recorded celebrity status:[34]

Figure 13. Napoleon Sarony, *Oscar Wilde* (1882). Courtesy of William Andrews Clark Memorial Library, University of California, Los Angeles.

Charles Dickens had started that custom when . . . he had refused to sit for photographer Burney until well paid. . . . But New York heard that Colonel Morse [a retired colonel who organized the lecture tour for the man producing *Patience* in America, Richard D'Oyly Carte] was so eager for Sarony to shoot his star that he waived the customary charge. "A picturesque subject indeed!" cried little Sarony, dancing about till his habitual red fez shook, as Wilde arrived holding a white cane across his fur lined overcoat. . . . As each pose was held Sarony would cease jabbering, turn and stare out of the window in rapt silence while an assistant took the picture.[35]

Although Sarony did not actually take the photograph, he defined photography and photographic art as a form of body-building. Sarony claimed ignorance of the photochemical aspects of photography, doing none of the printing and confining himself to setting up the camera and posing the sitter. As an admirer of Sarony put it, "[N]o one in New York could 'make a position' better."[36] If the mid-Victorian composition photographers defined photographic art as the ability to "make" a better body, Sarony literalized the technological manipulations of art-photography. As the copyright trial over these photographs would prove,

Daniel A. Novak

Figure 14. Napoleon Sarony, *Oscar Wilde* (1882). Courtesy of William Andrews Clark Memorial Library, University of California, Los Angeles.

Sarony's picture making made Wilde a "picturesque subject" and a fictional subject of Sarony's making.[37]

In interviews, Sarony expanded on his theory of the photographic model and photographic art. Although he said that "the art of posing is not posing," he demanded "a surrender of self on the part of the sitter"—in other words, that *he* be allowed to pose the sitter.[38] Posing therefore is only a photographic technique— or rather, *the* photographic technique—not a position of agency available to photographic sitters: "Once conscious, the sitter begins to pose, and falsely. . . . The moment a person is told to 'look natural,' at that moment he will look what he feels—perfectly idiotic. He feels he is posing—and posing is for professional models only. . . . Look at this face here—can you question that he was self-willed, head-strong, bound to be his own photographer? He forgot the art of not posing. Instead of lending himself to me as an artist, he would say imperiously: 'Take me this way.'"[39] For Sarony, the only way to produce a proper photographic likeness, the only way to produce an authentic photographic subject, was, paradoxically, for the sitter to surrender any identity, subjectivity, or consciousness that might make itself visible (fig. 14). Whereas Wilde was nothing if not a "professional" poser, Sarony would go out of his way to prove in a court of law that he, not Wilde, had authored the poses in the photographs.

Sarony sued the Burrow-Giles Lithographic Company for copying his "no. 18" portrait of Wilde without authorization (for a parallel example, see figs. 15 and 16), and the case came before the Supreme Court in December 1883. The court accepted the argument of Sarony's lawyer; his attorney validated the claim that photography was an art in itself by proving the photographer's ability to produce the sitter's body and pose as an original work of fiction. The portrait of Oscar Wilde, he contended, "is a useful, new, harmonious, characteristic, and graceful picture . . . made . . . entirely from [Sarony's] own original mental conception, to which he gave visible form by posing the said Oscar Wilde in front of the camera, selecting and arranging the costume, draperies, and other various accessories in said photograph, arranging and disposing the light and shade, suggesting and evoking the desired expression."[40] Making a "new" body, Sarony produced Wilde and his "pose" as a photographic fiction. Wilde's body became merely the abstract raw material that allowed Sarony's "original mental conception" to achieve a "visible form." Like Wilde's own artist's models, he became interesting to Sarony only when he was not himself.

Moreover, like the photographic negative, Wilde's negative body—a body that did not resist the impressions and projections of Sarony's "mental conception"—offered the opportunity to produce an infinite variety of "new [and] harmonious" photographic subjects. Rather than offering a likeness, Sarony's photograph offers an image that is "characteristic" not of Wilde but of Sarony's style. Likeness becomes not only irrelevant but also inimical to photographic art—an art that produces fictional and "characteristic" characters, not likenesses. Not only was Wilde's "expression" Sarony's suggestion, but it was also merely one of many inorganic and marginal props under Sarony's direction, along with "costume, draperies, and other various accessories." In the same manner as Vivian suggests in "The Decay of Lying" (1889, revised 1891) that "we are all of us made out of the same stuff" and that the only marks of difference between us are "dress, manner . . . [and] personal appearance," Sarony denied Wilde even the luxury of this attenuated subjectivity (*CW*, 8:15). Only an "accessory" to the innocent and legal exercise of photographic art, Wilde disappeared as an identifiable subject to reappear as the negative embodiment of Sarony's photographic intentions.

If we return briefly to 1895 and Wilde's first trial, in which he sued the Marquess of Queensberry for libel, we can see that this trial in many ways offered a reprise of Sarony's trial and the problems of authorship and identity, posing and being posed. But whereas Sarony sued to prove that he was the author of Wilde's

Daniel A. Novak

Figure 15. Napoleon Sarony, *Oscar Wilde*—image copied illegally (no. 11) (1882). Library of Congress, Washington, D.C.

Figure 16. Lithographed advertisement using Sarony's photograph of Wilde. Courtesy of William Andrews Clark Memorial Library, University of California, Los Angeles.

pose and that this pose was a form of fiction, Wilde sued the marquess for notoriously accusing him of "posing as a somdomite [*sic*]"—of circulating and imposing a fiction of a pose on the world. Wilde simultaneously disowned the pose that Queensberry circulated and asserted a proprietary interest in and authorship of his body and pose. Queensberry's accusation, of course, suggests that to pose as a sodomite was as bad as being a sodomite—that posing itself was a form of crime.[41] In the pose, then, the ethics of social registration and photographic aesthetics converged. If, for Sarony, posing was the ultimate aesthetic and photographic offense, then the trial extended Sarony's photographic ethic and aesthetic to its logical and legal conclusion. Paradoxically, only a subject who does not pose can become both a convincingly realistic photographic subject and an innocent civil subject.

Interestingly, this distinction between the posing and the posed, the material and the abstract is built into the title of *The Picture of Dorian Gray*, and the discourse of art-photography helps to illuminate Wilde's use of the word *picture* rather than *portrait*. The nineteenth-century photographic critic A. H. Wall drew a distinction between a portrait and a picture by associating a photograph and a portrait with a form of mechanical realism and a picture with language and narrative. An ordinary photograph, he argued, is "a mere portrait suggesting nothing beyond a by no means interesting face," while true photographic art must "make photographs *pictures*" by telling a story.[42] Perhaps more relevant to aestheticism is Charles Baudelaire, who offered an earlier articulation of a similar distinction in his *Salon de 1846*. While making a different distinction (between "historical" and "fictional" portraits that are realistic), he associated "picture" with fiction and narrative. In the French language, this distinction is rendered as *portrait* versus *tableau*: "The second method, which is the special province of the colorists, is to transform the portrait into a picture—a poem with all its accessories, a poem full of space and reverie. . . . Here imagination has a greater part to play."[43] Significantly, in arguing for the originality and fictionality of Sarony's portrait, Sarony's lawyer described the photograph of Wilde as a "picture." Wilde himself alludes to this distinction in his review of Harry Quilter's *Sententiae Artis*, titled "A 'Jolly' Art Critic" (1886). Paraphrasing Quilter's argument, Wilde writes that "[p]ortrait painting is a bad pursuit for an emotional artist as it destroys his personality and his sympathy; however, even for the emotional artist there is hope, as a portrait can be converted into a picture 'by adding to the likeness of the sitter some dramatic interest or some

Daniel A. Novak

picturesque adjunct'!" (*CW*, 13:113).[44] In *The Picture of Dorian Gray*, Wilde allegorizes this distinction between portrait and picture through the same logic of abstraction. The painting in the titular *Picture of Dorian Gray* performs the same kind of narrative and fictional work that both Wall and Baudelaire demanded of visual art.

Additionally, in letters and stories about photography, Wilde reproduces the distinction between portrait and picture and thus encourages an association between photographs and what Baudelaire and Wall called "pictures."[45] The photographed woman in Wilde's story "The Sphinx without a Secret" (1887), for example, retains the mysteriousness and indeterminacy in her photographed image, even though her life seemed to be a futile attempt to escape her own banality through deceit and fantasy (*CW*, 7:123–32). Wilde repeats this association between photographs and sphinxes in a letter to H. C. Pollitt (1899), thanking him for a photograph of Pollitt that he sent to Wilde but insisting that this sphinx or at least this photograph has a secret: "Thank you so much for your last photograph, which has just arrived. It is not a bit like the others, so I feel sure a good likeness. . . . Your personality becomes more and more mysterious, more and more wonderful, each portrait that I receive, but indeed all my life Sphinxes have crossed and recrossed my way."[46] Perversely defining photographic "likeness" as photographic difference, photographic identity with the nonidentity of a group of photographs, Wilde defines photographic realism as the possibility of multiple identities and bodies. Put another way, photographs reproduce secrecy rather than identifiable subjects. For Wilde, photographic "portraits" are "pictures" —a form of literature and a form of fiction.[47]

While Carson's assumption in Wilde's libel trial that *The Picture of Dorian Gray* was a photographic impression of Wilde's intentions appeared somewhat naïve, Basil Hallward's argument that all art is a form of self-portraiture seems to adhere to the same logic. As Basil says, "[E]very portrait that is painted with feeling is a portrait of the artist, not of the sitter. The sitter is merely the accident" (*CW*, 12:8). Even if Wilde's preface to the 1891 edition of his novel specifically rejects Basil's argument, announcing that "to reveal art and conceal the artist is art's aim," the novel returns again and again to the problem of authorship and the ways in which the artist is "revealed" or made visible (*CW*, 12:ix).[48] But if a portrait that does not represent its sitter seems hardly photographic, Basil's "portrait" is a *picture* and a *photographic* picture precisely because it exceeds its subject, not because it perfectly represents either his body or his identity. Instead, in Wilde's terms, the portrait is a "likeness" of Basil Hallward, a "portrait of the artist," precisely because it looks nothing like him.[49]

Of course, authorship (its traces and its reproducibility) is what *The Picture of Dorian Gray* productively puts into question. Just as Sarony claimed to have made a "new" and improved body through a form of photographic fiction, so too does Wilde's novel offer a similar narrative of body-building. Although the portrait of Dorian Gray has traditionally been understood as the gothic embodiment of his literally closeted sexuality, the novel clarifies that both the painting and Dorian are produced through a variety of artistic processes and by several authors.[50] Although Basil's portrait is not explicitly a photograph, it is described as a realistic representation, and critics have argued that Dorian Gray's pristine body is a "metaphor for photography" because he appears to be photographically frozen and preserved in time.[51] In the context of the photographic history and photographic discourse that I trace here, however, both the portrait and Dorian Gray's body represent two competing discourses and fantasies about photography in Victorian culture. In one sense, his body represents a fantasy about the innocence and inviolability of the photograph and photographic "truth." In this theory of the photograph, neither the past nor the future would be legible on his body, because, like the photograph, he represents the record and reproduction of a single moment in time and space. But in another sense, his body is photographic because it is at once impossible and "real," abstract, and material. As an embodiment of a photographic aesthetic, he is at once a pictorial fiction and an embodied reality, an abstract type and a "likeness" of an individual—or, to return to Carson's distinction, a "personality" and a "person."

Basil Hallward's painting, by comparison, articulates two Victorian theories of the photograph: first, it offers the fantasy that the photograph reveals not the body but the soul (a fantasy best represented by Nathaniel Hawthorne's *House of Seven Gables* [1851]); second, the painting literalizes the Victorian discourse around the photographic body as fragmented, grotesque, and unlike its "original." Even further, however, Dorian Gray's portrait resembles the products of art-photographers more than it does a normal painting. Like the photographic compositions of Rejlander and Robinson, his portrait is open to change and recomposition. More important, by seeming to change without the agency of an artist, the painting suggests the notion that the photograph is a product of the "sun." Henry Fox Talbot, one of the early inventors of photography, entitled his book of photographs *The Pencil of Nature*.[52] If Dorian Gray remarks incredu-

Daniel A. Novak

lously, "Surely a painted canvas could not alter" (*CW*, 12:130), then photographic art turns Wilde's wildly improbable gothic fiction into a technological reality. The technology of realism, then, has a great deal to teach us about Dorian Gray's impossible body and strange portrait.[53]

Literalizing Wilde's argument in "The Decay of Lying" that "Life imitates Art far more than Art imitates Life" and that "Life holds the mirror up to Art" (*CW*, 8:56), Dorian Gray becomes an exact or "photographic" reproduction of Basil's portrait.[54] Moreover, if the painting is read as an accurate reproduction of Dorian Gray's sexuality and subjectivity, it is also a representation produced by someone else. As he says to Basil before showing Basil the portrait, "[I]t is your own handiwork" (*CW*, 12:246).[55] But even as Basil discovers his own signature "in long letters of bright vermillion" (*CW*, 12:251) in the corner of the altered portrait, his mark of authorship merely marks the painting's reproducibility and the reproducibility of authorship. Having become the portrait, Dorian Gray turns Basil Hallward's painting into a reproducible work of art. In short, he turns painting into photography. Moreover, Dorian Gray inverts the problem of authorship explored in both the copyright and the libel trial. Whereas both of Wilde's trials attempted to halt a libelous circulation of a "pose," Dorian Gray's exchange of bodies with his portrait makes the reproduction a faithful "original" and the original portrait a pictorial slander.

Yet even if we interpret the portrait as a representation of an identity and a secret written by Basil, this secret is borrowed at a double remove. The painting is not simply Basil's representation of Dorian Gray; it also turns out to be a representation of Basil's secret.[56] As mentioned earlier, Carson used the end of the following quotation during the trial:

> I had drawn you as Paris in dainty armour, and as Adonis with huntsman's cloak and polished boar-spear. . . . One day, a fatal day I sometimes think, I determined to paint a wonderful portrait of you as you actually are, not in the costume of dead ages, but in your own dress and in your own time. Whether it was the Realism of the method, or the mere wonder of your personality, thus directly presented to me without mist or veil, I cannot tell. But I know that as I worked at it, every flake and film of colour seemed to me to reveal my secret. (*CW*, 12:184)

As a model, Dorian Gray has a family likeness to the larger family of models discussed earlier: Dickens's models, the models of art-photography, and Wilde's posers. Like these models, he has represented everything but himself.[57] Paradoxically, however, though Basil previously used Dorian Gray to embody allegorical subjects and "dead ages," "ideal, and remote," it is when Basil paints him as himself that he becomes even more "remote" from himself and thus more of an allegorical subject. Basil's photographic tendencies produce a portrait of the artist, not the model. The result of this realistic representation of Dorian Gray is an exposure of Basil's "secret." In the same way as the Victorians theorized photography and photographic art as a technology of abstraction, when Basil finally turns to "realism," his model becomes even more abstract. Moreover, the "realism of the method" does not represent Dorian's body or "person" but instead represents his abstract typicality—his "personality." In this convergence of realism and secrecy, photography and desire, the object of desire becomes a negative embodiment and a reproduction of the artist's sexuality.

Just as Sarony projected his "mental conception" onto Wilde to achieve the "desired expression," so too in the portrait does Basil Hallward "express" his desire in painting Dorian Gray. He gives "visible form" to his own desire while also helping both to make Dorian Gray aware of his own beauty and to make Dorian Gray an inexhaustible and universal object of desire. Earlier in the novel, Basil Hallward describes Dorian Gray in terms of abstraction: "But he is much more to me than a model or a sitter. . . . [H]is personality has suggested to me an entirely new manner of art, an entirely new mode of style. . . . I can now re-create life in a way that was hidden from me before. 'A dream of form in days of thought' . . . it is what Dorian Gray has been to me. The merely visible presence of this lad . . . his merely visible presence—ah! I wonder can you realize all that that means" (*CW*, 12:16–17). Dorian Gray's "visible presence" is valuable, then, precisely to the extent that he disappears into abstract form—to inspire a "new mode of style" and to become a "dream of form."[58] More than "a sitter," Dorian Gray is also less than a legible subject or an identifiable body. Dorian Gray's "visible presence" enables Basil, like Sarony, to give "visible form" to his own "mental conception." Like all of the other models I have discussed, Dorian Gray offers both an impossibly abstract or fictional body and an endlessly reproducible form. While Wilde's model in "London Models" absurdly offered to sit for "landscape," his protagonist makes that absurd fiction into artistic fact.

Basil Hallward, of course, is not the only author of Dorian Gray's subjectivity. Even the painter's portrait is indirectly produced by the influence of Lord Henry Wotton, Basil's friend and Dorian's tutor in the aesthetic life. In his first conver-

Daniel A. Novak

sation with Dorian Gray, Lord Henry entrances and persuades Dorian Gray precisely by claiming to reject "influence" or persuasion of any kind: "[A]ll influence is immoral . . . [b]ecause to influence a person is to give him one's own soul. . . . His sins, if there are such things as sins, are borrowed. He becomes an echo of some one else's music, an actor of a part that has not been written for him" (*CW*, 12:27). Of course, despite Lord Henry's call for "self-development" (*CW*, 12:27), Dorian Gray's reaction to his speech both psychologically and visually performs what Lord Henry describes as an unimaginative "borrowing" or imitation of subjectivity—a kind of mechanical reproduction of identity: "For nearly ten minutes he stood there, motionless, with parted lips, and eyes strangely bright. He was dimly conscious that entirely fresh influences were at work within him. Yet they seemed to him to have come really from himself. . . . [Lord Henry] was amazed at the sudden impression that his words had produced, and remembering a book that he had read when he was sixteen, a book which had revealed to him much that he had not known before, he wondered whether Dorian Gray was passing through a similar experience" (*CW*, 12:29–30). Like a photographic negative, Dorian Gray takes a "sudden impression" from Lord Henry's words and registers a particular expression. As Basil puts it, "I don't know what Harry has been saying to you, but he has certainly made you have the most wonderful expression" (*CW*, 12:31). And like the "desired expression" that Sarony projected into Wilde, Lord Henry makes a great first impression by awakening a new expression of desire in Dorian Gray. Catching and reproducing what Lord Henry had produced, Basil Hallward's portrait might be thought of as a reproduction at two removes—or perhaps three. Even Lord Henry's influence is borrowed from an entirely reproducible form and experience: "[A] book which had revealed to him much that he had not known before." The "poisonous" "yellow book" that Lord Henry gives to Dorian Gray later in the novel merely reinforces this pattern of literary reproducibility; in other words, the portrait is already a product of a literary and visual form of reproduction and reproducibility.

For Lord Henry, Dorian Gray offers an abstract form of raw material that can be made to embody any identity. Meditating on the pleasures and erotics of influence, Lord Henry argues, "To project one's soul into some gracious form. . . . He was a marvellous type, too, this lad . . . or could be fashioned into a marvellous type, at any rate. . . . There was nothing that one could not do with him" (*CW*, 12:57). Like Sarony's projecting his "mental conception" onto Wilde's "surrendered" body, or like Wilde's artists turning their models into art, Lord Henry's form of artistic re-creation depends on Dorian Gray remaining a perpetually open and abstract "form." As Lord Henry boasts later, "To a large extent the lad was his own creation" (*CW,* 12:91). Moreover, Lord Henry's "creation" remains abstract: "a marvellous *type*" (emphasis added).

As Lord Henry's product and as an impressible student, Dorian Gray appreciates the value and erotics of this artistic open-endedness. The most extensively narrated form of desire in the novel—his love for the actress Sibyl Vane—is described as a desire for an embodied negativity and flexibility: "I have seen her in every age and in every costume. Ordinary women never appeal to one's imagination. . . . How different an actress is! . . . She is more than an individual" (*CW,* 12:84, 87). Like Wilde's models, Sibyl Vane is only interesting when not herself. This point becomes clear in Dorian Gray's reply to Lord Henry's question, "When is she Sibyl Vane?" Dorian's answer is "Never" (*CW,* 12:86). In other words, his desire for Sibyl Vane is a model-desire—a desire for the negative capability of the model.[59] But when Sibyl Vane rejects the falseness of theatrical illusion for the "reality" of love ("You taught me what love really is" [*CW,* 12:137]), she violates both the aesthetic logic and the erotic logic of the novel, and the results are fatal. As soon as she attempts to embody her "proper" identity (an identity outside of her theatrical roles), she both ceases to be an object of desire and ceases to exist. "You are nothing to me now. . . . Without your art you are nothing. . . . What are you now? A third-rate actress with a pretty face" (*CW,* 12:138–39). Paradoxically, as soon as she appears as an individual, she becomes "nothing" and disappears as an eroticized body. Desire is defined only in terms of a desire for a body that is not a body—a body that can be anything and nothing and one that can be endlessly reproduced.

What, then, is sexuality in the age of technological reproducibility? If we assume that sexuality can be captured by the camera but that one's pose is produced and defined (and in one case legally owned) by someone else, then whose sexuality is it: the artist's or the model's? Or are sexuality, desire, and identity already constituted by a "photographic" logic of the kind that I articulate throughout this chapter? As I have tried to show, analyzing Wilde through the history and discourse of Victorian photography offers to redefine notions of identity, legibility, and sexuality. Whether we are researching photographs of Wilde, reading his essays on the artist's model, or attempting to make sense of Dorian Gray, we encounter the same spectral, anonymous, and abstract body. Perhaps the subtitle for the present volume provides a more concise explanation of how to

Daniel A. Novak

read these texts and images. Wilde's typicality and that of his characters is always in the process of being made and remade, deployed and redeployed through a photographic aesthetic of abstraction, composition, and recomposition. More simply, even when captured in the seemingly frozen time of photographic image, even when caught in the act by the photographic flash, sexuality in the age of technological reproducibility is always, by definition, in "the making."[60]

Notes

1. Walter Benjamin, "The Work of Art in the Age of Its Technological Reproducibility," *Selected Writings*, vol. 4, ed. Howard Eiland and Michael W. Jennings, trans. Edmund Jephcott and others (Cambridge: Belknap Press of Harvard University Press, 2003), 256.

2. On the Sarony trial and its relationship to Wilde and *The Picture of Dorian Gray*, see Jane Gaines, *Contested Culture: The Image, the Voice, and the Law* (Chapel Hill: University of North Carolina Press, 1991).

3. H. Montgomery Hyde, *Trials of Oscar Wilde*, 2nd ed. (New York: Dover, 1962), 112. I use this exchange from Hyde's version of the trials rather than Merlin Holland's more recent (and more accurate) transcript because it emphasizes the disagreement over the word *personality* that was an earlier part of this exchange. See Merlin Holland, *The Real Trial of Oscar Wilde* (New York: Harper-Collins, 2003), 85. See chapter 9 of the present volume for a critique of Hyde's version of the trials.

4. Michel Foucault, *The History of Sexuality*, vol. 1, *An Introduction*, trans. Robert Hurley (New York: Vintage, 1990), 42–43.

5. For a different account of Wilde's trials, his defense of male love, and the history of sexuality, see Linda Dowling, *Hellenism and Homosexuality in Victorian Oxford* (Ithaca, NY: Cornell University Press, 1994). Dowling argues both that Wilde had "deploy[ed] a new and powerful vocabulary of personal identity" and that this language and identity had been gradually developing through the nineteenth-century "triumph of Victorian Hellenism" (2–3). For a sophisticated critique of Foucault, the politics of resistance, and feminism, see Joan Cocks, *The Oppositional Imagination* (New York: Routledge, 1989).

6. Ed Cohen, *Talk on the Wilde Side: Towards a Genealogy of a Discourse on Male Sexualities* (New York: Routledge, 1993), 131. Cohen argues that the trials and the representation of the trials in newspapers "(re)produced the possibility for designating Wilde as a kind of sexual actor without explicitly referring to the specificity of his sexual acts, and thereby crystallized a new constellation of sexual meanings predicated upon 'personality' and not practices" (131). In Cohen's view, the trial "shifts the concern from the act to the actor" (146). Significantly, Cohen does not address this particular exchange from the trial, though he notes the various ways in which it was reported in the papers (162–64). See also Alan Sinfield, *The Wilde Century: Effeminacy, Oscar Wilde, and the Queer Moment* (London: Cassell, 1994).

7. Jeffrey Nunokawa, "The Disappearance of the Homosexual in *The Picture of Dorian Gray*," in *Professions of Desire: Lesbian and Gay Studies in Literature*, ed. George Haggerty and Bonnie Zimmerman (New York: Modern Language Association, 1995), 189. Nunokawa argues that homosexual desire in *Dorian Gray* is specifically constituted by the "disembodiment" of the desiring subject into a despecified Hellenic ideal, into the erotics of pedagogy, and into the vague agency of third-person narrative (186–88).

8. A. H. Wall, "'Composition' Photography: Searching for a Subject," *British Journal of Photography* 11 (1864): 8.

9. John Hollingshead, "A Counterfeit Presentment," *Household Words* 18 (3 July 1858): 72; the later quotation also appears on the same page.

10. Francis Galton, "Composite Portraits," *Journal of the Anthropological Institute of Great Britain and Ireland* 8 (1878–79): 133.

11. See Lewes, *Problems of Life and Mind:* "[F]iction [is] a necessary procedure of Research"; quoted in George Levine, "George Eliot's Hypothesis of Reality," *Nineteenth Century Fiction* 35 (1980): 5.

12. [Anon.,] "Typical Girl-Portrait by Galton's Method," *Photographic News,* 7 August 1885, 512.

13. Edgar C. Beall, M.D., *The Life Sexual: A Study of the Philosophy, Physiology, Science, Art and Hygiene of Love* (New York: Vim, 1905). For more on Beall, see Lisa K. Hamilton, "Oscar Wilde, New Women, and the Rhetoric of Effeminacy," in *Wilde Writings: Contextual Conditions,* ed. Joseph Bristow (Toronto: University of Toronto Press, 2003), 239–41.

14. The image is by Arnold Roth and the caption by Andy Borowitz; see *New Yorker,* 27 September 2004, 160.

15. Richard Ellmann, *Oscar Wilde* (Harmondsworth, UK: Penguin, 1988), 46.

16. Walter Pater, *The Renaissance: Studies in Art and Poetry, the 1893 Text,* ed. Donald L. Hill (Berkeley: University of California Press, 1980), 188–89; further page references appear in parentheses.

17. Charles Dickens, "The Ghost of Art," *Household Words* 17 (1850): 386. For further discussion of Dickens and the artist's model, see Daniel Novak, "'If Re-collecting Were Forgetting': Forged Bodies and Forgotten Labor in *Little Dorrit,*" *Novel: A Forum on Fiction* 31 (1997): 21–44.

18. In this sense, we can take Wilde's comment that the artist's model is "a sign of the decadence, the symbol of decay" literally ("The Relation of Dress to Art," *CW,* 14:70). The artist's model and his or her body are at the center of the aesthetic theory of fin-de-siècle decadence. On Wilde's version of the dandy, see Moe Meyer, "Under the Sign of Wilde," in *The Politics and Poetics of Camp,* ed. Moe Meyer (New York: Routledge, 1994), 75–107; and Ed Cohen, "Writing Gone Wilde: Homoerotic Desire in the Closet of Representation," *PMLA* 102, no. 5 (1987): 801–13. Both Meyer and Cohen argue that Wilde's dandyism represented a space of writing in which to "embody homoerotic desire." Meyer suggests that while "[a]estheticism was a theory . . . dandyism, on the other hand, offered a praxis" ("Under the Sign," 77–78).

19. Ellen Moers, *The Dandy: Brummell to Beerbohm* (New York: Viking, 1960), 296. Interestingly, Moers's description of fin-de-siècle dandyism echoes Nordau's figure of pastiche: "In the final analysis, their dandyism was a handful of mannerisms retrieved from the past" (314).

20. For more on Nordau and (in particular) Lee's response to *Degeneration,* see Richard Dellamora, "Productive Decadence, 'The Queer Comradeship of Outlawed Thought': Vernon Lee, Max Nordau, and Oscar Wilde," *New Literary History* 35 (2004): 529–46.

21. Max Nordau, *Degeneration* (Lincoln: University of Nebraska Press, 1968), 9.

22. Wilde's *Salomé,* of course, offers the most spectacular link between aestheticism and decapitation. Oscar Rejlander produced the raw material for his own image of Salomé, taking the *Head of John the Baptist* and *Salomé* separately. That is, Rejlander's photograph literalizes Nordau's critique, patching his bodies together in a "mythical mortuary"—in the fictional space of the photographic studio.

23. See Meyer, "Under the Sign." Meyer puts Wilde in the context of Delsarte's philosophy of gestures and bodily semiotics: "Situating desire in art, and art on the surfaces of the posed body

was a peculiarly Delsartean maneuver" (87). Meyer also maps a sexualized active/passive structure onto the artist/model relationship.

24. In "The Relation of Dress to Art," Wilde conjures a scene similar to the one Dickens offers in *Pictures from Italy.* See also Wilde's story "The Model Millionaire" (1887), in which he inverts Henry James's story "The Real Thing" (1893) by making an upper-class model perfectly and convincingly represent a beggar (*CW,* 7:135–44).

25. As Wilde writes, "the poor are completely unconscious of their picturesqueness" (*CW,* 14:126).

26. Wilde, "The Relation of Dress to Art: A Note in Black and White on Mr. Whistler's Lecture" (1885) (*CW,* 14:69–70). See also Wilde's "London Models," in which the painted body is a product of two separate models: "We must, however, distinguish between two kinds of models, those who sit for the figure and those who sit for the costume. . . . [T]he costume model is becoming rather wearisome in modern pictures. It is really very little use to dress up a London girl in Greek draperies and to paint her as a goddess. The robe may be the robe of Athens, but the face is usually the face of Brompton. . . . [W]e are shown every year a series of scenes from fancy dress balls which are called historical pictures" (*CW,* 14:129).

27. See Fredric Jameson, *Postmodernism, or, The Cultural Logic of Late Capitalism* (Durham, NC: Duke University Press, 1991). Jameson argues that pastiche is distinct from parody because in the postmodern era there is no coherent norm to target: "Pastiche is, like parody, the imitation of a peculiar or unique, idiosyncratic style. . . . But it is a neutral practice of such mimicry, without any of parody's ulterior motives, amputated of the satiric impulse, devoid of laughter and of any conviction that alongside the abnormal tongue you have momentarily borrowed, some healthy linguistic normality exists" (17). While Jameson reads the "disappearance of the individual subject" (16) as a symptom of postmodernism, I argue that this disappearance was the condition for Victorian literary, photographic, and economic fiction.

28. Roland Barthes, *S/Z,* trans. Richard Miller (New York: Hill and Wang, 1974), 55.

29. As Wilde writes in "The Relation of Dress to Art," "Popular is he, this poor peripatetic professor of posing, with those whose joy it is to paint the posthumous portrait of the last philanthropist who, in his lifetime, had neglected to be photographed" (*CW,* 14:70).

30. Even after the introduction of the Kodak camera in 1885, the professional studio was still the most important site for a photographic experience. By 1900, the roll film camera had become firmly established. It used a flexible film composed of a celluloid base and a gelatin emulsion. In February 1900, a camera maker employed by Kodak, Frank Brownell, invented the "Brownie" camera, which was essentially a cardboard box with a wood backing, costing only one dollar (or five shillings in England). This development brought photography into the hands of all but a few, and one hundred thousand of the "Brownies" were sold in their first year. Colin Ford, ed., *The Story of Popular Photography* (London: Century Hutchinson, 1989), 65. This meant that the photographer no longer needed to be an amateur chemist but could instead have the factory develop his or her film. The year 1900 saw the spread of such factories to Europe, and having one's film developed became increasingly easy. Josef Maria Eder, *History of Photography,* trans. Edward Epstean (New York: Columbia University Press, 1945), 442. Perhaps a more relevant shift in photographic technology, however, was marked by the move toward the larger format of the "cabinet card" and the introduction of "dry plates"—glass negatives that were sold presensitized with a gelatin emulsion (rather than the more troublesome collodion coating that had to be applied each time), which enabled professional photographers to dispense with the need to develop a plate as soon as it had been exposed. Although both photographers and consumers wanted the

larger format because it would allow for more detail and artistic effect, the popularity of the cabinet card was partly due to the fact that the larger negative greatly facilitated retouching. Photographic technology, then, continued to enable photographic fiction.

31. Sarony's photographs appear in Wilde's short story "The Canterville Ghost" (1887) as short-hand for American vulgarity and commodity culture: the ghost (Sir Simon) "was amusing himself by making satirical remarks on the large Saroni [sic] photographs of the United States Minister and his wife, which had now taken the place of the Canterville family pictures" (CW, 7:94).

32. Quoted in Gilson Willets, "Photography's Most Famous Chair," in The American Annual of Photography and Photographic Times Almanac for 1899, ed. Walter E. Woodbury (New York: Scovill and Adams, 1899), 60–61.

33. Lloyd Lewis and Henry Justin Smith, Oscar Wilde Discovers America (1882) (New York: Harcourt Brace and Company, 1936), 39. Whether other commercially sold photographs of Wilde existed before Sarony's is unclear. However, prior to his session with Sarony, at least one photograph was used to advertise Wilde's lecture tour. On 1 September 1881, a few months before his departure, an American newspaper (The Hour: Cartoon Supplement) printed a lithograph obviously taken from a photograph of Wilde by Elliot and Fry (plate 4—face front), showing a three-quarter portrait of Wilde in the fur coat that he bought for the American trip. The caption underneath reads "The Apostle of the Aesthetes." A photograph taken in this same sitting (plate 4) has been erroneously dated in some books as 1882, and in Oscar Wilde's London it is listed as a portrait of Wilde at the time of his first theatrical success—ten years later, in 1892: Wolf von Eckardt, Sander L. Gilman, and J. Edward Chamberlin, Oscar Wilde's London: A Scrapbook of Vices and Virtues, 1880–1900 (New York: Anchor, 1987), 77. The William Andrews Clark Memorial Library dates this photograph to March 1881. The Clark Library also holds the lithograph mentioned above. This photograph was probably sold to some extent and could have been printed with or without Wilde's knowledge or approval, since the photographers held the copyright. Because Americans were notorious for disregarding copyrights, the photographer was probably unaware of this lithograph.

34. William Allen, "Legal Tests of Photography-as-Art: Sarony and Others," History of Photography 10 (1986): 223.

35. Lewis and Smith, Oscar Wilde Discovers America, 39.

36. Ben L. Bassham, The Theatrical Photographs of Napoleon Sarony (Kent, OH: Kent State University Press, 1978), 14.

37. Sarony offers an anecdote about the American actress Adah Isaacs Mencken that stages the superiority of his direction over his subject's poses: "'Mr. Sarony,' she said, 'all attempts to photograph me as Mazeppa have been failures. Now I want you to take me in eight different poses, on condition that you allow me to pose myself.' I agreed to this on condition that she would allow me afterward to pose her in eight different attitudes. She said that was only fair, so we went to work. When the photographs were ready, I hunted her up in her dressing room at the theatre. I gave her those of her own posing first. Her exclamation was: 'They are perfectly horrible; I shall never have another photograph taken of myself as Mazeppa as long as I live.' Then I presented the photographs of my own posing. She threw her arms around me and exclaimed: 'Oh, you dear, delightful, little man, I am going to kiss you for that,' and she did." Bassham, The-atrical Photographs of Napoleon Sarony, 11. Apparently, even a professional actress could have a successful photographic experience only by not acting at all.

38. Quoted in Gilson Willets, "The Art of Not Posing—An Interview with Napoleon Sarony," The American Annual of Photography and Photographic Times (1896): 188–94.

39. Quoted in Willets, "Art of Not Posing," 189, 191.

Daniel A. Novak

40. Quoted in William Allen, "Legal Test of Photography-as-Art," 221–22. See also Rejlander on photographic authorship: "If a blind man dictates a story to another, who 'writes' it—who is the author? A silly question, you may think; yet I can get a parallel out of it for giving authorship and originality to a photographer. If my maid of all work, after I have posed myself before the looking-glass, takes off the cap of the lens when I cough, and replaces it at my grunt, has she taken the picture?" Oscar Rejlander, "Desultory Reflections on Photography and Art," *The Year Book of Photography and Photographic News Almanac* (1866), 45.

41. Cohen argues that the newspapers reported the accusation without the word *sodomite*, essentially making posing a crime (*Talk on the Wilde Side,* 146). See Alan Sinfield's similar reading: "'Oscar Wilde posing' stood for the whole idea" (*Wilde Century,* 3).

42. Wall continues, "In Rejlander's study a story is told." A. H. Wall, "Rejlander's Photographic Studies: Their Teachings and Suggestions," published in *Photographic Times and American Photographer* 16 (1886): 556. The quotation about making photographs into pictures is taken from a subsequent essay in this series, "Rejlander's Photographic Studies," *Photographic Times and American Photographer* 17 (1887): 73 (emphasis added). Wall repeats this distinction between *portrait* and *picture* often in his book *Artistic Landscape Photography* (Bradford, UK: Percy Lund; Country Press, 1896). Distinguishing artistic photography from mere "portraits" of objects, Wall writes, "I say pictures advisedly, because that is just the difference between the photographs of the present day and the photographs of the past. The superiority of the later efforts of photographers depended much more on the fact that, whereas in former time the photographer's aim was to produce a representation or a portrait of a particular scene, that of the modern photographer is to produce a picture. . . . It cannot be too frequently or emphatically stated that in all its best qualities, and however it is produced, a real picture is the outcome, not of a mechanical process but of intellectual study" (*Artistic Landscape Photography,* 27).

43. Charles Baudelaire, *Salon de 1846,* ed. David Kelley (Oxford, UK: Clarendon Press, 1975), 157. An English translation renders *roman* as "fiction"; Baudelaire, *Art in Paris: 1845–1862 Salons and Other Exhibitions Reviewed by Charles Baudelaire,* trans. and ed. Jonathan Mayne (London: Phaidon, 1985), 88–89.

44. Wilde, however, argues that, on the whole, the book "will not do" (*CW,* 8:115).

45. Wilde also draws a conventional association between photography and execution, but he seems to do so unconsciously. While describing the amorphous nature of objects in prison after his release, in a letter to Robert Ross dated 8 October 1897, he figures the house of execution as a photographic studio: "The difficulty is that the objects in prison have no shape or form. To take an example: The shed in which people are hanged is a little shed with a glass roof, like a photographer's studio on the sands at Margate. For eighteen months I thought it *was* the studio for photographing prisoners. There is no adjective to describe it. I call it hideous" (Wilde, *Complete Letters,* 956). In a morbid sense, Wilde's figuration extends Sarony's demand that his sitters "surrender" their consciousness to its extreme. I would suggest, however, that the photographer's studio is precisely the place where "the objects . . . have no shape or form."

46. Wilde to H. C. Pollitt, 19 January 1899, *Complete Letters,* 1103. In a previous letter to Pollitt, dated 31 December 1898, Wilde describes his photograph as Pollitt's representative in proxy: "I have come down to the Riviera, with your photograph, of course (the nice one in the Norfolk suit). . . . Of course, *you* should be here also" (*Complete Letters,* 1115). For more on letters in which Wilde mentions photography, see Sandra F. Siegel, "Wilde on Photographs: Four Unpublished Letters," *Wildean* 17 (2000): 12–47.

47. For the most part, Wilde defines photographs in these terms. However, in a review of George Sand's letters, he praises her by saying that "her heroes are not dead photographs; they

are great possibilities" ("The Letters of a Great Woman," *Pall Mall Gazette,* 6 March 1886, in *CW,* 13:49). See also his discussion of Fisher Unwin's *Warring Angels:* "[O]rdinary fiction, rejecting the beauty of form in order to realise the facts of life, seems often to miss that pleasure-giving power in virtue of which the arts exist. It would not, however, be fair to regard *Warring Angels* simply as a specimen of literary photography" ("Literary and Other Notes," *Woman's World,* February 1888, in *CW,* 13:283).

48. See also Wilde's reply to a hostile review of *The Picture of Dorian Gray* in the *Scots Observer:* "It will be to each man what he is himself. It is the spectator, and not life, that art really mirrors" ("To the Editor of the *Scots Observer,*" 23 July 1890, *Complete Letters,* 441). Wilde also wrote, "Each man sees his own sin in Dorian Gray. What Dorian Gray's sins are no one knows. He who finds them has brought them" ("To the Editor of the *Scots Observer,*" 9 July 1890, *Complete Letters,* 439).

49. Wilde, of course, rested his defense of *The Picture of Dorian Gray* precisely on the distance between author and text. As he wrote to the editor of the *Scots Observer,* "Your critic, then, sir, commits the absolutely unpardonable crime of trying to confuse the artist with his subject-matter. . . . One stands remote from one's subject-matter. One creates it, and one contemplates it. The further away the subject-matter is, the more freely can the artist work" (9 July 1890, *Complete Letters,* 439).

50. As Neil Bartlett points out, "Dorian Gray announces the significance of his portrait by hiding it. . . . In the course of his evil career he is proved guilty of adultery, debauchery. . . . Only one of his vices is hidden, only one sin cannot be named. Every word that Oscar Wilde wrote is about *it.*" Bartlett, *Who Was That Man? A Present for Mr. Oscar Wilde* (London: Serpent's Tail, 1988), 93–94. Contemporary response to the novel as "filthy" is perhaps the best example of the immediate association between the portrait and Dorian Gray's sexuality. After going to see the editor of the *St. James's Gazette,* Wilde spoke to the man who reviewed his novel. In response to Wilde's assertion that he meant "every word" of the novel, the reviewer (Samuel Jeyes) responds, "[A]ll I can say is that if you do mean them you are very likely to find yourself at Bow Street one of these days" (quoted in Ellmann, *Oscar Wilde,* 303). For a more complex reading of Dorian Gray's identification with the portrait and sexuality, see Eve Kosofsky Sedgwick, *Epistemology of the Closet* (Berkeley: University of California Press, 1990), 131–76.

51. See Wilde, *Picture of Dorian Gray* (*CW,* 12:31). See also Gaines, *Contested Culture,* 43.

52. Henry Fox Talbot, *The Pencil of Nature* (New York: Da Capo Press, 1969).

53. While I may seem to ignore the material distinction between painting and photography, I am more interested in the language used to describe the portrait of Dorian, which, I argue, is aligned with Victorian photographic discourse. Wilde, of course, argued for a conflation of the arts even as he privileged literature: "For there are not many arts, but one art merely: poem, picture, and Parthenon, sonnet and statue—are all in their essence the same, and he who knows one, knows all. But the poet is the supreme artist, for he is the master of colour and of form, and the real musician besides, and is lord over all life, and all arts" ("Mr. Whistler's Ten O'Clock" [1885], *CW,* 14:66).

54. Wilde, "Decay of Lying," 311.

55. For a different reading of Basil Hallward's production of Dorian Gray, see Robert Keefe, "Artist and Model in *The Picture of Dorian Gray,*" *Studies in the Novel* 5 (1973): 63–70. Keefe argues that "Dorian is not really a simple, affectionate boy at the beginning of his relationship with Basil" and links him to Narcissus (63–64).

56. See Cohen, "Writing Gone Wilde." Cohen points out that "Dorian . . . is a space for the constitution of male desire. . . . [He] provides the surface on which the characters project their

Daniel A. Novak

self-representations. His is the body on which Basil's . . . desires are inscribed" (806). See also Meyer's "Under the Sign" for the argument that "the artist's inscription . . . displaces and eliminates the model's 'true' identity by neutralizing Dorian's body surfaces in order to render him as the object of desire" (86). And see Robert Keefe's "Artist and Model" for the suggestion that "the fatal painting . . . is at least as much a study of Basil as it is a portrait of the model" (66).

57. See Nunokawa, "Disappearance of the Homosexual." Whereas Nunokawa points to the "processio[n] of homoerotic idols" (183) that parade through this passage and the text, I am placing Dorian's pictorial poses in the context of Wilde's theories of the negative body of the model—a theory that presupposes an evacuation of gender. That is, paradoxically, to be a "homoerotic idol," Dorian has to be capable of being anything and nothing.

58. Sedgwick places this passage of the distinction that both Wilde and Friedrich Wilhelm Nietzsche drew between Greek and Christian culture—a distinction between permission and prohibition of homosexual desire (*Epistemology of the Closet*, 136–40).

59. See Nunokawa, "Disappearance of the Homosexual." Nunokawa points out that while homosexual desire in the novel diffuses its subjects into "disembodied" figures, heterosexual desire "works to render its subject distinct. Love for Dorian Gray leads Sybil Vane to separate herself from the characters she plays onstage" (187). Of course, on the day that Dorian decides to propose to Sibyl, she plays Rosalind, and Dorian ecstatically describes her "in her boy's clothes": "She had never seemed to me more exquisite" (103). Sibyl's ability to be either, or, and both male and female—her ability to be anything and nothing—is what creates and sustains her erotic appeal.

60. In this way, Wilde becomes the site of what David M. Halperin describes as Foucault's notion of "queer politics": "Foucault's approach also opens up . . . the possibility of a *queer politics* defined not by the struggle to liberate a common, repressed, preexisting nature but by an ongoing process of self-constitution and self-transformation." Halperin, *Saint Foucault: Towards a Gay Hagiography* (New York: Oxford University Press, 1995), 122.

Salomé as Bombshell, or How Oscar Wilde Became an Anarchist

ERIN WILLIAMS HYMAN

O N 6 APRIL 1895, the painter Henri de Toulouse-Lautrec received a letter from the famed Montmartre dance-hall performer La Goulue asking him to paint two large canvases that would adorn the exterior of her funfair booth at the Foire du Trône. In deference to his old friend, who had been a subject of his previous work, he worked furiously to complete the commission within the week, in time to promote La Goulue's new act with an eye-catching advertisement. Whereas many of Lautrec's scenes endow forms of urban social life with a sense of the carnivalesque, here the carnival is imbued with overt political import, for the foreground of the right-hand panel is dominated by the portraits of two controversial figures: Oscar Wilde and Félix Fénéon, imagined as spectators of La Goulue's belly dance, alongside the figure of Lautrec (fig. 17). The Parisian funfairs "had a tradition of offering spectacles based on current political events," which Lautrec clearly drew on by connecting the two men as both aesthetes and outlaws, here spectators but each quite recently objects of public spectacle.[1]

On the one hand, Wilde had just lost his libel case against the Marquess of Queensberry, and on the same day that Lautrec had received his commission, Wilde had been arrested and charged with "committing indecent acts." On the other hand, Fénéon—esteemed art critic, quintessential aesthete and dandy,

Figure 17. Henri de Toulouse-Lautrec, *La danse mauresque ou les almées* (The Moorish Dance) (1895). Courtesy of Musée d'Orsay, Paris, France.

champion of the neo-impressionists, and editor of symbolist works and of the prominent literary journal *La revue blanche*—had earlier that year been acquitted as an anarchist conspirator in the "Trial of the Thirty." The trial, in which Fénéon had been tried along with Jean Grave, Sébastien Faure, and other anarchist theorists or writers, alongside eleven petty thieves, had turned Fénéon into a media celebrity. With rigid aplomb, his wit and ironic remarks outdid both prosecutor and judge, turning, in his biographer's words, "what was essentially a sinister drama into a sophisticated comedy."[2] For instance, the judge asserted, "It has been established that you surrounded yourself with [the anarchists] Cohen and Ortiz," to which Fénéon replied, "One can hardly be surrounded by two persons: you need at least three." Judge: "You were seen speaking with them behind a lamp-post!" Fénéon: "Can you tell me, Your Honor, where behind a lamp-post is?" (289–90). In each instance, the humor of Fénéon's replies lay in the way in which he showed the ambiguity and the unstable meanings of the judge's words, subverting the value of language as a transparent medium capable of seizing upon some "truth" about his "essence" as an anarchist. Thus, in numerous ways, Fénéon's verbal style—his wit and wordplay—paralleled Wilde's rhetorical gestures on the witness stand, although his ultimate acquittal shows that he was more able to elude legal definition as an anarchist than Wilde was as a homosexual.

Lautrec's portrait thus uses the two renowned figures to draw attention to La Goulue's publicity billboard yet at the same time makes an ironic comment on spectator and spectacle. He establishes a visual connection between Wilde and Fénéon, rendered in opposing profiles, but in doing so alludes to a much more profound connection between the two: both arguably their culture's most ardent advocates of "liberty in art," both seen as threats to the social order, both representing the ultimate in individualism for a fin-de-siècle public simultaneously ready to glorify and pillory them for it. Fénéon sensed clearly the connection that Lautrec was making; he later wrote, "I never actually posed [for the portrait], but I . . . was the prominent figure in the little soft felt hat next to Oscar Wilde, in the group of idlers around La Goulue's platform. It does seem that we two had something in common, though the comparison was not a flattering one for either of us."[3] That Fénéon should find the comparison unflattering may seem peculiar, since he was in no way averse to his association with Wilde. As editor of the La revue blanche, he published numerous articles defending the author and befriended Wilde during Wilde's later years in Paris. His aversion seems peculiar, that is, until one considers that what he may be pointing to is the way in which the portrait conflates anarchism and homosexuality. For Fénéon was indeed an avowed anarchist, embodying the aesthetic and political aspirations of the majority of French symbolists, and Wilde had long been taken by this avant-garde as another of their own, yet through their association in the painting (and the ironic humor of depicting a homosexual viewer of an orientalized striptease) there is a slippage between aestheticism, anarchism, and sexual subversion.

This slippage is not incidental. In the French context and even before his trials, Wilde was hailed as an aesthete-anarchist in circles where symbolism and decadence in the arts were synonymous with anarchist affinities; indeed, the production of Salomé in Paris in February 1896 could be seen as anarchist. If critic Joseph Donohue sees the composition of Salomé as "unconsciously prescient" of

Wilde's downfall—that is, that Salomé openly manifests an unlawful and perverse passion for which she must be destroyed by the power of the state—then the production of Salomé in Paris at the time of Wilde's imprisonment seemed to confirm this parallel, overtly allegorizing his predicament.[4] The production was more than simply an act of solidarity for a fellow artist; it was a representation of the open expression of sexual desire as an anarchic force capable of destabilizing a regime of power. Within the French context, the play and the polemic around it made the defense of homosexuality part of the anarchist struggle, placing erotic liberty squarely under the banner of libertarian politics.

Wilde's "Anarchist" Credentials

That Wilde should be considered an anarchist is perhaps nothing new. Twentieth-century critics have debated whether from a political viewpoint Wilde should be considered socialist, individualist, or anarchist primarily based on readings of his essay "The Soul of Man under Socialism" (1891). George Woodcock is the most prominent example of a critic whose reading of this piece and of "The Critic as Artist" (1890, revised 1891) insists that it comprises "individualist philosophic anarchism of the purest kind."[5] Other scholars, such as Sos Eltis, have followed Woodcock, citing other (somewhat scanty) evidence of Wilde's commitment to the anarchist cause, such as the fact that he signed George Bernard Shaw's petition in support of reprieve for the Chicago anarchists in 1886 (even though nothing else was heard from Wilde on the matter) and that he bailed anarchist John Barlas out of jail in 1891 after the poet had discharged a revolver outside of the House of Commons (even though Wilde's letter to Barlas indicates that this was a gesture of friendship for a fellow writer rather than a politically motivated action).[6] In an article entitled "Socialist or Socialite?" critic David Rose takes Woodcock and company to task for inferring too much from these incidents, as well as for attributing to "The Soul of Man" a broad political impact that it did not have. Rose remarks, "One is beginning to form a picture of Wilde assenting to left-wing positions only insofar as he could represent himself as spectator rather than participant."[7] Furthermore, in a detailed analysis of the journalistic context of the publication of "The Soul of Man," Josephine M. Guy suggests that "Wilde's essay is not serious," for "its paradoxes and reversals cannot bear the weight of detailed analysis."[8] She argues that the essay should be seen not as a fully fleshed-out political philosophy but as a topical contribution to an ongoing debate around fin-de-siècle individualism: "The political reference of Wilde's essay, and the humor derived from it, is thus much more topical than critics have realized, and it is precisely this topicality which may explain Wilde's relative lack of interest in the essay after 1891, and why also modern critics have struggled with its paradoxes" (79).

However, within the French context in the 1890s, "The Soul of Man" was neither published nor known among Wilde's admirers; in addition, as Rose points out, drawing conclusions from such scanty evidence as the Shaw petition or the Barlas episode is not well justified. Nevertheless, symbolism as a literary and artistic movement was already closely associated with anarchism in France, and Wilde's positions on art and the individual were easily assimilated into a movement in which aesthetic experimentalism and political radicalism mutually reinforced each other.

Symbolism as a literary movement is most often associated with the rejection of naturalism and with a turn toward subjective and esoteric concerns. Language, whether poetic or pictorial, should not name but evoke; mood, mystery, and altered states of consciousness are celebrated; art should depict not banal reality but the ideal. At the same time, however, symbolism was not purely hermetic and inward-turned; rather, its proponents quickly aligned their artistic endeavors with political aims. For instance, symbolist critic Remy de Gourmont could not have been more explicit in making a link between the two: "Symbolism can be translated literally by the word Freedom, and for the violent ones, by the word Anarchy."[9] Similarly, writer Stuart Merrill called symbolism "a libertarian movement in literature."[10]

The symbolists were not merely an extension of the Romantics, calling for political and cultural revolution; this was a generation that came of age after the disastrous French defeat to Germany in 1870 and the crushing of the Paris Commune, and they were nothing if not disillusioned by the call to mass politics. In anarchism, they claimed adherence to a model of individual insurrection that seemed all too analogous to their subjectivist view of art. The proliferation of bombings in Paris in the early 1890s, claimed by or attributed to anarchists, was widely supported by the literary and artistic avant-garde, who saw the anarchist bomb-thrower as the ultimate manifestation of the individual in revolt against a corrupt social order. Historian Jean Maitron states that "the chronological correspondence of symbolism and anarchism was cause for mutual sympathies. One was symbolist in literature and anarchist in politics."[11] But the fascination

Erin Williams Hyman

of the symbolists for anarchist acts of terror went beyond a simple recognition of an analogy between "art for art's sake" and "revolt for revolt's sake," or of a celebration of radical freedom and hyperindividualism. Figures such as Jean Grave, the foremost voice of anarchism in France at the end of the century, elaborated an analysis of the institutions of power and state coercion that radically critiqued the military, patriotism, marriage, bourgeois morality, and private property. Grave had close relations with Félix Fénéon, Remy de Gourmont, and Octave Mirbeau, and the journal Grave edited, *La révolte,* was widely read in symbolist circles (Stéphane Mallarmé, among others, was a subscriber). Anarchism was antimilitaristic, encouraging soldiers to desert; antinationalistic, denouncing the cult of the *patrie;* and antimarriage, in favor of sexual equality, birth control, and free and dissoluble unions between partners. Mikhail Bakunin's anarchist maxim "to destroy is to create" became a formula for avant-garde practice. Contemporary observer Ernest Raynaud makes clear that this desire for radical change is what brought symbolists and anarchists together in the 1880s:

> Symbolism is itself the expression of the generation that has arisen post 1870: a defeated generation, anxious and disillusioned, sickly and impressionable. Symbolism has profited from the mental distress created by the government and the series of scandals that leads one to need a change. So many people hope now for nothing other than an all-out reversal of the status quo. . . . This is why we are witnessing the collusion of aesthetes and anarchists. Both are appearing in public meetings to espouse their program to an audience that takes away from these intermingled discourses one point only: that it is a question of demolishing something.[12]

By the early 1890s, when Wilde was making numerous trips to the French capital, the associations between symbolists and anarchists had become well established. In the period between 1892 and 1894, when there was a spate of bomb attacks across the city, leading symbolist journals such as *Mercure de France* were lauding bomb-throwers such as Ravachol (the pseudonym of François Koenigstein) as a martyr and a poet. Wilde's associates in France, to whom he turned when composing *Salomé*—Stuart Merrill, Adolphe Retté, and Marcel Schwob—were self-proclaimed anarchists in this period, and Wilde's antibourgeois aestheticism and celebration of the individual were entirely in concert with the increasingly politicized views of this group. In 1893, the literary journal *L'ermitage* published a survey of dozens of literary and artistic figures, questioned on their view of the optimal form of social organization. Wilde responded, "Previously, I was a poet and a tyrant. Now I am an artist and an anarchist."[13] This ranked him among the "partisans of absolute liberty." The idea of the artist as the embodiment of an unfettered self-development that would point the way to social transformation was strongly embraced by the Parisian avant-garde.

Théâtre de l'Œuvre

This association strongly colors the history of the Théâtre de l'Œuvre, led by François-Aurélian Lugné-Poe, which was to stage Wilde's *Salomé* in 1896. Founded in 1893 on the heels of the short-lived Théâtre de l'Art, the Théâtre de l'Œuvre became the most prominent site of symbolist theatrical productions.[14] The company denounced the banality of naturalist theatrical representation and sought to re-create the dramatic experience as "the pretext for a dream."[15] The focus, above all, on lyric speech revealed the central tenet of symbolist theater: "[T]he word creates the scene as it creates everything else."[16]

Despite the apparent aestheticism of these views, however, upon the founding of the Théâtre de l'Œuvre by Lugné-Poe, Edouard Vuillard, and Camille Mauclair, the aesthetic aims of symbolist dramaturgy were noted as on a par with, or even subordinate to, the aim of social and political struggle. In a letter to *Mercure de France* in October 1893, Mauclair explains why the theater's founders chose Henrik Ibsen's *Enemy of the People* (1882) as their first production. Their primary motivation was the quest to "live violently," to "spark energies," to disseminate "libertarian ideas," and, above all, to promote the "individualist cause"; only secondarily did they desire to create a "scenic art of fiction, fantasy and dreams."[17] The expressed aim to create controversy and bring to the stage works that would bear directly upon contemporary social issues belies the obscurantism and esotericism often attributed to symbolist discourse.

Ibsen, championed as both a symbolist innovator and an anarchist inspiration, headed up the program of the first season. Staged at a moment of peak anarchist activity, the production of *An Enemy of the People* became an intensely politicized event. The play deals with one man's attempt to bring the truth to light in an attempt to safeguard the health of his town, while his efforts are stifled by corrupt authority and a hostile public. The protagonist, Dr. Stockmann, is represented as a man of ideas who asserts his freedom like a "dynamiter" against the malignant social order. In short, the production of the play at the Théâtre de l'Œuvre emphasized the similarity of Stockmann's predicament to the position of the symbolist avant-garde—the intellectual fighting for truth and artistic freedom in the face of the "imbecilic herd." On its opening night, the poet Laurent Tailhade introduced the production with a thirty-minute commentary extolling the virtues of revolt; his antagonistic and theatrical presentation aimed to implicate the audience directly in the conflict between the minority and the majority that is enacted in the play, as well as to frame the play's content explicitly in terms of contemporary controversies. The jeers and bravos that met Tailhade's introduction continued during the performance, in which, during the town meeting scene, the crowd of extras was divided into a bourgeois majority and an anarchist minority, with the audience cheering or booing the respective camps. As one critic puts it, "This interpretation of the text allowed the audience to actively participate in the production. This was not Ibsen's intention, but it successfully dramatized contemporary feelings about individualism and anarchy."[18]

The lecture by Tailhade was not all that had politicized the event. Some well-known anarchist sympathizers (including Fénéon) participated as extras in the crowd scenes; Lugné-Poe later recalled that during the intermissions and after the play, they engaged in "zealous" and "intransigent" political proselytizing, and when the company took the play subsequently to Brussels, "anarchist tracts rained down on the orchestra seats."[19] Following the opening night, the Théâtre de l'Œuvre was put under police surveillance, with several members of the company imprisoned, deported, or tracked; the next production, of *Âmes solitaires*, was cancelled by order of the police. What the example of Ibsen shows is not only how the Œuvre group polemicized a single play but also how the selection of plays that seemed to dramatize what they saw as their own struggle—that of an enlightened yet embattled minority against corrupt authority and public indifference—became their modus operandi. As a further example, the theater restaged *An Enemy of the People* in 1898; on that occasion, the conflict in the play was framed explicitly as a defense of Emile Zola in the Dreyfus Affair.

Thus, when Lugné-Poe determined to stage *Salomé* in 1896, not only was the staging of the banned work of an imprisoned author meant as an act of solidarity but also the content of the play was intended as an allegory of his predicament—Wilde, like Salomé, was being brutally punished for the open expression of unruly sexual desire. In the context of the Œuvre's politicized productions, the play stood as a manifesto of sexual freedom. Support for this assertion is apparent in the treatment of Wilde in the French press in 1895–96. Contrary to the general view that the French were more tolerant of Wilde's "crimes" than were the "puritanical" English, the mainstream French press excoriated Wilde as harshly as did anyone else. Most accounts present the case in highly nationalistic terms, casting aspersions on British virility and declaring that homosexuality was "deviant, marginal and foreign to the French nation."[20] An article published in *Le Figaro* on 6 April 1895 "identified *grivoiserie*—heterosexual humor and the display of the female body in popular entertainment—with a healthy, 'normal' male sexuality and then posited it as a trait of [French] national culture or character, as opposed to the doubtful masculinity of the British male."[21] This article—printed on the same day that Wilde was arrested and Lautrec received his commission from La Goulue—may have served as a subtext for Lautrec's comical juxtaposition of Wilde and Fénéon in the painting *The Moorish Dance*. In literary circles, even those writers who might have been expected to rally to Wilde's side feared any taint of the scandal. Nancy Erber observes, "[M]any in literary Paris took Wilde's arrest as an occasion not only to proclaim publicly their allegiance to the heterosexual moral order, but also to absolve themselves personally of any association with him and the deviance his name was coming to represent."[22]

Those commentators who took up Wilde's defense were essentially limited to the pages of symbolist literary journals such as *La plume, La revue blanche,* and *Mercure de France.* Often, the writers who most vigorously defended Wilde were those who were known for having strongly advocated anarchism as a program of individual and artistic freedom. For instance, Louis Lormel, who wrote an open letter of support to Wilde in April 1895, had one year earlier (in an article entitled "Art and Anarchism") hailed Emile Henry's bombing of the Café Terminus and argued for anarchism as a program of moral reform.[23] Laurent Tailhade, the provocative poet who had made the speech opening Ibsen's *Enemy of the People* calling for a revolt of the intellectual minority, used an article in the *Echo de Paris* to condemn French hypocrisy: "As if Wilde's actions were out of the ordinary! But frankly, there's nothing more common in our times [than] the cruising that takes place on the elegant boulevards of big cities [or in] the cafés. . . . Shall I pretend not to notice the elegant private clubs for lesbians [or] the sapphists who throng to certain taverns?"[24] And Octave Mirbeau, ever the anarchist polemicist, declared Wilde an original thinker and brilliant writer unjustly imprisoned "for acts which are neither crimes nor offenses against morality."[25]

Erin Williams Hyman

What all of these pieces have in common, along with the lengthy defense of Wilde by Paul Adam published in the *Revue blanche* under Fénéon's auspices, is that they not only object to the judgment of Wilde's behavior as "criminal" but also reject any argument that would cast his behavior as immoral. Lormel argues that Wilde's so-called crime is "a physiological act, no more or less reprehensible than any other" and asserts that "there is no immorality in it, as this word has for us no meaning."[26] Paul Adam, in his defense of Wilde, castigates the hypocrisy of public morality as it turns a blind eye to adultery while it is appalled by pederasty. Furthermore, he criticizes a nationalistic discourse that appropriates sexuality to the needs of the state. "Public opinion despises the man who prefers his own sentimental pleasure to the interests of the *patrie*," Adam accuses; "Love must exclusively produce new forces, new arms, new mothers."[27] At a time when France was facing falling birth rates and a "depopulation crisis," sexuality was being publicly discussed increasingly in terms of the military and security interests of the state. Meanwhile, anarchist activists were making the link between antimilitarism and antireproduction, promoting voluntary sterility as an act of civil disobedience. Adam's argument critiques this nationalist rhetoric, suggesting that the lack of tolerance for homosexuality is primarily because it is nonreproductive, and he defends it precisely for this reason. He even goes so far as to suggest ironically, through the ancient Greek example of battalions of warrior lovers, that the nationalists are denying themselves a sure-fire route to victory, for "with the taste for unisexual love, we would waste no time in regaining 'our place among the first rank of nations'" (458). Thus, most of the articles written in Wilde's defense not only cast aside arguments of law and morality as hypocritical and disingenuous but also tend to politicize his sexual preference in the context of a charged national debate around reproduction and state-sanctioned sexuality.

In November 1895, Stuart Merrill launched his campaign for Wilde's release, calling on writers to join him in petitioning Queen Victoria to have Wilde liberated from prison. Merrill claimed that Wilde was being incarcerated not for the vice imputed to him but out of bourgeois hatred of the "Beauty" he espoused, his iconoclasm, and the fact that he had declared himself an anarchist, hostile to bourgeois values. Merrill went so far as to call Wilde a martyr, echoing the kind of idealization that had accompanied anarchist bomb-throwers such as Ravachol, Vaillant, and Henry in the symbolist press as they went off to the guillotine.[28] As for the petition, France's most prominent literary personalities, such as

Edmond de Goncourt, Emile Zola, Maurice Barrès, and members of the Académie Française, refused to sign the petition; the only willing personalities came from within symbolist circles. The petition was thus a failure; Merrill admitted defeat in his "Epilogue pour Oscar Wilde" in *La plume* (1 January 1896).

In the context of this failed campaign to garner broader support for Wilde, the Théâtre de l'Œuvre staged *Salomé* the following month. In his memoirs, the theater's director, Lugné-Poe, stressed the legal dangers the company had to hazard in staging a play that was banned abroad by the English justice system because of Wilde's criminal status. Yet, he declares, he was determined: "Since no one else had moved to group together in an act of solidarity those who loved the artist, I disregarded any preliminary authorization and put on *Salome*, February 11, 1896, even though we were also threatened with reprisals . . . commercial this time and on French soil!"[29] Furthermore, because the theater had been previously under police surveillance for its anarchist activities, the company was not exactly above suspicion. Because of the risks involved, Lugné-Poe did not overtly publicize the event; indeed, one review praised his discretion and noted that the production was "almost a surprise."[30] Yet the subversive nature of putting on the play was clearly not only by virtue of the situation of its author; indeed, the theater company did not choose to put on *An Ideal Husband* in support of Wilde. Rather, insomuch as the content of the play dramatized excessive sexual desire and its threat to the state, its staging was a manifesto of libidinal freedom qua libertarian politics.

Though it is difficult to "reconstruct the performance with any accuracy," owing to the scanty first-hand accounts (as William Tydeman and Steven Price have noted in their book on the production history of *Salomé*),[31] certain details are revealing. Lugné-Poe relates the difficulty of finding a head of John the Baptist (Iokanaan) that would be sufficiently lifelike to make Salomé's climactic kiss scene plausible. Ultimately, he hit upon the idea of borrowing a wax head from the Musée Grevin. (Unfortunately, during the dress rehearsal, the head, brought in on a platter, rolled off the charger and shattered; it had to be glued back together for the performance.) Because later productions of the play were apparently marred by the appearance of a cardboard head of the prophet, the effort to bring in the wax head underscores the Théâtre de l'Œuvre's concern for rendering the kiss scene with a rivetingly lifelike attraction and repulsion.

Moreover, the press reviews of *Salomé* take note of the way in which the play foregrounds illicit sexuality. One review notes that Wilde changed the Salomé

Erin Williams Hyman

story to make her not a pawn of her mother but a subject acting to "quench her terrible desire to kiss the mouth of the prophet."[32] It also noted that Wilde added "other tragic stories like the death of the young captain that killed himself in front of the dancer because she doesn't love him." The role of the page in love with and mourning the young Syrian was played by a woman instead of a man so well, the critic for *Mercure de France* notes, that no one would suspect that this was "the dangerous passage."[33] As Regenia Gagnier has stated, "With *Salome,* Wilde expected . . . to confront Victorian audiences with their own sexuality. In the work that he felt was his best illustration of art for art's sake, through the figure of Salome, he portrayed sex for sex's sake, without purpose or production."[34] Gagnier has argued persuasively for the way in which the antiutilitarian and the nonpurposive unite aestheticism and sexual "deviancy" in this period; she claims that "aestheticism came to mean the irrational in both productive (art) and reproductive (sexuality) realms: an indication of the art world's divorce from middle-class life" (139). This embrace of the "irrational," the excessive, and the violent in the play could not but appeal to anarchist sympathizers, as it posits the castration of both secular and divine authority (embodied in Iokanaan and Herod). Salomé is no mere femme fatale; her anarchic passion ends in martyrdom, crushed under the shield of the law.

The theme of martyrdom was readily exploited. Press reviews of the play remark upon the fervor of the response to the performance, which received a lengthy standing ovation. In the words of one reviewer, "[T]hey acclaimed the drama and they acclaimed the name of Oscar Wilde with all the enthusiasm of admiration multiplied by indignation; we hope that some echo of this acclaim reaches the poet and that the sincerity of our sympathy will encourage him in the terrible experience he is undergoing."[35] The play was thus manifestly meant to send a message—to the imprisoned playwright, clearly, but also to the Parisian public—on the freedom of the artist and the unjustly repressive nature of social mores regarding sexual expression. "Morality can be defined as the ensemble of the prejudices of an epoch," wrote Adolphe Retté in *La plume;* "[T]hus, it is praiseworthy to eliminate it, at least in the domain of thought."[36]

If Wilde, as Gagnier puts it, "confirm[ed] that Salome was his personal fantasy of the triumph of love over the repressive forces of society" (169), then it seems that the Théâtre de l'Œuvre and Wilde's supporters in Paris also read it this way, in the key of an artistic and anarchistic struggle. Returning to the Toulouse-Lautrec portrait, we can see that the humor inherent in the portrait seems to be the counterpoint between La Goulue and Wilde—between two kinds of sexual spectacle: one that healthy, French *grivoiserie;* the other, suspect, "degenerate," and criminalized. But the inclusion of Fénéon as Wilde's counterpart suggests that Wilde's aestheticism, iconoclasm, and sexual subversion were of a piece with the anarchist position that Fénéon openly represented. If there remains some question as to the sincerity of Wilde's self-proclaimed anarchism, there is little doubt that to the symbolist-anarchist avant-garde in Paris, his cause and theirs were one and the same.

Notes

All translations from French texts are my own unless otherwise noted.

1. David Sweetman, *Explosive Acts: Toulouse-Lautrec, Oscar Wilde, Félix Fénéon and the Art and Anarchy of the Fin de Siècle* (New York: Simon and Schuster, 1999), 403.

2. Joan U. Halperin, *Félix Fénéon, Aesthete and Anarchist in Fin-de-Siècle Paris* (New Haven, CT: Yale University Press, 1988), 288; further page references appear in parentheses.

3. Marianne Ryan, ed., *Toulouse-Lautrec* (London: South Bank, 1991), 276.

4. Joseph Donohue, "Distance, Death and Desire in Salome," in *The Cambridge Companion to Oscar Wilde,* ed. Peter Raby (Cambridge: Cambridge University Press, 1997), 118–42.

5. George Woodcock, *The Paradox of Oscar Wilde* (London: T. V. Boardman, 1949), 151.

6. Sos Eltis, *Revising Wilde: Society and Subversion in the Plays of Oscar Wilde* (Oxford: Clarendon Press, 1996), 16–17. Shortly after Wilde's imprisonment on 25 May 1895, Fabian socialist George Bernard Shaw attempted to assemble a petition of signatories at a trade-union congress to protest the two-year sentence; he was unsuccessful in garnering support. On 31 December 1891, poet John Barlas was arrested outside the Speaker's House in the Palace of Westminster after firing a gun; he declared to the police that he was an anarchist who held Parliament in contempt. On 16 January 1892, Wilde posted a bond as surety for Barlas's good conduct. On these matters, see Margery M. Morgan, "Shaw and the Sex Reformers," *Shaw* 24 (2004): 96–111; and Karl Beckson, *The Oscar Wilde Encyclopedia* (New York: AMS Press, 1998), 19–20.

7. David Rose, "Oscar Wilde: Socialite or Socialist?" in *The Importance of Reinventing Oscar: Versions of Wilde during the Last 100 Years,* ed. Ewe Boker, Richard Corballis, and Julie Hibbard (Amsterdam: Rodopi, 2002), 43.

8. Josephine M. Guy, "'The Soul of Man under Socialism': A (Con)Textual History," *Wilde Writings: Contextual Conditions,* ed. Joseph Bristow (Toronto: University of Toronto Press, 2003), 77; further page reference appears in parentheses.

9. Remy de Gourmont, *L'idéalisme* (Paris: Mercure de France, 1893), 23.

10. Stuart Merrill, "Critique de poèmes," *La plume,* 1 June 1901, 409.

11. Jean Maitron, *Histoire du mouvement anarchiste en France, 1880–1914,* vol. 1 (Paris: Société Universitaire d'Éditions et de Librairie, 1951), 446.

12. Ernest Raynaud, *La mêlée symboliste (1870–1910): Portraits et souvenirs* (Paris: A. G. Nizet, 1971), 191.

13. "Autrefois, j'étais poète et tyran. Maintenant je suis artiste et anarchiste." "Referendum artistique et social," *L'ermitage* (July 1893): 21.

14. For more on the formation of the Œuvre and symbolist theater history, see Frantisek Deak, *Symbolist Theater: The Formation of an Avant-Garde* (Baltimore, MD: Johns Hopkins University Press, 1993); Patricia Ekert Boyer, *Artists and the Avant-Garde Theater in Paris, 1887–1900*, exhibition catalogue (Washington, DC: National Gallery of Art, 1998); John A. Henderson, *The First Avant-Garde, 1887–1894: Sources of the Modern French Theater* (London: George G. Harrap, 1971); Gertrude Jasper, *Adventure in the Theater: Lugné-Poe and the Théâtre de l'Œuvre to 1899* (New Brunswick, NJ: Rutgers University Press, 1947); Dorothy Knowles, *La réaction idéaliste au théâtre depuis 1890* (Paris: E. Droz, 1934); Gisèle Marie, *Le théâtre symboliste: Ses origines, ses sources, pionniers et réalisateurs* (Paris: A. G. Nizet, 1973); Jacques Robichez, *Le symbolisme au théâtre: Lugné-Poe et les débuts de l'Œuvre* (Paris: L'Arche, 1957).

15. Pierre Quillard, "De l'inutilité absolue de la mise-en-scène exacte," *Revue d'art dramatique* 21 (1891): 181–82.

16. "[L]a parole crée le décor comme le reste." Quillard, "De l'inutilité absolue," 181–82.

17. Camille Mauclair, "Théâtre de l'Œuvre," *Mercure de France* (October 1893): 191–92.

18. Frantisek Deak, *Symbolist Theater: The Formation of an Avant-Garde* (Baltimore, MD: Johns Hopkins University Press, 1993), 201.

19. Aurélien-François Lugné-Poe, *Acrobaties: Souvenirs et impressions de théâtre (1894–1902)* (Paris: Gallimard, 1931), 64.

20. Nancy Erber, "The French Trials of Oscar Wilde," *Journal of the History of Sexuality* 6 (1996): 565.

21. Erber, "French Trials," 565.

22. Erber, "French Trials," 565.

23. Louis Lormel, "L'art et l'anarchisme," *L'art littéraire* (March–April 1894): 33–35.

24. Quoted in Erber, "French Trials," 576.

25. Quoted in Erber, "French Trials," 574.

26. Louis Lormel, "A M. Oscar Wilde," *La plume*, 15 April 1895, 165.

27. Paul Adam, "L'assaut malicieux," *La revue bleue* 8 (1895): 461; further page reference appears in parentheses.

28. Stuart Merrill, "Tribune libre," *La plume*, 15 November 1895, 508–9.

29. Lugné-Poe, *Acrobaties*, 149.

30. Achille Segard, "Théâtres," *La plume*, 1 March 1896, 164.

31. William Tydeman and Steven Price, *Wilde: Salome* (Cambridge: Cambridge University Press, 1996), 28.

32. "[A]ssouvir le terrible désir qui l'a saisie de baiser sur la bouche le prophète Jean." Segard, "Théâtres," 164; the following quotation appears on the same page.

33. Jean de Tinan, "Théâtre de l'Œuvre," *Mercure de France* (March 1896): 416.

34. Regenia Gagnier, *Idylls of the Marketplace: Oscar Wilde and the Victorian Public* (Stanford: Stanford University Press, 1986), 165; further page references appear in parentheses.

35. De Tinan, "Théâtre de l'Œuvre," 416.

36. Adolphe Rette, "Chronique des livres," *La plume*, 15 October 1895, 474.

Oscar Wilde and the Politics
of Posthumous Sainthood

Hofmannsthal, Mirbeau, Proust

RICHARD A. KAYE

[T]hat under the glamour of myth and legend some stratum of historical fact may lie, is a proposition rendered extremely probable by the modern investigations into the mythopoeic spirit in non-Christian times.

—Oscar Wilde, "The Rise of Historical Criticism"
(composed 1879, published 1905)

IN A 1905 ESSAY entitled "Sebastian Melmoth," the Austrian poet, playwright, and critic Hugo von Hofmannsthal cautions against what he construes as the widespread tendency to detach Oscar Wilde the man from Wilde the writer, a conception that posits the one as a tragic social miscreant and the other as a splendid literary success. Hofmannsthal's essay seeks to rescue Wilde from the countless contemporary distortions that had adhered to him, variously depicting Wilde as an apolitical aesthete, an unwitting victim of social prejudice and persecution, the author of "marvelously polished words," the luxuriant Society gadfly, a brazen litigant against the Marquess of Queensberry, a prisoner degradingly forced into filthy jailhouse baths, and a saintly rebel who violated boundaries.[1] Each of these roles, taken in isolation, is fraudulent or at least inadequate for Hofmannsthal, who insists that "Wilde's fate and Wilde's character" are not "two different entities" (302). Most outlandish for Hofmannsthal is a pervasive ideal-izing framework in which the playwright ossifies into a superhuman or hagio-graphic legend. "They talk of an aesthete transformed into a new man, a believer, almost a saint," scoffs Hofmannsthal of Wilde's new acolytes; "They have devel-oped the habit of saying certain things about certain romanticists, and such things are too easily repeated. They should not be repeated" (302).

Perhaps the most vivid image in Hofmannsthal's stringent essay—one that distills this critic's paramount point about Wilde's filling the role of perpetrator of his own destruction as much as that of passive target of others' malevolence—comes at the brutal summa of a string of tantalizing contradictions. Wilde, writes Hofmannsthal, "glittered, enchanted, offended, seduced, betrayed and was be-trayed, stabbed others' hearts and was himself stabbed in the heart" (301). The last of these traits, which offers us Wilde as a bloody tormentor as much as a tor-mented castoff, is a telling image. For throughout his life Wilde identified with a specific martyr, St. Sebastian (evoked in the title of Hofmannsthal's essay), a martyr whose exquisite, arrow-ridden body is familiar from hundreds of depic-tions by Renaissance artists. Hofmannsthal's strenuous effort to liberate Wilde from the fetters of a purifying saintliness reveals the increasingly complex and contradictory status of martyrdom at the beginning of the previous century. Wilde's status as saint or martyr—a status powerfully given historical, aesthetic, and corporeal force in the specific figure of Sebastian that Wilde embraced throughout his life—helped to determine the writer's twentieth-century fortunes.

As Hofmannsthal grasped, the playwright's devotees were eager to place a saintly halo over Wilde immediately after his three-act trial, locating in Wilde a potent political figure whose force depended on the consecrations of religious authority. In a furious 1895 philippic published shortly after the verdict of gross indecency, "À propos of 'Hard Labor,'" the left-wing French writer Octave Mirbeau salutes Wilde and a "thousand other martyrs" who suffered at the hands of British justice.[2] This sense of Wilde as exemplary martyr, often on behalf of unusual causes, continued after his death in Paris on 30 November 1900. In an endorse-ment of a rational policy of eugenics (one that would allow for "abnormality" as a welcome aspect of a natural schema), Edith Lees Ellis (along with her spouse, Havelock Ellis, a pioneering campaigner for legal reform on matters of sexual freedom) declared in 1911 that Oscar Wilde denoted a "martyr to unscientific leg-islation," by which she evidently meant a legal apparatus in which nonnormative forms of sexuality were misunderstood as contrary to nature rather than being seen as natural phenomena.[3] Arthur Ransome—in the introduction to his study *Oscar Wilde* (1912), one of the first appreciative estimations of the writer that appeared after Wilde's death—imagined someone asking him to define Wilde "in a few words" and having to reply, "One cannot define in a sentence a man whom it has taken God several millions of years to make."[4] For the hagiographic Ransome, Wilde represented a hallowed member of an elect group of men who "live their lives like flames, hurrying to death through their own enjoyment and expenditure alike of their bodies and brains" (21). Such associations with divine self-martyrdom—redolent of both innocent, sublime victimhood and valiant activism on behalf of a disreputable cause—hovered over the name of Oscar Wilde in his last years and in the decades after his death.

The aesthetic and Decadent movements' penchant for an overwrought rhetoric that drew on religious language is a much-noted aspect of fin-de-siècle literary culture. (Such rhetorical strategies may even have played a part in late-Victorian pornographic culture. Consider how the 1893 novel *Teleny, or the Reverse of the Medal,* a scabrous work that Wilde may have had a hand in authoring, endows its glamorous hero with a "heavenly figure.")[5] Moreover, Wilde's self-identification with the Christian martyr Sebastian and his devotees' attraction to that role coincided with a new, psychological conception of martyrdom, one that construed heroic Christian renunciation and self-sacrifice as a diminished, masochistic condition. Religious faith, in this psychoanalytic conceptualization, represented a displacement of a potentially violent neurosis. Thus, the nineteenth-century French physician Jean-Martin Charcot authored an 1885 essay, *La foi qui guérit* (Faith-Healing), in which the celebrated analyst diagnosed Christian saints and martyrs such as Francis of Assisi and Teresa de Avila as "undeniable hysterics."[6] Charcot was baffled that these neurotics were considered experts at curing hysteria in others. He stressed the neurotic and specifically masochistic dimension in Christian devotion, a view of Christianity and of martyrdom in particular as developmental stages that had its literary parallels in late nineteenth-century writings linked to aestheticism. Such a conception is apparent, for example, in Walter Pater's 1885 novel about Antonine Rome, *Marius the Epicurean,* in which the eponymous hero passes through a host of tantalizing philosophies and religions —primitive paganism, Cynicism, Stoicism, Epicureanism, and ultimately Christian martyrdom. Yet not even in martyrdom can Marius reject the rich sum of his experience, since the state of martyred suffering implies the surrender to a single,

Richard A. Kaye

closed system. Pater's schema predicts a later psychoanalytic perspective on intense religious faith as just another (temporary) psychological state.

In *The Future of an Illusion* (1927), Freud placed a corresponding stress on the psychological basis for religious faith when he claimed that "religious belief" was "comparable to childhood neurosis" and when he offered the hope that "mankind will surmount this neurotic phase, just as so many children grow out of their similar neurosis."[7] In an earlier essay, "The Economic Problem in Masochism" (1924), Freud conceived of masochism as frequently having a "feminine" dimension in men, whom he theorized as needing to assume the erotic position of a debased female to reenact an oedipal struggle with a father invariably constructed as punitive.[8] The tensions between Decadent aesthetics and innovative psychological theoretical models are apparent across Europe, most notoriously in Max Nordau's best-selling *Degeneration* (1892), in which Wilde's "genius" is diagnosed as an exaggerated form of illness.[9] In 1919, a medical thesis described the heroine of Mirbeau's 1899 novel *Le jardin de supplice* (The Torture Garden)—a work of insistent Decadent characteristics that Wilde found both "quite awful" and "wonderful"— as "a degenerate hysteric with a deep perversion of the sexual instinct."[10]

The Wilde who took hold of the imagination of others in the years after his death stood at the crossroads of these contrasting and intensely overdetermined conceptions of Decadent writing and aestheticism, dissident forms of sexuality, and martyrdom, in which traditional notions of Christian renunciation rubbed up against a disease-seeking psychological formulation. However much sainthood and martyrdom seemed characterized by a paradox that simultaneously evoked heroic self-sacrifice and masochistic longing, there was a more socially positive function for a newly fashioned popular "martyr" such as Wilde. For Wilde's role as suffering Christian hero spoke less of the writer's status as a model for his followers' behavior than of his enduring role as the leader of a certain kind of community or fellowship—namely, sexual dissidents throughout modern history. This conception of sainthood as not so much exemplary as communal in its function harks back to medieval cults of sainthood, in which saints often served, through their charismatic hold over followers, chiefly as builders of devotional communities and only secondarily as exemplary models. As recently as 1965, Vatican II accentuated the issue of fellowship in elaborating on what was most palpably authentic in the cult of Christian saints. As John S. Hawley has noted of this long-standing tradition, medieval saints strove to create a "sacred family" through their "luminous" behavior.[11] Similarly, Wilde's reputation as a modern secular saint is inextricably bound up with his role as a politically generative figure, an architect of a self-conscious community of "inverts." That role is complicated and sometimes undermined, however, by a new medical comprehension of martyrdom, in which a martyr's willingness to sacrifice himself for a cause and a people is represented as the most morbid of compulsions—most notably, in Freud's theory of the "death drive" (Thanatos), outlined in *Beyond the Pleasure Principle* (1914).[12]

Three instructive instances in the history of Wilde's European reception accentuate this role of martyr not only during his lifetime but also (and especially) in the decades after his death. The first is Hofmannsthal's essay, a neglected, remarkably unsentimental yet appreciative meditation on the writer that critiques what Hofmannsthal considered a widespread sanctification of Wilde. The second, which further expands on this tangled political component in Wilde's posthumous incarnations, consists of Mirbeau's recurring engagement with Wilde and his legacy. In Mirbeau's writings, one finds a diverse and complex comprehension of the Irish author. In his semiautobiographical *Sebastien Roch* (1890), a work that Wilde may have read while revising *The Picture of Dorian Gray* for publication in a single volume, the anti-Catholic Mirbeau (an ally of the anarchist cause) excoriates French Catholic officialdom as a sexually sadistic regiment by drawing on the myths, images, and language of martyrdom to represent its hero in hyperpolitical terms. Mirbeau's friendship with Wilde during the years of the Dreyfus case prompted Mirbeau to write his bold defense of Wilde as well as a glowing review of *The Picture of Dorian Gray* (1890, revised 1891), followed by a lightly satirical portrait of the author in Mirbeau's biting Society novel *Le journal d'une femme de chambre,* which he completed in March 1900, eight months before Wilde's death in Paris. (During his lifetime, Wilde appeared as a fictional character in several novels, but Mirbeau's work is arguably the first published work of fiction to include Wilde as a character after Wilde's demise.) In this satiric narrative, a send-up of haute-bourgeois French society, Mirbeau gives Wilde the part of a prophet of aestheticism who transfixes his audiences with the credo of a new *philosophe.* In *Le journal d'une femme de chambre,* Wilde has a spectral socioreligious power as an aesthete of uncanny powers, Sir Harry Kimberly, whose dinner-party lectures create comically stupefied acolytes.

The third example I consider here—and one that places similar emphasis on Wilde as builder of community—is Marcel Proust's allusion to Wilde in the

Richard A. Kaye

Sodom et Gomorrhe section of *À la recherche du temps perdu* (Remembrance of Things Past) (1913–27). Although, as numerous scholars have noted, *À la recherche du temps perdu* has several revealing references to Wilde (the figure of Charlus has long been identified by critics as a stand-in for him), one passage is a striking set piece beyond its simple allusiveness to the playwright.[13] It is, significantly, the longest sentence in all of Proust's multivolume work, a searching rumination in which Marcel broods on the historical and social conditions of the persecuted homosexual, whom Marcel analogizes in racialist terms as akin to the maligned Jewish people. Syntactically, the unnamed figure of Wilde generates Proust's coiling sentence. The extravagance of this sentence—a Proustian fantasy of a heterosexual male's far-ranging, empathetic inquiry into the conditions of the homosexual male—offers a view of Wilde as a figure who cannot be named but nonetheless serves as a signal moment in the narrator's understanding of the male "invert" and his imagined secret counterworld.

The examples from Hofmannsthal, Mirbeau, and Proust evoking Wilde's position should focus our attention on Wilde as an assertive (albeit sometimes unwitting) leader of a fraternity of aesthetes of same-sex tastes. What links these three examples in the history of Wilde's reception is that in each of these European writers' works, Wilde is the overseer of not merely a privileged, brittle London coterie but an international, self-consciously constituted community of aesthetically sensitive "inverts." These three instances in the history of comprehensions of Wilde on the part of non-English-speaking writers should serve to suggest the ways in which an exalted, sometimes semidisguised rhetoric of sainthood determined Wilde's twentieth-century afterlife. Wilde has continued to resonate as a politically potent martyr in contemporary culture. In Todd Haynes's 1998 film *Velvet Goldmine,* for example, Wilde is explicitly invoked as the patron saint of a musical and erotic counterculture—Glam Rock, specifically, but also an entire youth movement. Wilde's "sainthood" has become a kind of secular canonization on behalf of the cause of sexual and cultural dissidence. Even when the playwright is construed in de-idealizing terms, as in Terry Eagleton's 1989 play *Saint Oscar* (which presents Wilde as an arrogantly detached toff who turns his back on the working classes and his Irish compatriots), a rhetoric of sainthood prevails. As we shall see, that diminished conception of Wilde finds an antidote in Peter Ackroyd's 1983 fictional re-creation of Wilde's last days.

Still, in the twenty-first century, the notion of Wilde as martyr continues to hold sway. In Neil McKenna's biography, *The Secret Life of Oscar Wilde* (2003), a work that fulsomely catalogues a recklessly priapic Wilde's innumerable erotic assignations and love affairs as a kind of riposte to Richard Ellmann's influential humanist study, *Oscar Wilde* (1987), the playwright nonetheless retains his position as "the greatest 'martyr' to the cause of Uranian love."[14] McKenna's account concludes triumphantly with the declaration that "[a] hundred years and many monstrous martyrdoms later, Oscar's men are outcast men no more and the love that dared not speak its name has at last found its joyful voice." Only the quotation marks that McKenna employs for the word *martyr* intimate that martyrdom might be a problematic ideal. In a post-9/11 era of massive terrorist acts by self-proclaimed "martyrs," the idea of martyrdom has become a troubled ideal, having moved as far as possible from its status in earlier epochs, in which martyrs were unassailably heroic heroes (although, to be sure, the power of contemporary "martyrs" to take on a time-honored role as builders of vast communities of adherents is no less pronounced).

"Like dear St. Francis of Assisi, I am wedded to Poverty: but in my case the marriage is not a success," Wilde quipped toward the end of his life.[15] Yet well before his three catastrophic trials, Wilde helped to shape his reputation as sacred victim through his self-identification with another saint, the martyr Sebastian, the third-century Praetorian soldier who, on coming to the aid of two Christian soldiers, revealed himself to be a Christian. Although Wilde's love of the martyred Roman saint was dramatically signaled with his choice of the *nom de voyage* "Sebastian Melmoth" on leaving Reading Gaol in May 1897, his interest in this particular martyr dated back to a youthful visit to Genoa. The Oxford undergraduate composed a sonnet to John Keats while in the Italian port town; in the sonnet, he compared the poet to St. Sebastian ("Fair as Sebastian and as early slain"; Wilde, "The Grave of Keats," *CW*, 11:157). In his 1877 essay entitled "The Tomb of Keats," in which he first published his sonnet, Wilde compared the Romantic poet to a "Priest of Beauty slain before his time," one who evoked "the vision of Guido [Reni]'s St. Sebastian" (*CW*, 14:3). Wilde imagined a youth "with red lips, bound by his evil enemies to a tree, and though pierced by arrows, raising his eyes with a divine, impassioned gaze towards the Eternal Beauty of the opening heavens" (*CW*, 14:3–4).[16] The writer's embrace of the martyr was the culmination of decades of nineteenth-century worship in which the Roman martyr functioned less as a cult homoerotic totem, the proprietary martyr familiar to fin-de-siècle Decadents, than as a widely available emblem of feminized masculinity, androgyny, working-class consciousness, erotic disorder, and passive but sublime submission.

Richard A. Kaye

Because nineteenth-century writers viewed Sebastian's arrow-ridden body in far more than religiously symbolic terms, as that of a penetrated male who is beatifically ecstatic and not merely submissive, Sebastian would seem to render flagrant the tacit masochism evident in a certain strain of Victorian masculinity. A favorite subject in Renaissance painting, where he is typically represented as an ephebe-like male, Sebastian emerged as a martyr of keen appeal for turn-of-the-century writers and artists, doubtless because of the metaphorical associations of his arrow-penetrated state, a condition of polymorphous perversity in that Sebastian would seem to be a figure, like the nineteenth-century vampire, who revels in an exposed body of newly generated orifices. Beyond such symbolic associations, Sebastian seemed to offer a needed sensual strain to exalted Christian ideals. In the third volume of *The Renaissance in Italy* (1887), John Addington Symonds turned rhapsodic in describing a depiction of St. Sebastian by Giovanni Antonio Bazzi, a work that Symonds saw as a perfect "hybrid" of Hellenic beauty and the "Christian sentiment of martyrdom."[17] Furthermore, Sebastian had a special resonance in a period saturated in medical models, in which self-revelation was a fundamental aspect of sexuality. Legend had it that Sebastian dramatically declared his Christian faith and was therefore punished by the emperor Diocletian with an execution by arrows. For late-Victorian writers of Decadent leanings, this "confession" served as a metaphorical sexual self-revelation. What Wilde contributed to this nineteenth-century cult of Sebastian was an aestheticization of martyrdom; what his posthumous followers offered was a sense of Wilde as risk-taking leader of a newly constituted breed of erotically dissident men.[18]

Hofmannsthal's Wilde: Inescapable Martyrdom

That Hugo von Hofmannsthal was a perennially conflicted writer of aestheticist inclinations and that his literary career posthumously intersected with Wilde's in that he collaborated with Richard Strauss, the composer who adopted Wilde's *Salomé* for opera, complicate Hofmannsthal's investment in Wilde. (Hofmannsthal's 1922 collection of aphorisms, the "Book of Friends," reads like a distillation of Wildean paradoxes, Goethe's *Maxims and Reflections,* and Novalis's *Fragments.*)[19] The essay "Sebastian Melmoth" suggests at once a fascination with Wilde and a timorous dread at the public versions then being disseminated on the Irish writer's behalf.[20] At the same time, Hofmannsthal's response is tempered by a canny detachment from the uses to which Wilde's name would be put. Hofmannsthal's "Sebastian Melmoth" begins with a consideration of what its author sees as Wilde's three key public personae. According to Hofmannsthal, "it was the fate of this man to bear three successive names: Oscar Wilde, C[.]3[.]3[.]3[.], Sebastian Melmoth" (301). For Hofmannsthal, the "sound" of the first of these personae suggests only splendour, pride, seduction," with a "fine brow, sensual lips, moist, magnificent, impudent eyes—a mask of Bacchus" (301). The second is the "mask behind which Oscar Wilde concealed his face, ravaged by gaol and the signs of approaching death, so as to live out a few more years of his life in the dark" (301). The name Sebastian Melmoth "sounds terrifying, one of those marks which society brands with a fiery iron into the naked human shoulder" (301). The third of Wilde's sobriquets, according to Hofmannsthal's account, is the "name of a ghost, a half-forgotten Balzacian character . . . a wretched costumier's domino hired to conceal a slow death from the eyes of mankind" (301). Significantly, the last of these names is the one that Hofmannsthal chose for the title of his essay, as if the most garish and pathetic of Wilde's three selves (in Hofmannsthal's terms) had eclipsed all others.

In an important passage, Hofmannsthal argues that the sobriquet of aesthete, strictly speaking, is unsuitable for Wilde. "People say," Hofmannsthal insists, "'He was an aesthete, and suddenly unfortunate entanglements overwhelmed him, a snare of unfortunate entanglements.' . . . An aesthete! This signifies nothing" (303). Rather, for Hofmannsthal, Pater (Wilde's mentor) was the one who "was an aesthete, a man who lived by the enjoyment and re-creation of beauty," one whose "attitude towards life was one of reserve and reverence, full of propriety" (303). In Hofmannsthal's view, an "aesthete, by nature, is steeped in propriety," whereas Wilde was a "figure of impropriety, tragic impropriety" (303). Of course, recent critics such as Richard Dellamora have demonstrated just how ideologically dissident within a Victorian cultural context Pater's aestheticism was,[21] but the more important point here is the way in which Hofmannsthal seeks to fashion a Wilde of meaningful improprieties, whose relationship with reality, Hofmannsthal insists, was always conflicted: "[Wilde's] aestheticism had a convulsive quality. The jewels among which he professed voluptuously to delve were death-dimmed eyes, petrified because they could not bear the sight of life. Incessantly he felt the threat of life directed towards him. He was forever surrounded by a tragic air of horror. He kept challenging life unceasingly. He insulted reality. And he senses life lying in wait in order to spring upon him out

Richard A. Kaye

of the darkness" (303). Hofmannsthal's Wilde thus enters into fierce combat with a vicious reality that ultimately defeats him. Interestingly, this "reality" is not exactly a set of historical actualities, obstacles, or challenges but rather something approximating unalterable fate wedded to an abiding personal flaw. Yet in "Sebastian Melmoth," Hofmannsthal insists that reality for Wilde was most terribly pronounced at "the moment when he (over whom no one but his fate had any power)—against the pleading of his friends and almost to the horror of his enemies—turned and denounced Queensberry" (304). At that moment, Hofmannsthal concludes, the "mask of Bacchus with its full, beautifully curved lips must have been transformed in an unforgettable manner into the seeing-blind Oedipus or the raging Ajax" (304). The sensual allurements of Hellenic culture evoked in the figure of Bacchus thereby give way to the sobering truths of Greek tragedy—which, for Hofmannsthal, is the central narrative in Wilde's story.

Despite its attempt at rescuing Wilde from a tangle of posthumously created personae, Hofmannsthal's essay ultimately enacts the cul-de-sac in understanding —and in doing so comprises yet another highly functional distortion—that Hofmannsthal so sharply critiques in Wilde's posthumous public reception. Hofmannsthal ultimately could not escape his sense of Wilde as a tragic figure who aggressively acted as public miscreant, a troublemaker against a pudibund culture whose body had been cast ritualistically before a condemning public. Hofmannsthal concludes his essay by taking an Olympian, quasi-anthropological view, noting that

> [t]here are certain islands whose savage inhabitants pierce the bodies of their dead relatives with poisoned arrows, to make sure that they are dead. This is an ingenious way of expressing metaphorically a profound thought and of paying homage to the profundity of nature without much ado. For in truth the slowly killing poisons and the elixir of gently smouldering bliss all lie side by side in our living body. No one thing can be excluded, none considered too insignificant to become a very great power. Seen from the viewpoint of life, there is not one thing extraneous to the Whole. Everything is everywhere. Everything partakes of the dance of life.
>
> In the words of the Jalal-ud-din Rumi, "He who knows the power of the dance of life fears not death. For he knows that love kills." (304–5)

This extraordinary conclusion reads like a funeral rite, in which Wilde's death falls into a series of revealing increments. Wilde, a priest of love, becomes the focus of an obscure, possibly pagan ritual in which his metaphorical body is pierced yet also serves to elicit the loving concern of relatives. Wilde the religious figure endures. Indeed, the reference to the thirteenth-century Persian poet and Sufi theologian Rumi (whose name literally means "Majesty of Religion") consigns Wilde to an apotheosis in the deathless spiritual realm of world mysticism.

Octave Mirbeau's Oscar Wilde: Aestheticism, Martyrdom, Conversion

"His soul seems to have wandered in fearsome places"—so wrote Wilde in late May 1899 of Octave Mirbeau, who had become a friend in the writer's Paris years and whose novel *Le jardin de supplice* Wilde described as a "terrible little book . . . a *Sadique* joy in pain pulses in it."[22] Mirbeau, who after early years as a political reactionary gradually became a committed anarchist and a fierce supporter of Dreyfus, composed in novels such as *Le jardin de supplice* what might be termed a politically conscious form of Decadent writing. His depiction of many sadistic acts and depravities suggests the inability of complex, modern social systems to quell what the novelist intimates are natural, violent inclinations. Wilde's debt to Mirbeau may have been long-standing. *Sebastien Roch,* a lyrical bildungsroman about a tormented young man and the traumas of Catholic education in Belle Epoque France, suggests certain affinities with Wilde's *Picture of Dorian Gray.* (Mirbeau's novel was published in France in the months between the magazine and book editions of *Dorian Gray.*) *Sebastien Roch* is at once a novel of education and an instructive pendant to Wilde's story of embattled youth. Mirbeau's Sebastian, a half orphan with a hypersensitive character, would seem to suffer from the same temptations of the senses that afflict his contemporary Dorian Gray. Like Dorian, with his cloak adorned with the symbols of St. Sebastian, Sebastien Roch palpably invokes the name of his patron saint, though more overtly through his name and actions. "Intoxicated" with a local girl named Marguerite, he feels a bond "so intimate, so magnetic," that "very often, if she bumped against the edge of a piece of furniture or pricked her fingers on a needle, he immediately felt the same physical pain."[23] But after his maltreatment by priests at a remote Jesuit school, his tortures become terrifying and morbid:

> Left to his own devices for most of the time, seated or lying on his bed, his body inactive, he was also scarcely able to defend himself. Against the temp-

Richard A. Kaye

tations which assailed him, more numerous and precise each day, against the unbridled madness of the impure images inflaming his brain, scourging his flesh, driving him to shameful relapses, immediately followed by self-disgust and bouts of prostration, during which his soul sank down as if into death. Afterwards, he would fall into an agitated painful sleep, interspersed with nightmares and a feeling of suffocation; his dreams were terrible, as if he were emerging from the heavy, terrifying darkness of a would-be suicide. (183)

Such passages harbor some of the never-quite-explicit allusiveness to unnamed sinfulness that become increasingly prevalent in *The Picture of Dorian Gray*, as Dorian's sins increase and their precise details become elliptically unstated. Yet in its critique of a beleaguered youth, Mirbeau's novel represents a forcefully naturalistic literary model against which *The Picture of Dorian Gray* militates. For Mirbeau's Sebastian suffers the torments resulting not from a supernatural Faustian bargain in which he aims for eternal youth but from the explicitly detailed torments of the sadistic priest, Father de Kern, who sexually attacks him. It is a forcefully naturalistic scheme that dominates *Sebastien Roch*, in a novel that culminates in its hero's death on the battlefield. Mirbeau's literary artistry represents a politically conscious version of Decadent literature, as exemplified in *Le jardin de supplice*, where dissolute acts simultaneously represent a titillating display of sexual sadomasochistic games and an indictment of bourgeois social smugness. A similar social critique animates *Le journal d'une femme de chambre* (Diary of a Chambermaid), whose low-born heroine Célestine details the degradations of servant life.[24] However, Mirbeau makes clear that Célestine is no sexual innocent, as when, in the novel's opening pages, she observes, "I dote on nothing so much as on white leather knee-breeches tightly fitting nervous thighs." In its similar stress on destroyed sexual innocence and on the social obstacles to its doomed protagonist's fate, *Sebastien Roch* narrates its hero's pitiful decline, a fall that functions as a proleptic meditation on Wilde's *Picture of Dorian Gray*. (Significantly, Mirbeau's admiring review of *Dorian Gray* hailed it as a novel that exposed the perils of societal tyranny, with Mirbeau asserting, "In reading *The Picture of Dorian Gray*, I have never before felt so sharply the horror of social repression.")[25]

In *Diary of a Chambermaid*, both the historical Wilde and his lover Alfred Douglas make a transparent appearance in the characters of Sir Harry Kimberly, described as a "symbolist musician," and "his young friend Lucien Satorys, as beautiful as a woman, as supple as a peau de Suede glove, as slender and blonde as a cigar" (191). Kimberly is a drawing-room virtuoso who, in a key scene at a dinner party, expounds his aestheticist principles with oracular force: his "look and gestures, and even the orchid that adorned the buttonhole of his coat, expressed the most ardent ecstasy" (199). He delivers a lengthy talk in which he tells of John-Giotto Farfadetti, a poet, who "sang in his verses the marvelous symbols that his friend Fredric-Ossian Pingleton painted on his canvases, that the glory of the poet was inseparable from that of the painter, and that their works and their immortal geniuses had come to be confounded in one and same adoration" (200–201). Both men fall in love with the spectral spirit of Botticellina, the subject of their aesthetic masterpieces, and when she finally appears to them out of the painter's canvas, the painter collapses, as he "buried his nails in his flesh . . . while the blood streamed from him as from a fountain" (204–5). When Kimberly pauses in the midst of this speech (a kind of comic retelling of *The Picture of Dorian Gray,* in which Basil Hallward and Lord Henry Wotton are united in the shared love of an immortal woman), "[t]he silence was religious. Something sacred hovered over the table"—and indeed, when he concludes his speech, the other guests "rose from the table in religious silence, but thrilled through and through. In the *salon* Kimberly was closely surrounded and warmly congratulated. The looks of all the women converged radiantly upon his painted face, surrounding it with a halo of ecstasies" (201). Here aestheticism has taken on a transformative religious power for female acolytes who yearn for conversion and shiver to such information as "[s]ouls have no sex" (205). Aestheticism, resembling Christian doctrine, has as its ideal proselytizer a Svengali-like dinner guest.

The Longest Sentence: Proust, Wilde, and the "Race" of Inverts

Marcel Proust's biographers have tended to accentuate the French writer's detachment from his British contemporary, epitomized in the French novelist's apparent disappointment on first meeting Wilde. Noting that Wilde and Proust's initial encounter at the home of Mme. Arthur Baignères was inauspicious (Wilde reportedly made disparaging remarks about Proust's heavy furniture), George Painter hazards that Wilde "failed to impress Proust," while a more recent biographer, Jean Yves Tadié, speaks of "Proust's lack of sympathy" for the writer.[26] Most recently, Michael Lucey has supplied a trenchant interpretation of Proust's complex denigration of what Proust terms, in a remarkable letter quoted by Lucey, Wilde's "banal aestheticism," a characterization of Wilde's aesthetic that entails, as Lucey notes, a naïve confusion of Wilde with the speaker Vivian in "The Decay of Lying" (1889, revised 1891).[27] Yet if Wilde as a theorist of art disappointed the French writer, in offering Wilde a place in the longest sentence in *Sodom et Gomorrhe* (1921–22), Proust is positively grandiloquent in his evocation of Wilde—in fact, Proust feelingly conceives of Wilde as signifying the most poignant example, at once exemplum and leader (in Marcel's eyes), of an entire "race." In the *roman fleuve* ("river-novel") that comprises *À la recherche du temps perdu,* the sentence invoking Wilde offers the greatest *fleuve* of all.

The passage, amounting to 1,858 words, is generated by Marcel's attempt at characterizing the Baron de Charlus's sexuality, likening it to that of a "race of beings, less contradictory than they appear to be, whose ideal is virile because their temperament is virile" and describing them as inevitably drawn to men who are not "inverts." There then follows a lengthy meditation on this "race" or "freemasonry" of secretive men who are loathed by society: what Lucey terms, in a discussion of similar passages in *Sodom et Gomorrhe,* a "pseudo-sociological digression" (*Never Say I,* 221). Proust's sentence (from the 2004 translation by John Sturrock) is as follows:

> Their only honor is precarious, their only liberty provisional until the crime be discovered; their only position unstable, as for the poet who was yesterday being fêted in every drawing-room and applauded in every theater in London, only to be driven on the morrow from every lodging-house, unable to find a pillow on which to lay his head, turning the millstone like Samson and saying, like him, "The two sexes will die each on its own side," excluded even, save at times of high misfortune, when the majority rally around the victim, like the Jews around Dreyfus, from the sympathy—sometimes from the company— of their own kind, who are disgusted to be made to see themselves as they are, depicted in a mirror that no longer flatters them but brings out all the blemishes that they had not wanted to remark in themselves and makes them understand that what they had been calling their love (to which, by playing on the word, they had annexed, out of a social sense, all that poetry, painting, music, chivalry, and asceticism have been able to add to love) stems not from an ideal of beauty that they have chosen, but from an incurable malady; like the Jews once again (save those few who wish to associate only with those of their own race, and who have the ritual words and hallowed jokes constantly on their lips), shunning one another, seeking out those who are the most opposed to themselves, who want nothing to do with them, forgiving when rebuffed, elated when indulged; yet also brought together with their own kind

by the ostracism that afflicts them, the opprobrium into which they have fallen, having finally acquired, by a persecution similar to that of Israel, the physical and moral characteristics of a race, sometimes beautiful, often ghastly, finding (despite all the ridicule that he who mixes more with and is better assimilated to the opposing race, and is relatively, on the surface, less inverted, heaps on him who has remained more so) relief in the frequentation of their own kind, a support even in their existence, so that, while denying that they are a race (the name of which is the gravest insult), they willingly unmask those who succeed in concealing that they belong to it, less in order to hurt them, to which they have no objection, than to excuse themselves, and going in search, like a doctor of appendicitis, of inversion, even in history, taking pleasure in reminding you that Socrates was one of them, just as the Israelites tell you that Jesus was a Jew, without reflecting that no one was abnormal when homosexuality was the norm, and no one anti-Christian before Christ, that opprobrium alone makes the crime, for it has allowed to survive only those who were recalcitrant to all preaching, all example, all punishment, by virtue of an innate disposition so special that it repels other men more (even though it may be accompanied by lofty moral qualities) than certain vices that contradict it, such as theft, cruelty, or bad faith, which are better understood and thus more readily excused by the common run of men; forming a freemasonry far more extensive, more effective, and less suspected than that of the lodges, for it rests on an identity of tastes, of needs, of habits, of dangers, of apprenticeship, of knowledge, of commerce and of vocabulary, in which even the members who do not wish to know one another at once recognize one another by natural or conventional signs, whether involuntary or deliberate, which indicate to the beggar one of his own kind in the great nobleman whose carriage door is closing, to the father in his daughter's fiancé, to the man who had wanted to be cured, or to confess, or to be defended, in the doctor or the priest or the lawyer of whom he has gone in search; all of them obliged to protect their secret, yet having their share in a secret of others which the rest of humanity does not suspect, and which means that for them the most improbable cloak-and-dagger stories seem true; for in this fabulous, anachronistic life, the ambassador is friends with the convict; the prince, with a certain freedom of manner lent him by his aristocratic upbringing, which no fearful petty bourgeois could have, when he comes out from the duchess, goes off to confer with the ruffian, a reprobate version of the human collectivity, but a significant portion, suspected in places where it is not, flaunted, insolent, unpunished in places where it goes undetected; numbering adherents everywhere, among the common people, in the army, in the temple, in prison, on the throne; living, finally, a great number of them at least, in a

Richard A. Kaye

dangerous, caressing intimacy with the men of the other race, provoking them, playing with them by speaking of their vice as if it were not theirs, a game made easy by the blindness or falseness of the others, a game that may be prolonged for years, up until the day of the scandal when these animal-tamers are devoured; obliged until then to keep their lives hidden, to avert their gaze from where they would like to be fixing it, to fix their gaze on what they would like to avert it from, to change the gender of many of the adjectives in their vocabulary, a small social constraint compared with the inner restraint that their vice, or what is improperly so called, imposes on them, in respect no longer of others but of themselves, and in such a way that it does not appear to them to be a vice.[28]

This sentence is a richly meaningful plentitude: an extravagantly protracted meditation on homosexual persecution, an eruption of sympathetic emotion into verbal logorrhea at the injustice of maltreatment of "inverts," a panoramic evocation of persecution of homosexuals across classes and throughout epochs of history. What is initially striking in this essayistic passage is Proust's cognizance, through Marcel's voice, of the unnamed Wilde as a pivotal, emblematic figure in the history of same-sex eroticism. That Wilde is tacitly evoked along with Jesus and Dreyfus adds to a sense of the playwright's magnitude as a monumental historical figure, although, to be sure, Marcel's reluctance to identify Wilde by name is itself a secrecy-enforcing excess of protective tact that duplicates the socially mandated repressions that the passage otherwise laments. (Although, as Emily Eells discovered while preparing an edition of *Sodom et Gomorrhe*, Proust originally cited Wilde by name in his working notes for this passage but then deleted Wilde's name in the published version of the novel.[29]) Arguably, Wilde continues to reappear in the sentence after his initial appearance, since the reference to "a game that may be kept up for years until the day of the scandal" may be an allusion to the writer's celebrity status followed by public opprobrium, just as the reference to the man who leaves a duchess's party to associate with a "ruffian" evokes the specific, damning revelations of Wilde's last trial, in which telegraph boys exposed the playwright's fondness for working-class men.

Moreover, in Proust's sentence, Wilde functions not only as an initial, focused moment in Marcel's baffled understanding of a "homosexual race" but also as a dominant case of universal homosexual maltreatment. The case of Wilde does not merely appear to generate the multiple insights of Marcel's unbroken sentence;

Wilde also emerges as an inadvertent builder of a certain kind of community of "inverts" who rally around their unjustly convicted "leader" (as the Jews here are said to have rallied around the unjustly convicted Dreyfus). Indeed, the sentence approximates a syntactic embodiment of Wilde's influence as a heroic martyr of biblical authority who, through his suffering, organizes a self-conscious if scattered community of inverts, for whom Wilde represents a recurrently influential figure. In a sense, Marcel needs Wilde to inaugurate and organize the disparately composed "race" of inverts that his meditation conjures up—men who, like Wilde, have the unique ability to cross class and professional barriers in a playful game of "perilous intimacy." In answer to the obvious question of why Proust requires such an extravagantly protracted sentence of multiple subordinate clauses (as opposed, say, to several sentences), one might respond that this sentence contains in a single whole the vast community of "inverts" whose history, characteristics, and fortunes it taxonomizes. Marcel, like Wilde, creates a "freemasonry" of homosexual men, linked by a common "taste," through a syntactic accommodation of their largely secret history. And this "race" of men harbors something in addition to a history: one finds in this passage, with its reference to "an identity of tastes, of needs, of habits, of dangers, of apprenticeship, of knowledge, of commerce, and of vocabulary," a conception of a richly coded homosexual subculture, one that has "annexed, out of a social sense, all that poetry, painting, music, chivalry, and asceticism have been able to add to love." Lest one think that this subcultural entity actually rests on or is given a foundational unity in a philosophy of aestheticism, the narrator concludes that this coterie may believe it is searching for an ideal of beauty but in fact is linked by a shared "malady." Indeed, the rousing movement of this sentence—in which inverts are initially described in negative terms as lacking honor but then in the last words gain a kind of agency as they see their affliction as not a vice—is somewhat undermined by the simple eroticism of their bond. Writing only of the first part of this sentence, Leo Bersani has marveled that "[w]e might almost see here a Queer Nation poised for revolution—even though these improbable comrades don't share a faith or an ideology, only a desire."[30] Bersani goes on to note that in Proust "the person disappears in his or her desire, a desire that seeks more of the same, partially dissolving subjects into a communal homo-ness."

Beyond Marcel's dream of communal cohesion, a striking aspect of the passage is its implicit positing of disparate and even contradictory theories of homosexuality. The heterosexually identified, often voyeuristic Marcel, tempera-

Richard A. Kaye

mentally incapable of adopting a single explanation for homosexuality, seems to flail about for a sustaining theory for same-sex desire, variously conceiving of it as a taste, a malady, a secret club, a racial category with the immutable characteristics of a race, a vice, a sin—no, none of these, or perhaps all of these. Undoubtedly, the most outlandish of Marcel's graspings at causalities is his analogical conceit that homosexuals have the "physical and moral" attributes of a "race" like the Jewish "race." Of course, the notion that Jews comprise a racial group is a staple of anti-Semitic thinking regarding what in fact is a religious or ethnic affiliation, no less so now than in the period in which Proust was writing *Sodom et Gomorrhe.* Yet with a rapid adjustment that suggests the searching processes not so much of consciousness as of deliberate mental reflection, the passage that begins with the unquestioning use of the term *crime* concludes with the comment that what inverts call "their vice" in actuality "does not appear to them a vice." By ultimately not construing homosexuality in legal or moral terms, Marcel thus helps to legitimize a new scientific vocabulary in the understanding of what was formerly moralistically or criminally understood. Further, Marcel offers shrewdly perceptive observations, such as his notion that in other historical epochs, such as classical Greece, what the nineteenth century would term "abnormal" was in fact socially normative, thus rendering the modern-day homosexual's search for historical "role models" a meaningless adventure. Homosexuality, as it is understood by Marcel's contemporaries, is at heart anachronistic, according to Marcel, for although it is a malady it is also a "fabulous," democratizing one, which allows a "prince" to become friends with a "convict."

If the sentence has a theme or argument, it would seem to be that there are two oppressions afflicting the male homosexual, that of a punitive society that will not allow him to express his desires and—more important for Marcel, given the way this becomes the primary thrust of the last third of the sentence—that of the secretly homosexual man who engages in a game in which he torments his fellow homosexuals. There is, in fact, a sort of psychological theory embedded in the passage, in which the despising of homosexuality stems from the need to punish one's homosexual brethren. In an important sense, then, Proust's protean sentence functions as a kind of microcosm of *Sodom et Gomorrhe,* in which the nature of homosexuality shifts wildly. (That the passage is central to the whole of *Sodom et Gomorrhe* is suggested by the fact that the poem by Alfred de Vigny, "La colère de Samson," that Proust is quoting when he writes that "[t]he two sexes shall die each on its own side" also contains the line that was the inspiration for the title of Proust's volume: "Soon withdrawing into a hideous kingdom, / Woman will have Gomorrah and Man will have Sodom.")[31] Yet it is the nameless ghost of the "poet" Wilde that functions as a true focus and cause in the sentence —a sentence that always verges on an endlessness that the tantalizing problem of homosexuality here seems to require. In Proust's *Sodom et Gomorrhe*, then, we can see the culmination of a process in the decades after the playwright's death whereby Wilde emerges as a thoroughly secularized figure, yet one who serves the same role as that of a cult-generating, glorified Christian hero.

Wilde's New Martyrologies

Although I have been focusing on Wilde's posthumous role as "homosexual saint" and "martyr," the discourse of sometimes-martyrdom floats free of specific issues of sexuality as new roles emerge for Wilde. In a recent history of youth culture, Jon Savage, while not exactly declaring Wilde a martyr for teen culture, nonetheless sees him as having a suprahistorical importance in the birth of youth rebellion, hyperbolically noting that the "verdict of his trial stopped British modernism in its tracks."[32] For Savage, Wilde is the original patron saint of teenage group consciousness and, especially through the figure of Dorian Gray, of several generations of diverse teen cults. Such cults, argues Savage, encompass such highly disciplined organizations as the Boy Scouts and Hitler Youth and culminate in the antiestablishmentarian 1950s Beatniks and in matinee idols such as James Dean.

None of these newly conceived roles for Wilde is more prominent—or difficult to sustain—than the conception of Wilde as a martyr for Ireland. To be sure, recent critics have successfully explored Wilde's complex relation to Irish nationalism—most notably, Vicky Mahaffey, who convincingly argues that the writer's experimental style was forged out of a struggle with an Irish national heritage.[33] In a more recent study, A. N. Wilson links Wilde with the Irish nationalist hero Roger Casement, noting that "Casement died, liked that other vilified Irish Protestant homosexual, Oscar Wilde, having been received into the Roman Catholic Church."[34] But the idea of Wilde as an unacknowledged martyr for the cause of nationalist Ireland is a fairly recent notion. Nowhere is this connection more elaborated on than in the critic Terry Eagleton's play *Saint Oscar*, first performed in 1989 by the Field Day Theatre Company in Derry and starring Stephen Rae in the title role. In his introduction to the published version of the

Richard A. Kaye

play, Eagleton declares, with blunt swagger, that he has chosen to "avoid writing a 'gay' play about Wilde because as a heterosexual I am inevitably something of an outsider in such matters," adding that "Wilde was perverse in much more than a sexual sense."[35] Whatever Eagleton may mean by a "gay play," his *Saint Oscar* moralizes quite energetically about Wilde's sexuality. With the performance reproducing a large image of a St. Sebastian by Guido Reni, which Wilde admired in "The Grave of Keats," as a backdrop, the drama depicts Wilde as suffering a series of reprimands, all of them curiously approximate to Eagleton's notion of Wilde as an apolitical aesthete. Moreover, Eagleton imagines Wilde as a slave to his ungovernable erotic urges, masochistically drawn to Douglas. Early in the play, Wilde remarks of Douglas (known in the drama by his nickname, Bosie), "One flash of his eyes, or better still his thighs, and I fall instantly to appreciating his finer points. Hard though they are to remember. I love him as the torturer's victim loves the knife that will put him out of his agony; as Saint Sebastian loved the arrows" (19). In *Saint Oscar,* Eagleton fashions not only a masochistic Wilde but also an ideal hunk-cum-executioner in Douglas. Martyrdom as deliberate sexual self-torture is integral to Eagleton's conception of Wilde, at the same time that the playwright emerges as a would-be saint for Ireland. Yet no cause other than self-advancement animates Eagleton's Wilde. We are asked to believe that the author of "The Soul of Man under Socialism," when told by a friend that the police have severely beaten citizens at a Trafalgar Square protest, would respond with a cold joke about disliking the "naturalistic" setting of the square. Ultimately, Wilde is here martyred to Eagleton's strained conception of him as a sex-obsessed decadent and therefore failed political radical.

Despite its failure to imagine Wilde as both aesthete and socialist, as a sexual radical alert to the economic inequities of his time, Eagleton's *Saint Oscar* does highlight the historical shift in the representation of martyrdom, whereby the role of exemplary sufferer is increasingly construed as one that veils deep psychic compulsions. As we have seen, martyrdom as a metaphor for Wilde's life, although especially efficacious in helping to present the writer as a community-building activist, has its limits, particularly when such representations duplicate banal psychological conceptions.[36] For, as I have suggested, beginning in Wilde's own time, martyrdom increasingly came to accrue a set of negative psychic associations, in which exemplary self-sacrifice emerges as a death-courting impulse. Such associations draw strength from what is arguably one of Freud's least persuasive theoretical contentions—that humans are composed of various "drives," the death drive chief among them, which relentlessly draw them into particular psychic and sexual trajectories. Such negative associations of martyrdom have continued to become entangled with conservative conceptions of homosexual desire, in which same-sex preferences must inevitably lead to a self-willed isolation and morbidity.

That Wilde may have courted, even as he sometimes resisted, the role of martyr is entertained in one of the more brilliant works to reimagine him and his life. Peter Ackroyd's *Last Testament of Oscar Wilde* (1983), which takes the form of a diary that Wilde might have written in the last days of his life, makes a point of Wilde's deliberate self-fashioning as a Christian saint. Early in the novel, Wilde recalls his school days:

> It was then that I learned the first secret of the imagination: an amusing fantasy had more reality than a commonplace truth. And another secret was revealed to me also: I made them laugh, and then they could not hurt me. Although like all children they found their greatest pleasure in vulgar sarcasm —they called me "Grey Cow" because of the pallor of my skin—I would draw the sting from that sarcasm by becoming more extravagant than they could possibly have foreseen. I would twist my limbs into the contorted attitudes of Christian martyrs depicted on the windows of the chapel—unfortunately, I seem to be in the same position now—and they were amused.[37]

This sense of martyrdom as a potentially useful act, deliberately performed before an audience of peers (and, through laughter, potential followers), comically upends a commonplace tradition in which Wilde is seen either as self-destructively welcoming his misfortunes or as the passive vector of social opprobrium. It is the fantasy of martyrdom that Ackroyd's Wilde embraces, one that becomes ironically "unfortunate" when he finds himself a symbolic outcast in his last days. It is a fantasy, as well, that may suggest the exhaustion of the martyr role in the representation of Oscar Wilde's fate. As we enter a new century of Wilde-worship, we may want to entertain other fantasies to evoke Wilde's claim on our imaginations.

Notes

1. Hugo von Hofmannsthal, "Sebastian Melmoth," in *Selected Prose,* trans. Mary Hottinger, Tania Stern, and James Stern (New York: Pantheon Books, 1952), 303; further page references appear in parentheses.

Richard A. Kaye

2. Octave Mirbeau, "À propos de 'Hard Labor,'" *Le journal*, 16 June 1895, reprinted in *Pour Oscar Wilde* (Rouen: Elizabeth Bruner, Libraire à Rouen, Association des Amis d'Hugnes Rebell, 1994), 45 (my translation).

3. Mrs. Havelock Ellis [Edith Lees Ellis], "Eugenics and the Mystical Outlook" (1911), in *Nineteenth-Century Writings on Homosexuality*, ed. Chris White (London: Routledge, 1999), 114.

4. Arthur Ransome, *Oscar Wilde: A Critical Study*, 2nd ed. (London: Methuen, 1913), 23; further page reference appears in parentheses.

5. *Teleny: A Novel Attributed to Oscar Wilde*, ed. Winston Leyland (1893; repr., San Francisco, CA: Gay Sunshine Press, 1984), 5.

6. Jean-Martin Charcot, *La foi qui guérit* (1885; repr., Paris: Félix Alcan, 1897).

7. Sigmund Freud, *The Future of an Illusion*, trans. James Strachey (1927; repr., New York: Norton, 1961), 53.

8. Sigmund Freud, "The Economic Problem in Masochism" (1924), in *General Psychological Theory: Papers on Metapsychology*, trans. James Strachey (New York: Collier Books, 1963), 190–201.

9. Max Nordau, *Degeneration* (1892; repr., Lincoln: University of Nebraska Press, 1993).

10. Cited in Pierre Michel and Jean-Francois Nivet, *Octave Mirbeau: L'imprécateur au cœur fidèle* (Paris: Séguier, 1990), 124. Wilde's comments on the novel, which he calls *Le jardin des supplices*, appear in a letter to Frank Harris from late May 1899, in Wilde, *The Complete Letters*, ed. Merlin Holland and Rupert Hart-Davis (London: Fourth Estate, 2000), 1146.

11. John S. Hawley, introduction to *Saints and Virtues*, ed. John Stratton Hawley (Berkeley: University of California Press, 1987), xi–xxiv.

12. Sigmund Freud, *Beyond the Pleasure Principle*, in *The Standard Edition of the Collected Psychological Works of Sigmund Freud*, ed. James Strachey, 24 vols. (London: Hogarth Press, 1953–74), 18:38.

13. Michael Lucey, *Never Say I: Sexuality and the First Person in Colette, Gide, and Proust* (Durham, NC: Duke University Press, 2006), 202.

14. Neil McKenna, *The Secret Life of Oscar Wilde* (London: Century, 2003), 465; the later quotation also appears on this page.

15. Wilde to Frances Forbes-Robertson, mid-May 1899, *Complete Letters*, 1145.

16. Wilde sent a copy of "The Grave of Keats" to Lord Houghton, whose edition of Keats's *Life and Letters* appeared in 1848. In the letter enclosed with his poem, Wilde states, "Someway standing by his grave I felt that he *too* was a Martyr, and worthy to lie in the City of Martyrs. I thought of him as a Priest of Beauty slain before his time, a lovely Sebastian killed by the arrows of a lying and unjust tongue." Wilde to Lord Houghton, c. 17 May 1877, *Complete Letters*, 49.

17. John Addington Symonds, *Renaissance in Italy* (7 vols.), vol. 3, *The Fine Arts* (London: Smith, Elder, 1887), 501.

18. Numerous writers also focused on Sebastian's close relation to the emperor Diocletian, a relation that even the Catholic Church's Acta-Sanctorum stressed as intimate, with its comment that Sebastian was "dearly beloved by the Emperors Diocletian and Maximian." That he was once a saint invoked against the plague during medieval times helped determine his position as a signifier of same-sex eros at a historical moment when such desires were being defined medically. Crucial too, was the ambiguity of Sebastian's position, his evident delight in his arrow-besieged fate and in his isolation. Unlike earlier Classical and biblical "myths" of homoerotic desire familiar to Victorians—Zeus and Ganymede, Damon and Pythias, Hadrian and Antinous, Jonathan and David (all reducible to romances)—Sebastian's archetypal pose was as a Romantic icon, an image of radical isolationism, that hinted at an irretrievable homoerotic identity. Julia

Kristeva has suggestively attempted to discern in Sebastian an erotico-existential quality by conjuring up the neologistic category of the "soulosexual"—a man, she writes, who "will undergo martyrdom in order to maintain the fantasy that there exists a power, as well as its masochistic obverse, pacification, total 'feminization.'" Kristeva, *Tales of Love*, trans. Leon S. Roudie (New York: Columbia University Press, 1987), 78. For a discussion of St. Sebastian's role in nineteenth-century culture, see Richard A. Kaye, "'Determined Raptures': St. Sebastian and the Victorian Discourse of Decadence," *Victorian Literature and Culture* 27 (1999): 269–303.

19. Hofmannsthal, "Book of Friends," in *Selected Prose*, 349–74.

20. The sobriquet "Sebastian Melmoth" referred to one of Wilde's favorite novels, *Melmoth the Wanderer* (1820), written by Wilde's great-uncle, Charles Marturin, and simultaneously evoked the saint whose appeal to the playwright was lifelong and powerful.

21. Richard Dellamora, *Masculine Desire: The Sexual Politics of Victorian Aestheticism* (Chapel Hill: University of North Carolina Press, 1990).

22. Wilde to Frank Harris, late May 1899, *Complete Letters*, 1146.

23. Octave Mirbeau, *Sebastien Roch*, trans. Nicoletta Simborowski (1890; repr., London: Dedalus, 2000), 33; further page references appear in parentheses.

24. Octave Mirbeau, *The Diary of a Chambermaid*, trans. Anon. (New York: HarperCollins, 2006); further page references appear in parentheses.

25. Octave Mirbeau, "Sur un livre," *Le journal*, 6 July 1895, reprinted in *Pour Oscar Wilde*, 52.

26. George Painter, *Proust: The Early Years* (Boston: Little Brown, 1959), 209; Jean-Yves Tadié, *Marcel Proust* (New York: Viking, 1996), 124.

27. Lucey, *Never Say I*, 205; further page references appear in parentheses.

28. Marcel Proust, *Sodom and Gomorrah*, trans. John Sturrock (London: Allen Lane, 2002), 17–19.

29. Emily Eells, *Proust's Cup of Tea: Homoeroticism and Victorian Culture* (Burlington: Ashgate, 2002), 80.

30. Leo Bersani, *Homos* (Cambridge, MA: Harvard University Press, 1995), 149; the later quotation also appears on this page.

31. "Bientôt, se retirant dans un hideux royaume, / La Femme aura Gomorrhe et l'Homme aura Sodome." Alfred de Vigny, "The Anger of Samson," in *Les destinées* (Paris: Société d'Edition d'Enseignement Supérieur, 1964), 86.

32. Jon Savage, *Teenage: The Creation of Youth Culture* (New York: Viking, 2007), 30.

33. Vicki Mahaffey, *States of Desire: Wilde, Yeats, Joyce and the Irish Experiment* (Oxford: Oxford University Press, 1998).

34. A. N. Wilson, *After the Victorians: The Decline of Britain in the World* (New York: Farrar Straus and Giroux, 2005), 112.

35. Terry Eagleton, *Saint Oscar* (Derry: Field Day, 1989), xi; further page references appear in parentheses. See also chapter 10 of the present volume.

36. For an extended critique of conservative psycho-biographical approaches to Wilde, see Richard A. Kaye, "Gay Studies, Queer Theory, and Oscar Wilde," in *Palgrave Advances in Oscar Wilde Studies*, ed. Frederick S. Roden (Basingstoke, UK: Palgrave, 2004), 189–223.

37. Peter Ackroyd, *The Last Testament of Oscar Wilde* (New York: Harper and Row, 1983), 24.

Richard A. Kaye

The Trouble with Oskar

*Wilde's Legacy for the Early Homosexual
Rights Movement in Germany*

YVONNE IVORY

> For a long time in Germany Oskar Wilde was nothing more than an advertisement for homosexuality. Then, after his death, his books came into fashion. Hysterical women let their nerves be whipped raw by the sadistic atmosphere of *Salomé*; young men and women paraded their sparkling Wildean paradoxes like rings or brooches; ... the name Wilde even made the very passion for which the poet was locked up seem respectable. Now I do not want to do Wilde an injustice, but in the face of such fatuous raptures someone needs to say for once and for all what he was really about, this poser whom I hate, and yet love.
>
> —Peter Hamecher, "Gegen Oskar Wilde"

A CT 2 OF Oscar Wilde's *The Importance of Being Earnest* (1895) opens on a
scene of Cecily Cardew watering flowers. She is called to task by her governess, Miss Prism, for wasting her time on such a "utilitarian occupation," especially when the "intellectual pleasures" of German grammar await her:

> CECILY. But I don't like German. It isn't at all a becoming language. I know
> very well that I look quite plain after my German lesson.
> MISS PRISM. Child, you know how anxious your guardian is that you should
> improve yourself in every way. He laid particular stress on your German,
> as he was leaving for town yesterday. Indeed, he always lays stress on your
> German when he is leaving for town. (*CW*, 6:67–68)

For Cecily as for her guardian, Jack Worthing, the German language clearly represents everything that is the opposite of beauty and pleasure: it is a source of plainness in women, can be enjoyed only by the likes of the spinsterish Miss Prism, and guarantees that a young woman will not be led into any kind of temptation. We can catch a glimpse of Wilde's attitude toward the language in these lines: he may have had a German governess as a young boy, two parents who were fluent in the language, and a great admiration for certain German philosophers and writers, but he was never as enthusiastic about German as he was about French.[1] His German was certainly "competent" when he was a young man, but he neglected it as he grew older.[2] Only when he was a prisoner in Reading Gaol did he take up German once again, finding "a good mental tonic" in the study of "a language one had forgotten."[3] Echoing Cecily's assessment of the language, he writes in November 1896 to Robert Ross, "I am going to take up the study of German: indeed *this* seems to be the proper place for such a study" (*Complete Letters*, 669; emphasis added).

Wilde not only associated the German language with austerity and penance but also found its country of origin less than charming. We can be sure of only two trips that he ever made to Germany: he briefly visited Bad Kreuznach in July 1889, and he spent several weeks in Homburg in July 1892, "taking the waters" —as he told William Archer—with Lord Alfred Douglas (*Complete Letters*, 534).[4] On the first occasion, he wrote to Ross, "I am actually in Germany! I had an invitation to come here . . . and I thought it would be a superb opportunity for forgetting the language. . . . The Rhine is of course tedious, the vineyards are formal and dull, and as far as I can judge, the inhabitants of Germany are American" (*Complete Letters*, 409). On the second occasion, when he took the rest-cure, he sent a postcard to the French poet Pierre Louÿs, complaining of being hugely bored and "*horriblement triste*" at having had five doctors force him to give up smoking (*Complete Letters*, 530).

Given Wilde's boredom with all things German, his distaste for Germany, and his eagerness to forget the German language, it is ironic that the German-speaking world was where his name and reputation, tarnished by the scandal of 1895, would first be remembered and even redeemed. There his wife, Constance, would find refuge with their children after having fled England,[5] and there his works would begin again to command respect and—more important for his executor, Ross—significant receipts.[6] For at the dawn of the twentieth century, while Oscar Wilde was still something of a pariah in England, he was the subject of an extraordinary renaissance in the German-speaking world. Between 1901 and 1906, works pulled from the shelves of London booksellers many years earlier were translated into German at a prodigious rate; his plays—especially *Salomé* —became required viewing on the stages of Berlin, Munich, and Vienna; and journalists—when not writing biographical pieces about the misunderstood "Englishman"—struggled to keep current their reviews of all this output.

Scholars have often placed this early German Wilde revival firmly in the context of contemporary nationalist debates between Britain and Germany, arguing that Wilde was merely a convenient figure for Germans who wished to portray theirs as the more enlightened society.[7] Other researchers have focused on the quality of the early translations or on Wilde's reception among contemporary artists and writers in the German-speaking world.[8] But a significant aspect of Wilde's rich afterlife in Germany has been neglected by critics: his legacy for the early homosexual rights movement.

The trials of 1895, a watershed year, ushered in an entirely new moment in the history of homosexual rights in Germany. Yet the Wilde who became notorious in 1895 embodied ideas that were already percolating in emancipatory—especially anarchic-individualistic—discourses on sexuality in the early 1890s. In this regard, Wilde facilitated continuities rather than signaled ruptures in the history of homosexuality in Germany. Finally, these two tendencies for the most part line up with the two most important—and often clashing—blocs of the homosexual rights movement: Magnus Hirschfeld's Scientific-Humanitarian Committee and Adolf Brand's Gemeinschaft der Eigenen (Community of the Self-Owners).[9] In their treatment of Wilde, the two movements made public their ideological differences; Wilde's being championed by the former group ultimately led to his being rejected by the latter—by the very organization, ironically, whose ideas best reflected his own philosophy.

Wilde's Early Reception in Austria and Germany

It is generally accepted that Max Nordau, a Hungarian-born physician and influential Zionist, was the first author to write extensively about Wilde for the German-speaking world.[10] His 1892 study *Entartung* (Degeneration) contains a section on Wilde in which he condemns the Irishman as an egomaniac and Wilde's aesthetic agenda as degenerate—as morally insane.[11] A more reasoned discussion of Wilde's oeuvre can be found in the influential 1894 essay "Decadence" by Hermann Bahr, the renowned Austrian publisher and literary critic.[12] Although Bahr might be seen to be contributing to the thrust of Nordau's argument when he categorizes Wilde as the English Robert de Montesquiou,[13] he does not condemn Wilde in the same manner as Nordau does. In his memoirs he would even go so far as to praise "Wilde's magnificent 'Soul of Man under Socialism' [1891], which quite simply and quite completely expresses our most fundamental principles—it stands as the powerful creed of an entire generation."[14] Ultimately, Bahr was responsible for popularizing Wilde's work among Austrian intellectuals, recommending *Intentions* (1891) to his friends Hugo von Hofmannsthal and Leopold Andrian, for instance, and publishing "The Decay of Lying" ("Der Verfall des Lügens") in his journal *Die Zeit*.[15]

"The Decay of Lying" (1889, revised 1891), which appeared in the same issue of *Die Zeit* as Bahr's "Decadence" essay, was the first work by Wilde ever to be published in German.[16] Before this, only a single aphorism by Wilde (a quip on art and anarchism) had appeared in German.[17] Surprisingly few of Wilde's works were translated into German while he was alive: the aphorism in 1893; "The Decay of Lying" in 1894; and in 1897, the preface to *Dorian Gray*—published as aphorisms on art—and an extract from "The Soul of Man under Socialism."[18] That same year, *The Canterville Ghost* appeared as an illustrated book—possibly the first of Wilde's works to be printed without concealment of the author's name following the 1895 scandal.[19] Finally, in 1900, German periodical readers could enjoy "The Truth of Masks" (1885, revised 1891), "The Selfish Giant" (1888), *Salomé* (1892), and excerpts from *The Ballad of Reading Gaol* (1898).[20]

Hedwig Lachmann's translation of *Salomé,* which was printed in the *Wiener Rundschau* with reproductions of two of Aubrey Beardsley's illustrations from the 1894 English edition, was a critical success.[21] Within months of its appearance, private performances of the play took place in Munich and Breslau.[22] The following year, on 15 November 1902, an invitation-only performance took place in Berlin's Kleines Theater under the direction of a twenty-nine-year-old Max Reinhardt, and this performance is considered by theater historians to be the play's true German premiere. In the audience sat composer Richard Strauss, giant of German letters Stefan George, and the most influential German theater critic of the early twentieth century, Alfred Kerr.[23] As Max Meyerfeld put it in his 1903 essay "Oscar Wilde in Deutschland," "as ridiculous as this may sound, it was on this afternoon that Oscar Wilde was really *discovered* in the capital of the German Empire."[24]

A veritable "Salomania" took hold of the German-speaking world in 1903, an obsession that was stoked by Strauss's 1905 operatic reworking of Wilde's play.[25] Robert Ross would later reflect on the period:

> In 1901, within a year of the author's death, [*Salomé*] was produced in Berlin; from that moment it has held the European stage. It has run for a longer consecutive period in Germany than any play by any Englishman, not excepting Shakespeare.... During May 1905 the play was produced in England for the first time.... My friends the dramatic critics ... fell on *Salomé* with ... vigour.... Unaware of what was taking place in Germany, they spoke of the play as having been "dragged from obscurity." The Official Receiver in Bankruptcy and myself were, however, better informed. And much pleasure has been derived from reading those criticisms, all carefully preserved along with the list of receipts which were simultaneously pouring in from the German performances.[26]

Salomé, then, was at the heart of the Wilde revival in Germany. In its wake, and in the wake of Wilde's death, came translations of *The Picture of Dorian Gray* (1890, revised 1891), the society comedies, the fairy tales, and the short stories. Whereas there had been only a handful of longer articles about Wilde in German-language periodicals and newspapers throughout the 1890s (his trial and conviction had been widely reported but for the most part only in short news bulletins), between 1902 and 1906 Wilde's name was everywhere.[27] Even if we rely on the flawed count of the German periodicals index of the day, the man who had inspired no articles in 1896 was the subject of twenty-two in 1903.[28] Indeed, several of Wilde's works appeared during these years in German before they had ever been published in English. In his introduction to the excerpts of "Epistola: In Carcere et Vinculis" (Letter: In Prison and in Chains) that appeared in *Die neue Rundschau* in 1905, Max Meyerfeld claimed that this was the first time Wilde's letter had ever been published; it was accompanied by several other previously unpublished letters that had been written to Ross while Wilde was in prison.[29] Similarly, in 1907, the first edition of *A Florentine Tragedy* (without Thomas Sturge Moore's extra scenes) appeared as "Eine florentinische Tragödie," also in *Die neue Rundschau* and translated by Max Meyerfeld.[30]

Meyerfeld was to the German reception of Wilde in the first decade of the twentieth century what Hermann Bahr had been to the Austrian reception of Wilde in the last decade of the nineteenth. Meyerfeld's excellent command of English and working relationship with Ross gave him broad access to primary materials and a unique perspective on Wilde's work.[31] In the years following his short but important 1903 essay "Oscar Wilde in Deutschland," he published an annual review essay on the previous twelve months' cache of literature in German on and by Wilde.[32] Meyerfeld pulls no punches in these reviews: he scolds Robert Harborough Sherard for including fabrications in his 1902 memoir about Wilde; he criticizes authors for insisting on spelling Oscar with a *k* no matter how often he has told them it should be spelled with a *c;* and he is quick to chide critics for claiming to be Wilde experts when they have done nothing more than read Sherard's unreliable reminiscences or André Gide's memoir.[33]

But he saves his most scathing remarks for Wilde's translators. Franz Blei, Ida and Arthur Roessler, Felix Paul Greve—some of the most important translators of the early twentieth century—are at the receiving end of Meyerfeld's reproofs.[34] They do not appreciate the subtleties of the English language, he complains; Wilde's sophisticated wit is beyond them; and they do not even know enough about Wilde's cultural context to realize that the famous American author was not James Henry but Henry James or that Margaret Oliphant "didn't wear trousers" (Greve had referred to her as "Mr. Oliphani").[35] Only Hedwig Lachmann, the translator of *Salomé;* Else Otten, who worked on *The Ballad of Reading Gaol;* and Gustav Landauer, who collaborated with Lachmann on translating "The Soul of Man," are singled out for praise.[36] One of the worst efforts, for Meyerfeld, is Hermann Freiherr von Teschenberg's rendering of Robert Harborough Sherard's *Oscar Wilde: The Story of an Unhappy Friendship* (1902): "The translation of this volume really ought to be passed over with the silence of the grave, because it sins against the German language; but I feel it my duty to mention it, to say it in a forthright manner to Freiherr von Teschenberg; all the more so, as the director of the Neues Theater clearly found it beneath himself to remove the highly entertaining errors from [von Teschenberg's translation of] *A Woman of No Importance* [1893] or even to clean up the language of that play."[37]

Wilde's Reception among German Homosexuals

Hermann Freiherr von Teschenberg functions as a node connecting Wilde's London circle with what Rainer Kohlmayer has characterized as the German "Homosexuellenmilieu" (circle of homosexuals) that championed Wilde's writings at the turn of the century.[38] An open and practicing homosexual, von Teschenberg had left his native Vienna at the age of twenty to avoid the fallout of a scandal that arose when he was caught kissing a member of the imperial guard in public. He fled to England, where during the early 1890s he appears to have become an acquaintance of Wilde's.[39] Hirschfeld's biographer Charlotte Wolff goes too far, though, when she describes von Teschenberg as a "close friend of Oscar Wilde."[40] He is not mentioned in any of Wilde's letters; and judging by von Teschenberg's short 1903 article "Memories of Oscar Wilde," their friendship was far from intimate.[41] The reminiscence comprises only two vignettes of Wilde, both of which are written from the point of view of a distant observer. In the first, von Teschenberg describes Wilde entertaining guests at a party before his fall; in the second— which plagiarizes an earlier piece by Eugen Wilhelm—von Teschenberg tells of how he watched Wilde, now "dead to the world," walking through the Coliseum in Rome.[42] That von Teschenberg exaggerated his connections to Wilde is also clear from Hirschfeld's 1911 eulogy, in which he claimed that his late friend had personally tried to mediate between Wilde and the Marquess of Queensberry in 1895 and had "tried—with little success, sadly—to secure a more just sentence for the unlucky poet."[43]

Upon his return to Germany in 1898, von Teschenberg became one of the most active members of Hirschfeld's Scientific-Humanitarian Committee, the organization founded in 1897 to enlighten the public about homosexuality and to lobby for the lifting of §175 (Paragraph 175), the law that banned sexual relations between men in Imperial Germany.[44] He was one of the few men willing to publicly acknowledge his homosexuality, and he was often engaged to speak about his "case."[45] When Hirschfeld was working on a study of *Tranvestiten* (transvestites), von Teschenberg made available for publication a photograph of himself in drag (fig. 18), which he wanted to see appear in print alongside his full name, claiming that the image revealed his "true nature."[46] He was, in short, one of the most visible homosexuals in turn-of-the-century Berlin.

By the time of his death in 1911, von Teschenberg had translated not only Sherard's book and *A Woman of No Importance* but also *The Importance of Being Earnest, An Ideal Husband* (1895), *Lady Windermere's Fan* (1892), and *Salomé* (composed in French in 1892).[47] All of these titles had appeared in Max Spohr Verlag, the Leipzig publishing house that specialized in works dealing with homosexuality.[48] Spohr had published almost all of Wilde's major works by 1903; those not rendered into German by von Teschenberg were translated by Johannes Gaulke, another associate of Hirschfeld's—and another inadequate translator of Wilde, in Max Meyerfeld's opinion.[49] By far the lion's share of Wilde's works

Figure 18. Hermann Freiherr von Teschenberg, a *soi-disant* acquaintance of Oscar Wilde, and one of his early translators into German. Von Teschenberg supplied this photo to Magnus Hirschfeld in the hope that it would help educate the world about the "true nature" of some men. Von Teschenberg's real name was printed alongside the image. (Hirschfeld, *Geschlechtskunde,* 4:624) Courtesy of Schwules Archiv, Berlin.

that appeared in German in the first years of the twentieth century, then, were either translated, published, or illustrated by men with close ties to the homosexual rights movement in general, and to Hirschfeld's committee in particular.[50]

In 1903 Meyerfeld dismissed the efforts of von Teschenberg, Gaulke, and Spohr as the literary equivalent of fast food ("literarischer Schnellbetrieb").[51] He worried about the simple production values used by Spohr in its editions of Wilde: "Once upon a time in London, Wilde's books appeared in magnificent editions. . . . Is it really necessary for them to be clad in the beggar's costume of a green wrapper now that they are in a foreign country?"[52] What he found more troubling, however, was the fact that Max Spohr Verlag was primarily known for its promotion of books that dealt with homosexuality: "I would have thought Wilde had already paid dearly . . . for [his sins.] Is he, even in death, to remain oppressed by the millstone of his past? I don't really know this publishing house, I just know that they specialize in homosexual literature. Do we really have to lock up

Yvonne Ivory

the works of this poor poet in the same cage with all of those psycho-pathological studies?"[53] Two years later, however, Meyerfeld could rejoice in the fact that the Wilde renaissance in Germany had led to Wilde's finally being pried from the clutches of his "debased defenders"—a comment made in response to translator Arthur Roessler's claim that "Wilde mania" was "probably engineered by the committee of organized homosexuals for their own purposes."[54]

Roessler's and Meyerfeld's comments highlight the fact that in the minds of many Germans, Oscar Wilde was inextricably linked with the German homosexual rights movement, just as Spohr's list suggests that the German homosexual rights movement was inextricably linked with Wilde. Historical and autobiographical narratives that deal with the rise of that movement tend to emphasize this link, suggesting causal connections between the Wilde scandal of 1895 and, say, the formation of the Scientific-Humanitarian Committee in 1897 or the appearance of the world's first "gay" magazine, *Der Eigene,* in 1896. A causal relationship can more easily be seen in the case of the committee, largely because the man behind it, Magnus Hirschfeld, later recalled having been inspired by the Wilde trials. Hirschfeld claims that he was driven to found the organization by two equally important factors: the suicide of a patient and the "trial that was at that time under way in England against the poet Oskar Wilde."[55] Those responsible for the Gemeinschaft der Eigenen, in contrast, never acknowledged the role played by the Wilde case in the emergence of their organization, and they went so far as to avoid all mention of his name for a number of years.

Hirschfeld's circle was inspired by Wilde and used his case and his name strategically to publicize the plight of homosexuals. Upon Wilde's conviction, Hirschfeld and his friend Leo Berg publicly protested the author's imprisonment.[56] Shortly thereafter, Hirschfeld set about writing his first defense of same-sex love, *Sappho und Sokrates.* In that text, he uses Wilde's case to argue for legal reform, protesting that "the married man who corrupts his children's governess goes unpunished, just like the countess who has an amorous relationship with her maid. And the brilliant writer Oskar Wilde, who has devoted himself to Lord Alfred Douglas in passionate love, is, on the word of a couple of prostitutes, delivered up to the most severe humiliations and abuses of Wandsworth prison. . . . And all because of a passion which he shares with Socrates, Michel Angelo, and Shakespeare."[57] *Sappho und Sokrates* was published by Max Spohr Verlag in 1896, several months before Hirschfeld founded the Scientific-Humanitarian Committee with Spohr and others.

II. Abrechnung.*)

Für den Fonds zur **Befreiung der Homosexuellen**
gingen bei dem wissenschaftlich-humanitären Comité ein:

1898			Mk.
Febr. 25.	Cassa-Bestand		407.—
März 2.	Spende von S. M. 100 aus Essen a. R.		5.—
„ 21.	„ „ J. R. Forster, Zürich.		
		5 Frcs. =	4.—
„ 30.	„ „ Dorian Gray aus Monte		
		Carlo 100 Frcs. =	·80.—
April 2.	„ „ . P. S. in München . .		10.—
„ 13.	„ „ X. Z. 2285 aus Berlin .		25.—
„ 17.	„ „ E. W. H. in L. . . .		5.—
Mai 10.	„ „ E. O. in H.		1.70
„ 19.	„ „ „Viribus unitis" 20 fl. =		34.—
	„ „ Dorian Gray in Wien		
		30 fl. =	51.—

The committee's initial project was a petition calling for the repeal of §175. This they circulated (perhaps cleverly, in light of the Wilde trials) among prominent writers and artists, many of whom signed it promptly. By the time the committee brought out the first of its *Jahrbücher für sexuelle Zwischenstufen* in 1899, hundreds had signed the petition.[58] These were often prominent individuals who had no personal stake in the repeal of §175 but saw the injustice of the law; they signed their names openly. In this sense, Wilde's fate advanced the cause in Germany. Subscribers to the journal had to be more circumspect, however: the first issue of the *Jahrbuch* lists the names of contributors to the cause alongside the amount of their contribution. While most individuals were content to use simply their initials, some resorted to pseudonyms. In 1899, the pseudonym of choice was "Dorian Gray" (fig. 19).

The use of the fictional dandy's name as a pseudonym points to what is perhaps one of the most obvious legacies left by Wilde for the German homosexuals who followed him: a suggestive moniker that is instantly legible but ultimately functions as an impenetrable mask. "Dorian Gray" and "Oskar Wilde" remained code names well into the twentieth century not only in membership rolls but also in personal ads (fig. 20);[59] in the 1920s, advertisements appeared regularly in the gay press for one of Berlin's first and most popular gay bars, the "Dorian Gray Café."[60]

The publishing agenda and success of Max Spohr; the petition against §175 and the strategies used to circulate it; the founding of the Scientific-Humanitarian

Yvonne Ivory

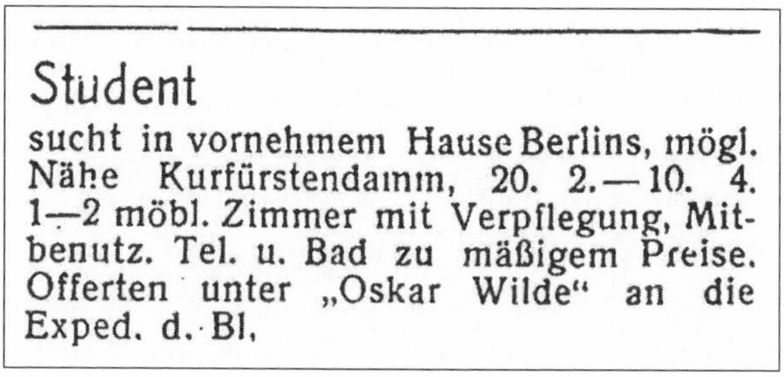

Student
sucht in vornehmem Hause Berlins, mögl. Nähe Kurfürstendamm, 20. 2.—10. 4. 1—2 möbl. Zimmer mit Verpflegung, Mitbenutz. Tel. u. Bad zu mäßigem Preise. Offerten unter „Oskar Wilde“ an die Exped. d. Bl.

Figure 20. A personal ad from *Der Eigene* in which the code word "Oskar Wilde" is used by a student looking for lodgings in Berlin. (*Der Eigene* 7, no. 11 [1920]: 8. Courtesy of Schwules Archiv, Berlin.

Committee; the writing and publication of *Sappho und Sokrates;* the appearance of the *Jahrbuch für sexuelle Zwischenstufen;* the emergence of homosexual Dorian Grays all over Germany—these are phenomena that are difficult to imagine without the precedent of the Wilde scandal. But while Wilde must be recognized as the inspiration for certain events that were to define the early German homosexual rights movement, his case can also be said simply to continue a discussion already in progress among German radical individualists regarding freedom of sexual expression. German portrayals of Wilde both during and after his trials often classified him as an "individualist," and they compared him explicitly to Friedrich Nietzsche. The philosophy of Nietzsche became the basis for the magazine that Adolf Brand founded in 1896, *Der Eigene,* and for the group that grew up around the publication, the Gemeinschaft der Eigenen.

Whereas the Scientific-Humanitarian Committee often emphasized the physical drives of the homosexual and foregrounded medical discourses on same-sex desire, Brand and his circle championed what they called Platonic love: intellectual, supportive, chaste relationships between men that had a strong romantic and aesthetic component but were never overtly physical. Brand derived the neologism "Eigene" from concepts outlined in the radical Max Stirner's individualist-anarchist tract *The Ego and His Own* (1845).[61] In Brand's words, "Whoever has always attentively read the leading articles of the journal long since knows of course that *Der Eigene* stands on the basis of individualist anarchism and that for it the *weltanschauung* of Max Stirner and Friedrich Nietzsche is the great working program of the future. For *Der Eigene* represents the right of personal freedom and sovereignty of the individual to the farthest consequence."[62] Given that fictional and factual accounts of male same-sex friendship and eroticism, photos and drawings of young male nudes, and political and social commentaries written from the perspective of love between men make up the bulk of the pieces that appeared in *Der Eigene* over the decades, the "farthest consequence" of the "sovereignty of the individual" for Brand would seem to encompass exclusively homosocial and homoerotic relations between men; "der Eigene" would seem to be Brand's nonpathologizing name for the homosexual.

An appeal to philosophies of unfettered individualism was Brand's main tactic in his attempt to provide an alternative to the pathologizing legal and medical discourses of sexuality current in turn-of-the-century Germany. In this he was joined by the homosexual poet John Henry Mackay, who had been working on a biography of Max Stirner since the 1880s and was responsible for the Stirner revival of the early 1890s. Thanks in large part to them, by the time of the Wilde trials the connection between radical individualism and love between men had already become quite well established in the German-speaking world.[63] The connection was so widely accepted, in fact, that in one of the few longer contemporary German newspaper articles on the Wilde trials, the socialist Eduard Bernstein could characterize the debate about homosexuality as a tussle between "ultra-puritanical moralizing" and "an extreme definition of freedom borrowed from radical philosophy."[64] Bernstein's observation allows us to see beyond the usual image of moralizers arguing with scientists in the realm of same-sex desire in the late nineteenth century, such that we can recognize the strength of contemporary radical anarchist-individualist voices in the debate.

That Wilde's philosophy of individualism, particularly as expressed in "The Soul of Man under Socialism," fit neatly into the emerging German discourse of emotional self-realization can be seen in several other responses to his trial.[65] The first book-length publication about the Wilde trials to appear in any language was Oskar Sero's *The Wilde Case and the Problem of Homosexuality*.[66] In this book, Sero compares Wilde to Nietzsche and describes the kinds of readers who can fully appreciate *Dorian Gray* as "free personalities" (19, 21, 88). Similarly, in an essay that appeared at around the same time, Johannes Gaulke claims that Wilde was an anarchist and that the guiding principle of his life was "self-development."[67] Gaulke suggests that the "orgies" that Wilde was fond of having with fellow aristocrats were simply the result of his being an "Ich-Mensch" (an "I" person) whose goal was always to be more fully himself (185). Gaulke's ideas about Wilde's self-realization project are repeated in four strikingly similar essays between 1896 and 1901.[68] In 1897, he added an essay on *The Picture of Dorian Gray* to his repertoire; in this essay, he argues that the novel is profoundly homosexual and that Lord Henry Wotton flirts with homosexuality in an effort to expand his persona-

Yvonne Ivory

lity.[69] The longevity in German intellectual history of the association of Wilde with radical experimental individualism is clear from Carl Sternheim's 1925 play, *Oskar Wilde: Sein Drama*.[70] Sternheim uses as the play's epigraph a Wilde quotation about the necessity of individualism in all areas of life (6), and he celebrates Wilde as an "anti-authoritarian individualist" who rejected psychiatry because it destroyed all uniqueness in the individual (83).

Wilde's consistent reception in Germany as a radical individualist with homosexual leanings should have made him an honorary member of *Der Eigene*'s pantheon. After all, the early issues of the journal are replete with tributes to Nietzsche, a figure with whom Brand's contemporaries often compared Wilde. *Der Eigene*'s essays, too, are very much in the style of Wilde and deal with issues close to Wilde's heart—with the individualism of Christ, for instance. And the editors of *Der Eigene* went to great lengths to rebut Max Nordau's negative evaluation of egocentrism, an evaluation that had in large part been based on an analysis of Wilde's character. Yet Wilde's name remained curiously absent from the publication, a fact that can only be attributed to Adolf Brand's general avoidance of topics that could in any way sully his chaste portrayals of love between men. The Gemeinschaft der Eigenen was clearly no place for a man who had been branded a criminal, whose martyrdom had become the rallying cry of Hirschfeld's committee, and whose works had been translated into German by the country's most notorious transvestite.

Wilde was excluded, too, when Brand published the first anthology of world literature celebrating love between men in 1900.[71] Only upon Wilde's death did one of the most prolific contributors to *Der Eigene*, Peter Hamecher, publish a piece about the Irishman. In "Oskar Wilde im Elend!" (Oscar Wilde in Misery), Hamecher laments the fact that this great man died destitute, and he refers readers to several German editions of Wilde's works as well as to Sero's 1896 account of the Wilde trials.[72] Hamecher's article did not appear in *Der Eigene*, however, but in the more popular and mainstream periodical *Die Gesellschaft*. Nevertheless, it suggests that although members of the Gemeinschaft der Eigenen did not embrace Wilde, they followed his story closely.

Not until six years after his death was Wilde's name even mentioned in the pages of a Gemeinschaft der Eigenen publication—and then only to undermine the Irishman's commitment to individualism. In "Gegen Oskar Wilde" (Against Oscar Wilde), Peter Hamecher lays out the case against Wilde, an author whose work he loves but whose actions he claims to hate.[73] Hamecher takes aim at the

Scientific-Humanitarian Committee when he argues that the problem with Wilde is that "for a long time in Germany he has been nothing more than an advertisement for homosexuality" (34). He goes on to analyze Wilde's commitment to individualism, which he finds overly "superficial" and "narcissistic" (35). Had Wilde been able to marry his individualistic philosophy to a strategy for improving the lot of humankind, he would have been worth emulating. As it is, he shows how a well-developed personality unmoored from reality constitutes a threat to mankind. The article makes plain that the Gemeinschaft cannot read Wilde outside the context of his usefulness to and uses by the Scientific-Humanitarian Committee. Moreover, it suggests that the resonances between Wilde's writings and the writings of such philosophers of individualism as Nietzsche or Stirner are always trumped by his sin of having committed a physical homosexual act and having moved love between men out of the ethereal and aesthetic realm to which the Gemeinschaft would have it belong. A final critique of Wilde appeared in *Der Eigene* in 1925. Here Ewald Tscheck echoes the sentiments of Hamecher, arguing that André Gide's insights into homosexuality and individualism were profound, while Wilde's understanding of those matters was always only superficial.[74] Tscheck draws an even more direct line between Wilde and Hirschfeld, whom he ridicules throughout the piece.

The reception of Wilde among Germans engaged in the early homosexual rights movement had little to do with his writings and everything to do with his biography. This is the one element of his treatment by the Scientific-Humanitarian Committee and the Gemeinschaft der Eigenen that is shared and consistent. Apart from this, Wilde not only meant different things to each group but also was treated very differently by each. Hirschfeld's circle never left off writing about Wilde—discussing his problems with the law and with blackmailers in the first volume of their journal, offering two separate articles on him in their second, and publishing all of his works in quick succession. Brand's circle, meanwhile, distanced themselves from him ever more emphatically over the years. The more important Wilde became for the Scientific-Humanitarian Committee, the less attractive he became for the Gemeinschaft der Eigenen. Through Hirschfeld's works, Wilde became associated with prevailing medical models of homosexuality —models rejected by Brand's cohorts as mechanical, unromantic, and degrading to man-loving men. In the pages of the *Jahrbuch*, Wilde was often portrayed as a victim or as a martyr; the Gemeinschaft der Eigenen wanted an *Übermensch*. Instead of looking to his writings, they responded to a Wilde refracted through the publications and politics of the Scientific-Humanitarian Committee; instead of bolstering their arguments about self-realization by leaning on the rich defenses of anarchy and individualism that can be found in such essays as "The Soul of Man under Socialism" and "Pen, Pencil, and Poison" (1889, revised 1891), they insisted on producing a Wilde whose proximity to criminality and pathology made him unfit to grace the pages of *Der Eigene*. And ultimately, instead of seeing Oscar Wilde the individualist, they could only see that individual whose creation was perhaps one of the most enduring legacies of the early homosexual rights movement in Germany: Oscar Wilde the type.

Notes

I would like to express my thanks to UCLA's Center for Seventeenth- and Eighteenth-Century Studies, the William Andrews Clark Memorial Library, and Joseph Bristow, organizers and gracious hosts of the conference at which a version of this chapter was first presented. My thanks, too, to Jennifer Schaffner of the Clark Library for speedily tracking down rare early German editions of Wilde's works for me.

1. For the Wilde family's links to the German-speaking world (including his father's medical studies in Berlin, Heidelberg, and Vienna and his mother's translations of German novels), see Merlin Holland, *The Wilde Album* (New York: Henry Holt, 1997), 9, 16, 18; Richard Ellmann, *Oscar Wilde* (New York: Knopf, 1988), 14, 18, 20; and Barbara Belford, *Oscar Wilde: A Certain Genius* (New York: Random House, 2000), 11–12, 19. The depth of Wilde's engagement with the German tradition can be sensed from a cursory glance at his writings: the commonplace book that Wilde kept at Oxford shows that he was familiar with the work of Dürer, Kant, and Hegel; his essay on historical criticism (1879) looks at Fichte and Hegel; and he was an admirer of Goethe, Lessing, Schlegel, Schiller, and Winckelmann. See *Oscar Wilde's Oxford Notebook: A Portrait of a Mind in the Making,* ed. Philip E. Smith II and Michael S. Helfand (New York: Oxford University Press, 1989). On Wilde's personal encounters with Germans and their culture, see also Ellmann, *Oscar Wilde,* 47, 73, 78; and Belford, *Oscar Wilde,* 289.

2. Ellmann, *Oscar Wilde,* 27. Robert Harborough Sherard claims that Wilde needed to refer only to a small dictionary while reading Heinrich Heine on train journeys during lecture tours. Also, when first married, Wilde tried to talk Constance into learning the language so that they could share new books. Ellmann, *Oscar Wilde,* 255; Patrick Bridgwater, "Oscar Wilde and Germany: Germany and Oscar Wilde," in Bridgwater, *Anglo-German Interactions in the Literature of the 1890s* (Oxford: Legenda, 1999), 45.

3. He requested from the authorities a copy of Ollendorff's *German Method* ("priceless") and its key, as well as a German-English dictionary and Goethe's *Faust* in the original. Wilde to More Adey, 16 December 1896, *The Complete Letters of Oscar Wilde,* ed. Merlin Holland and Rupert Hart-Davis (New York: Henry Holt and Company, 2000), 672, 673n; further page references appear in parentheses.

4. As for the rest of the German-speaking world, there is no record of Wilde visiting Austria-Hungary, but he did spend some time in Switzerland. Wilde called that country "vulgar" (Ellmann, *Oscar Wilde,* 235) in a conversation with Otho and Constance Lloyd in February 1883,

which suggests that he had passed through the country on one of his trips to Italy or Greece. At the prospect of spending a month at a friend's villa on Lake Geneva in early 1899, he wrote to Frank Harris, "Switzerland is close at hand, and I feel rather depressed at the prospect. . . . I dread the cold and the lack of coloured, moving, beautiful life" (*Complete Letters*, 1126). Wilde's stay may have allowed him to escape the harassing bills he faced at hotels on the French Riviera, but the price to his spirits was great: his host was "unsocial, taciturn, wretched"; the Swiss wines he was served were "most horrid" (Wilde to Robert Ross, 21 March 1899, *Complete Letters*, 1134), even "revolting" (Wilde to Reginald Turner, 20 March 1899, *Complete Letters*, 1132); and the Swiss themselves "so ugly to look at that it conveys melancholy into all my days" (Wilde to More Adey, March 1899, *Complete Letters*, 1129). For Wilde's trips to Germany, see Belford, *Oscar Wilde*, 178–79; and Ellmann, *Oscar Wilde*, 377, 391.

5. Despite Wilde's complaints about the country (see note 4 above), Constance sent her two sons to Switzerland at the onset of her husband's scandal. She later followed them there, and before her death in 1897, the family spent considerable amounts of time in Heidelberg and in the Black Forest region. See Holland, *Wilde Album*, 168, 180.

6. Robert Ross, preface to Oscar Wilde, *Salomé, La Sainte Courtisane, and A Florentine Tragedy* (London: Methuen, 1909), xii.

7. Robert Blackburn, "'The Unutterable and the Dream': Aspects of Wilde's Reception in Central Europe, 1900–1920," *Irish Studies Review* 11 (1995): 30–35; Bridgwater, "Oscar Wilde and Germany," 64. Contemporary German commentators suggested that sentencing a man such as Wilde to two years' hard labor was a barbaric policy and proved that England was less civilized than Germany. M. Handl, "Der Wilde-Process: Ein Epilog," *Die Zeit: Wiener Wochenschrift für Politik, Volkswirtschaft, Wissenschaft und Kunst* 37 (1895): 166–68; Johannes Gaulke, "Oscar Wilde," *Die Gegenwart* 12 (1896): 184–87; Max Meyerfeld, "Erinnerungen an Oscar Wilde," *Die neue Rundschau* 14 (1903): 400–407; Max Meyerfeld, "Oscar Wilde in Deutschland," *Das litterarische Echo* 5 (1903): 458–62.

8. Several scholars have recently made significant contributions to our understanding of Wilde's reception in Germany. Patrick Bridgwater, while emphasizing the resonances between Wilde and Nietzsche, places Wilde's impact in the German-speaking world squarely in the context of a general reception of the British aesthetic movement ("Oscar Wilde and Germany"); Rainer Kohlmayer offers an invaluable and thorough translation and performance history of Wilde's plays in his *Oscar Wilde in Deutschland und Österreich* (Tübingen: Niemeyer, 1996); and W. Eugene Davis's essay on the early reception of *Salome* in the German press provides not only a detailed production history of the play and translations of its most important reviews but also a subtle analysis of the myriad ways in which it was read by different German interest groups. Davis, "Oscar Wilde, *Salomé*, and the German Press, 1902–1905," *English Literature in Transition* 44 (2001): 149–80.

9. Brand's neologism "Eigener" is notoriously difficult to translate. John Lauritson and David Thorstad render the name "The Special," as does Walter Fähnders, while George L. Mosse prefers "The Personalist." Hubert Kennedy translates the name as "The Self-Owner"—a clumsy phrase that nevertheless perhaps comes closest to conveying the range of ideas (characteristic, idiosyncratic, own, strange, self, separate, and so forth) suggested by the German word and prefix *eigen*. John Lauritson and David Thorstad, *The Early Homosexual Rights Movement, 1864–1933* (New York: Times Change Press, 1974), 19; Walter Fähnders, "Anarchism and Homosexuality in Wilhelmine Germany: Senna Hoy, Erich Mühsam, John Henry Mackay," *Journal of Homosexuality* 29 (1995): 117–53; George L. Mosse, *Nationalism and Sexuality: Respectability and Abnormal Sexuality in Modern Europe* (New York: Howard Fertig, 1997), 42; Hubert Kennedy and Harry Oosterhuis,

eds., *Homosexuality and Male Bonding in Pre-Nazi Germany* (New York: Hayworth Press, 1991), 2.

10. Bridgwater, "Oscar Wilde and Germany," 59–64.

11. Max Nordau, *Entartung*, 2nd ed., 2 vols. (Berlin: C. Duncker, 1893), 1:133–43.

12. Hermann Bahr, "Decadence," *Die Zeit: Wiener Wochenschrift für Politik, Volkswirtschaft, Wissenschaft und Kunst* 6 (1894): 87–89.

13. De Montesquiou is thought to have been the model for Des Esseintes, the aestheticist antihero of J.-K. Huysmans's *À rebours* (1884), the antirealist novel whose influence can be felt in *The Picture of Dorian Gray*.

14. Hermann Bahr, *Prophet der Moderne: Tagebücher, 1888–1904* (Vienna: Böhlau, 1987), 200. Most translations from the German in the present article are my own; exceptions should be clear from the language of the volume cited.

15. Wilde's *Intentions* was published simultaneously in London and in New York in May 1891. Wilde was keen to have the volume appear on the Continent, and that summer he authorized William Heinemann to bring out an edition in Germany. This edition—still in the original English —was published in Leipzig in October 1891. Wilde, *Complete Letters*, 454, 486n, 487. "The Decay of Lying" thus was the first work to appear in German. Oscar Wilde, "Der Verfall des Lügens," trans. Francis Maro, *Die Zeit: Wiener Wochenschrift für Politik, Volkswirtschaft, Wissenschaft und Kunst* 6 (1894): 95–96; 7 (1894): 111–12; 8 (1894): 126–28.

16. My discussion of Wilde's German reception owes a great debt to Markus Hänsel-Hohenhausen's excellent bibliography, *Die frühe deutschsprachige Oscar-Wilde-Rezeption (1893– 1906)* (Egelsbach: Hänsel-Hohenhausen, 1990).

17. The aphorism is quoted in a report on a survey conducted by the French magazine *L'ermitage*. The editors had asked ninety-nine internationally known authors and artists for their ideas on the subject of freedom and discipline. Wilde is reported to have quipped, "I was formerly a poet and a tyrant; now I'm an artist and an anarchist!" "Noch eine internationale Abstimmung," *Freie Bühne für den Entwicklungskampf der Zeit (Die neue Rundschau)* 4 (1893): 957.

18. The aphorisms appeared under the title "Art" (Oscar Wilde, "Kunst," *Wiener Rundschau* 1 [1897]: 335–36), while "The Soul of Man" excerpt was entitled "The Artist and the Public" (Oscar Wilde, "Künstler und Publikum," trans. G. Adam, *Wiener Rundschau* 1 [1897]: 496–98).

19. Oscar Wilde, *Der Geist von Canterville*, trans. A. M. von B[öhn] (Munich: Brügel, 1897). This edition, with illustrations by Fritz Erler, was limited to only sixty copies and is the first Wilde work that appeared in book form in German. The stigma still associated with Wilde's name in 1897 may account for the facts that Böhn used only his initials to identify himself and that the publisher's imprint did not appear on the volume. This was in all likelihood an unauthorized edition, as neither Wilde nor Ross makes mention of it in their correspondence, despite Wilde's continual efforts to make as much money as possible off his works during these years. I am extremely grateful to Bronwyn Hannon, curator of acquisitions in Special Collections at Hofstra University, for her detailed description of that university's copy of this rare volume.

20. Oscar Wilde, "Die Wahrheit der Maske," *Wiener Rundschau* 4 (1900): 112–17; "Der selbstsüchtige Riese," *Die Gesellschaft* 16 (1900): 28–32; "Salome," trans. Hedwig Lachmann, *Wiener Rundschau* 4 (1900): 189–212; "Aus der Ballade des Stockhauses zu Reading. Von C.3.3. (Zellennummer Oscar Wildes)," trans. Arthur Holitscher, *Wiener Rundschau* 20, no. 4 (1900): 345–49. According to Hänsel-Hohenhausen, Arthur Holitscher's German translation of *The Ballad of Reading Gaol* appeared in book form in 1898 (*Oscar-Wilde-Rezeption*, 21). While it is not unlikely that Holitscher had completed a translation of the poem by this date—his translation was excerpted in the *Wiener Rundschau* early in 1900—there seems to be no other evidence of an 1898 book publication. The Clark Library has two copies of the volume to which Hänsel-Hohenhausen

appears to be referring (number 26 in Juncker's Orplidbücher series, with illustrations by Otto Schmalhausen), both of which can be firmly dated to 1923, thanks to a publisher's note in the front matter. The same note does, however, claim that this is the "fifth luxury printing" of the volume, opening up the possibility that there were printings before 1923.

21. Rudolf Defieber, *Oscar Wilde: Der Mann und sein Werk im Spiegel der deutschen Kritik und sein Einfluß auf die deutsche Literatur* (Heidelberg: Friedrich Schulze, 1934), 29–33; Max Meyerfeld, "Wilde, Wilde, Wilde . . . ," *Das litterarische Echo* 14 (1905): 985–90; Max Meyerfeld, "Wilde-Nachlese," *Das litterarische Echo* 17 (1906): 1225–29.

22. There has been some debate over which was the first performance, but it was probably first staged in Munich in March, then in Breslau in May. Blackburn, "Unutterable," 30; Defieber, *Oscar Wilde*, 29; E. Freund, "Bühnentelegraph: Breslau," *Bühne und Welt* 5 (1902): 258; Sander L. Gilman, *Disease and Representation* (Ithaca, NY: Cornell University Press, 1988), 158; Kohlmayer, *Oscar Wilde in Deutschland*, 9n; Davis, "Wilde, *Salomé*, and the German Press," 152; Steven Price and William Tydeman, *Wilde: Salome* (Cambridge: Cambridge University Press, 1996).

23. Davis, "Wilde, *Salomé*, and the German Press," 154; Kohlmayer, *Oscar Wilde in Deutschland*, 9.

24. Meyerfeld, "Oscar Wilde in Deutschland," 459; emphasis added.

25. See, for instance, Marie Becker's important 1901 essay on representations of Salomé in art and literature, "Salome in der Kunst des letzten Jahrtausends," *Bühne und Welt* 4 (1901): 201–9.

26. Oddly, Ross seems in this comment to be confusing the Breslau and Munich productions of 1901 with the more important Berlin production of 1902. See Ross, preface to Oscar Wilde, *Salomé*, x–xii.

27. The coverage of the Wilde trials in the German media has yet to be treated fully. Even when scholars have mentioned in passing the fact that the trials garnered a lot of attention, bibliographical detail remains scant and close analysis of the reportage is lacking altogether. See Gilman, *Disease*, 158; Günter Dworek, "'Für Freiheit und Recht': Justiz, Sexualwissenschaft und schwule Emanzipation, 1871–1896," in *Die Geschichte des §175: Strafrecht gegen Homosexuelle*, ed. Manfred Baumgardt et al. (Berlin: Rosa Winkel, 1990), 58. My own brief survey of coverage by the most important German newspaper of the day, the staid *Vossische Zeitung*, found twenty-two separate items on the Wilde affair between April and June 1895. The editorializing in some of the pieces invites further investigation.

28. Felix Dietrich, ed., *Bibliographie der deutschen Zeitschriften-Literatur*, 128 vols. (Leipzig: Felix Dietrich, 1896–1967), 1:179, 12:329, 13:318. The count might be considered flawed, as the index came into being in the mid-1890s and excluded many influential periodicals during its first years. Moreover, to merit inclusion in the index, an author or his work had to constitute the primary focus of an article—a rare occurrence in Wilde's case.

29. Oscar Wilde, "*De Profundis*: Aufzeichnungen und Briefe aus dem Zuchthause in Reading," trans. Max Meyerfeld, *Die neue Rundschau* 16 (1905): 87, 88–104, 163–91. These letters, with corrected dates, appeared in the second English-language edition of *De Profundis* in 1908. See Robert Ross, "A Prefatory Dedication to Dr. Max Meyerfeld," in Wilde, *De Profundis*, 2nd ed. (London: Methuen, 1908), vii–xvi.

30. Oscar Wilde, "Eine Florentinische Tragödie," trans. Max Meyerfeld, *Die neue Rundschau* 18 (1907): 1075–89.

31. Ellmann, *Oscar Wilde*, 584; Max Meyerfeld, "Gedenkblätter, Robert Ross," *Das litterarische Echo* 21 (1919): 779–85. Ross dedicated the 1908 expanded edition of *De Profundis* to Meyerfeld, observing that the letter would never have been published had it not been for the German scholar's persistence (vii).

Yvonne Ivory

32. Max Meyerfeld, "Von und über Oscar Wilde," *Das litterarische Echo* 15 (1904): 541–44; Meyerfeld, "Wilde, Wilde, Wilde" (1905); Meyerfeld, "Wilde-Nachlese" (1906).

33. Meyerfeld, "Von und über," 541–42; Meyerfeld, "Wilde-Nachlese," 1227.

34. Meyerfeld, "Oscar Wilde in Deutschland," 460–61; Meyerfeld, "Wilde, Wilde, Wilde," 987–88; Meyerfeld, "Wilde-Nachlese," 1226.

35. Meyerfeld, "Von und über," 542; Meyerfeld, "Wilde, Wilde, Wilde," 987.

36. Meyerfeld, "Von und über," 543; Meyerfeld, "Wilde, Wilde, Wilde," 987.

37. Meyerfeld, "Von und über," 541. Von Teschenberg, a barrister and the son of an Austrian minister, grew up speaking German. See Charlotte Wolff, *Magnus Hirschfeld: A Portrait of a Pioneer in Sexology* (London: Quartet Books, 1986), 42; Magnus Hirschfeld, *Geschlechtskunde: Auf Grund dreissigjähriger Forschung und Erfahrung*, 5 vols. (Stuttgart: Julius Püttmann, 1926–30), 1:357. Nevertheless, Meyerfeld is not alone in his criticism of von Teschenberg's style, grammar, and syntax; Rainer Kohlmayer presents a particularly strong case against von Teschenberg as a translator, providing numerous examples of stilted, prolix, prudish, and dated phrasing in von Teschenberg's 1903 rendering of *The Importance of Being Earnest* (*Ernst sein!*). Kohlmayer, *Oscar Wilde* (Tübingen: Max Niemeyer, 1996), 127–47, 188, 194, 385. Whereas Kohlmayer is willing to chalk some of these peculiarities up to the translator's Austrian dialect, others can only be explained, he finds, "by a lack of linguistic competence in German" (93).

38. Kohlmayer, *Oscar Wilde in Deutschland*, 127.

39. Hirschfeld, *Geschlechtskunde*, 1:357–58; Hermann Freiherr v. Teschenberg, "Erinnerungen an Oscar Wilde," *Theater* 1 (1903): 28–29.

40. Wolff, *Hirschfeld*, 105.

41. One circumstance that does vouch for von Teschenberg's closer ties to Wilde's circle is the fact that his translation of *The Importance of Being Earnest* appears to have been based on a previously unpublished manuscript of that play; he can only have received such a manuscript from Robert Ross. Kohlmayer, *Oscar Wilde in Deutschland*, 63, 127, 188n; Russell Jackson, introduction to *The Importance of Being Earnest*, by Oscar Wilde (London: Benn, 1980), xliii. Vyvyan Holland relied heavily on von Teschenberg's translation when collating the first four-act edition of the play in 1957. Vyvyan Holland, foreword to Wilde, *The Importance of Being Earnest* (London: Methuen, 1957), xii.

42. Teschenberg, "Erinnerungen," 29. It is very likely that von Teschenberg never saw Wilde in Rome but was relying on an obituary by the lawyer and activist Eugen Wilhelm (Numa Prätorius) published two years earlier (Numa Prätorius, "Oskar Wilde," *Jahrbuch für sexuelle Zwischenstufen* 3 [1901]: 265–74). In that less-than-accurate piece—Wilhelm christens Wilde "Oskar Flakertie Wills" (265) and claims that he died at the Salpetrière with Lord Alfred Douglas at his side (271)—the author describes having seen Wilde once at the Coliseum. In his derivative piece, von Teschenberg even uses the same adjectives as Wilhelm to describe Wilde's appearance as well as his surroundings (Teschenberg, "Erinnerungen," 29; Numa Prätorius, "Oskar Wilde," 272).

43. Wissenschaftlich-humanitäres Comitée, "Komitee-Mitteilungen," *Jahrbuch für sexuelle Zwischenstufen* 12 (1912): 244.

44. Hirschfeld, *Geschlechtskunde*, 1:357–58; Wolff, *Hirschfeld*, 42, 105.

45. Wissenschaftlich-humanitäres Comitée, "Komitee-Mitteilungen," 245.

46. Hirschfeld, *Geschlechtskunde*, 4:624–25.

47. Robert Harborough Sherard, *Oscar Wilde: Die Geschichte einer unglücklichen Freundschaft*, trans. Hermann Freiherr von Teschenberg (Minden: J. C. C. Bruns, [1902?]); Oscar Wilde, *Ernst sein!* trans. Herman Freiherr von Teschenberg (Leipzig: Spohr, 1903); *Lady Windermere's Fächer*, trans. Hermann Freiherr von Teschenberg and Leo Pavia (Leipzig: Spohr, 1902); *Eine Frau ohne*

Bedeutung, trans. Herman Freiherr von Teschenberg and Leo Pavia (Leipzig: Spohr, 1902); *Ein idealer Gatte*, trans. Herman Freiherr von Teschenberg and Leo Pavia (Leipzig: Spohr, 1903); *Salome*, trans. Herman Freiherr von Teschenberg and Leo Pavia (Leipzig: Spohr, 1903).

48. Max Spohr, too, was a founding member of Hirschfeld's Scientific-Humanitarian Committee. Manfred Herzer, "Das Wissenschaftlich-humantiäre Komitee," in *Goodbye to Berlin? 100 Jahre Schwulenbewegung: Eine Ausstellung des schwulen Museums und der Akademie der Künste*, ed. Monika Hingst et al. (Berlin: Rosa Winkel, 1997), 37–48.

49. Meyerfeld, "Von und über," 542. On Gaulke's translation of *Dorian Gray*, Meyerfeld had this to say: "Gaulke . . . should be sued for his treatment of Dorian Gray, which sets a record for ignorance of English and abuse of German." Gaulke by this time had also translated "The Portrait of Mr. W.H." (1889) and Wilde's short stories. Oscar Wilde, *Das Sonnettenproblem des Herrn W.H.*, trans. and with an introduction by Johannes Gaulke (Leipzig: Spohr, 1902); Oscar Wilde, *Der glückliche Prinz und andere Erzählungen*, trans. Johannes Gaulke (Leipzig: Spohr, 1903).

50. An attractive illustrated edition of Hedwig Lachmann's *Salome* translation appeared in Insel Verlag in 1902. The illustrations, strongly reminiscent of the work of Aubrey Beardsley, were executed by Marcus Behmer, a member of Hirschfeld's committee. Behmer, a homosexual, is also remembered for his erotic drawings celebrating the phallus. Andreas Sternweiler, "Kunstbetrieb und Homosexualität," in Hingst, *Goodbye to Berlin?* 64.

51. Meyerfeld, "Oscar Wilde in Deutschland," 460.

52. Meyerfeld, "Oscar Wilde in Deutschland," 462. Apparently, Spohr did not think its series was "clad in . . . beggar's costume." The endpapers of the 1903 Spohr edition of *Salome* include the following notice: "In the near future, the same publisher will be bringing out all further works by Oscar Wilde in an equally beautiful edition."

53. Meyerfeld, "Oscar Wilde in Deutschland," 462.

54. Meyerfeld, "Wilde, Wilde, Wilde," 986.

55. Hirschfeld, *Geschlechtskunde*, 3:680; Baumgardt et al., *Die Geschichte des §175*, 56n. Hirschfeld's memories may not be 100 percent reliable, however. He goes on to claim that Wilde was at that time (1895) well known in Germany because of the popularity of his plays (*Geschlechtskunde*, 3:680). This was, of course, not the case.

56. Wolff, *Hirschfeld*, 48.

57. Magnus Hirschfeld, *Sappho und Sokrates: Wie erklärt sich die Liebe der Männer und Frauen zu Personen des eigenen Geschlechts?* 2nd ed. (Leipzig: Spohr, 1902), 35.

58. Wissenschaftlich-humanitäres Comitée, ed., *Jahrbuch für sexuelle Zwischenstufen* (Leipzig: Spohr, 1899–). The *Jahrbuch* was partly a medical, partly a sociocultural, and partly a historical journal of homosexuality. Its second issue contained two essays on Wilde.

59. Marita Keilson-Lauritz, *Die Geschichte der eigenen Geschichte* (Berlin: Rosa Winkel, 1997), 311n.

60. Luginsland [Adolf Brand], "Dielen-Bummel," in *Emanzipation hinter der Weltstadt: Adolf Brand und die Gemeinschaft der Eigenen. Katalog zur Ausstellung vom 7 Oktober bis 17 November 2000 in Berlin Friedrichshagen*, ed. Marita Keilson-Lauritz and Rolf F. Lang (Berlin-Friedrichshagen: Rolf F. Lang, 2000), 103; Curt Moreck [Konrad Haemmerling], *Führer durch das lasterhafte Berlin* (1931; repr., Berlin: Nicolaische, 1996), 159, 165.

61. Max Stirner, *Der Einzige und sein Eigentum* (1845; repr., Leipzig: Reclam, 1893).

62. Quoted in Kennedy and Oosterhuis, *Homosexuality*, 22. That *Der Eigene* could trace its roots to Stirner's tract was a matter of public record from the time of Fürst von Bülow's 1907 libel trial against Brand. Summarizing the trial in 1909, Erich Wulffen states that "[Brand] was the

founder of the Gemeinschaft der Eigenen and quite early on he started to publish a newsletter named *Der Eigene*. According to Brand, this was based on Stirner's book *The Ego and His Own.*" Erich Wulffen, *Der Sexualverbrecher: Ein Handbuch für Juristen, Verwaltungsbeamte und Ärzte* (Berlin: Dr. P. Langenscheidt, 1910), 605.

63. Erin Williams Hyman has explored similar links between homosexuality and individualist-anarchist movements in the context of Wilde's career. See chapter 3 of the present volume.

64. Eduard Bernstein, "Die Beurtheilung des widernormalen Geschlechtsverkehrs," *Die neue Zeit* 13, no. 34 (1895): 229.

65. Wilde's position in this work is that individualism is not the antithesis of socialism but that socialism is a stage on the road toward an ideal society in which individualism will flourish. Socialism, by stripping the wealthy of their possessions, will at last bring about a society in which "we shall have true, beautiful, healthy Individualism. Nobody will waste his life in accumulating things. One will live." Wilde, "The Soul of Man under Socialism," *CW*, 8:285.

66. Oskar Sero, *Der Fall Wilde und das Problem der Homosexualität: Ein Prozess und ein Interview* (Leipzig: Spohr, 1896); further page references appear in parentheses. The author's name is a pseudonym. The last name is probably an anagram of "Eros"; his first would seem to be paying tribute to Wilde.

67. Gaulke, "Oscar Wilde," *Die Gegenwart*, 186, 184; further page reference appears in parentheses.

68. Johannes Gaulke, "Oskar Wilde," *Die neue Zeit* 15 (1897): 143–48; Gaulke, "Oscar Wilde," *Stimmen der Gegenwart* 10 (1901): 283–88; Gaulke, "Oskar Wilde," *Das Magazin für Litteratur* 1 (1901): 3–8; Gaulke, "Fragmente aus Oskar Wilde's *Dorian Gray*," *Das Magazin für Litteratur* 37 (1901): 879–84.

69. Johannes Gaulke, "Oskar Wilde's *Dorian Gray*," *Jahrbuch für sexuelle Zwischenstufen* 3 (1901): 276, 279. Other early-twentieth-century critics who saw expansive individualism as a crucial aspect of Wilde's work include Ernst Heilborn, Samuel Lublinski, Arthur Sewett, and Alois Stockmann; see Defieber, *Oscar Wilde*, 14, 15, 21, 62. Rudolf Defieber uses each of them to bolster his argument that Wilde had a "thoroughly negative" (128) influence on German art because of his anti-Christian individualistic ideology.

70. Carl Sternheim, *Oskar Wilde: Sein Drama* (Potsdam: Gustav Kiepenheuer, 1925); further page references appear in parentheses.

71. Elisarion von Kupffer, *Lieblingminne und Freundesliebe in der Weltliteratur*, ed. Marita Keilson-Lauritz (1900; repr., Berlin: Rosa Winkel, 1995).

72. Peter Hamecher, "Oscar Wilde im Elend!" *Die Gesellschaft* 1 (1901): 128.

73. Peter Hamecher, "Gegen Oskar Wilde," *Die Gemeinschaft der Eigenen* 3 (1906): 34–36; further page references appear in parentheses.

74. St. Ch. von Waldecke [Ewald Tscheck], "André Gide, 'Corydon,'" *Der Eigene* 10 (1925): 430.

Staking Salomé

*The Literary Forefathers and Choreographic Daughters
of Oscar Wilde's "Hysterical and Perverted Creature"*

JULIE TOWNSEND

Leaving [Cairo], I sought everywhere traces of Cleopatra. In a fragment
of ancient carving done by a Greek sculptor, I saw her head. Dreamy
and willful, it is indeed the Oriental character. This Grecian artist, who
perished many centuries ago, understood the nature of the great lovers
of Asia, the profound and terrible passions of those queens, Balkis,
Shamiram, the Marys of Magdala. . . .

Thus does the Orient revere, even though she [Cleopatra] be an
enemy, one of the great lovers of Asia. The Occident would make of
her, undoubtedly, *a hysterical and perverted creature,* such as Oscar
Wilde makes the young and chaste Salome.

—Armen Ohanian, *The Dancer of Shamahka*

THE TITLE OF this chapter was inspired by Armen Ohanian's autobiographical
novel *The Dancer of Shamahka* (published in French in 1918 and translated
into English four years later). In addition to its direct reference to Oscar Wilde's
play *Salomé* (originally written in French in 1892), Ohanian's narrative is worth
consideration because it provides a thought-provoking critique of, as well as
a cultural context for, the many Salomés that I consider here. *The Dancer of
Shamahka* self-consciously debunks several of the literary myths that characterized
representations of the Orient, Eastern women, and dancers in the nineteenth

and early twentieth centuries. Ohanian's novel appealed to her European audience by providing an insider's view into the world so often portrayed as ahistorical and impenetrable. This roman à clef recounts Ohanian's childhood in Armenia, her family's flight through the Caucasus in the face of the Russian invasion, and her life in a Muslim harem in Tehran after she was abandoned by her Armenian husband and separated from her family. After being taken in by a Muslim family, she learned traditional Persian dances. Just before World War I, she moved to Paris, where she befriended Anatole France, Natalie Barney, and Auguste Rodin and was brought under the protection of the Duchess Clermont-Tonnerre. Ohanian participated in the "Persian Nights" performances at the "Tout-Paris" music hall, and throughout her stay in Europe she gave lectures and published on Middle Eastern dance and poetry.

Ohanian's autobiographical narrative ends in Cairo as she prepares to travel to France for a dancing tour. There she surveys the colonial city and berates the European tourists in Egypt for ruining the East.[1] Ohanian's romanticized vision of the Orient in many ways mimics the French and British Orientalist tradition against which she is writing; in the following passage, she continues with an appraisal of the colonial revision of the belly dance:

> Thus in Cairo one evening I saw, with sick incredulous eyes, one of our most sacred dances degraded into a bestiality horrible and revolting. It was our poem of the mystery of and pain of motherhood, which all true Asiatic men watch with reverence and humility, in the far-away corners of Asia where the destructive breath of the Occident has not yet penetrated. . . . Such is our Asiatic veneration of motherhood, that there are countries and tribes whose most binding oath is sworn upon the stomach, because it is from this sacred cup that humanity is issued.
>
> But the spirit of the Occident had touched this holy dance, and it became the horrible *danse du ventre,* the *hoochie-koochie.* To me, a nauseating revelation of unsuspected depths of human bestiality, to others it was amusing. I heard the lean Europeans chuckling, I saw lascivious smiles upon even the lips of Asiatics, and I fled. (262)

Ohanian's decidedly antimodernist prose both elaborates her nostalgia for a lost mythological era and develops an assessment of the deleterious ways in which colonialism reads and represents the Orient. By focusing her analysis on the subjects of women and of women dancing, Ohanian strikes at the heart of French Orientalist literature even while invoking many of its conventions.

If we sought an emblem to characterize the Orient of nineteenth-century French literature, then Salomé would surely be at the top of the list. But of all the appalling examples of perverse Orientalism, why did Ohanian make specific reference to Wilde's *Salomé?* A perusal of late-nineteenth-century French literature suggests that there was much at stake in the figure that the gospels call "the daughter of Herodias" (Matthew 14:6); in fact, more than a dozen well-known French versions appeared between 1843 and 1913.[2] For early-twentieth-century dancers, such as Ohanian, the figure of Salomé spoke specifically to the question of whether dance was a proper form of art or a mere pretext for prostitution. It also addressed a pressing inquiry about feminine agency: Was Salomé a feminist heroine who usurped the power of kings to clear her mother's name? Was she the victim of Herod and Hérodiade's scheme to kill John the Baptist? Or, was she, as Wilde portrays her, a young girl driven mad by her unchecked desire?

The biblical stories of Salomé offer little information on this much-debated figure: Herodias had been married to Philip but left him to marry his brother Herod, often referred to as the Tetrarch.[3] John the Baptist, also called by his Hebrew name Iokanaan in nineteenth-century texts, denounced this marriage as incestuous. Herod had John the Baptist imprisoned but was afraid to execute him. On the night of Herod's birthday celebration, Salomé, Herodias's daughter from the previous marriage, danced for Herod; her dance so pleased him that he offered her a reward of her choosing. She, at the instruction of her mother, requested the head of John the Baptist on a charger.[4] Almost two millennia later, the figure of Salomé became a standard but highly contested icon in nineteenth-century French literature and early-twentieth-century dance. Literary works and dance performances employed the Salomé story as a means of giving voice to what were acutely sensitive cultural debates at the time: the supremacy of artistic power in the face of political and religious authoritarianism; the assertion of female agency in the face of patriarchal authority; and the unapologetic expression of sexual desire in the face of cultural taboo and injunction.

To sort out the centrality of the figure of Salomé in Wilde's time, we need to look back to a few nineteenth-century male writers—notably, Gustave Flaubert, Stéphane Mallarmé, and J.-K. Huysmans—whose works he assuredly knew. Each of these writers made the daughter of Herodias into an icon that served polemical artistic aims. Yet numerous critics have bemoaned scholars' reliance on viewing Wilde's experimental play solely in relation to the French sources that appear to have been his main influences. Regenia Gagnier, Steven Price, William Tydeman, and Joseph Donohue share the view that it is distracting to look at the various French Salomés to interpret his 1892 French-language drama.[5] Gagnier, for one, distrusts the critical tradition—first articulated in the *Pall Mall Gazette*'s review of the French 1893 edition of Wilde's one-act tragedy—that claims that "*Salome* is the daughter of too many fathers. She is the victim of heredity."[6] This method of approaching the drama, Gagnier maintains, tends to occlude the "subversive themes of the play."[7] However, the various literary Salomés help to show why Wilde's version of this figure impacted the choreographic representations that I take up later in my discussion. My readings thus concentrate on the rhetorical and narrative strategies of the literature and choreography not so much to confirm the discernible presence of French texts in Wilde's drama (which, in any case, is clear) as to explore the position that his work occupies in an almost century-long discussion among artists and dancers about how and why Salomé might emerge as an emblem of aesthetic, political, and sexual insubordination.

Close examination of a few scenes from these works reveals that they share a series of representational strategies—including narrative disruption, containment, and impenetrability—that are essential both to the deciphering of Wilde's tragedy and to an understanding of the importance of Salomé among early modern dancers. My analyses of these passages focus on how each writer sets out to represent the revolutionary eroticism embodied in Salomé and her dance. If a pattern emerges from these examples, it is one that shows that Salomé abstains, on the one hand, from the sexual-political corruption of the Tetrarch and his court and, on the other hand, from the oppressive patriarchal religion voiced by Iokanaan. As a consequence, she is able to exercise ultimate authority over both despotic power (Herod) and divine power (John the Baptist).[8] In the literary tradition that I trace here, Salomé served the purpose of Decadent and symbolist male writers who sought to distance their aesthetics from bourgeois commodification of the arts and mass consumerism. Salomé became the medium through which the avant-garde male author could imagine (somewhat presumptively) setting himself apart as a separate class, as a figure who could topple corrupt power and replace the divine voice with his own art.

Salomé in Nineteenth-Century French Literature

Four prominent French versions of Salomé had a discernible impact on aspects of Wilde's drama: Gustave Flaubert's *Salammbô* (1862); Stéphane Mallarmé's

"Hérodiade" (1864, revised 1867); Flaubert's "Hérodias" (from *Trois contes;* 1877); and J.-K. Huysmans's *À rebours* (1884). These three highly influential French authors represented Salomé and the Salomé story through a variety of narrative viewpoints and literary forms. These works serve as a kind of catalogue of stylistic and representational strategies with which Wilde would later engage in his *Salomé*.

Although not technically a story about Salomé, Flaubert's *Salammbô* set the tone for later representations of this biblical figure.[9] *Salammbô*, set in ancient Carthage, recounts the story of an ongoing war; the novel is weighed down by hundreds of pages describing monumental ruins, complex weaponry, and terrible portraits of warriors for hire. Salammbô, eponymous heroine and daughter of the Carthaginian general Hamilcar, is less a protagonist than she is an elusive and seductive image whose sporadic appearances serve as a respite from the archaic prose. In the face of her father's military defeat, Salammbô, despite her desire to become a priestess, becomes a pawn in her father's war. When the war turns for the worse, Salammbô agrees to sacrifice her virginity to her father's enemy, Mathô, in exchange for the "goddess' veil," a symbol of the health of the state. Her dance is a movement against the deteriorating ruins of her society and a trope for ruins insofar as it, as dance, is in a state of disappearance. In terms of narrative movement, her dance scene stalls the progression of the novel while simultaneously providing the event that enables some sort of narrative progression. Before trading her virginity for the goddess's veil to save "the health of the Republic and of her father," Salammbô follows the priest Schahabarim's orders to dance as a ritual that leads her delivery to Mathô.[10] Her dance is at once a respite from the incessant repetition of the war scenes and an essential component of the war narrative because it serves as the ritual entrance of Salammbô into this military history both as a participant and as part of the available spoils of war. Her performance is displayed only to her nursemaid, Taanach, and the omniscient narrator. The site of the dance is sealed off by Taanach, who covers the walls with tapestries "because Salammbô didn't want to be seen, even by the walls."[11] In a cinematic scene that casts the reader as voyeur, Salammbô dances with the ailing national python before delivering her body to her father's enemy, Mathô:

> Salammbô unfastened her ear-rings, her necklace, her bracelets, and her long white simar. . . . The music went on outside; it consisted of three notes ever the same, hurried and frenzied; the string grated, the flute blew. . . . Salammbô,

with a swaying of her whole body, chanted prayers, and her garments fell one after another around her.

The heavy tapestry trembled, and the python's head appeared above the cord that supported it. The serpent descended slowly, like a drop of water flowing along a wall.... [H]e rose perfectly erect; then his eyes, more brilliant than carbuncles, darted upon Salammbô. A horror of cold, or perhaps a feeling of shame, at first made her hesitate. But she recalled Schahabarim's orders and advanced; the python turned downwards, and resting the centre of its body upon the nape of her neck, allowed its head and tail to hang like a broken necklace with both ends trailing to the ground. Salammbô rolled it around her sides, under her arms and between her knees.... [S]he threw herself back beneath the rays of the moon. The white light seemed to envelop her in a silver mist, the prints of her humid steps shone upon the flagstones, stars quivered in the depth of the water.... [S]he felt herself dying, and with the tip of its tail, the serpent gently beat her thigh; the music became still, it fell.[12]

This seduction scene not only facilitates but also frustrates the reader's position as voyeur. The simultaneous deployment and interruption of sexual imagery result in a tension between rupture and containment. The repetitive, rhythmic music juxtaposed with the adjectives *hurried* and *frenzied* (*"précipitée"* and *"furieuse"*) create the expectation of sameness and the threat of unpredictability while achieving an atmosphere of sexual anticipation. Salammbô's undressing is provoked by the music, but her calm and calculated prayers and preparations resist the increasingly frantic and seductive rhythms. The systematic removal of her jewelry, clothing, and scarf suggests an undoing of restraints, a letting loose of that which has been limited, controlled, tied up. Flaubert's prose reflects Salammbô's syncopated rhythm as she both creates and is re-created by the dance. The structural rigor of semicolons gives way to commas and a consequent shortening of phrasing, of breath. This provokes acceleration within the repetition, which is interrupted by a paragraph break and the entrance of the snake. The python promptly limits Salammbô's unchaining as a "broken necklace" (*"collier rompu"*), a replacement of her jewelry that, in its brokenness, retains a trace of her having been momentarily freed from restraint; it is, however, equally a sign of her having been undone during the dance and a foreshadowing of what is to come in her later scene with Mathô.

The eroticism of the scene stems not only from the voyeuristic fantasy it produces but also from the circumstances of Salammbô's dance. She voluntarily sacrifices her virginity in the name of her country and father—thus, the subversion of patriarchal authority is sanctioned by a larger patriarchal cause. This sacrifice of Salammbô's chastity, religion, and desire to be a priestess coincides with her rite of passage into masculine sexuality. The untying, disrobing, and freeing in the first paragraph turns into the constriction of the dance with the snake, to which she initially responds with "[a] horror of cold, or perhaps a feeling of shame"—or so speculates the narrator.[13] Salammbô's agency remains ambiguous throughout the scene, the dance seems to be happening to her rather than driven by her: "she felt herself dying."[14]

This scene, both narrative and imagistic, betrays itself by failing to deliver the body that it offers. First, the prospect of Salammbô's revealing herself and her desire is suppressed by her reliance on Shahabarim's orders; her sexual initiation remains under the control of systems of patriarchal state and religion. Second, she is physically hidden by the accoutrements of her dance scene. Salammbô's body, the supposed object of desire, is all but absent from the scene: her clothing falls around her, the snake encircles her arms and legs, she leaves moist footprints on the ground, and the light of the moon surrounds her. Like a negative for a photograph, all that frames her is emphasized over her body itself. Flaubert reveals Salammbô to us only through the signs of her absence. Her image is registered only insofar as she is reflected in the things around her: the moon, the snake, the music, and the footprints on the floor. She becomes this series of signs rather than an agent interacting with them.

Several aspects of Flaubert's narrative set the tone for the Salomés that proliferated later in the century. Salammbô's desire to remain outside of the masculine sexual economy and her subsequent role as a pivotal figure in matters of the state and of religion reappeared in a variety of Salomé stories. Similarly, Flaubert's luxurious descriptions and his focus on all that surrounds the dancing body rather than on the body itself provided the narrative model for the Salomé figures that follow.

In my next example, Stéphane Mallarmé's "Hérodiade" (1864–67), Salomé is the explicit subject of the poem, yet her name has been replaced with that of her mother and the poem ignores the biblical story entirely; Mallarmé concentrates instead on the figure of Salomé/Hérodiade as an icon of beauty.[15] In other words, Mallarmé replaced Salomé with Hérodiade, thus collapsing the mother and daughter. While this may have been an interesting interpretation of the biblical story in which Salomé is in fact the mouthpiece of her mother, Mallarmé's explanation for his choice suggests another, rather amusing reason for the change;

his choice stemmed from his preference for the word "Hérodiade," which sounds like *grenade* (pomegranate), an image that figures prominently in symbolist poetry. In an 1865 letter to Eugène Lefébure, Mallarmé writes,

> The most beautiful page of my work will be that which contains only this divine name *Hérodiade*. The little inspiration I have had, I owe to this name, and I believe that if my heroine had been called Salomé, I would have invented this word that is as dark and red as an open pomegranate: *Hérodiade*. For the rest, my intent is to create a being purely dreamt and absolutely independent of history. You understand me. I do not even invoke all the paintings of da Vinci's students or of all the Florentines who have had this mistress and have called her like me.[16]

Mallarmé's treatment of Salomé noticeably unpins her from the specificity of her historical time and place but also from her literary legacy. In representing this well-known myth, he stages the scene between Hérodiade/Salomé and the nurse in the princess's chambers; the well-worn story disappears entirely, and Mallarmé transposes it into a series of dramatic monologues that resist both narrative and psychology.

Although Mallarmé's poem sets up as a dramatic scene between two characters, there is very little interaction. What little there is, though, is significant for our look at Wilde. There are three key exchanges between Hérodiade and the nursemaid. In the first, when the nurse asks to kiss her mistress's hand, Hérodiade exclaims, "Get back!"[17] Then the nurse offers perfumes, to which Hérodiade replies, "Leave there the perfumes! Do you not know that I hate them?"[18] Finally, the nurse tries to replace a fallen tress of Hérodiade's hair, and Hérodiade orders her, "Stop your crime."[19] For a reader familiar with the Wilde version of Salomé, these exchanges resemble the dialogue between Salomé and Iokanaan in which Salomé repeatedly asks to touch Iokanaan, who, in turn, refuses her advances. For the most part, though, Mallarmé's poem focuses on Hérodiade alone.

In the poem, Hérodiade's desire to remain chaste and thus disconnected from the heterosexual economies of marriage is a transposition of her attempts to escape history—in other words, to become both infinite and impersonal. If Flaubert's Salammbô must enter into the masculine sexual economy, then Mallarmé's Hérodiade must increasingly seal herself off from interaction or reproduction; she elaborates, instead, a sterile, masturbatory sexuality that brings her increasingly closer to an ideal object of beauty.

Yes, it's for me, for me that I flower, deserted!
You know it, gardens of amethyst, hid
Endlessly in cunning abysses and dazzled,
Ignored gold, keeping your antique light
Under the sombre sleep of a primaeval soil,
You stones whence my eyes like pure jewels
Borrow their melodious brightness, and you
Metals which give my youthful tresses
A fatal splendour and their massive sway!

. . . .

I love virginity's horror, and I would
Live in the terror that my locks inspire

. . . .

I think myself alone in my monotonous country
And, around me, all lives in the idolatry
Of a mirror, reflecting in its sleeping calm
Herodias of the clear diamond look. . . .
Oh! supreme joy, yes, I know it, I am alone.[20]

This section of the poem marks Hérodiade's encapsulation of the self into a
work of art and a subsequent dissipation of that self into all things. Unlike most
nineteenth-century versions of Salomé, which tend to retain narrative elements
of the biblical story, Mallarmé's poem removes Salomé/Hérodiade from her historical context or literary history. Rather than becoming a victim of narrative,
Mallarmé's Salomé seals herself into poetry as an icon or symbol, untouched by
the pessimism of literary realism or naturalism. The first lines of this excerpt
construct reversals of the subject/object relationship as her eyes "borrow" ("*empruntent*") from jewels and the metals "give" ("*donnez*") to her hair. Through
her physical qualities, she merges with the reflection or trace of the object. The
hardness of the amethyst, stones, jewels, and metals ("*améthyste*," "*pierres*," "*bijoux*," and "*métaux*") becomes the source of visual and aural musicality through
their reflective qualities as well as through the internal rhymes, assonance, allit-
eration, and rhythms: "*sombre sommeil*," "*terre première*," "*yeux . . . bijoux*,"
"*chevelure . . . splendeur*." Hérodiade's luminous body echoes that which surrounds
her and separates her from history. If Salammbô seals herself off from even the
walls, then Hérodiade, it would seem, renounces herself as a separate being from
all that encompasses her and instead becomes one with the scene. As the body

Julie Townsend

becomes nothing but the trace of the thing, the corporeal becomes a site of monumental rather than mortal space.

Passing through the states of opacity and reflection, Hérodiade "of the clear diamond look" ("*au clair regard de diamant*") becomes, finally, transparent, the recipient and reflector of light. Mallarmé has taken the figure of Salomé and veiled her practically to the point of nonrecognition; thus, he elevates Salomé from her status as narrative strategy to that of an icon, entirely separate from all the narrative accoutrements that usually define her.

It is worth noting here a couple of points in relation to Wilde's play. First, Wilde's Salomé, like Mallarmé's, seems inseparable from the things that surround her. The moon is the most obvious example. Several characters in Wilde's drama mistake the moon for Salomé. Mallarmé's exchanges between the nursemaid and Salomé may also have found echoes in Wilde's play. In a more profound way, though, Salomé's body, in particular her dance, seems oddly absent from the texts. Mallarmé leaves it out entirely, and Wilde relegates it to a single stage direction without any specificity as to the style of the dance. Mallarmé's "Hérodiade" shifts Salomé from a literary figure based on a biblical one to an icon removed from narrative or history.

If these earlier versions focused on strategies of containment and isolation of the dancing—or not dancing—body, then my next example, Flaubert's "Hérodias" from *Trois contes*, represents Salomé's dance as a problem of reading. Of the literary works that I am considering here, Flaubert's "Hérodias" seems to be the most researched in relation to the biblical origins of Salomé in her position in the history of art. Additionally, Flaubert's *conte* self-consciously identifies itself as part of a web of Salomé narratives and imagery in his own historical moment. As Françoise Meltzer notes,

> Flaubert himself was overwhelmed by Moreau's vision and began research for his *Hérodias* in the same month of the same year. So we have come full circle. Flaubert's verbal depiction of Salammbô inspires Moreau's paintings of Salome, which in turn help to motivate Flaubert's story of Salome. . . . It is this symbiotic relationship between writing and painting that Salome provides— both in her biblical "origins" and in the countless depictions her story has generated—and Huysmans' prose rendition thus from the outset demonstrates the extent to which "writing" may be seen, like painting, as a form of augmented iconization.[21]

Flaubert sets "Hérodias" against a backdrop of a fortressed citadel buttressed by piled-up houses, a zigzagging road, many-angled ramparts, and terraced roofs. This impassable physical and geographic space mirrors the multiple ethnic and religious backgrounds of the many minor characters who offer arguments to Herod about how to garner favor with Caesar, what to do with Iokanaan, and whether to believe that the wandering prophet is to be taken as the son of God. Additionally, swarms of people, including hostile soldiers and well-wishers alike, inhabit the city and its surrounding territory; these images of lively, passion-inspired crowds contrast Flaubert's descriptions of the aging Tetrarch and his wife, Hérodias. Throughout the narrative, Flaubert presents us with contradictory information and never really gives us the tools with which to sort out the confusion: Iokanaan, for example, cannot determine whether he should resist his imprisonment or whether it is fate that he should be martyred to make way for the savior. In several instances, translators misunderstand statements and thus relay inaccurate information from one character to another; Herod is alternately lecherous and impotent; there are arguments among the Jews as to whether Herod's marriage to Hérodias is incestuous or not; and Herod does not know that Hérodias has sent for her daughter, so he, unknowingly, lusts after Salomé at a distance before he knows that she is his stepdaughter. This entire version, it seems, is about failures of interpretation—in fact, at times even the narrator cannot decipher the scene:

> A young girl had just come in. . . . Upon the dais she took off her veil. It was Herodias, as she used to look in her youth. Then she began to dance. Her feet slipped back and forth, to the rhythm of the flute and a pair of castanets. Her arms curved round in invitation to someone who always eluded her. She pursued him, lighter than a butterfly . . . and seemed on the point of flying away. . . . Despair had followed hope. Her attitudes expressed sighs, and her whole body such languor that one could not tell whether she was mourning for a god or swooning in his embrace. With eyes half closed, she twisted her waist, made her belly ripple like the swell of the sea, made her breasts quiver, while her expression remained fixed, and her feet never stood still.[22]

Not for another two paragraphs does Flaubert name Salomé. Herod is unclear on the identity of this girl, he does not recognize her as the young woman after whom he lusted earlier in the story (even the narrator cannot properly read the dance), and he does not know what story Salomé recounts in her dance—whether she mourns a god or swoons in his arms. As is typical of Salomé dance scenes,

Figure 21. Bas-relief of Salomé dancing on her hands, Rouen Cathedral. Courtesy of Yvan Leclerc.

all the spectators misconstrue her dance as one of sexual seduction; in this regard, she unwittingly plays the part well. But the disorder that Salomé will cause pertains to the order of religious and political power as much as to sexual order and the incest taboo. Flaubert encodes the form of Salomé's disorder in her dance: "She sprang up on her hands, heels in the air, crossed the dais in that way, like some great beetle; and suddenly stopped. Her neck and spine were at right angles. . . . Her lips were painted, her eyebrows very black, her eyes almost frightening, and the drops on her forehead looked like a vapour on white marble."[23] Salomé's initial seduction degenerates into a kind of corporeal chaos—the body is reversed, beetle-like, and her face inhuman. She declares in a childlike voice, "'I want you to give me on a dish the head . . . ' She had forgotten the name, but then went on with a smile, 'Iaokanann's head!' The Tetrarque collapsed, shattered."[24] The image of Salomé dancing on her hands, transformed not only from seductive girl-woman to beetle but also broken, with her neck and spine at right angles, was inspired by a bas-relief at the Rouen Cathedral (fig. 21). This image of a reversed Salomé appears in a variety of comments on the story. Most notably, Jean Cocteau was disappointed that Ida Rubinstein did not dance on her hands (as Flaubert describes) in her 1912 performance of Salomé.[25]

In Flaubert's "Hérodias," the narrative elements adhere more closely to the biblical versions than most other nineteenth-century Salomés do, yet the stamp of the era certainly informs the style and psychological context of the story. In Flaubert's *conte,* Salomé is the puppet of her mother, but she clearly takes a perverse pleasure in her performance—insofar as she is unreadable to the audience. Although Flaubert's Hérodias seems to fit a much more conventional idea of the story, his emphasis on confusion and problems of interpretation as well as horrifying reversals points to the still-unresolved problem of the figure of Salomé among nineteenth-century writers. This aspect of narrative confusion is a central characteristic of Wilde's play.

But the most often discussed narrative influence on Wilde's Salomé is Huysmans's *À rebours,* which invokes the Salomé story through two of Gustave Moreau's paintings, "Salomé Dancing before Herod" (1874) and "The Apparition" (1876).[26] Huysmans's notoriously antirealist narrative is a kind of character study of Des Esseintes, an antisocial aesthete who retreats from Paris to a country home where he cultivates his senses through the collection and study of hothouse flowers, exotic perfumes, and early Catholic literature. In *À rebours,* Des Esseintes's idiosyncratic perspective lies conspicuously between the reader and the object, accentuating the distance between the reader and the object of his reflection. The Salomé story lends itself to this aesthetic because she is available only as an image of seduction, never as a participant in sexual acts. By focusing on static images and the well-worn plot of a story already familiar to Des Esseintes and readers, Huysmans refuses to rely on causal relationships and focuses instead on the image as discrete entity. The immobile, stalled narrative appears in opposition to the dance, which floats just behind this static language. Huysmans's prose highlights the distance between prosaic representation and the body in performance. The few active, present-tense verbs refer to individual body parts and hence isolate the movement to the breast, arms, or feet. Meltzer argues that Huysmans has given "Salome full life"; in fact, she notes that "[t]he verbs are overwhelmingly of motion: glides, stretched, holding, rouse, begins, rise, fall, hardening, whirling . . . the play of light upon them: glitter, fiery, sparks, spangled, ablaze, dazzling, speckled. . . . Huysmans's passage is entirely in the present tense (unlike most of the rest of the novel), thus reinforcing the immediacy of the drama . . . giving us a Salome who moves, who actually dances."[27] Although Meltzer's study makes a compelling case, I would suggest quite a different reading of the passage from *À rebours.* Rather than delivering to the reader a fully alive, dancing body, the narrative alludes to the body through its focus on the accoutrements that surround Salomé. By elaborating static images, Huysmans refuses the causal relationships that a representation of the dancing body would demand and focuses instead on images as discrete entities. The descriptions of Moreau's paintings emphasize pure image over any seduction into a plot or psychology that would connote heterosexual romance. Huysmans's account of the dance begins with a sentence that includes Salomé's body, but the paragraph then puts the dancing body increasingly under erasure and replaces it with a description of the costume:

> With a withdrawn, solemn . . . expression on her face, she begins the lascivious dance which is to rouse the aged Herod's dormant senses; her breasts rise and fall, the nipples hardening at the touch of her whirling necklaces; the strings of diamonds glitter against her moist flesh; her bracelets, her belts, her rings all spit out fiery sparks; and across her triumphal robe, sewn with pearls, patterned with silver, spangled with gold, the jeweled cuirass, of which every chain is a precious stone, seems to be ablaze with little snakes of fire, swarming over the matte flesh, over the tea-rose skin, like gorgeous insects with dazzling shards, mottled with carmine, spotted with pale yellow, speckled with steel blue, striped with peacock green.[28]

Traces of the organic disappear by the end of the passage. By systematically erasing the dancer's body, narrative movement retreats into the arbitrary play of light on the surface of Salomé's jeweled accoutrements. In addition to the disappearance of the dancer's body, throughout the novel there is a suppression of the body of the spectator. Des Esseintes' fantasies rest solidly within the realm of the cerebral. Huysmans's prose denies movement not only to the dancer but also to the spectator. This immobility and stalling of narrative mask the implied mobility of dance, which threatens to break through the static prose, though it does not succeed in doing so.

The dancer in Huysmans's À rebours, then, provokes movement and stasis with seemingly equal force. The resulting paralysis prohibits the establishment of a narrative position that holds authority for anyone other than the viewer or reader. By encasing the dancer in the frame and limiting aesthetic experience to the imagination of the viewer (in other words, by removing it from any historical or social context), Huysmans removes the danseuse from models of desire in which she circulates among heterosexual male spectators. The narrative strategy of stasis or elaborately framed movement strips away the narrative elements that make Salomé a plot device; instead, Salomé becomes an emblem, a symbol, a trope. In some ways, Huysmans's use of painting to frustrate narrative parallels Mallarmé's use of poetry rather than prose; but it is unlike Mallarmé's poem in that Huysmans does not develop a character.

Wilde's Stake in Salomé

Art patron Harry Graf Kessler, in his correspondence regarding a possible production of *Salomé,* recounts the following of his conversations with American modern dancer Ruth St. Denis in 1906: "St. Denis is utterly opposed to [Wilde's] *Salome*—a whole crowd of objections, two of which are deep-rooted. She says that in any case it's a *purely literary* work (people can think differently if they wish to) in which the *dance can only be an incidental feature,* however people arrange things. And secondly, *she herself* has already conceived a *completely different Salome* (or Herodias), one in which the dance and the production correspond."[29] Although the production featuring St. Denis was abandoned, her sentiments may indeed have reflected the thoughts of many dancers. So far in the literary representations that we have considered—*Salammbô,* "Hérodiade," "Hérodias," and *À rebours*—the Salomé figure has been the object of the text even if she has been veiled or, in some cases, rendered an unattainable figure. In these writings, the reader's attention (whether literary, sexual, or aesthetic) focuses on the discursive appearance or disappearance of Salomé's body or her dance. Although the ways in which Wilde draws upon previous literary versions are clear, his depictions of Salomé and Iokanaan also exhibit noticeable shifts away from his acknowledged antecedents.

The most obvious departure from the French tradition is Wilde's choice of drama rather than prose or poetry. But this choice is not simply a new genre for the Salomé story. Both Flaubert and Huysmans challenge the conventions of both the novel in particular and prose writing in general with their depictions of Salammbô and Salomé, which elaborate on stasis, obscurity, and absence rather than the development or clarification of characters and plots. The genre of drama allows Wilde, like Mallarmé, to forgo an organizing narrator, thereby putting the onus of point of view on the characters and that of interpretation on the reader. But unlike Mallarmé's poem, which represents the Salomé figure as isolated from the family and state dramas that surround her, Wilde maintains

Julie Townsend

the basic plot of the biblical stories. In Wilde's play, each character seems to seek to position him- or herself as the narrator, and each character narrates his or her own position through a series of images, which for the most part fail to correspond with other characters' descriptions of the same items. The contradictory descriptions of the moon, Iokanaan, and Salomé construct disembodied, often paratactic, linguistic frames rather than cause/effect relationships.

If we look, for example, at the moon in Wilde's text, then we see a new manifestation of the problem of reading or interpretation. Each character in the play "reads" the moon differently and appeals, futilely, to others for confirmation: the Page of Herodias says, "How strange the moon seems! She is like a woman rising from a tomb. She is like a dead woman."[30] By comparison, the Young Syrian says, "She is like a little princess who wears a yellow veil. . . . One might fancy she was dancing" (S, 1). And Herod says, "The moon has a strange look to-night. Has she not a strange look? She is like a mad woman, a mad woman who is seeking everywhere for lovers" (S, 27–28). The Page of Herodias and the Young Syrian construct their similes in parallel grammatical forms that seem to render the images both interchangeable and in juxtaposition to one another. The drama thus begins with this challenge to meaning and continues as characters speak of mirrors, shadows, and reflections as well as double entendres, such as "I cannot tell" (S, 2, 3). Herodias resists the vagaries of comparison in her reply: "No; the moon is like the moon, that is all" (S, 28).

These competing descriptions speak, I think, to the problem of interpretation that haunts the earlier French writings about Salomé. In Mallarmé's poem, Salomé becomes increasingly diffuse and finally dissipates into a reflection of all that surrounds her; later, Flaubert, in his *conte*, gives us an unsure narrator who draws attention to the ambiguities of Salomé's performance. Besides the contradictory descriptions of the moon and of Iokanaan's body, several characters in Wilde's *Salomé* offer arbitrary symbolic readings of omens: there are often gaps between characters' appearances as described by others and their self-proclaimed state. Herodias, for example, declares that Herod is "ill" (S, 31), while the soldiers remark that he has a "sombre aspect" and "sombre look" (S, 3, 47). At the same time, the Tetrarch declares, "To-night I am happy. I am exceeding happy. Never have I been so happy" (S, 47). Even though most characters in the play make simple, straightforward statements that are nonetheless contradictory, they, apart from Salomé and Herodias, agree that they do not understand what Iokanaan is saying.

In the midst of seemingly circular and banal discussions on the countenance of the moon or the dovelike qualities of Salome's feet, Iokanaan interrupts with metaphorical and allegorical diatribes that contrast with the style of the rest of the play. Take, for example, this statement of his: "The centaurs have hidden themselves in the rivers, and the nymphs have left the rivers, and are lying beneath the leaves in the forests" (*S*, 11). While Iokanaan confuses his listeners and while the various pages and servants mimic each others' similes, Salomé elaborates a double strategy of rhetorical substitution. Not only do her several attempts to seduce Iokanaan result in the substitution of his white body with his black hair and then with his red lips, but she also takes on the desiring gaze of which she is the object, thus substituting Iokanaan for herself. In this remarkable rhetorical feat, Salomé terrifies the Page and the Young Syrian with her erotic deconstruction of Iokanaan: "Thy hair is horrible. It is covered with mire and dust. It is like a crown of thorns placed on thy head. It is like a knot of serpents coiled round thy neck. I love not thy hair. . . . It is thy mouth that I desire, Iokanaan. Thy mouth is like a band of scarlet on a tower of ivory. It is like a pomegranate cut in twain with a knife of ivory. The pomegranate flowers that blossom in the gardens of Tyre, and are redder than roses, are not so red" (*S*, 23). Salomé's lines to Iokanaan might serve as literary vengeance for all the nineteenth-century Salomés who have suffered the pornographic descriptions of their bodies and dances by so many lecherous writers—though unlike other versions, at the end of Wilde's play, Herod orders his guards to kill Salomé. Of course, Salomé's vivid descriptions and similes of Iokanaan's hair, mouth, and lips lend themselves most easily to a homoerotic reading insofar as readers or spectators receive a parceled and eroticized representation that closely resembles descriptions of women in erotic or pornographic writing in the nineteenth century. Additionally, though, these passages in the play seem to be both an elaboration upon and a reversal of earlier descriptions both of Flaubert's *Salammbô* and of Salomé in Huysmans's *À rebours*. In Flaubert's and Huysmans's respective works, the woman's body finally disappears amid the elaborate prose that describes all that surrounds and encircles her. By comparison, in Wilde's *Salomé* we see an elaboration (perhaps an ironic one) in which Salomé's excessive descriptions finally obscure the very object of her desire. This cacophony of contradictory and illegible imagery, none of which helps the reader or listener understand anything beyond the basic plot, participates in this tradition of literary Salomés who seduce the reader into trying to interpret her, only to forestall, in the end, her legibility.

Julie Townsend

Wilde's *Salomé*, which had been associated with scandal from the moment the Lord Chamberlain's office forbade its performance in London in 1892 on the grounds of its "half biblical" and "half pornographic" nature, remained controversial well into the twentieth century.[31] Beyond that, the textual ambiguities and the proximity of the publication of the English edition of *Salome* in 1894 and Wilde's trial in 1895 contributed to the scandal that followed most productions or attempted productions of the play. Scholarship on the performance history of Wilde's *Salomé* has focused largely on Maud Allan's performances and the subsequent libel trials involving Noel Pemberton Billing in 1918.[32] Dancer Ida Rubinstein also performed a scandalous version of Wilde's tragedy in Saint Petersburg in 1907. After having the play translated into Russian, commissioning a new score for the dance of the seven veils, and working with Michel Fokine on the choreography, Rubinstein was forbidden by the synod from pronouncing a word of Wilde's drama on stage and from using any representation of the head of John the Baptist. Rubinstein nonetheless succeeded in pulling off the performance in 1908 by distributing copies of the play in advance and holding an empty platter on which she hallucinated the head of the prophet.[33] Ironically, we do not often hear about how modern dancers engaged the Salomé myth when they employed their own visions of the story.[34] Some of the most prominent avant-garde and early modern dancers revisited Salomé in their performances.

Choreographic Challenges

Because of its notorious history, Wilde's *Salomé* often serves as the benchmark for considering performances of Salomé more generally. As we have seen, dancers such as Maud Allan and Ida Rubinstein knew the play well and, like most readers, had strong feelings one way or the other about it. As many dance historians attest, the period from 1890 to 1920 was one of utter upheaval in the world of dance.[35] The French obsession with dancers had persisted despite the degeneration of classical ballet into mere formula. The rise of modern dance as a new art form was accompanied by the increased popularity and ubiquity of music-hall performances of the cancan, striptease, and belly dance. All of these developments ushered in a revitalized debate on dance aesthetics—and for the first time, women's essays and autobiographies took a prominent part in this discussion. Not surprisingly, many dancers took up the figure of Salomé. On the one hand, she was a figure of the burgeoning avant-garde, while, on the other hand, many dancers felt that they, like Salomé, had been maligned by both mainstream and avant-garde representations, which often portrayed dancers as prostitutes and femmes fatales—in short, as "perverse and hysterical creatures."

Loïe Fuller was responsible for the most influential and, ironically, least well-received revisions of Salomé in the early twentieth century. Fuller presented her experimental dances at the Folies-Bergère, and her early performances in the 1890s were a spectacle unlike any seen before.[36] Revolutionary costumes surrounded her entire body with mobile fabric, and her pioneer work in the use of electric rather than gas lights created prismatic effects on the stage. Rejecting narrative and traditional scenery, Fuller typically performed a series of short dances: *The Serpentine, The Butterfly,* and *The Violet* (all 1892), to name a few. These object-based dances removed the thing (serpent, butterfly, or flower) from any recognizable scenario or storyline. The performance metaphorically conjured the image of these objects and animals but removed them from any narrative reference. Her bodily motions were hidden from view, and she faced only the audience for her bow. Her billowy and voluminous costumes covered her body from the neck down. Using prosthetic extensions on her arms and effects of light and shadow from electric lighting, Fuller further obscured her body. In addition to inventing in 1892 what her contemporaries for the first time styled "modern dance" and developing many techniques that are still part of stage lighting, Fuller married antirealist representation to technology.

Fuller's dances removed any narrative reference or metaphorical relationship between social institutions and her performance, and she did this with technology as an integral part of the performance. Mallarmé, in his often-cited set of articles on theatre, *Crayonné au théâtre* (1886–96), holds Fuller up as an emblem for symbolism. Certainly, her challenges to Romantic and realist narrative, as well as her tendency to cover her body with yards of draped fabric, characterize her performances as a stark departure from the storylines of Romantic ballet and the highly sexualized aesthetic of the popular music-hall. If Fuller's work exercised several structural or formal parallels with symbolist and perhaps Decadent literature, then her approach to the Salomé narrative reveals a marked contrast to the examples we have considered thus far.

Fuller took up the figure of Salomé twice in her career. On both occasions, she radically altered the narrative and performed the piece as a series of dances rather than as a story per se. Rather than turning to nineteenth-century versions of Salomé, Fuller, in 1895, drew her dance from the thirteenth-century writer

Figure 22. Photograph of Loïe Fuller dancing as Salomé (1895). Courtesy of Réunion des Musées Nationaux/Art Resource, New York.

and illustrator Jacques de Voragine, for whom Salomé was an innocent pawn of Herod and Hérodias, who used her dance as a pretext to kill John the Baptist (fig. 22). Fuller's scenario reads as follows:

> Except for Salomé, the characters don't change from the role given to them by tradition: Herod, weary, irresolute, quivering with lust; Herodias uncertain of her power, worried, thirsting for vengeance; John the Baptist, minister of souls, tender and so stirring that upon approach, Salomé is under his spell; so, a miracle of faith substitutes for the legendary Salomé, drunk with blood and voluptuousness, a mystical Salomé almost chaste. It is for John the Baptist that she dances; it is for his protection that she begs against the eager desire of the tetrarque; and when Herod, driven wild with impatience, orders the decapitation—only then does Salomé cede, sacrifice herself, offer herself in exchange for grace; but the irreparable has already been committed; triumphantly, the executioner holds the bloody head encircled with the martyr's halo, and, at the terrifying apparition, Salomé collapses, thunderstruck.[37]

This version, which makes a single substitution—of one Salomé for another—puts the dance in entirely new light. If the dance is, instead of a seduction, a religious plea for the prophet's protection, then Herod nonetheless reads the dance as a sexual invitation and demands a sexual favor while decapitating the intended audience. This scenario, with its semicolons and discrete images, mirrors Fuller's staging by presenting the story through a series of tableaux rather than as a seamless narrative. Her challenges to narrative and her critique of Herod's inability to decipher the dance engage with structural elements of previous versions even as she reverses the traits of Salomé.

Despite her compelling revision, Fuller's 1895 *Salomé* was a bust. Critic Roger Marx gave one of the few positive reviews: "In the dance executed at Herod's command, Loïe Fuller is covered in orange gauze. . . . [S]he throws it aside and makes it zigzag, with the swiftness of a lightning bolt, amongst the electric spotlights. . . . [W]ith a satanic coquettery, she agitates the golden scarves . . . and once the fatal design [of Herod] is understood, there are no more gracious poses, but large and menacing gestures that call upon the deities of vengeance."[38] In general, though, audiences were disappointed to find that Fuller's performance involved quite a bit of pantomime and not as much technological artistry as they had come to expect from her.[39]

Luckily, Fuller was never easily dissuaded. Her later Salomé, written by Florent Schmitt based on a poem by Robert d'Humières, met with a better response and became the model for several important Salomé performances. Like Fuller's earlier productions, her 1907 *Tragédie de Salomé* was noted for its highly technological scenery, of which critic Jules Claretie wrote, "Loie Fuller has made studies in a special laboratory of all the effects of light that transform the stage. . . . [S]he has succeeded . . . in giving the actual appearance of the storm, a glimpse of the moonbeams cast upon the waves, of the horror of a sea of blood. . . . The light in a weird way changes the appearance of the picturesque country."[40] The Schmitt and d'Humières revision of the story takes on a very dark twist: "Herod watches Salomé dance on the terrace of his palace. John the Baptist rises to hurl his curses at Herodias. Herodias plies Salomé with jewels and takes Salomé's clothes away from her; John, seeing this, covers Salomé with his cape; Herod then decapitates John and Salomé throws the head into the sea; The bloody head then reappears in the sky"[41] and haunts Salomé, whose dance of fear provokes an earthquake, after which the rubble of the citadel buries her.[42] The performance relied heavily on colored lights and projected landscapes as décor. Once again, Fuller constructed her *Salomé* around a series of tableaux-type dances. This version, like the 1895 one, recasts Salomé by connecting with John the Baptist and putting her in conflict with Herodias.

Although reviews for the 1907 version were not as cruel as earlier ones, most critics were silent on the subject of Fuller's last Salomé. At forty-five years old and quite heavy for a dancer, Fuller may have demanded that her audience employ considerable imagination in viewing her as the youthful Salomé. The importance of this version, though, was revealed later; it inspired both Sergei Diaghilev's 1913 *Salomé* featuring Tamara Karsavina at the Paris Opera House and Ida Rubinstein's 1919 restaging at a post–World War I fund-raising gala.

Despite several attempts, dancers could not seem to live up to audiences' expectation of Salomé. Assuredly, Fuller and others offered interesting revisions of the Salomé story. But ultimately, none of them successfully recuperated Salomé from the clutches of so many nineteenth-century Herods. Perhaps Salomé, like the Orient, as Ohanian suggests, has been ruined. Just as the Schmitt and d'Humières's version revised Salomé as a heroine who tries to intervene in the story of decapitation and fails, so too did Fuller, Rubinstein, and others try— and, in the eyes of the public, fail—to recuperate this biblical figure for women dancers. It is interesting to speculate on why these dancers, who could have just shed their veils to impress the crowd, as many others did, decided instead to pursue a much more tragic Salomé, one who not only fails to achieve her purpose but is then also haunted by her failure.

Coda

Perhaps Oscar Wilde's Herod really did kill Salomé, and so it would have been better to let her lie. But rather than end on such a pessimistic note, I would like to close with a brief discussion of one of Fuller's films, which successfully took up Orientalist tropes, though not the Salomé figure, to challenge normative sexual roles and bourgeois morality.

Fuller's 1920 film *Le lys de la vie* (The Lily of Life), based on a short story by Queen Marie of Rumania, is perhaps the most explicit development of the use of Orientalist imagery to develop what we would now call a queer aesthetic. The fairy-tale film is complete with two competing princesses and a prince, love and disappointment, magical lands, and a voyage in search of—as the title suggests— the lily of life. The story is frequently disrupted with scenes and images that are peripheral to the overall narrative. The interior of the princess's castle is a site of wandering desire and a mixture of all variety of personas and paraphernalia. The cast of the film includes African servants dressed in ancient Egyptian costumes, a pet monkey and dog, and a dwarf. The set is constructed of animal skins and statues, as well as golden and semitransparent draperies. In contrast to the overarching heterosexual marriage plot, the general atmosphere is one of wandering flirtation and erotic tension: the princesses and the African servants exchange loaded glances, the monkey flirts with a dog and with the head of a bearskin rug, one of the princesses caresses the head of a dwarf in her bedchambers, and a kiss between Princess Mora and the prince is mirrored with a parallel screen of two black children kissing.

The disruptive narrative elements and free-floating sexual desires that appear throughout the film emphasize how Fuller redeployed the representational strategies of late-nineteenth-century Orientalist literature to explore, rather than narrow the scope of, feminine desire and the power of the dancing body. Salomé seems to have been too laden with cultural expectations to function as truly radical by the time dancers began to take up the story.

Notes

All translations from the French are the author's unless otherwise indicated.

1. Armen Ohanian, *The Dancer of Shamahka*, trans. Rose Wilder Lane (New York: E. P. Dutton, 1923), 252, 255 (quoted as the epigraph to this chapter; emphasis added); further page references appear in parentheses.

2. Heinrich Heine's *Atta Troll* (1847) may have set off the trend of Salomé stories. Versions of the biblical myth can be found in the works of Théodore de Banville, Gustave Flaubert, Ernest Renan, Stéphane Mallarmé, J.-K. Huysmans, Jules Laforgue, Bernard Lazare, Catulle Mendès, Albert Samain, and Guillaume Apollinaire.

3. The name "Salome" does not appear in the New Testament; Flavius Josephus, the first-century Jewish historian, was the one who gave her the name "Salome," in *Jewish Antiquities* (c. 94).

4. In *Salome and the Dance of Writing: Portraits of Mimesis in Literature* (Chicago: University of Chicago Press, 1987), Françoise Meltzer offers one of the most compelling critical explorations of the Salomé figure. In her book, Meltzer performs an informative reading of the biblical texts.

5. Critical works that make the argument that readings of Wilde's play have been limited by a critical focus on French influences include Regenia Gagnier, *Idylls of the Marketplace: Oscar Wilde and the Victorian Public* (Stanford: Stanford University Press, 1986); Steven Price and William Tydeman, *Wilde: Salome* (Cambridge: Cambridge University Press, 1996); and Joseph Donohue, "Distance, Death and Desire in *Salome*," in *The Cambridge Companion to Oscar Wilde*, ed. Peter Raby (Cambridge: Cambridge University Press, 1997), 118–42.

6. Gagnier, *Idylls of the Marketplace*, 165. The review that Gagnier quotes appeared in the *Pall Mall Gazette* on 27 February 1893.

7. Gagnier, *Idylls of the Marketplace*, 165. Meltzer, to my mind, answers this type of critical concern by showing how the various versions of Salomé participate in an ongoing artistic conversation about literary genres and the "frames" that situate writing in relation to painting. I would go further to say that contextualizing the Wilde version among the versions of other writers (and dancers for that matter) helps us to see the historical, aesthetic, and literary debate that developed through the course of these manifestations of Salomé.

8. See Gagnier, *Idylls of the Marketplace*, 166–68, for a formulation of this argument that is specific to Wilde's play.

9. Additionally, Meltzer writes that *Salammbô* was a likely inspiration for Gustave Moreau's paintings *Salomé Dancing before Herod* (1874), *The Apparition* (1876), and *Salomé Dancing* (1876), which inspired the Salomé passages in Huysmans's *À rebours*. See Meltzer, *Salome and the Dance of Writing*, 19.

10. "[L]e salut de la République et de son père." Flaubert, *Salammbô* (Paris: Gallimard, 1970), 290.

11. "[C]ar Salammbô ne voulait pas être vue, même par les murailles." Flaubert, *Salammbô* (1970), 294.

12. Gustave Flaubert, *Salammbô*, trans. J. S. Chartres (London: J. M. Dent, 1931), 164–65. The original French passage reads as follows:

> Salammbô défit ses pendants d'oreilles, son collier, ses bracelets, sa longue simarre blanche. . . . La musique au dehors continuait; c'était trois notes, toujours les mêmes, précipitées, furieuses; les cordes grinçaient, la flûte ronflait. . . . Salammbô, avec un balancement de tout son corps, psalmodiait des prières, et ses vêtements, les uns après les autres, tombaient autour d'elle.
>
> La lourde tapisserie trembla, et par-dessus la corde qui la supportait, la tête du python apparut. Il descendit lentement, comme un goutte d'eau qui coule le long d'un mur, . . . il se leva tout droit; et ses yeux, plus brilliants que des escarboucles, se dardaient sur Salammbô. (Flaubert, *Salammbô* [1970], 295–96)

13. "[L]'horreur du froid ou une pudeur" (1970), 286.

14. "[E]lle se sentait mourir" (1970). 296.

15. For a more in-depth analysis of dance metaphors in symbolist poetry and an analysis of what role "Hérodiade" played in the development of a symbolist concept of dance, see Julie Townsend, "Synaesthetics: Symbolism, Dance, and the Failure of Metaphor," *Yale Journal of Criticism* 18 (2005): 126–48.

16. "La plus belle page de mon œuvre sera celle qui ne contiendra que ce mon divin *Hérodiade*. Le peu d'inspiration que j'ai eu, je le dois à ce nom, et je crois que si mon heroine s'était appelée Salomé, j'eusse inventée ce mot somber, et rouge comme une grenade ouverte, *Hérodiade*. Du reste, je tienes à en faire un être purement rêvé et absolument independent de l'histoire. Vous me comprenez. Je n'invoque meme pas tous les tableaux des élèves du Vinci et de tous les Florentines que ont eu cette maîtresse et l'ont appelée comme moi." Stéphane Mallarmé, *Correspondance, 1862–1871*, ed. Henri Mondor (Paris: Gallimard, 1959), 154.

17. "Reculez." Stéphane Mallarmé, "Hérodiade," *Œuvres complètes* (Paris: Gallimard, 1945), 44.

18. "Laisse là ces parfums! Ne sais-tu que je les hais?" Mallarmé, *Œuvres complètes*, 45.

19. "Arrête dans ton crime." Mallarmé, *Œuvres complètes*, 45.

20. Stéphane Mallarmé, *Poems*, trans. Roger Fry (London: Chatto and Windus, 1938), 85–87. The original French passage from Mallarmé's *Œuvres complètes* reads as follows:

> Oui, c'est pour moi, pour moi, que je fleuris, déserte!
> Vous le savez, jardins d'améthyste, enfouis

Sans fin dans de savants abîmes éblouis,
Ors ignorés, gardant votre antique lumière
Sous le sombre sommeil d'une terre première,
Vous, pierres où mes yeux comme de purs bijoux
Empruntent leur clarté mélodieuse, et vous,
Métaux qui donnez à ma jeune chevelure
Une splendeur fatale et sa massive allure!

. . . .

J'aime l'horreur d'être vierge et je veux
Vivre parmi l'effroi que me font mes cheveux

. . . .

Je me crois seule en ma monotone patrie
Et tout, autour de moi, vit dans l'idolâtrie
D'un miroir qui reflète en son calme dormant
Hérodiade au clair regard de diamant. . . .
Ô charme dernier, oui! je le sens, je suis seule. (47–48)

21. Meltzer, *Salome and the Dance of Writing,* 19.

22. Gustave Flaubert, "Herodias," in *Three Tales,* trans. A. J. Krailsheimer (Oxford: Oxford University Press, 1991), 101–3. The original French passage from Gustave Flaubert, "Hérodias," *Œuvres complètes* (Paris: Editions Gallimard, 1952), reads as follows:

Une jeune fille venait d'entrer. . . . Sur le haut de l'estrade, elle retira son voile. C'était Hérodias, comme autrefois dans sa jeunesse. Puis elle se mit à danser. Ses pieds passaient l'un devant l'autre, au rythme de la flûte et d'une paire de crotales. Ses bras arrondis appelaient quelqu'un, qui s'enfuyait toujours. Elle le poursuivait, plus légère qu'un papillon . . . et semblait prête à s'envoler. . . . L'accablement avait suivi l'espoir. Ses attitudes exprimaient des soupirs, et toute sa personne une telle langueur qu'on ne savait pas si elle pleurait un dieu, ou se souriait dans sa caresse. Les paupières entre-closes, elle se tordait la taille, balançait son ventre avec des ondulations de houle, faisait trembler ses deux seins, et son visage demeurait immobile, et ses pieds n'arrêtaient pas. (2:675–76)

23. Flaubert, "Herodias," trans. Krailsheimer, 103. The original French passage from Flaubert's "Hérodias," *Œuvres complètes,* reads as follows: "Elle se jeta sur les mains, les talons en l'air, parcourut ainsi l'estrade comme un grand scarabée; et s'arrêta, brusquement. Sa nuque et ses vertèbres faisaient un angle droit. . . . Ses lèvres étaient peintes, ses sourciles très noirs, ses yeux presque terribles, et des gouttelettes à son front semblaient une vapeur sur du marbre blanc" (2:676).

24. Flaubert, "Herodias," trans. Krailsheimer, 103. The original French passage from Flaubert's "Hérodias," *Œuvres complètes,* reads as follows: "'Je veux que tu me donnes dans un plat, la tête . . . ' Elle avait oublié le nom, mais reprit en souriant: 'la tête de Ioakanaan!' Le Tétrarque s'affaissa sur lui-même, écrasé" (2:676).

25. Price and Tydeman, *Wilde: Salome,* 147.

26. In addition to Meltzer's *Salome and the Dance of Writing,* see the following important analyses of Huysmans's novel: Charles Bernheimer, "Fetishism and Decadence: Salome's Severed Heads," in *Fetishism as Cultural Discourse,* ed. Emily Apter and William Pietz (Ithaca, NY: Cornell University Press, 1993), 62–83; and Rita Felski, "The Counterdiscourse of the Feminine in Three Texts by Wilde, Huysmans, and Sacher-Masoch," *PMLA* 106 (1991): 1094–1105.

27. Meltzer, *Salome and the Dance of Writing*, 20.

28. J.-K. Huysmans, *Against Nature*, trans. Robert Baldick (Harmondsworth: Penguin Books, 1959), 64. The original French passage from Huysmans, *À rebours* (Paris: Gallimard, 1977), reads as follows: "La face recueillie, solennelle, presque auguste, elle commence la lubrique danse qui doit réveiller les sens assoupis du vieil Hérode; ses seins ondulent et, au frottement de ses colliers qui tourbillonnent, leurs bouts se dressent; sur la moiteur de sa peau les diamants, attachés, scintillent; ses bracelets, ses ceintures, ses bagues, crachent des étincelles; sur sa robe triomphale, couturée de perles, ramagée d'argent, lamée d'or, la cuirasse des orfèvreries dont chaque maille est une pierre, entre en combustion, croise des serpenteaux de feu, grouille sur la chair mate, sur la peau rose thé, ainsi que des insectes splendides aux élytres éblouissants, marbrés de carmin, ponctués de jaune aurore, diaprés de bleu d'acier, tigrés de vert paon" (143).

29. Hugo von Hofmannsthal, *Harry Graf Kessler Briefwechsel, 1898–1929*, ed. Hilde Burger (Frankfurt: Insel, 1968), 135–36, quoted in Price and Tydeman, *Wilde: Salome*, 139.

30. Oscar Wilde, *Salome*, trans. Alfred Douglas (1894; repr., New York: Dover, 1967); further page references are given in parentheses, with *S* indicating this facsimile edition (as discussed in the preface to the present volume).

31. Edward Pigott, examiner of plays at the Lord Chamberlain's office, described Wilde's play—a "miracle of impudence"—in these terms; see John Russell Stephens, *The Censorship of English Drama, 1824–1901* (Cambridge: Cambridge University Press, 1980), 112.

32. For a thorough study of these trials, see Michael Kettle, *Salome's Last Veil: The Libel Case of the Century* (London: Hart-Davis, 1977). Kettle's research is also taken up by Philip Hoare in *Oscar Wilde's Last Stand: Decadence, Conspiracy, and the Most Outrageous Trial of the Century* (London: Duckworth, 1997). For further discussion of the controversy about Allan's performance provoked by British parliamentarian Noel Pemberton-Billing, see chapter 7 of the present volume.

33. Jacques Depaulis, *Ida Rubinstein: Une inconnue jadis célèbre* (Paris: H. Champion, 1995), 57–58.

34. Richard Bizot gives an overview of several performances in "The Turn-of-the-Century Salome Era: High- and Pop-Culture Variations on the Dance of the Seven Veils," *Choreography and Dance* 2 (1992): 71–87.

35. See, for example, Jack Anderson, *Ballet and Modern Dance: A Concise History* (Princeton, NJ: Princeton Book Co., 1986).

36. This section draws upon my chapter "Alchemic Visions and Technological Advances: Sexual Morphology in Loïe Fuller's Dances," in *Dancing Desires: Choreographing Sexualities On and Off the Stage*, ed. Jane Desmond (Madison: University of Wisconsin Press, 2001), 73–96.

37. Giovanni Lista, *Loïe Fuller: Danseuse de la belle époque* (Paris: Art Somogy, 1994), 224.

38. Quoted in Lista, *Loïe Fuller*, 226.

39. In addition to the disappointed reviews, the magazine *La vie parisienne* continued a long tradition of critiquing dancer's bodies with this most inelegant description, which appeared under the heading "The Undressed of the Year": "To Loïe Fuller, the pompon award—if not in nudity, then in electricity. . . . There was something for every taste; now blonde, now redheaded, now pink, now green. . . . [W]e can brag of having ogled a multi-colored woman." Quoted in Lista, *Loïe Fuller*, 230. Needless to say, Fuller was humiliated.

40. Quoted in Loïe Fuller, *Fifteen Years of a Dancer's Life with Some Account of Her Distinguished Friends* (Boston: Small, Maynard, 1913), 282–83.

41. Lista, *Loïe Fuller*, 456.

42. Depaulis, *Ida Rubinstein*, 223.

"Surely You Are Not Claiming to Be More Homosexual than I?"

Claude Cahun and Oscar Wilde

LIZZIE THYNNE

D URING THE German occupation of Jersey, Claude Cahun[1] (1894–1954), the French avant-garde photographer and writer, would go for walks with her partner and collaborator Suzanne Malherbe (1892–1972) to search for materials that they could use in their resistance campaign that was designed to spread demoralization and defeatism among the German troops. Cahun recalls finding a page from a German magazine featuring the photograph of a triumphant, marching regiment. She realized that by hiding half of the image, she could completely change its meaning: without their exultant faces, the legs and boots of the soldiers covered in mud appeared extremely exhausted. Carefully cutting the photograph, she describes how, having signed it with the "ritornello" she and her partner used, she "looked for an aesthetic way of presenting it. I found a pretty frame of the right size. It contained a photo of Oscar Wilde and Alfred Douglas —the whole thing dating from so long ago I had almost forgotten it—I don't know why I had kept it except that we weren't short of cupboard space either in Nantes or here. I opened the frame, substituted the boots for the 1892 photo and stuck it together again."[2] The couple then sneaked into an empty house that they knew was about to be occupied by German troops. They attached the picture to a wall where Cahun hoped it would be discovered after the soldiers' arrival so the troops would think that a member of their company had made it.

Cahun narrates this incident in a letter to her friend Gaston Ferdière in 1946, the year after she and Malherbe had been released from St. Helier Prison at the Liberation on 8 May 1945. It suggests the irrelevance to her, at that moment, of the memory of Oscar Wilde but at the same time gives a wry nod to the aestheticism that she associates with him. The pretty frame, after all, has its uses, and its meanings can be interrogated and made to serve an urgent political purpose through juxtaposition with the base, filthy boots. This emblematic story evokes some of the tensions and continuities between a modernist practice in which objects and images may be dramatically recontextualized or reframed to disrupt or empty out their original significance (here exemplified by Cahun's photomontage) and the fin-de-siècle culture from which it emerges. This chapter explores connections between the work of Cahun, now known mainly as a surrealist photographer, and the heritage of Oscar Wilde. The relationship shifted over time, as Cahun's art and thinking evolved, in the context of the profound social and political changes following both world wars and alongside the art and thinking of the surrealists with whom she finally associated herself in the 1930s. A key figure in Cahun's engagement with the Decadent tradition is Salomé, a persona she often adopted and alluded to in her writing and photography. Cahun's reappropriation of some of the same icons and themes that Wilde had utilized from nineteenth-century French literature provides a telling glimpse of how modern homosexual and gendered identities were being forged and resisted out of that tradition.

The photographic portraits produced by Claude Cahun with Suzanne Malherbe have become the subject of critical interest since the early 1990s because of their sustained play with identity and gender, anticipating the concerns of contemporary artists and foregrounding the construction of subjectivity through the image.[3] Her work, much of it long hidden and neglected, seems to exemplify recent theorizations of gender as performance. As far as is known, many of the couple's portraits were scarcely exhibited in their lifetime, except in the form of photomontages accompanying Cahun's text of her experimental autobiographical work, *Aveux non avenus* (Cancelled Confessions), published in 1930. Born Lucy Schwob, Cahun was known to her contemporaries principally as a writer of poetry, prose, and essays often published in literary journals, including the prestigious

Mercure de France. For a long time after her death, she was thought to have been the male author of *Les paris sont ouverts* (Place Your Bets): a booklet, issued in 1934, that explores the nature of revolutionary art and defends avant-garde practice in the face of the Soviet and French Communist Parties' endorsement of socialist realism.[4] Suzanne Malherbe, her lover and stepsister to whom she was linked from the age of fifteen, worked under the pseudonym "Marcel Moore"; a graphic artist, she produced posters, stage sets, illustrations, and possibly some of Cahun's costumes. Long thought to have been self-portraits, the extensive archive of images of Cahun is now viewed as the product of the partnership of Cahun and Moore (without whom many of these photographs could not have been taken).[5] Well before the First Surrealist Manifesto was published in 1924, Cahun and Moore were the first women to start using photography in a sustained way (one that drew critically on psychoanalysis) to go beyond normative social identities and radically destabilize the genre of auto-portraiture as well as the representation of gender within it.[6]

The Multiplication of Personalities

Cahun's connections with Wilde have a particular resonance because he was an associate of her uncle, the symbolist writer Marcel Schwob, among other leading French literary figures including André Gide, Paul Valéry, and Pierre Louÿs. Schwob was a significant critic as well as a writer who had a strong interest in British literature, translating some of the works of Robert Louis Stevenson (whom he much admired), *Hamlet* (with Sarah Bernhardt as the eponymous protagonist) in 1905, and Wilde's "Selfish Giant" (1888). He was also the cofounder of the prestigious literary journal *Mercure de France.* Having largely rejected the suggested amendments of other Parisian friends such as Stuart Merrill and Adolphe Retté, Wilde entrusted the final corrections to the French text of his play, *Salomé*, to Schwob before it went to the publishers.[7] *Salomé* had made Wilde more popular in France—not least, perhaps, because the 1892 banning of the play in England, just before it was due to have its first performance with Sarah Bernhardt in the lead role, highlighted British hypocrisy. By the time the French translation of *The Picture of Dorian Gray* (1890, revised 1891) was published in 1895, Wilde's trials were under way and provided the opportunity for certain critics to attack and dismiss his work in France, as in England, by conflating his oeuvre with the scandalous revelations of his sexual life. One such critic, Jules Huret, questioned whether French literature could be enriched by the translating the work of this "*esthète 'de porc'*" (swinish aesthete).[8] He linked the plot of *The Picture of Dorian Gray* with the trial in progress, claiming that "in the end one sees that Oscar Wilde has not so much imagination as he has vices, and that he was only writing documentation."[9] Huret's derogatory allusions in the same article to not only Marcel Schwob but also the poet and novelist Catulle Mendes as friends of Wilde's provoked both of them to challenge him to a duel.

Cahun's relationship to the memory of her uncle and his circle was deeply ambivalent. Her adoption of the name of her paternal grandmother, Mathilde Cahun, was in part an attempt to establish her separate literary identity and detach herself from the Schwob legacy. The extended series of self-portraits that she produced with Moore are in many ways an articulation of the French symbolists' and British aesthetes' negation of the authentic and transparent singular subject. She often drew on characters deployed by those traditions, including Medusa, the Harlequin, and, notably, Salomé. The fact that this series was produced within the context of a collaborative lesbian relationship also means that it goes beyond "the romantic myth of the individual artist, communicated through the heightened selfhood of dandyism."[10]

Cahun's essay on Schwob makes clear that she sees the author as inaccessible behind the personae that he created: "Marcel Schwob was more egotistical than the most egotistical, transposing himself, in the manner of an actor, into each of his heroes."[11] Her opening description of her uncle, however, might apply as much to herself and the strategies she endlessly adopted to defer self-identification and the possibility of self-revelation: "There are certain men whose real life escapes us. Even if we knew the external movements of these hermetic beings with great precision and in the smallest detail, they would still be like a dead clock of which we have lost the key."[12] If her uncle had not suffered an early death, he "might . . . have let down the masks and spoken for himself."[13] Only through the life of his imagination, Cahun claims, can we know Schwob—a comment that mirrors the concept of his series of tales of legendary figures, including the Edinburgh murderers Messieurs Burke and Hare, in *Vies imaginaires* (Imaginary Lives) (1896). Schwob's introduction to this book is an attack on the generalizing tendencies of realism, its attempts to identify social types, and its preoccupation with veracity: "Art is opposed to general ideas, describes only the individual, desires only the unique. It does not classify; it *de*classifies."[14] The singular, bizarre, and often perverse aspects of the chosen "lives" are the springboard for fantastic and often darkly humorous tales. The interest of *Vies imaginaires* lies in a fascination with the transgressive, if not murderous, actions of its protagonists such as Clodia—the "shameless matron" who poisons her husband, loves only her "beardless and womanish" brother, Clodius, and is herself murdered, after debauching herself in the Roman underworld.[15] Clodia, like Wilde's beautiful, seductive Dorian Gray, comes to a bad end, but her incestuous narcissism is not condemned but merely presented as part of the decadence of the ancient world, to which the moral norms of bourgeois society do not apply.

Wilde's earlier seminal essay "The Decay of Lying" (1889, revised 1891)—which, as Richard Ellmann says, had become "the *locus classicus* of the converging aesthetic idea of writers everywhere"[16]—also argues the case for an art freed from the demands of moral didacticism and truthfulness. In this essay, which stages a conversation on aesthetics between Cyril and Vivian, Wilde's dialogue form allows his essay to be ironically self-reflexive. Even while we suspect that Wilde is advocating many of the aestheticist views held by his main spokesman, Vivian, the use of the fictional persona allows him to distance himself from any absolute identification with what the character says, thus disavowing any assumptions of sincerity while at the same time illustrating its key arguments about the worthlessness of art imitating life. The distantiation is further achieved when Vivian spells out his ideas to Cyril in the form of an article titled "The Decay of Lying" that he has written for the *Retrospective Review*, a magazine produced by his club, "The Tired Hedonists" (*CW*, 8:7). The article satirizes the realist novelist and promotes aesthetic doctrine: "Art takes life as part of her rough material, recreates it, and refashions it with fresh forms, is absolutely indifferent to fact, invents, imagines, dreams and keeps between herself and reality the impenetrable barrier of beautiful style, of decorative and ideal treatment" (*CW*, 8:22).

Although Vivian's doctrine (which is also Wilde's) is heavily imbued with an adherence to a Romantic notion of transcendental beauty, its stress on the independence of art from life helped to open the way for a complete break with mimeticism and the emergence of a modernist practice that emphasizes the status of art as representation and as form unshackled from the demands of verisimilitude. Cahun was able to exploit this aspect of aestheticism in her work, freeing it from any judgment "by any external standard of resemblance" (*CW*, 8:31), thus exemplifying Dorian Gray's (and Wilde's) opinion that insincerity is "a method by which we may multiply our personalities" (*CW*, 12:229).[17] Far from revealing an authentic image of herself, her series of portraits render her identity

Lizzie Thynne

Figure 23. Claude Cahun (and Marcel Moore), untitled, c. 1921. Courtesy of Soizic Audouard.

opaque and create a visual analogue for the aestheticist ideas espoused by both Wilde and Schwob that art should provide not a mirror but a mask. It is impossible to identify the real Cahun from her series of personae featuring masculine and feminine traits—from, for example, the dandy (fig. 23) to the weightlifter to the ageing masked figure in a nightdress standing on a cemetery wall.[18] In every instance, the artifice of these poses and mise-en-scène comes to the fore. Even a brief glance at the images of Cahun from her youth to old age reveals that she maintained a lifelong concern with how the subject can be transformed through the image by the manipulation of hair, clothing, posture, and setting. Cahun's strategy of constantly rearranging the poses, props, and set within the same frame also has the effect of underlining the status of the photograph as representation and thus questions its relationship to any external reality: a strategy that is the visual equivalent of the literary techniques used by Wilde to throw into relief the artifice of his characters' speech.

The 1921 portrait of Cahun in the black velvet suit and white cravat subversively appropriates and critiques the dandy, mimicking the pose of Wilde the aesthete in the 1882 Napoleon Sarony photographs.[19] Far from picturesque, her image is boldly confrontational. It is not beautiful but rather grotesque in a conventional sense, not an "ideal treatment" but instead a persona neutered by the shaving of her head.[20] Among the many connotations of the shaved head is its Jewishness, since it evokes the ritual of Orthodox women. Moreover, it suggests the idea of punishment because in many European conflicts hair removal has historically been the punishment of prisoners, adulterers, and women who consort with the enemy. In this portrait, Cahun appropriates the dandy's garb and mimics the pose of one hand on hip but also contradicts that aesthetic pose by clenching the other fist, thereby giving the figure a much more ambivalent identity. What scholars have not observed is how this striking image connects with two others that have very similar framing, location, and backdrop and in which the rearrangement of objects in the frame draws attention to the frame itself as the field of representation.[21] The first shows Cahun as a sailor, an image that presents another masculine *travestie* (fig. 24). The second is the picture of the artist in a feminine outfit, a décolleté wrap, which exposes her nude shoulders (fig. 25). Across all of these three images, certain elements remain constant while others vary, with some items arranged within the same frame to create new meanings. The simple cloth backdrop, for example, changes from a single sheet in the dandy photograph to two overlapping ones in the sailor picture and is finally repeated as the décolleté wrap on her shoulders in the third image.[22] Moreover, in the final image, Cahun is lower in the frame, and instead of staring, her eyes are averted from the camera in a more conventionally feminine pose. Interestingly, the key element that remains constant is the shaven head of the subject, which de-sexes it and serves to interrogate the gendered clothes, preventing them from anchoring the subject as either male or female. The setting is also apparently the same one in each image: the skirting board included in each frame emphasizes the incongruous staging in a space marked as private—each a scene of fantasy that is being performed in a domestic environment rather than a professional studio with an illusionistic or neutral background.[23]

The refusal to anchor the subject in any essential identity but instead to emphasize the possibility of play, performance, and the artistic reinvention of self undoubtedly made aestheticism attractive to those like Cahun and Wilde whose sexuality placed them outside social acceptability. Much of Wilde's work, as

Lizzie Thynne

Figure 24. Claude Cahun (and Marcel Moore), untitled, c. 1920. Courtesy of Soizic Audouard.

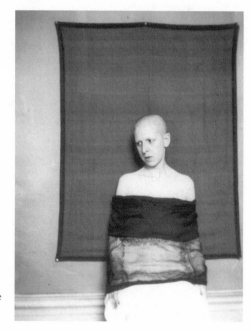

Figure 25. Claude Cahun (and Marcel Moore), untitled, c. 1921. Courtesy of the Jersey Heritage Trust, JHT 00041/m.

countless critics have remarked, is an ironic questioning and mimicry of dominant Victorian forms of social categorization and sense-making, whether it be in the light-hearted mode of *The Importance of Being Earnest* (1895), the Decadent philosophy (derived from Walter Pater) of Lord Henry Wotton in *The Picture of Dorian Gray,* or the irreverent rhetoric of essays such as "The Decay of Lying." In her famous 1960 study, Ellen Moers shows that the dandy tradition in its social and literary expressions—from Regency dandy Beau Brummell to French *Symboliste* Charles Baudelaire, as well as that vividly embodied by Wilde—is based on parody, with all the connotations of inauthenticity that that implies.[24] Jonathan Fryer comments about Wilde's Oxford days, "[H]e acquired a wardrobe of formal clothes, punctiliously following the codes set down by Society about what was appropriate for day, evening, town or country. It is no wonder that, in some quarters he began to acquire a reputation as a parvenu and a snob. Yet soon the loudness of the checks of some of his leisure wear and the flamboyance of his neckties indicated he was aping the English gentleman, rather than trying to pass for one. . . . [H]e was becoming a dandy dilettante in disguise."[25] The effect of the public investigations of Wilde's sexuality was indelibly to link his external appearance (that is, his flamboyant, effeminate dress, and his poses) with homosexuality, the dandy image being locked to a single referent. Wilde's conviction and imprisonment were not only a personal and professional disaster but also meant that his work became identified with a homosexuality seen as immoral and perverse. As Alan Sinfield has argued, the trials of 1895 cemented Wilde's effeminate image as what a homosexual looked like: "[A]t that point the entire, vaguely disconcerting nexus of effeminacy, leisure, idleness, immorality, luxury, insouciance, decadence and aestheticism which Wilde was perceived variously as instantiating was transformed into a brilliantly precise image."[26]

The trials undoubtedly helped to piece together a modern homosexual identity, which could be appropriated by queers in the fight for social recognition. Yet at the same time, the construction of "an Oscar Wilde" as a homosexual in the aftermath of the trials worked against the radical undermining of identity that Wilde's life and work exemplify. Both his own history and much of his writing throw into question any fit between external appearance and an essential self. The widely publicized prosecution of the novel *The Well of Loneliness* for obscenity in 1928 had a similar effect to Wilde's trials in fixing perceptions of what a lesbian was. In her courageous novel, which was banned from further circulation in Britain, English writer Radclyffe Hall earnestly adopted the singular category of the essentialist female invert from sexological discourse, thus confirming public suspicions that the lesbian was indeed a mannish woman.[27] By contrast, Cahun/Moore's photography questions the image as a means of categorization and identification. In its paradox, humor, and performativity, Cahun's work—rather than Hall's controversial fiction—perpetuates and develops the subversive dissimulation of Wilde's aestheticism for a modern, if not postmodern, audience.

"Daniel Douglas" and 47,000 Perverts

Cahun mainly settled on the name "Claude Cahun" as her artistic alias beginning around 1916, when she was twenty-four. "Cahun" was gender-ambiguous, and as she observed many years later, the name was that of her "obscure Jewish relatives with whom [she] felt more affinity"[28] than with the memory of her father or with Marcel Schwob. Her decision to choose this name was a brave move in the anti-Semitic climate of wartime France not least because she had already suffered from anti-Semitic bullying at the time of the Dreyfus Affair (1894–1906).[29] It was also about 1916 that she cropped her hair for the first time and took on a more distinctly boyish appearance: a look that culminated in the bald-headed photographs taken in the early 1920s, as previously discussed.[30] Yet "Claude Cahun" was not her only pseudonym from this period. First, there was "Claude Courlis," the name under which she published her first text, *Vues et visions* (Views and Visions), which Moore illustrated.[31] Secondly, there was "Daniel Douglas," a name she used in several articles written for the Nantes journal *La gerbe* from 1918 to 1920.[32] "Courlis," from the French for *curlew*, is an allusion to her beaked nose, and the joining of "Daniel," a Jewish first name, with the surname of Lord Alfred Douglas may have been intended as an ironic conjuncture of the monstrous: either the Jew with the noble Englishman or the Jew with the renegade "Bosie" (Alfred Douglas's nickname), the "other" of Oscar Wilde, who led Wilde to his perdition. The adoption of "Douglas" may have formed part of her rebellion against the paternal heritage represented by both Schwob and Wilde. In other words, "Douglas" might be thought of as a mimicry of the bad boy who felt himself constantly in the shadow of his more famous and more talented older lover, not to mention the fact that he was locked in a bitter Oedipal struggle with his father, the Marquess of Queensberry, whose accusation that Wilde was a sodomite had spurred the Irish author into suing the aristocrat for criminal libel.

Quotations from Douglas, among other writers, including Gide, Plato, and Shakespeare, preface sections of Cahun's manuscript that she entitled "Les jeux uraniens" (Uranian games), also called "Amor Amicitae" (The Love of Friendship), written in 1913 and unpublished. The fact that the quotations are handwritten suggests that they are an addition to the original text; they have the effect of placing it in a context of homosexual writing. The manuscript has a handwritten notice with a rather adolescent tone on the first page, written in English: "Trespassers will be prosecuted." This warning may have been intended to apply not only to those readers who consult the document without permission but also those who trespass against "Uranian games."[33] The opening sentence begins the exploration of the theme: "Better than love, friendship is an art."[34] The text, however, is also prefaced by a quotation from Douglas's best-known poem, "Two Loves" (1892), which contains the famous line—which Wilde cited during the trials—"The Love that dare not speak its name."[35] (This unspeakable love is, of course, homosexuality.) Cahun's quotation from Douglas's fine poem suggests that the friendship alluded to is not just love in the abstract but specifically homosexual love: "I pray thee, speak me sooth, / What is thy name? He said: My name is Love."[36]

"Les jeux uraniens" is Cahun's first attempt as a young writer to explore the languages of homosexuality inherited from the Decadent tradition. It takes the form of a dialogue, written in the masculine first person, between a friend and his loved one. The two titles of the piece refer to two dominant ways of constructing same-sex love: first, through the modern science of sexology, and second, through the traditions of the ancient Greeks, particularly that of *pæderastia,* the love of men for boys. "Urnings" were defined by the German lawyer and classical scholar Karl Heinrich Ulrichs (1825–1895) as "individuals among us whose body is built like a male, and at the same time, whose sexual drive is directed towards men"; the love of Urnings he "termed *Uranian* love or man-manly love."[37] Ulrichs's work was very influential in the emerging discipline of sexology, and both Richard von Krafft-Ebing and Havelock Ellis, whose work Cahun later translated, drew on Ulrich's writings. Classical culture also provided ways of figuring the attraction of like for like in the myths concerning the characters of Narcissus, Hermaphrodite, Salmacis, and Sappho, which Freud was able to draw on in his construction of psychic narratives in the emerging field of psychoanalysis. Homosexuality was often defined as narcissism during this period.[38] "Les jeux uraniens" introduces the play with this theme, which was to become a major trope of Cahun's work, both affirming and interrogating it as a metaphor for homosexuality.[39] The text is dedicated to R. M.—that is, Renée Mathilde (Lucy Schwob's middle names)—from her friend (*ami*) Claude Cahun, suggesting an exchange with the self, yet a self that is already a split subject. If the dialogue of lover and beloved presented here, as François Leperlier, biographer and editor of her oeuvre, argues, is "a variation of the narcissistic relationship,"[40] then it also questions the idea that this relationship is merely *self*-love. In other words, the title, the preface, and the dedication in this work present a circuit of desire that moves between and across the pair as well as showing one as the creation of the other, simultaneously shadow and model. The speaker moves from contemplation of the self to gazing at the other: "These are the reflections I had yesterday, looking closely at my eyes in the oval mirror. . . . [Y]ou came up behind me; you leant on my shoulder; suddenly the mist of your breath condensed on the tarnished glass, and when the cloud had evaporated your image had replaced mine."[41]

The photograph of Cahun as Harlequin shows the subject poised beside a mirror (fig. 26). In countless nineteenth-century representations of a woman at her toilette, the subject gazes at herself in a mirror while her body is on display for the viewer.[42] Here, however, Cahun stares at the viewer while her reflection gazes to the right out of the frame behind her. Read in conjunction with a matching photograph of Moore,[43] the Harlequin photograph becomes a double portrait, revealing the reflected Harlequin's gaze as a look at another, the lover. In a symmetrical composition, Moore stands to the right of a mirror in which we see her reflection gazing off to the left, as if at the reflected Cahun. Thus, not only does the Harlequin/Cahun not look at herself, but her reflection gazes at another, her lover. The effect is to enclose the viewer in the circle of the lovers' looks—their reflections look at each other and they look at us.

In many ways, in *The Picture of Dorian Gray,* the protagonist's love of his youthful image is shown to lead to his downfall and descent into excessive decadence, including his unspecified, malign influence on young men and frequenting of underworld scenes of vice. Wilde's novel thus appears to affirm the construction of homosexuality as a sterile and amoral form of narcissism. But another reading suggests that the repression of the "Love that dare not speak its name" is what causes Dorian's restless and doomed search for pleasure. Dorian's fatal attraction to artist Basil Hallward's portrait of him is at least partly because of Hallward's projection of his hidden desire for Dorian into his painting. Wilde also mocked the myth of Narcissus elsewhere;[44] when asked by the prosecuting

counsel, Edward Carson, at his trial whether he had ever adored a young man
madly, he replied, to loud laughter, "I have never given adoration to anybody
except myself."[45]

Significantly, Cahun began using Douglas's name after she saw him in court
in London in 1918, when she went to report on a widely publicized case brought
by the actress and dancer Maud Allan in connection with her private performance of Wilde's *Salomé.* (Even though the Lord Chancellor, Edward Piggot-
Smyth, had declined to grant a license to Wilde's play in 1892, the drama could
be presented before private audiences, as it was in 1905, 1906, and 1911 by the New
Stage Club, the Literary Theatre Society, and the New Players, respectively.)[46]
Allan brought the case against Independent MP Noel Pemberton Billing after a
paper he edited, the *Vigilante,* implied that the production would attract perverts. Douglas, having by this time vehemently renounced homosexuality and
repudiated his relationship with Wilde, was called as a witness for the defense to
testify to his former lover's perverse intentions in writing the play. *Salomé,* which

Wilde originally wrote in French, was based on a story of female transgression that had become emblematic in the culture, and the play was well received in France on its publication.[47] It was translated into English by Alfred Douglas. As both Erin Williams Hyman and Julie Townsend remind us in the present volume, the play was banned in England on the grounds that it violated censorship laws because it depicted biblical characters (see chapters 3 and 6). The drama enjoyed its first production when François-Aurélian Lugné-Poe's Théâtre de l'Œuvre staged it in Paris in 1896.

The proceedings of Allan's case were published in detail in the London *Times* from 30 May to 5 June 1918. The reports of the case provide a fascinating glimpse not only of how Wilde's work and reputation could be mobilized to spread paranoia about a queer fifth column during World War I but also of how lesbianism by association was made visible in an attempt to demonize enemies threatening Britain from within.[48] In many respects, as Michael Kettle and Philip Hoare have shown, the Billing case echoes the trajectory of Wilde's trials because the occasion for Allan's prosecution was also a response to the slur of homosexuality.[49] The paragraph in the *Vigilante*, which was the basis for Allan's charge of obscene libel, was headed "The Cult of the Clitoris." Billing's offensively worded article implied that those people attending Allan's performance of *Salomé* were members of this supposed cult and that their names could be found in the "black book" of 47,000 perverts that Billing's associate, Harold Spencer, who also testified at the hearing, said had been compiled by the German secret service because their vices made them vulnerable to manipulation by the enemy.[50]

Billing's tactic in his defense was to attempt to conflate Allan, the performer, both with Salomé, her character, and by association with the discreditable Wilde, the author. To prove his point, Billing argued that Allan's interest in the role of Salomé arose from the hereditary sadism in her family, which had apparently led her brother to be convicted of the murder and rape of two young women. On this view, while some sufferers act on this hereditary instinct by becoming criminals, others are drawn to the representation of the acts they dare not perform in real life. Thus, when toying with the bleeding head of John the Baptist, Allan was committing an "act of sadism in pantomime."[51] She must, moreover, have possessed the personal knowledge of the acts depicted to perform them. In particular, Billing's defense implied that the fact that Allan had understood the term *clitoris* sufficiently well to bring her charge of libel was itself evidence of incriminating knowledge of unnatural practices. As Billing asserted, "out of 24 people who were shown that libel including many professional men who were shown that libel only one of them who happened to be a barrister, understood what it meant."[52] Allan lost the case, despite the unconvincing nature of the accusations made against her and the contradictory and hypocritical testimony provided by the likes of Douglas, a Catholic priest, Spencer, and the medical evidence relating to perversion. As with Wilde, Allan never recovered from the consequences, and her stage career largely came to an end.

Cahun's report of the Billing trial is necessarily much briefer than the daily reports in the British press. Although she notes that the title of the article that had given rise to the case for obscene libel was censored in the English newspapers, she omits mentioning "The Cult of the Clitoris" in name, possibly because of its unsuitability for publication in the *Mercure de France* (although one assumes that she must have heard the many references to the clitoris if she attended the whole trial). Instead, she describes Billing's diatribe rather wryly as "apparently a medical term describing the morals of all the people taking part or attending the play."[53] Her report consists of extracts from the proceedings that she relates verbatim and with very little comment, choosing to focus on those aspects of the proceedings that she thinks will be of interest to her French literary audience. After drawing an analogy with Gustave Flaubert's prosecution for publishing his novel *Madame Bovary* (1857), which also took place in wartime, she announces that she will concentrate on the parts of the interrogation that deal with the literary aspects of the trial and with the private life of Oscar Wilde.

Cahun gives relatively little space to the long cross-examination of Maud Allan, although, as I argue below, her knowledge of Allan's performance at the trial has interesting parallels with her 1925 novella "Salomé the Skeptic." She includes at length the testimony of Douglas and prefaces this section with an apparently sympathetic reference to him, as a witness on whom Billing was depending to win his literary and moral case: "[N]o doubt he was expecting a lot from an ageing, discouraged man who by now is at the mercy of anyone who comes along armed with the name of Wilde."[54] Billing's deployment of Douglas, not surprisingly, backfired. During the past six years, Douglas had attempted to discredit both Wilde's literary and moral status at every possible juncture. In large part, his anger toward his former lover was directed against Wilde's literary executor, Robert Ross, who had divulged information about Wilde's hostile sentiments toward "Bosie" to Arthur Ransome, whose critical study of the Irish author appeared in 1912. In particular, Douglas took exception to Ransome's dis-

Lizzie Thynne

closure of those parts of the autobiographical document that Wilde had completed in prison and that Ross had published, in tactfully abridged form, in 1905, under the title *De Profundis*. Ransome intimated that in the complete text of *De Profundis*, Wilde referred to Douglas in the most uncomplimentary ways and regarded Douglas as responsible for encouraging the perilous failed libel suit against Queensberry. When Douglas, who converted to Catholicism in 1911, had tried to sue Ransome's publisher, he had experienced the humiliation of hearing the defense read long, condemnatory passages from the unpublished sections of Wilde's prison document. Thereafter, he remained for many years intensely antipathetic toward Wilde's reputation, doing his utmost to impugn not only his former lover's but also Ross's name. Little wonder that during the Billing trial, Douglas called Wilde "the greatest force for evil in Europe in 350 years."[55]

Moreover, Douglas argued that *Salomé* was inherently immoral and influenced by the work of Austrian sexologist Richard von Krafft-Ebing, which he claimed Wilde was reading at the time of writing. Predictably, Allan's counsel then produced letters from Wilde and Douglas incriminating Douglas in the very homosexual perversions that he had been arguing informed Wilde's entire oeuvre and *Salomé* in particular. Cahun's footnote explaining one of the letters produced is rather less sympathetic to both members of the couple: "It was a rather impertinent letter written by Lord Douglas to Mr. Labonchere [*sic*], director of the journal *Truth,* from the period during which Douglas and Wilde bragged of wanting to sodomize the world."[56] This remark may be addressed to the sensibilities of the readership of the *Mercure de France,* in which many of Cahun's fictional works and essays were published in the teens and twenties, but it also suggests some disapproval of both men's lack of discretion. Cahun's explorations of homosexual desire are never made sexually explicit in her work; rather, as we have seen, they are often veiled and metaphoric. She had seen the fate that had befallen Wilde and, in this case, Maud Allan, for their defiance of Victorian morality. Although French society was less overtly censorious of creative work, Cahun took pains to make her writings and photography inaccessible to any reductive autobiographical interpretation, as the elliptical title "Cancelled Confessions" suggests.[57] Cahun concludes by noting the judge's remarks to "Bosie" in his summing-up:

> [H]e said he hoped that this ardent repentance was sincere and that his [Bosie's] regret in the part played in the dishonorable acts that led Wilde to his downfall

was authentic. It was never too late to put it right. He then showed the passages of Salomé written by Lord Douglas himself. Seated by the door, the Lord jumped up and shouted at the top of his voice: "[Y]ou have no right to say I wrote those words! You are a liar!" He was seized by policemen as he spoke and thrown out. The judge said he was merely repeating the assertion made by the witness himself.[58]

Cahun ends her piece by refusing any other comment than to say the best response is to laugh with Judge Darling, "the wise man of the trial."[59] Kettle comments that Darling's tendency to make jokes at the expense of the defendants brought before him made him understandably unpopular. Cahun, however, clearly appreciated the judge's disdain for hypocrisy and the sense of the absurd that he displayed. Indeed, in 1944 she deployed the same tactic of "black humor"[60] in her trial for resisting the German occupation, using it to debunk the absurdities of Nazi logic.[61]

"They Imagine I Am in Love with It"

In *Salomé,* Wilde's contribution to this long obsession with a murderous female figure was to reassert the representation of her as the ultimate castrating woman who takes her revenge for her unrequited lust by securing the decapitation of John the Baptist, renamed Iokanaan in an ineffectual bow to his sanctified status. Wilde exploits to the full the possibilities for hyperbolic description of Iokanaan's person in Salomé's speeches, in which she eulogizes in turn his body, his hair, and, finally, his mouth, which she longs to kiss, achieving her desire only when Herod reluctantly consents to her wish to have the prophet's decapitated head on a silver platter in return for dancing the dance of the seven veils.[62] In her perverse desire, Wilde's Salomé bears little relation to the biblical figure of Salomé who is prompted by her mother (Herodias), rather than by her own lust, to ask for the head of the Baptist. Wilde's initial title for the play, "The Decapitation of Salome,"[63] also drew attention to the punishment of the heroine for her deadly passion.

Allusions to Salomé abound in Cahun's work, and the character has a particular resonance for Cahun, as a figure around whom a complex nexus of discourses about gender, sexuality, and art revolved. In 1925, Cahun dedicated a version of the Salomé story, "Salomé the Skeptic," to "O.W." (Oscar Wilde). This is one of the ironic, parodying portraits of legendary female figures in the series entitled "Heroines," in which each character inhabits a cultural narrative not of her own making, which she is forced to act out though it does not match the complexity of her desires.[64] Cahun's protagonists include Delilah, Eve, Sophie the symbolist, Judith, Sappho, Marguerite the incestuous sister, and Salmacis. Each is dedicated to another writer or artist, who is evoked in the relevant narrative. Salmacis ("the Suffragette") is dedicated to Claude: Salmacis becomes the frustrated Hermaphrodite, a man living in a woman's body, whose only means of escape is to think of going to the house of Narcissus. Sophie, having learned to symbolize and act out her sadomasochistic desires as a young child with her playmate Paul, is certainly not interested in his "banal desire for marriage" by the time she is twenty.[65] Many of the leading characters are seductresses overcome with passion or forbidden desire, either being sterile or, as with Salomé, having no feelings for men. The series is a paradoxical, witty appropriation and inversion of dominant cultural stereotypes about femininity and homosexuality, including Freudian ones, in which the protagonists interrogate their representation in the first person. The women normally represented as castrating seductresses such as Delilah have no interest in the opposite sex in this series, while those represented traditionally as innocent turn out to be the reverse: Cinderella thus becomes an accomplished dominatrix who knows that the prince can be pleasured with pitiless hard heels.

"Salomé the Skeptic" is a short, densely allusive piece that references Wilde's arguments about how life imitates art, as well as playing with Freud's influential theory of the castration complex. Cahun's Salomé is an actress who cares only for "the dream," that is, her own fantasy that she cannot find represented.[66] She is as indifferent to the head of John the Baptist as she has become to both art and life and, in fact, has difficulty distinguishing between them.[67] One feels that Cahun would have concurred with illustrator Aubrey Beardsley's insubordinate view of Wilde's play. The tone of the rather malicious drawings that Beardsley produced for the 1894 English edition of *Salome* provide a camp counterpoint to Wilde's overheated drama.[68] In many of Beardsley's arresting illustrations, the ambiguously gendered appearance of Salome, among other characters, allows for a homoerotic reading that underlines the analogy between Salome's desire for what she cannot have—the love of a holy man—and "the Love that dare not speak its name." In the first unbidden illustration that Beardsley did for the play, inscribed with her words "J'ai baisé ta bouche Iokanaan," Salome's face is distinctly masculine and her erect snakelike locks mirror the flaccid ones of her

victim (fig. 27). Cahun's Salomé's lack of interest in the prophet, in contrast to
her uncontrollable lust for him in Wilde's version, may also be read as suggesting
that men are not what arouse her passions: "When as erotic sleepwalker, I will
have changed my skin seven times for his pleasure, I will wake up and order that
they bring me the head of the prophet *Whatshisname* on a silver platter (I forget
his name: never mind! My stepfather will understand). . . . It appears I must take
it in my hands and kiss it. . . . I really don't give a damn."[69] She is repelled by the

painted cardboard head that she is first presented with in the theatre, "dripping with red—like a piece of fresh pork on the butcher's stall" (148). Her last line underlines that her interests lie elsewhere: "If I vibrate to other vibrations from yours, must you conclude that my flesh is insensitive?" (149).

While Cahun's Salomé is a satire of Wilde's protagonist (and in many ways, the performance of the dance of the seven veils had become a burlesque cliché by the 1920s), her novella also highlights the importance to both the fictional character and her author of Wilde's refusal to submit to the dictates of realism. Cahun prefaces her narrative with an epigraph from André Gide, in which he quotes Wilde as saying, "That evening, when he returned to his village and they asked him, as on other evenings: Come on! Tell us: What did you see? He answered:—I saw nothing."[70] In Gide's recollection, this is how Wilde concludes an unwritten story, which depicts a man who is a habitual teller of tales. When this character sees nothing but the everyday world, he invents fantastic sights of mermaids and fauns; when, however, one day he actually sees these sights, he says to his eager audience that he has seen nothing.

Once she has quoted Gide's remark, Cahun opens "Salomé the Skeptic" as follows: "How strange people are who *believe that it has happened!*" (148). She dismisses realist art, in which art slavishly imitates life: "[H]ow could I admire their color reproductions, I who never loved their originals?" (148). She then goes on to attack other schools of art: idealists, *maudits,* and those who claim to re-create "the other life that surges . . . behind closed eyelids" (148). (This might be a reference to the surrealists, given the importance they placed on dreams and the unconscious.) The repeated phrase that Salomé mocks in her monologue— "they believe that it has happened" (148)—also suggests another reading. This is not only a critique of those who are duped by art into believing that the events it depicts are real or directly correlate to actual behavior but also refers to the castration complex. Decapitation, as Freud notes, is associated with castration.[71] The decapitated head often features in Cahun's work, as in the series of images of her head under a bell jar, entitled "Studies for a Keepsake,"[72] in which her intense, wistful expression belies the idea that she is dead even though her head is apparently detached from her body and contained under glass. In the photomontage preceding Part 7 of *Cancelled Confessions,* the idea of castration is both evoked and denied; a headless female torso sits upright above a pair of scissors, but her decapitation is contradicted by the presence of a much larger image of Cahun's head, androgynously made-up, hovering above the torso. On the right, another headless torso of a Classical statue, with one breast, has a curlew's head growing from its base. In the text following this photomontage, Cahun recounts a nightmare: she imagines herself cutting off curlews' beaks (another reference to the beaked nose she had inherited from her father); the allusion to the castration of the father is reiterated when she encounters him on a railway line:

> I have overtaken my father and seek to convince him, through whatever idea I can think of in the tumult, of my genius, of my bravura. . . . But I don't have time. His train comes in and doesn't slow down. ("Your mother will be worried") . . . Something falls which I am still holding on to, my arm now slackened, by a bit of warm and viscous flesh. Despair—and stronger, horror —freeze me and yet despite myself I see, half relieved: it's a jointed wooden artist's mannequin that clings to my fingers.[73]

The horror that she experiences at her father's castration references the horror Freud describes that the boy is supposed to experience at the sight of the female genitals, the lack of the penis causing a fear of his own castration. Here, however, the narrator feels that she has been responsible for the castration by her overbearing, unfeminine behavior in trying to persuade her father of her "genius." This fear is assuaged for her by a transmutation of the severed penis in her hand into a mannequin, an object that is not flesh but symbolizes her artistic status, a reassuring alternative to the phallus (like the snakes on Medusa's head). Allusions to the Salomé legend continue throughout the chapter. In a section entitled "Salomé Vanquished," the narrator appears to speak in the voice of Salomé, echoing the character's speeches to Iokanaan in Wilde's play and lamenting the Baptist's refusal to return her look or her desire. She then, in another witty inversion of the story, appears to settle for his hand: "I am hardly ambitious. Your mouth is too high up for me. But (out of stubbornness) . . . I kiss your hand Iokanann! The whiteness of hands, of all skin visible or guessed at."[74] In the photomontage that prefaces the chapter, a hand is featured protruding from a pair of lips. The hand is often transformed in Cahun's work—it is not only a phallic symbol but also, in the endless blurring of boundaries between fake and authentic, an alternative to the penis as a prime sexual organ and signifier of sexual difference. The section entitled "Salomé Vanquished" concludes with the narrator contemplating suicide—burning the haunted house she inhabits, where she can never see her reflection in Iokanaan's eyes—and there are painful variations on this theme for the rest of the chapter.

Lizzie Thynne

If the Salomé of *Cancelled Confessions* finds no recognition from the male figures at whom her desires are directed, then the Salomé of "Heroines" takes a different line in her aspiration to transcend sexual difference and its imprisoning representation. She refuses to accept that "it has happened"—that is, that the decapitation of the prophet has occurred. She does not know why she wanted his head in the first place, unless it was an idea that Herod, who seems to be a bit of a psychoanalyst, has read in her unconscious (he has made her describe her dreams to him, she says). The idea of her own castration, symbolized in Wilde's play by her beheading—"the blood like mine" that is soiling her—she also dismisses as bad theater. These aspects of Cahun's narrative recall Allan's refusal in her court case to concur with Billing that Salomé is a sadist who is sexually excited by the dead head or, as he tries to imply, that Allan has any knowledge of or connection with the acts depicted in the play. Allan refused the conflation of her life and art; to Billing's persistent attempt to identify her with her role, she retorted, "Does that make me the part because I act it? Of course not."[75] In Cahun's revisions of the story, Salomé cannot be the vengeful, castrating woman of legend. Thus, she must leave behind both the art that represents her and a life that requires her to reenact endlessly a narrative in which she must acquire a dead head (phallus) for which she has no desire and an aesthetic repugnance. For Cahun, as both lesbian and artist, a new life required the creation of a new art that had the autonomy that Wilde wanted for it but would also fracture in both form and content the cultural myths of the nineteenth century and the emerging ones of the twentieth.

Notes

All translations from the French are the author's unless otherwise indicated.

    1. The quotation that serves as the chapter title, "Tu n'as pourtant la prétention d'être plus pédéraste que moi?" is from Claude Cahun, *Aveux non avenus,* in Cahun, *Écrits,* ed. François Leperlier (Paris: Jean Michel Place, 2002), 223.

    2. "Je . . . cherchai une présentation esthétique. Je trouvai un joli cadre à la taille voulue. Il contenait une photo d'Oscar Wilde et Alfred Douglas—l'ensemble datait de si loin que je l'avais presque oublié, gardé je ne sais pourquoi si ce n'est que la place dans les placards ne manquait ni à Nantes ni ici. J'ouvris le cadre, substituai la photo des bottes à la photo de 1892 et recollai." "Lettre à Gaston Ferdière," in Cahun, *Écrits,* 681. The meaning of the "ritornello" she refers to here is not entirely clear—it refers either to the German Romantic verse she mentions looking for a few paragraphs earlier in this letter or to the phrase "Ohne Ende" (Without End), which Cahun and Moore often used for these purposes. They had appropriated this from the Nazi slogan "Schrecken ohne Ende oder Ende mit Shrecken" (terror without end or an end to terror).

3. Abigail Solomon-Godeau comments that Cahun's work has affinities with "contemporary feminist theorizations of the stakes (and difficulty) in feminine self-representation: elaborating on the one hand, the problem of excessive proximity to the body and, on the other hand, a painful alienation from it." Solomon-Godeau, "Surrealist Confessions," *Afterimage* 19, no. 8 (March 1992): 13.

4. The study of Cahun's work was greatly facilitated by the publication of the first biography of her: François Leperlier's *Claude Cahun: L'écart et la metamorphose* (Paris: Jean Michel Place, 2002; rev. ed., Paris: Fayard, 2006). Leperlier's groundbreaking work uncovered details of Cahun's life that had long disappeared under numerous mistaken assumptions, including the idea that she was a man and had died in a concentration camp.

5. The largest collection of photographs, manuscripts, and other documents by Claude Cahun and Marcel Moore is held by the Jersey Heritage Trust and appears in Louise Downie, ed., *Don't Kiss Me: The Art of Claude Cahun and Marcel Moore* (London: Tate Publishing, in association with the Jersey Heritage Trust, 2006). This collection can also be accessed via the art and archives databases at www.jerseyheritagetrust.jeron.je; reference numbers to Cahun/Moore's work in this article refer to these databases, unless otherwise indicated.

6. See Jennifer Shaw, "Singular Plural: Collaborative Self-Images in Claude Cahun's *Aveux non avenus*" and Tirza True Latimer, "Looking Like a Lesbian: Portraiture and Sexual Identity in 1920s Paris," in *The Modern Woman Revisited: Paris between the Wars,* ed. Whitney Chadwick and Tirza True Latimer (New Brunswick, NJ: Rutgers University Press, 2003), 155–67 and 127–43; and Laura Bailey, "Creative Collaborations within Same-Sex Partnerships: The Domestic Dandyism of Claude Cahun and Gluck," MA diss., University of Sussex, 2003.

7. Schwob confided to Arthur Ransome some years later that "he thought he would have spoiled the spontaneity and character of Wilde's style if he had tried to harmonize it with the diction demanded by the French academy." Quoted in Christine Satzinger, *The French Influences on Oscar Wilde's* The Picture of Dorian Gray *and* Salomé (Lewiston, NY: Edwin Mellen Press, 2004), 205.

8. Huret, *Le Figaro,* 13 April 1895, quoted in Sylvain Goudemare, *Marcel Schwob ou les vies imaginaries* (Paris: Le Cherche Midi, 2000), 186. The phrase is a play on the French term of abuse "*espèce de porc*" (swine).

9. "On s'aperçoit enfin qu'Oscar Wilde avait moins d'imagination que des vices, et qu'il ne travaillait que sur documents." Goudemare, *Marcel Schwob,* 186.

10. Bailey, "Creative Collaborations," 9.

11. "Plus égoïste que les plus égoïstes, Marcel Schwob l'a été en se transposant à la manière des acteurs, dans chacun de ses héros." Claude Cahun, "Marcel Schwob," *La gerbe* 20 (May 1920), in Cahun, *Écrits,* 475.

12. "Il y certains hommes dont la véritable vie nous échappe. Nous aurons beau connaître dans toute leur précision et leur moindre détail les mouvements extérieurs de ces êtres hermétiques, ils resteront pour nous l'horloge morte dont on a perdu la clef." Cahun, *Écrits,* 473.

13. "S'il avait vécu peut-être, déposant les masques, eût-il parlé pout lui-même." Cahun, *Écrits,* 475.

14. Marcel Schwob, *Vies imaginaires,* in *The King in the Golden Mask and Other Writings,* ed. Iain White (Manchester, UK: Carcanet New Press, 1982), 115.

15. "Clodia, Shameless Matron," in Schwob, *Vies imaginaires,*134–36.

16. Richard Ellmann, *Oscar Wilde* (Harmondsworth, UK: Penguin, 1987), 287.

17. This opinion is attributed to Dorian Gray by the narrator at the end of a passage in which he has, however, already affirmed the view as his own.

18. Cahun poses as a weightlifter wearing a top emblazoned with the motto "Don't Kiss Me I'm in Training" in a series of photographs taken c. 1927 (see JHT/1995/00041/0 and JHT/2003/00001/004); she is posed on her garden wall with St. Brelade's cemetery in the background in five photographs taken c. 1947 (JHT/1995/00031/n, JHT1995/00036h, JHT/1995/00031a, JHT/1995/00031/e, and JHT/1995/00036/g). In the first of these cemetery photographs, she is holding up a blank mask to her face and is wearing a white shift, a single black glove, and a chain-like necklace; in the second, she wears the same outfit but without the mask and is clutching her right breast; in the last three, she is in masculine attire—trousers, high boots, and jacket— posing first with a small model skull in her hand, then holding up the blank mask, and third, in a mock dandy stance, her head thrown back, jacket open, cigarette in hand, and long-haired cat at her feet.

19. The most striking similarity in pose to Cahun's dandy portrait is with the photograph of Wilde taken by Napoleon Sarony in early January 1882, numbered BX1-N.4 in the William Andrews Clark Memorial Library collection (http://www.humnet.ucla.edu/humnet/clarklib/wildphot/sarony.htm, accessed 28 January 2007). A comparison of these images with that Sarony photograph and a previously unpublished photograph of Cahun in an Edwardian woman's traveling suit is in Laura "Lou" Bailey and Lizzie Thynne, "Beyond Representation: Claude Cahun's Monstrous Mischief-Making," History of Photography (Summer 2005): 137–38.

20. Jennifer Blessing underlines the links between Cahun and both Wilde and Charles Baudelaire. In the 1921 portrait of Cahun in the dark jacket and velvet pants, Blessing notes that "her head [is] shaved in the style of Baudelaire" and comments that the literary elaboration of the dandy was deeply misogynistic and therefore required "a particular kind of self-reflexivity and self-consciousness for Cahun as a female subject." Blessing, "Claude Cahun: Dandy Provocateuse," in Dandies: Fashion and Finesse in Art and Culture, ed. Susan Fillin-Yeh (New York: New York University Press, 2001), 194–95. Several other contemporary lesbian artists, including Romaine Brooks, embraced the dandy ethos, although in a much less critical way than Cahun did; see Latimer, "Looking Like a Lesbian," 132–33.

21. By drawing attention to the frame, Cahun and Moore subvert the photograph as a means of categorization and identification, defying the tendency of both sexological and psychoanalytic discourse to fix the meaning of bodies and sexual identities; see Bailey and Thynne, "Beyond Representation."

22. These three images are reconstructed as part of a sequence choreographed by Lea Anderson in my film Playing a Part: The Story of Claude Cahun (Brighton: University of Sussex, 2004), which underlines the ways in which identity is transformed across some of Cahun's images through the rearrangement of a few simple props.

23. Cahun's extant work does not clarify whether there was a final intended framing of each subject or, if so, what it should be; there is little evidence of these portraits having been exhibited or published as single images. The collection in the Jersey Heritage Trust sometimes includes wide shots and close-ups of the same setup, and some of the photographs were subjected to further cropping for inclusion in the photomontages of Aveux non avenus, 1930.

24. See Ellen Moers, The Dandy: Brummel to Beerbohm (London: Secker, 1960); and Jessica R. Feldman, Gender on the Divide: The Dandy in Modernist Literature (Ithaca, NY: Cornell University Press, 1993).

25. Jonathan Fryer, "Dandyism, Decadence and Dissent: Style and Sensibility among Wilde's Coterie," in The Wilde Years: Oscar Wilde and the Art of His Time, ed. Tomoko Sato and Lionel Lambourne (London: Barbican Art Galleries, 2000), 54.

26. Alan Sinfield, *The Wilde Century: Effeminacy, Oscar Wilde and The Queer Moment* (New York: Columbia University Press, 1994), 3.

27. See Laura Doan's invaluable study, *Fashioning Sapphism: The Origins of a Modern English Lesbian Culture* (New York: Columbia University Press, 2001).

28. "[L]e nom de l'obscurs parents juifs (Cahun) avec qui je me sentais plus d'affinités." Claude Cahun, "Lettre à Paul Levy" [1950], in Cahun, *Écrits,* 711.

29. Leperlier notes that the young Lucy Schwob suffered anti-Semitic harassment by her classmates in 1906 when the Dreyfus case reopened and as a result was sent to school at Parson's Mead in Surrey, England, in 1907–8; see his introduction to Cahun, *Écrits,* 11. Captain Alfred Dreyfus was a Jewish officer in the French Army who was wrongly convicted of passing military secrets to the German Embassy in Paris on the basis of dubious evidence. He was finally exonerated on 12 July 1906, after having served several years' imprisonment on Devil's Island.

30. Cahun's interest in male personae might be interpreted as signifying that she was what we might now call transgender. However, such an interpretation categorizes her work and defines her in ways that contradict the spectrum of transformations that run through her output, of which gender is only a single facet. She continued to use her given name, Lucy Schwob, on some publications into the 1920s.

31. *Vues et visions* was published in the *Mercure de France* on 16 May 1914 but had been written in April–May 1912, when Cahun was eighteen. Having originally dedicated this text to Marcel Moore, Cahun sent a copy to André Breton's wife, Jacqueline Lamba, in 1939, with a very affectionate inscription, "Pour Jacqueline Mathilde Lamba, son amie, Lucy Mathilde Schwob," which links them through their matching middle names, echoing the parallel narrations in the text. In her note to Lamba, she dismisses the work as puerile, particularly in the light of "the exceptional hours" they spent together during Lamba's recent visit with her daughter Aube, those "mysterious days of leap year" ("année bissextile"), about which she says, "I had to do away with my alibis, trasvestissements and armour," suggesting a period of close intimacy between them (Cahun, *Écrits,* 20). The beautiful, enigmatic photograph of Lamba with a bare torso, taken through a pane of glass during this visit, is the only frontal nude in Cahun's work—at least, what has survived of it.

32. These articles include "Au plus beau des anges" and "Cigarettes" (both in *La gerbe* 3 [December 1918]), "La Sorbonne en fête" (*La gerbe* 5 [February 1919]), and "L'amour Aveugle" (*La gerbe* 12 [September 1919]).

33. The manuscript of "Les jeux uraniens" is held at the Jersey Museum, St. Helier; hereafter cited as "Les jeux uraniens" manuscript. Extracts from this work are also reproduced in Cahun, *Écrits,* 487–95, under the title "Amor amicitae."

34. "Les jeux uraniens" manuscript, f. 2.

35. The phrase "The Love that dare not speak its name" first appeared in Alfred Douglas's "Two Loves" in John Francis Bloxam's magazine, *The Chameleon* (1894); the poem is reprinted in Brian Reade, ed., *Sexual Heretics: Male Homosexuality in English Literature from 1850 to 1900* (London: Routledge and Kegan Paul, 1970), 162. The poem had been used as part of the evidence against Wilde in his trial; he denied that it made any improper suggestion and at the same time showed up his interrogator, Carson, who attributed a homoerotic verse by Shakespeare to Wilde. On this matter, see chapter 9 in the present volume.

36. The quotation from Douglas's "Two Loves" is followed by one from the poetry of Percy Bysshe Shelley that makes the same point:

> If any should be curious to discover
> Whether to you I am a friend or lover,

Let him read Shakespeare's sonnets, taking thence
A whetstone for their dull intelligence
That tears and will not cut.

Shelley, "Passages of the Poem, or Connected Therewith," in Shelley, *Poetical Works*, ed. Thomas Hutchinson (London: Oxford University Press, 1967), 428. Hutchinson's text presents "them" instead of "him." Shelley's poem, which is related to "Epipsychidion" (1821), first appeared in *Relics of Shelley*, ed. Richard Garnett (London: Moxon, 1862).

37. Karl Heinrich Ulrichs, *The Riddle of "Man-Manly" Love* (1864), trans. Michael A. Lombardi-Nash, 2 vols. (New York: Prometheus Books, 1994), 1:34. The Oxbridge group of pederastic poets, to which Lord Alfred Douglas belonged, was subsequently dubbed "Uranian" by Timothy d'Arch Smith in *Love in Earnest: Some Notes on the Lives and Writings of the English "Uranian" Poets from 1889 to 1930* (London: Routledge, 1970).

38. Carolyn J. Dean, in one of the most stimulating articles about Cahun's work, cites the following example of the tendency to see homosexuality as narcissistic, sterile, and existing "for its own sake": "In his preface to Willy's *Le troisième sexe*, Louis Estève noted that 'in its blind pursuit of sensual joy, homosexuality is only an aestheticized form of egotism' that threatens the 'judicious altruism' on which 'civilisation is based.'" Dean, "Claude Cahun's Double," *Yale French Studies* 90 (1996): 77.

39. One of the earliest extant photographs of Cahun and Moore together shows them posed side by side, reflected in a large mirror above a mantelpiece and looking out at the viewer; see JHT/2003/0001/011.

40. Cahun, *Écrits*, 488.

41. "Les jeux uraniens" manuscript, f. 87. "Voila les réflexions que je faisais hier mirant de près mes yeux dans un miroir ovale . . . Tu vins derrière moi, tu te penches sur mon épaule; soudain la buée de ton haleine se condensa sur la glace ternie, et quand ce nuage fut évaporé, ton image avait remplacé la mienne."

42. Latimer cites the painting *A Kiss in the Glass* (1885) by Antoine Magaud as an example of the cliché of narcissistic femininity reiterated in late-nineteenth- and early-twentieth-century art, which she contrasts with the Harlequin portrait, in which Cahun "maintains both a literal and symbolic distance from her proper reflection." Latimer, "Looking Like a Lesbian," 135).

43. The medium close-up photograph of Moore beside the mirror is number 267 in the catalogue of the Musée de l'Art Moderne exhibition, *Claude Cahun: Photographe* (Paris: Jean Michel Place, 1995). For another discussion of the connection between these two portraits, see Bailey, "Creative Collaborations," 20–23. There is a different version of the Moore portrait setup in the Jersey collection: JHT/1995/00024/h.

44. André Gide recalls Wilde accusing him of "listening with his eyes." Wilde continued by inverting the myth of Narcissus to draw an analogy with Gide: he told the French writer that the river into which Narcissus gazed "was in love with him but only because it could see the reflection of its waters in Narcissus' eyes." Gide, "Oscar Wilde," in *Œuvres complètes d'André Gide*, ed. L. Martin-Chauffier, 15 vols. (Paris: Nrf, 1932–39), 3:477.

45. Ellmann, *Oscar Wilde*, 422.

46. For a chronology of selected productions of the play, see William Tydeman and Steve Price, eds., *Wilde: Salome* (Cambridge: Cambridge University Press, 1996), 184–85.

47. By 1912, no fewer than 2,789 French poets had tried their lyrics on the daughter of Herodias, as had Stéphane Mallarmé, Maurice Maeterlinck, and Gustave Flaubert; on this topic, see Michel Décaudin, "Mythe de fin de siècle: Salomé," *Comparative Literary Studies* 4 (1967): 109,

quoted in Toni Bentley, *Sisters of Salomé* (New Haven, CT: Yale University Press, 2002), 26. Wilde's version was heavily indebted to Flaubert's "Hérodias." See Satzinger, *French Influences;* see also chapter 6 in the present volume.

48. For analyses of the trial and its reporting, see Lucy Bland, "Trial by Sexology? Maud Allan, Salome and the 'Cult of the Clitoris Case,'" in *Sexology in Culture: Labelling Bodies and Desires,* ed. Lucy Bland and Laura Doan (London: Polity Press, 1998), 183–98; and Alison Oram, "'A Sudden Orgy of Decadence': Writing about Sex between Women in the Interwar Popular Press," in *Sapphic Modernities: Sexuality, Women and National Culture,* ed. Laura Doan and Jane Garrity (Basingstoke, UK: Palgrave Macmillan, 2006), 165–80.

49. See Michael Kettle, *Salome's Last Veil: The Libel Case of the Century* (London: Hart-Davis, 1977); and Philip Hoare, *Wilde's Last Stand: Decadence, Conspiracy and the First World War* (London: Duckworth, 1997).

50. The ulterior motive for targeting Allan was a political attack on Herbert Asquith, the Liberal leader, for whose wife, Margot Asquith, Allan had performed. Margot Asquith was also rumored to be a lesbian: "[T]he wives of men in a supreme position were entangled in lesbian ecstasy where the most sacred secrets of state were being betrayed." Quoted in Kettle, *Salome's Last Veil,* 80.

51. Quoted in Kettle, *Salome's Last Veil,* 80.

52. Quoted in Kettle, *Salome's Last Veil,* 61.

53. "[C]'est, paraît-il, un terme médicale qualifiant les mœurs de toute personne ayant pris part ou assisté aux représentations." Cahun, "La Salomé d'Oscar Wilde, le procès Billing et les 47000 pervertis du livre noir," *Mercure de France,* 406 (May 1918), in Cahun, *Écrits,* 451.

54. "Sans doute ésperait-il beaucoup d'un homme vieilli, découragé, à la merci désormais du premier venu armé du nom de Wilde." Cahun, *Écrits,* 455.

55. "[L]a plus grande force du mal en Europe depuis 350 ans." Quoted in Cahun, *Écrits,* 455.

56. "Il s'agit d'une lettre assez impertinente écrite par Lord Douglas à Mr Labonchere [*sic*], directeur du journal *Truth,* a l'époque où Douglas et Wilde se vantaient de vouloir sodomiser le monde." Cahun, *Écrits,* 457n4. Henry Labouchère (Cahun misspells his name) was the author of the clause in the 1885 Criminal Law Amendment Act, which banned all intimate relations between men in England.

57. There are very few direct references to the exact nature of her relationship with Suzanne Malherbe (or with other women) anywhere in Cahun's writing, although Malherbe figures as a constant presence in her more documentary writing after the Second World War. After leaving Paris to settle in Jersey in 1937, the pair was known locally as "the Schwob sisters" (which is what they were by their parents' marriage). Even when they were arrested by the Germans, their sexuality appears not to have been made an issue in their prosecution for undermining the morale of the German troops. Ironically, only in their letters, passed secretly to each other on Jeyes toilet paper while incarcerated in St. Helier prison after their condemnation, do their terms of endearment reveal the amorous nature of their lifelong union. The extant prison letters between Cahun and Moore are held at the Jersey Museum.

58. "[I]l dit ésperer que ce repentir bruyant était sincere, et véritable le regret de la part prise aux actes déshonorants qui avaient conduit Wilde à sa perte. Il n'était jamais trop tard pour se corriger. Puis le juge montra des passages de Salomé écrits par Lord Alfred Douglas lui-même. Assis près de la porte, le Lord s'élança, criant de sa voix la plus haute: 'Vous n'avez pas le droit de dire que j'ai écrit ces mots! Vous êtes un menteur! . . .' Il fut saisi par des *policemen* au beau milieu de son discours, et explusé. Le Juge fit remarquer qu'il avait simplement répété l'assertion

Lizzie Thynne

du témoin." Cahun, "La Salomé d'Oscar Wilde," in *Écrits*, 459. Darling was also the judge at the case that Douglas had brought against Arthur Ransome's publisher, which he lost.

59. "[L]e sage du procès." Cahun, *Écrits*, 459.

60. "Black humor" is a term used in French (*l'humour noir*) as well as British and American English to refer to a dark kind of wit that responds to the uncomfortable or shocking by transforming it into a joke incorporating that which is feared. André Breton draws on Freud's analysis of the way humor can be used to turn trauma into a source of amusement in his *Anthologie de l'humour noir* (Paris: Pauvert, 1966).

61. See Lizzie Thynne, "Action Indirecte: Politique, identité et subversion chez Claude Cahun et Marcel Moore dans la résistance contre l'occupation nazie de Jersey," in *Paragraphes*, 27 (Montreal: University of Montreal Press, 2007); also forthcoming in an English version as "Indirect Action: Politics and the Subversion of Identity in Claude Cahun and Marcel Moore's Resistance to the Occupation of Jersey," *Papers of Surrealism* 8 (2008): http://www.surrealismcentre.ac.uk/papersofsurrealism/index.html.

62. The homoerotic possibilities of the play were subsequently brought out in a 1922 film starring Alia Nazimova, directed by Charles Bryant, and performed as high camp by a mainly gay male cast, including a distinctly effeminate Page who, because he is jealous, very clearly does not want the Young Syrian to look at Salomé (see chapter 6 in the present volume).

63. Ellmann, *Oscar Wilde*, 325.

64. Some of the stories of the "Heroines" series were published, including Eve, Delilah, Judith, Helen, Sappho, Marguerite, and Salomé in *Mercure de France* 639 (February 1925) and "Sophie La Symboliste" and "La Belle" in *Le journal littéraire* 45 (28 February 1925). Five others—Penelope, Mary, Cinderella, the unknown princess, Salmacis, and the one who is not a hero ("the Mad Virgin")—were not published in Cahun's lifetime but appear in Cahun, *Écrits*, 127–59.

65. Cahun, "Sophie la Symboliste," in *Écrits*, 154.

66. Leperlier suggests that "le rêve" (the dream) resembles Jacques Lacan's famous definition of the imaginary, that is, the form of identification with the ideal mirror image of the self that occurs in the child's unconscious before it enters into the symbolic realm of language. Leperlier, *Claude Cahun*, 58.

67. Miranda Welby Everard, in her exploration of the centrality of the theatrical metaphor in Cahun's work, suggests that Cahun may have seen both Allan's performance of Salomé while in London and Georges Pitoëff's production of *Salomé* at the Théâtre Comédie, Champs-Elysées, in 1922, in which Pitoëff's spouse, Ludmilla, played Salomé as "a pale mysterious figure with her silvery veils showing not too much interest in her lifeless trophy, unlike the Wildean character who yearns to kiss the prophet's mouth, dead or alive." Everard, "Imaging the Actor: The Theatre of Claude Cahun," *Oxford Art Journal* 29, no. 1 (2006): 12.

68. While the similarities between Moore's and Beardsley's respective works are clear, such as in Moore's illustrations for *Vues et visions* (1916), the parallels between the English artist's work and the portraits of Cahun are also striking. The grotesque, bald-headed, and masked figures who appear in Aubrey Beardsley's illustrations in the 1894 English version of *Salome*, with which Moore was undoubtedly familiar, might also have influenced the personae Cahun adopted, including the 1921 "dandy" portrait. Cahun shared Beardsley's parodic and Decadent approach to figures from Classical mythology. Chris Snodgrass observes that in Beardsley's work—in contrast to earlier more idealized versions of the figure—the androgyne is "far from evincing romanticized resolution," since "the anatomically explicit hermaphrodite emphasized starkly graphic self-contradiction." Snodgrass, *Aubrey Beardsley: Dandy of the Grotesque* (Oxford:

Oxford University Press, 1995), 58. On Beardsley's title page for *Salome,* for example, Pan is shown as a satanic hermaphrodite. Cahun's Salmacis, "the first woman who willingly makes herself sterile," forms a union with Hermaphrodite; while they have no desire to procreate, they are nonetheless filled with lust, and "eternally unsatisfied this strange, shameless couple assaults male and female, attracted, repelled, passive, active, across thirsts and disgusts, with horrid rifts and jealous of itself." Cahun, "Heroines," in *Écrits,* 155.

69. Cahun, "Heroines," in *Écrits,* 149; further page references appear in parentheses.

70. "Ce soir-là, quand il rentra dans son village et qu'on lui demanda comme les autres soirs: Allons! Raconte: Qu'as tu vu? Il répondit:—Je n'ai rien vu." Gide, "Oscar Wilde," 479.

71. According to Sigmund Freud, Medusa's head is cut off and produces the fear of castration in the viewer (turning him to stone), but because her head is covered in live snakes, symbolic of the penis, it also disavows this fear. Freud similarly interprets the story of Judith and her beheading of Holofernes as dealing with the vengeful castration of the virgin who envies the penis of the man who has deflowered her. See Freud, "Medusa's Head" and "The Taboo of Virginity," in *The Standard Edition of the Psychological Works of Sigmund Freud,* ed. and trans. James Strachey, 24 vols. (London: Hogarth Press and the Institute of Psychoanalysis, 1953–74), 11:207 and 18:274.

72. See JHT/1995/00027/o–r.

73. Cahun, *Disavowals or Cancelled Confessions,* trans. Susan de Muth (London: Tate Publishing, 2007), 137.

74. Cahun, *Disavowals or Cancelled Confessions,* 144.

75. Quoted in Kettle, *Salome's Last Veil,* 81.

Lizzie Thynne

Oscar Wilde's
AN IDEAL HUSBAND
and W. Somerset Maugham's
THE CONSTANT WIFE

A Dialogue

LAUREL BRAKE

IN A SUGGESTIVE essay in *The Cambridge Companion to Oscar Wilde*, Richard Cave explores "some lines of influence" of Wilde's drama on twentieth-century theater, but for some reason Cave judges W. Somerset Maugham's and Noel Coward's conscious reworking of Wilde's comedies as superficial and thus fit to set aside.[1] I argue, however, that the line from Wilde to Maugham is especially strong and complicated and that Maugham adopted Wildean structures as well as diction in *The Constant Wife* (1926) to critique twentieth-century social values no less profoundly than Wilde probed those of the nineteenth century in *An Ideal Husband* (1895). When Maugham began his career as a playwright just before the turn of the century (from 1898 onward), he looked to Wilde's theatrical models, ones described by Anthony Curtis as "temporarily out of service" at the time.[2] After Maugham's first commercial success in 1907 with *Lady Frederick*, Maugham decided to go for a structure more free of melodrama and farce than nineteenth-century models offered,[3] but long after this date—in the 1920s—he still engaged in a robust dialogue with Wilde. This intertextuality helps define the continuation of a Wildean tradition of drama, apparently unscathed, surviving the trials, Wilde's imprisonment, and death and moving smartly into the twentieth century in Maugham's *Penelope* (1909) and its redaction, *The Constant Wife*.

In particular, my discussion focuses on the ways in which Maugham's great 1926 drama crafts a playful inversion of aspects of Wilde's *An Ideal Husband*. Maugham produces a wry and searching investigation of constancy in wives set in the 1920s that complements Wilde's focus on the ideal husband in the 1890s. But even as Maugham's play regenders *An Ideal Husband*, it also imitates another work—one planned by Wilde and realized by Frank Harris—in which Wilde directly points the way to Maugham's cameo of constancy in modern women. While it is possible, as Curtis suggests, that Maugham's choice of title of *The Constant Wife* echoes George Farquhar's *The Constant Couple* (1699), Maugham is more likely to have drawn on a combination of Wildean models for the titles and substance of his two constant wife plays.[4]

In this regard, numerous similarities between the playwrights and the 1895 and 1926 dramas immediately spring to mind. This is a dialogue between male authors who, in their 1895 and 1926 works, are idiosyncratic in their representation of gender difference and largely sympathetic toward the advancement of women. Moreover, both of these playwrights were bisexual, both married, and both, at these dates, were not (in our idiom) "out." Gerald Kelly's portrait of a dandified Maugham in 1911 suggests the younger man's identification at the time with a Wildean persona (see fig. 28).[5] Likewise, both plays are drawing-room comedies, produced for the commercial theater, and both of these works are inter alia about marriage as well as the woman/man question. Wilde produced his play in the immediate wake of what had just been named the "New Woman"[6] and following long-standing debate in the press about the social, intellectual, and legal status of women and about the nature of marriage. At the same time, nineteenth-century writers (from George Gordon Byron and Percy Bysshe Shelley onward, including Alfred Tennyson, Charles Kingsley, and John Henry Newman) were envisaging the lineaments of masculinities, both homosexual and heterosexual. Wilde was not unique in this respect; among his contemporaries, Walter Pater, John Addington Symonds, Thomas Hardy, and others were engaged in rethinking masculinity during the fin de siècle, while Maugham's 1909 and 1926 plays on marriage, sexuality, and gender sit among other modernist texts and images that take up these subjects, including those of Pablo Picasso, D. H. Lawrence, and Virginia Woolf, to name but a few.

If one compares the lists of dramatis personae, then the relation of echo and inversion of Wilde's 1895 drama in Maugham's 1926 play is unmistakable, if not obvious. At the center of each work is a married couple, but in *An Ideal Husband*

Laurel Brake

Figure 28. Gerald Kelly *The Jester* (W. Somerset Maugham) (1911). Courtesy of National Portrait Gallery, London/ Art Resource, New York.

the main figure in the action is the husband (Sir Robert Chiltern), while in the Maugham work it is the wife (Constance) around whom the play's structure turns. Sir Robert's goal of the attainment of power through wealth (to which end his insider trading is dedicated) is also Constance's project. Whereas Wilde is dealing with the higher echelons of London Society—the elite known as the "upper ten thousand," comprising lords, ladies, baronets, diplomats, and members of government (signified by their titles, humorously derived from southern English place-names such as Chiltern, Basildon, Caversham, and Goring)—Maugham's social register is lower, in keeping with the postwar 1920s, but it also reflects Wilde in its association with English locales. All of the main characters' names in *The Constant Wife* (save one) use the same device. Middleton, the family name of the central couple, is found in Warwickshire, Norfolk, West Sussex, Northampton-shire, Durham, and Manchester. Kersal, the family name of the silk merchant lover, is in Nottinghamshire. Durham, the mistress's married name, is in York-shire. Meanwhile, Culver (Constance's maiden name, the family name of her sister and mother) is located in Culverthorpe, Lincolnshire. The exception is Barbara Fawcett, the professional woman; her origins are politically allusive, referring to Millicent Garrett Fawcett (1847–1929), suffrage leader and cofounder of Newnham College, Cambridge.

This shift of social status from the distinctly upper-class world of Wilde's play to the upper-middle-class society of Maugham's is signified by the surname (Middleton) of Maugham's central couple and by the fact that John Middleton works at all. Critics of Wilde's plays illustrate the distinction between the social world of Wilde's drama and that of Maugham's. Peter Raby, for example, comments on what Wilde leaves out of his four society comedies from the 1890s: "No one, apart from the servants, works, or wishes to work in these plays."[7] Alan Sinfield goes further; arguing that Wilde's concept of work is gendered in its juxtaposition of MP Sir Robert and the dandyish, unemployed Goring, Sinfield views Sir Robert's profession as a member of Parliament ironically as "manly earnestness under contest from [the upper-class] effeminate idleness [of Goring]."[8] Sir Robert's claim to the upper classes is tenuous, albeit established through a combination of birth, marriage, title, position in government, and money (acquired late and illicitly). In the 1890s, his "job" (if we give it that name) was one of the few that members of the aristocracy could do without loss of so-cial status, and the family name Wilde assigns to him, Chiltern, is explicitly if ironically associated with parliamentary traditions—of resignation from office.[9]

In The Constant Wife, by comparison, John Middleton's class is pegged by his middle-class profession—namely, that of surgeon. The early distinction between surgeons and physicians, one that mapped onto the middle and upper classes as well, was still meaningful in the 1920s. Even in the early twentieth century, sur-geons were associated with blood and the crude practices of barber surgeons, the hybridity of general practice, and the cheap acquisition of medical qualifications via apprenticeships, while physicians were linked with university degrees and their medical practice was confined to internal medicine. The two validating colleges (the one for surgeons, the other for physicians) remained serious rivals.

Wilde's echo of Hamlet's betrayal in An Ideal Husband (echoed in Gertrude, the first name of Sir Robert's pure-minded spouse) is countered by Maugham's Constance: a first name that ironically bespeaks her version of loyalty to her hus-band. This name, however, is also a direct reference—for those theatergoers who

Laurel Brake

remained alert to Wilde's personal history—to the circumstances of Constance Wilde, his wife, whose ordeal and behavior in coming to know her husband's secrets had by the 1920s become public knowledge.[10]

The rest of Maugham's characters in *The Constant Wife* are also tellingly connected to Wilde's play. Just as Wilde's male protagonist has a sister (Mabel Chiltern), so too does Constance, Maugham's female lead, but Martha Culver's moral indignation is her only trait and function in the play, and her role is limited and rhetorical: "I don't think anyone can accuse me of not being frank," she boasts, to which her mother retorts, "Frankness of course is the pose of the moment. It is often a very effective screen for one's thoughts."[11] In comparison with Wilde's Mabel, whose alliance with Goring suggests the possibility of moderately experimental marriage arrangements, Martha remains a spinster whose humorless feminism denies her participation in a marriage plot that would propel her into the future. The relation of each of these two characters to the solutions of their respective play's problems is structurally and ideologically expressed. In *An Ideal Husband,* Mabel is part of the last episode and lines of the play. The two couples—first, Mabel and Goring, and second, Lady Chiltern and Sir Robert —are structurally parallel in their intimate relation to each other, as sisters and as best friends. They also share the final scene and lines in a mirror-image of new and established marital expectation. Mabel firmly rejects the prospect of Goring as "an ideal husband!" (*CW,* 5:238). "Oh, I don't think I should like that," she adds. "It sounds like something in the next world" (*CW,* 5:238). For her part, she agrees to be "a real wife," as a corrective to her sister and brother-in-law's marriage (*CW,* 5:239). In Maugham's play, by comparison, Constance's sister Martha is dispatched toward the beginning of act 3, as superfluous to the denouement, from which Maugham excludes her. Martha's declamatory, off-the-shelf truisms betraying a caricatured feminism appear crude and simplistic compared with the exquisite and feminist torture that Constance doles out to her adulterous husband and his lover in a succession of episodes that unfold toward the end.

Maugham adds a more fully fledged New Woman to *The Constant Wife,* one who extends the limited versions of this topical figure represented by Mabel and Martha. She is the quiet and underdeveloped career woman Barbara Fawcett, whose family name associates her with the veteran suffrage leader Millicent Fawcett, from Wilde's generation, who was still alive at the time. The Fawcett reference also extends the feminist framework to John Middleton, the adulterous husband of the constant wife, a medical man whose affair is conducted under cover of medical "consultations," ones that coyly permit physical contact:

> MARIE-LOUISE [*with presence of mind*]: John, I wonder if you'd mind looking at my knee for a minute. It's been rather painful for the last day or two.
>
> JOHN: Of course not. Come into my consulting-room. These knee-caps are troublesome things when you once get them out of order.
>
> MARTHA [*firmly*]: I'll wait for you. You won't be long, will you? (285)

Millicent Fawcett's sister, a medical pioneer, is the link between the New Woman character (Barbara Fawcett) and the surgeon. As the first Englishwoman to qualify as a doctor in Britain, Elizabeth Garrett Anderson (née Fawcett; 1836–1917) was forced to fight for access to medical education in England against gender restrictions of a conservative male profession. Maugham's use of this famous family name therefore links the Victorian and modern periods, reinforces his careful revision of Wilde's comedy, and provides a device for signaling the feminist framework of his 1926 drama. As a result, John Middleton's Society-based medical practice is glancingly set against Anderson's serious medical vocation. Likewise, Barbara Fawcett's resonant example as a new, working, and independent woman is set against Wilde's Mabel and Lady Chiltern, who, even at their best, show the political limitations of their time and circle. Wilde's and Maugham's respective plays, however, belong to the same arc of history, placed as they are at either end of the New Woman controversy and the suffrage campaigns, both of which took place before the full accession of women to the vote in 1928. A contemporary review of *The Constant Wife* attests to this historical framework in its identification of Maugham's play with two elements of modernity that map onto Wilde's 1895 drama: first, the woman question; and second, journalism, with its twin characteristics of topicality and ephemerality. "Mr. Maugham's play is a journalistic piece," writes St. John Ervine in 1927; "it deals with a topic of the time: equality of the sexes."[12] In making this remark, Ervine recognizes the play's accessibility while warning his readers of its nonclassical, political character, as well as its raciness.

In his 1926 work, Maugham also replicates the pairing of the principal protagonists in *An Ideal Husband* with Marie-Louise, Constance's same-sex confidante, mirroring Goring's relationship to Sir Robert in Wilde's play. Although Goring and Marie-Louise are both fashionable and trivial, Goring additionally has a dramatic weight and serious role in the action and memorable, epigram-matic lines, while Marie-Louise's frivolity and triviality comprise the whole of her character, and her dramatic purpose consists of that contrast with Constance. Goring's dandyism, however, is accompanied by qualities that complement and echo Sir Robert's. Regenia Gagnier, for example, links "Goring's insistence on staying out of politics" with "Chiltern's corrupt luxuriousness and hypocritical idealism" within politics.[13] Similarly, Sinfield, noting the absence of a third, alter-native figure in this play ("the conventionally active man is written out"), com-ments on the unique link of the binary relationship—or balance—between the idle dandy Goring and the manly active Sir Robert.[14]

Moreover, in *An Ideal Husband*, another absentee (not the "conventionally active man"), Baron Arnheim, also connects the two men. An exquisitely culti-vated and rich financier, Arnheim is the offstage referent of Goring's dandyism and Robert's power. Significantly located by Wilde outside of England, on the Continent, Arnheim is free to function as the symbol of outlawed and evil prac-tices. Corrupt in his financial dealings, he buys the young and poor Sir Robert's state secrets, illicitly setting up the fortunes of the onstage member of Parliament. Moreover, Arnheim succeeds Goring as the sexualized lover of Mrs. Cheveley, the blackmailing femme fatale whom Richard Dellamora suggestively calls "the 'bad' dandy" of the drama, since her epigrammatic wit can prove as incisive as Goring's sparkling dialogue.[15] Her "Lamia-like" appearance and "highly coloured" lips—as the stage directions describe her—vividly show that she is not merely danger-ous to Sir Robert's public career (since she threatens to expose his corrupt dealings in the past with a foreign financier) (*CW*, 5:150, 7) but is also the potential rival of both Mabel (for Goring's attentions) and Gertrude (for Robert's soul). Her lineage and legacy from Baron Arnheim (deceased by the time the play's narra-tive opens) include her exotic fortune, and her attempt at blackmailing Sir Robert in light of her knowledge of his questionable past underlines her alliance of evil and power. Baron Arnheim thus reveals the negative reaches of Sir Robert's and Goring's lives onstage. By contrast, in *The Constant Wife*, Marie-Louise's bubbling and transparent stupidities, moral shallowness, scheming materialism, and be-jeweled frocks provide a strong dramatic alternative to the tailored and controlled Constance. Certainly, the male model of friendship in Wilde's play is far closer and deeper than that between the women in Maugham's play, notwithstanding the hint in Wilde's drama of Goring's potential sexual rivalry with his friend for Gertrude, Chiltern's spouse, which is aired but undeveloped (see *CW*, 5:221–13).[16]

The tension between male homosocial friendship and heterosexual rivalry in Wilde's comedy is picked up by Maugham and located in the women: Constance's best friend is also her sexual competitor and her husband's mistress. In Maugham's mirror-image of *An Ideal Husband*, centered on the woman protagonist, Constance, Marie-Louise does shadow Goring, but as Constance's husband's "secret," she also bears comparison with Mrs. Cheveley. If Marie-Louise seems lightweight with respect to Goring, then she appears positively weak in parallel with Mrs. Cheveley, whose insight, glamour, experience, intellect, age, and unmarried state permit her a freedom and power echoed in Maugham not by Marie-Louise but by Constance. In this respect, in *The Constant Wife*, Maugham has transferred the power of Wilde's female interloper in *An Ideal Husband* to the wife, who exists both inside the family and at the center of the stage.

In *The Constant Wife*, we can see that Wilde's Mrs. Cheveley is structurally matched by Maugham's silk merchant, Bernard Kersal. While he, too, is an outsider, he enters the play from Japan (highly fashionable at the time) rather than the morally dubious Continent. Like Mrs. Cheveley—who is Gertrude's former schoolfellow, Goring's ex-girlfriend, and Baron Arnheim's ex-mistress— Kersal originates from the past and serves (or threatens) to introduce that largely unseemly past into the present. In *An Ideal Husband*, the main plot in the present turns on political blackmail involving Sir Robert's corrupt dealings with Baron Arnheim, which promise to determine the political future of the main protagonist.[17]

Whereas Wilde's Mrs. Cheveley is a potent force from the past that successfully stalks and haunts the present, the role of the past in Maugham's play is secondary, contained, and more benign. *The Constant Wife* is less about men haunted by secrets from the past than about the nature of contemporary marriage. The intrigue and farce of Wilde's *An Ideal Husband*, which are the structural correlatives of the irrational secrets threatening its polished social surfaces, have their analogues in Maugham's play in the comedic stage business of surmise and gossip, involving all of the characters except the supremely logical Constance. In light of the inexorable force of the rational that fuels the action of Maugham's play, the idle meddling and earnest morality are rendered ineffectual in determining the convolutions of the plot, let alone its resolution. Thus vitiated, they simply dissolve. *The Constant Wife* is suffused by the trope of reason, within which power lies—and female power at that, not a gender normally associated with power or reason in the 1920s. Maugham's location of these qualities in Constance

Laurel Brake

recalls Mabel Chiltern as a notable exception to this rule. Constance's lover, Kersal, is a safe if sleek functionary whose role is instrumental and delimited to a single note: to desire Constance and to make love to her, first decorously on-stage, then briefly offstage (at the races), and finally, in a strictly controlled time span, to consummate the affair "abroad." If, like Mabel, however, Constance as the rational woman is a demonstrable power in the courtship, her one-note lover is notably less rounded than Goring and is not her match. This aspect of the play works to enhance the matchless sovereignty of Constance, allowing her to prevail over her husband and family, and to carry the audience with her neat resolution. If in 1895 Wilde and Mabel are forced to comply with the social con-straints of courtship and marriage (below which Mabel's rational self bubbles) to consummate their relationship, then in Maugham's 1926 play Constance is free to fashion her own life, in which she can exist quite openly, replete with em-ployment, economic independence, and a controlled affair, after which she will return to the marital home:

> CONSTANCE [to her husband and mother]: He's adored me for fifteen years. There's something in that long devotion which gives me a funny little feel-ing in my heart. I should like to do something to show him that I'm not ungrateful. You see, in six weeks he goes back to Japan. There is no chance of his coming to England again for seven years. I'm thirty-six now and he adores me; in seven years I shall be forty-three. A woman of forty-three is often charming, but it's seldom that a man of fifty-five is crazy about her. I came to the conclusion that it must be now or never and I asked him if he'd like me to spend these last six weeks with him in Italy. (357)

Kersal's merchant status merely hints at the vulgarity of the deceased baron's financial speculations in Wilde's work; the question of money is more distinct in Marie-Louise's husband, Mortimer Durham, a city man, who (like Sir Robert and Baron Arnheim) is hell-bent on becoming a millionaire. The moneyed middle class and the nouveau riche are critiqued as well as comically displayed in both dramas. The relation between the younger, widowed Mrs. Cheveley and her sugar daddy Baron Arnheim in *An Ideal Husband* finds an echo in *The Constant Wife* in Marie-Louise's marriage to her doting, much older, and very wealthy husband, Mortimer. But where Wilde imbricates the anti-Semitism of his time by equat-ing Arnheim's name and nationality with money-dealing and sharp practices, Maugham's Mortimer is an English vulgarian, part of the new rich middle class.

One last element remains in this series of comparisons. In act 3 of Wilde's play, there is the dispute that Lord Goring engages in with Mrs. Cheveley about the item of jewelry that she lost at a party the previous night. It turns out that the "diamond snake-brooch with a ruby" that she tries to recover from Lord Goring's safekeeping happens to be a gift that he made to his cousin as a wedding-gift (*CW*, 5:181). By revealing to Mrs. Cheveley how the jewelry can also serve as a bracelet (one that clamps around her wrist), Lord Goring exposes her as a thief. This aspect of Wilde's plot reemerges in Maugham's drama through the device of John Middleton's lost (and found) cigarette case: a sharply observed characteristic appurtenance, linking the dandy of the 1890s with the surgeon of the 1920s. Wilde's piece of jewelry is as redolent of the lower reaches of the femme fatale/dandy/financier nexus of decadence in the 1890s as Maugham's cigarette case is of the stylish, wealthy, sexual libertines of the 1920s.[18]

Then again, the trajectories and emphases of Wilde's 1895 and Maugham's 1926 dramas differ significantly, even if their characters and subjects overlap. Besides marriage, *An Ideal Husband* raises typical Wildean and late nineteenth-century matters, among which the relation of private to public life is prominent.[19] These are matters presented penultimately as rivals, a competition that domestic life loses.[20] Indeed, the domestic along with the familial territory of marriage in Wilde's play is resolutely secondary to other customary and characteristic topics of the time: work versus idleness; the earnest versus the dandified/insouciant; the threat of blackmail and scandalous secrets (largely male); and serious rivalry between women. In dramatizing the "problem" of the "fallen" man in *An Ideal Husband*, Wilde apparently simply inverts the woman question into an analysis of the social and sexual nature of men, but this bold move also allows the play to engage with some of the most vehemently debated aspects of the woman question. While Sir Robert's leak of Cabinet decisions and his affiliation with insider dealing are clearly located in politics, they result in a trope of (potential) public disgrace, which might equally result from revelation of a (homo)sexual liaison.

The subject of the "fallen" man was a topic of the day with respect to sexual conduct. It was raised to prominence in the 1880s and 1890s by advocates of "social purity" as a solution to the problem of the "double standard," by which women were required to be chaste before marriage, whereas men were permitted to have a "past." Wilde's play was a response to this vociferous group of vigilantes of social purity, which comprised media and renowned public men as well as feminists.[21] Disseminated by *The Heavenly Twins*, a popular novel by Sarah Grand

Laurel Brake

that was much reprinted between 1893 and 1895, "social purity" imposed on men the same standards of purity before marriage pertaining to women.[22] In this respect, Wilde's defense of Robert Chiltern is the reverse: to allow imperfections—particularly "pasts"—to both men and women. Sir Robert's triumph represents Wilde's denial of lifelong culpability and serves as a defense of forgiveness and of charity and love, which are here notably identified with the male protagonist's position. The power of men in the period in part conventionally derived from the alleged character of their (hetero)sexuality, the biological force of desire, and the tribute to its uncontrollability that the double standard allowed; Wilde translates this freedom into male weakness. This ingenious argument in defense of men's weakness is recommended in the play by a man (Goring) to a woman (Lady Chiltern). It amounts to a witty and brilliant retort to the "social purity" party, a retort that, given the necessary attachment of campaigning feminists to sexual respectability, few women would care to make publicly, however much they advocated it.[23] As John Stokes sees it, the idea that Wilde had "social purity" and a didactic aim in view in this play is borne out by his definition of the subject of the play: "[T]he difference in the way in which a man loves a woman from that in which a woman loves a man."[24]

As other commentators have suggested, however, the position to which Lady Chiltern is forced to retreat from her former idolatry of her husband and her liberated participation in the Women's Liberal Association is abject and Ruskinian, amounting to a high-flown iteration of the separate spheres argument (see *CW*, 5:98).[25] In act 2, Sir Robert insists to her that a man's love is "wider, larger, more human than a woman's" (*CW*, 5:132), and in act 4, Goring tells her that "[a] man's life is of more value than a woman's. It has larger issues, wider scope, greater ambitions. A woman's life revolves in curves of emotions. It is upon lines of intellect that a man's life progresses. . . . A woman who can keep a man's love, and love him in return, has done all the world wants of women, or should want of them" (*CW*, 5:228–29). To these words she dramatically assents in a series of retreats, first from her demand of her husband's moral perfection, then from her demand of his withdrawal from public life.

While feminism and the woman question pervade Wilde's play, the apparently triumphant female protagonist in *An Ideal Husband* (who routs Mrs. Cheveley and keeps her man) has change imposed upon her, and the fallen woman, in striking contrast to the fallen man, is exposed and sent packing.[26] Despite its grounded feminism, the world and authority of Wilde's drama remain resolutely predominantly male. It is largely a play in which men (and, by extension, the male world of power and politics) possess validity and authority. This aspect of *An Ideal Husband* is unsurprising, perhaps, in a work that self-consciously engages in critical dialogue on behalf of men (ones with secrets of any kind) with a range of feminist writers, including not only Sarah Grand (who, as I note above, advocated social purity) but also Ella D'Arcy (who was closely linked with the aesthetic and Decadent circles in which Wilde moved).[27] On the whole, Wilde's life and writing were strongly supportive of activist women and the variety of feminist struggles for education, suffrage, dress reform, and social change of the day.[28] But *An Ideal Husband*, I suggest, is an example where Wilde's agenda as a sexualized man made him "come out" publicly (and vehemently) against "social purity," thus allying himself uncharacteristically against those particular New Women advocating that policy.[29]

Wilde was also not alone among male fin-de-siècle writers to assume a posture of what we may call reflexive masculinity. *An Ideal Husband* is only one of several titles by male writers between 1890 and 1895—including Thomas Hardy's *Tess of the D'Urbervilles: A Pure Woman* (1891) and *Jude the Obscure* (1894–95), George Gissing's *The Odd Women* (1893), and Grant Allen's *The Woman Who Did* (1895) as well as George Bernard Shaw's and Henrik Ibsen's plays—that explicitly address the nature of sexuality and gender and social formations such as marriage, free union, and, in Shaw's work, female prostitution.[30] Maugham, some thirty years after *An Ideal Husband,* in constructing a parallel cameo of the constant wife, extricates several recognizable elements—including social purity, marriage, male secrets, idleness and work, and earnestness and the urban. *The Constant Wife,* however, construes them quite differently, since it retains a focus on the woman question in a marriage setting. In this 1926 drama, the public world is shorn away, and we are left with an unadulterated domestic comedy, one confined to the domestic sphere. While Maugham's play is less rich and brilliant than Wilde's, it provides the satisfactions of a well-worked, accretive, ever-deepening dramatization of a single issue—the need for equalities within marriage.

The story of Maugham's indebtedness to Wilde's play began well before 1926, when *The Constant Wife* first opened in New York City.[31] Maugham had reworked this play from an earlier script called *Penelope,* which opened 9 January 1909 at the Comedy Theatre in London, starring Marie Tempest; *Penelope* was written within living memory of Wilde's drama.[32] In his 1909 drama, Maugham picks up on a classical reference to Penelope that emerges very early in *An Ideal Husband*. Wilde's allusion to the spouse of Odysseus invokes the traditional gender roles, which his 1895 comedy go on to disrupt, modify, and endorse. Referring to Baron Arnheim, Sir Robert says that "he knew men and cities well, like the old Greek," to which Mrs. Cheveley replies, "[W]ithout the dreadful disadvantage of having a Penelope waiting at home for him" (*CW*, 5:20). From this piece of dialogue, I suggest, Maugham was prompted to consider the figure of the constant wife, whom Penelope embodies. In this early 1909 play by Maugham, the source of Penelope's deportment in the management of her straying husband is not Penelope herself but a man—the tellingly named Golightly—who counsels his daughter, on the basis of his knowledge of male desire, to appear to withhold her affection from her husband indefinitely to keep his love fresh.[33] Although both Penelope and her successor, Constance, in *The Constant Wife* retain the constancy of Homer's Penelope, by 1926 James Joyce had reinvoked and rethought Homer's trope in *Ulysses* (1918–22), which concludes with *his* Penelope's ironic and lyrical "Yes."[34]

Maugham's plays of 1909 and 1926 also draw on other Wilde-related work, including an August 1894 scenario for a play by Wilde, which he sketched for actor-manager George Alexander in a letter, and its later dramatization in 1900 by Frank Harris as *Mr. and Mrs. Daventry*. Soon after writing *An Ideal Husband* (before it was produced and while he was working on *The Importance of Being Earnest*) Wilde planned a play on the complementary notion of the constant wife. While this was a project that he did not complete, he allowed Harris to develop it after selling him (and several others) the scenario.[35] Harris's play appeared on the London stage at the Royalty Theatre in October 1900, when Maugham was twenty-six. With Mrs. Patrick Campbell in the lead, it had a reasonable success, running for 116 performances into 1901. It remained unpublished until 1956, when H. Montgomery Hyde found prompt copies in the library of the Victoria and Albert Museum, London, and created an edition. So although Maugham would not have had the text of *Mr. and Mrs. Daventry* to hand in 1909 or 1926, it is likely that—given the gossip in which the play was rumored to be connected with Wilde—he saw this play in the autumn of 1900 and read reviews that also intimated the connection.[36] Maugham was a great theatergoer in this period, and he already moved in theatrical circles.[37] From 1903, when Maugham met Max Beerbohm (the satirist who came to know Wilde through his half brother, the actor-manager Herbert Beerbohm Tree), the young playwright had direct contact with Wilde's circle. And when in 1907 Reggie Turner reviewed *Lady Frederick* (Maugham's debut in London's West End),[38] Maugham became close friends with one of Wilde's intimate companions who had been with him when he died. By 1908 Maugham had met Ada Leverson, a loyal supporter of Wilde's, who remained intimate with Maugham through 1911. In 1909, therefore, Maugham's link to Wilde and his network of close friends was direct.

That Maugham knew of Harris's play based on Wilde's scenario is certain, given the close resemblance of *Mr. and Mrs. Daventry* to Maugham's subsequent work. There are two clear ideas that Maugham drew from Harris's play for *The Constant Wife.* First, there is the notion of the knowing wife who tolerates and covers up for an adulterous couple, one of whom is her husband. In a scene in act 2 (this scene became notorious at the time), Mrs. Daventry, concealed behind a screen, watches her husband kiss his mistress in the Daventry home. Then, revealing her presence when the woman's husband walks into the room, she covers up for the couple and apologizes for keeping his wife from the general company. In the scenario, Wilde provides a bit of dialogue: "I am afraid I have kept Lady X up too late; we were trying an absurd experiment in thought reading."[39] Second, in the scenario (as in Maugham's play), Mrs. Daventry takes a lover with whom she plans to go away; in Harris's dramatization, they travel to the Continent together (again, a detail made much of in Maugham's drama, as Constance is particularly keen to go to Italy with Kersal). In addition, Maugham mischievously acknowledges Harris's play (and its Wildean origins) in *Penelope* through characters' names, which are significantly translated to other Wildean idioms in *The Constant Wife.* In the earlier drama, the name of Penelope's old-fashioned and lascivious uncle (Davenport Barlow) recalls Daventry, and Penelope's Irish family name (O'Farrell) echoes Wilde's Irish middle name O'Flahertie. Both of these names disappear in *The Constant Wife,* in which the Penelope figure is called Constance Middleton and the uncle is deleted along with the rest of Constance's male relations.

It may appear surprising that the adultery is experienced by the knowing wife, the guilty pair, and the audience far more directly in Wilde's plan and the Daventry plot than in either of the Maugham plays. This aspect of Maugham's drama may be attributed to the naturalistic theater in Britain at the turn of the century in the wake of the English problem play and the controversial impact of Ibsen's works on the London stage.[40] While the location of the telltale cigarette case makes clear that Maugham's John Middleton and Marie-Louise shared a bed on the previous night, the passion of the affair is distanced and offstage, with only its comic dalliances viewed by the audience of the 1920s. In both Wilde's scenario and Harris's play, the kisses between Mr. Daventry and Lady Langham of act 2, witnessed illicitly by Mrs. Daventry and salaciously by the audience, present bare passion for all to see. Wilde's notion of the affair was far more radical both in its dramaturgy and in its substance than Maugham's: "I want the sheer passion of love to dominate everything. No morbid self-sacrifice. No renunciation—a sheer flame of love between a man and a woman."[41]

In addition to Wilde's scenario and Harris's play, there is a third Wildean text on which Maugham may have drawn. In 1897, after his release from prison, Wilde began work on a play based on the scenario. Now allegedly referred to as *Constance* by Wilde, its title is markedly similar to that of Maugham's 1926 drama. According to Hyde, Wilde named the play after his wife, "who was an essentially 'good' woman like the Mrs. Daventry in the play."[42] The apparent reference to Constance Wilde that Maugham makes in his title is therefore real enough, as is shown not only by this apparent reference to Wilde in Maugham's very Wildean play but also by its possible echo of Wilde's actual title in 1897 for a version of the Daventry play that possesses two salient plotlines adopted by Maugham. Moreover, although a text of *Constance* did not emerge until a French edition by Guillot de Saix and de Briel in 1954,[43] knowledge of its existence and its title was published in 1916, in Frank Harris's *Life and Confessions of Oscar Wilde,* after Maugham wrote *Penelope* but before he penned *The Constant Wife,* with its referential title. Harris mentioned it again in his autobiography, *My Life and Loves,* published in 1922. Maugham, with his longstanding interest in Wilde and as a friend of Harris's, was likely to have read both. Maugham may thus have known of both the Wildean origins of Harris's *Mr. and Mrs. Daventry* and the existence of Wilde's own version, *Constance,* when he set out to transform his early play *Penelope*—whose title had already invoked Wilde's reference to Homer's constant wife—into *The Constant Wife* of 1926.

Unlike Wilde's Gertrude Chiltern in *An Ideal Husband,* the key characteristics of Constance Middleton in *The Constant Wife* are not ignorance and idealism but knowledge/knowingness and strategic practicality. She is nothing if not self-possessed. At the same time, Constance maintains (to considerable comic effect) her mask of *not* knowing with great difficulty in the face of those determined to tell her. In this later feminist climate of the mid-1920s, just before the suffrage acts that were to grant women the full right to vote in both the United States and the United Kingdom, Constance's cool attempts to manage her marriage are assailed repeatedly by her flapper sister, her witty but transparently purposeful mother, and her tacitly compassionate friend in business. Whereas in Wilde's 1895 play, the male dandy Goring is the character who is predictably taxed with "idleness" by his father, in his 1926 drama Maugham is able credibly to introduce into a West End comedy the advantages of paid work for women. While not "earnest" (the gloss that Wilde memorably put on the alternative to idleness in *The Importance of Being Earnest*), Maugham's Constance reluctantly decides to abandon the leisure of a dependent, middle-class, married woman for the independence that economic power offers, an independence gained by entry into interior design, a career only recently beginning to be pursued by women.

The power of labor is an argument rendered familiar by this period through the dissemination of Karl Marx's economic philosophy; Maugham's echo of John Stuart Mill's position that the economic dependence of middle-class women on their husbands is akin to prostitution is reinvigorated by Constance in light of Marx's emphasis on production and productivity. For Constance, the transaction between prostitute and client involves the sale of sex, which, she alleges, in the case of middle-class marriage, is often not sustained: a situation that leaves the wife dependent without fulfilling her function, and the husband seeking sex elsewhere while having to support his redundant partner. Despite the wit of Maugham's intellectual gymnastics, more than one critic of the day was repelled by this cool analysis and inversion of the biosocial functions of marriage.[44] Whereas in *Penelope* the female protagonist is tutored by her father in the rules of self-preservation in marriage, in *The Constant Wife* Constance is the expert manager of this institution, and she functions as a tutor to them all. A partial explanation for this change of dramatic tack lies in what Cyril Connolly observed was "the astringent anti-romantic influence of Maupassant" on Maugham from the year 1919.[45]

The formal transfer of idleness from Wilde's male to Maugham's female, however, is not merely neat. It illustrates how overdetermined Wilde's defense of "idleness" is in his play, being located in the character of a man of independent wealth. Goring's voluntary leisure, unlike that experienced by (nonworking) married women, is not compromised by dependence on another individual. It is not only gendered, given the possibility of independently wealthy women, but is also a class characteristic; in this way, it is part of the class location of his play, which in turn is related to Wilde's Society audience at the time. In *An Ideal*

Husband, Wilde's desire to critique evangelical morality and the criterion of use-fulness and his desire to celebrate art, imagination, and antiutilitarian useless-ness result in a critique of paid work, which inscribes the ambivalence of the upper middle class toward paid work at the time—work by men as well as by women. Work was the unwelcome imposition of public demands on private time. In this context, Caversham's notion of "useful" public duty (that is, that Goring should go into Parliament) is firmly resisted as "dull" (*CW,* 5:198), and at the end of the play, it comes as little surprise that Goring readily accepts the "domestic" career to which Caversham consigns him: "Your career will have to be entirely domestic" (*CW,* 5:238).

The dependence of Wilde's case for uselessness on the economic freedom of a wealthy member of the aristocracy is perhaps the cost of the relative realism of society comedy. If set in a lower social register, then such "idleness" would be hardly possible for middle- and working-class males. Wilde's partiality for leisure, however, is of course gender-specific as well as class-specific, in that for the ma-jority of women of his day (of all classes), the cost of the economic dependence of married women on their husbands was very high, as feminists since Mary Wollstonecraft had been arguing. Such dependency included a curtailment of opportunity—which in other settings Wilde repeatedly and publicly regretted, in concert with the wide dissemination in the 1890s of the cases for women's education, suffrage, and paid work. Although not the dominant reading, the high moral and political cost of Lady Chiltern's economic and emotional de-pendence on her husband by the end of the play would have been clear to Wilde's New Women and radical friends among the audience of *An Ideal Husband.*

In contrast, in Maugham's play, once knowledge of her husband's affair is forced on Constance Middleton, she undertakes a critical review of her life. The privilege that she exacts for her unavoidable knowledge is her husband's agree-ment to her taking up paid work. Unlike *An Ideal Husband,* in which neither Gertrude's nor Mabel Chiltern's "idleness" nor the possibility of female employ-ment is mooted, in *The Constant Wife* paid work and the economic indepen-dence it brings are the most important factors in Constance Middleton's sense of liberation. Although the first two acts of Maugham's drama steal upon the au-dience easily, without arousing suspicion of ensuing events, the third act involves the calibrated and compelling gradual revelation of the lengths to which men and women may amicably pursue sexual equality.

In this third act, Maugham defamiliarizes male marital infidelity by relocating it as female behavior of a wife. In its objectification as a model for female imitation, Robert Middleton's affair with Marie-Louise appears demeaning to his wife and her husband and seems risible in its conduct: apparently covert, it proves visible to all and sundry. Constance's reenactment with Kersal is, by contrast, negotiated with her husband, visible to her family, and above all an act arising from self-knowledge rather than self-delusion. Her earned vacation of six weeks, which she spends separately from her husband (because he does not "like" Italy), is shown step by step as the product of rational behavior based on his example. Thus, Constance insists on her right for a change in sexual partner, which may, within six weeks, invigorate her sexualized self, in abeyance for a decade after the first intoxication of the marriage had (naturally) ended by mutual consent. During that period, "love," she explains, had been replaced by "devotion" (324–25). Neither, she implies, is she about to abandon her constancy. The uncomfortable and gradually revealing third act leaves male deception within marriage, conventionally naturalized, neither deceitful nor singular, thrown into relief as it is by female appropriation—the departure of the independent wife, who is now paying her way at home and at leisure, with her selected lover.

The logical, calm playing out of the parallel to male infidelity in the open, together with the establishment of Constance's right to return to the marital home upon the completion of the six-week sojourn with her lover, set the outcome of *The Constant Wife* in dramatic contrast with Gertrude Chiltern's abject embrace of a life conventionally subordinate to that of her husband and his greater work. To be sure, in both Wilde's 1895 and Maugham's 1926 play, separation is mooted, hinting at the possibility of marital breakdown and divorce, but the grounds are quite distinct. In *An Ideal Husband,* Gertrude threatens to leave because of the discrepancy between her idealistic expectations and his conduct in the past—*his* flawed state; in *The Constant Wife,* the challenge is for John Middleton to accept his wife's right to live as sexually emancipated a life as he does.

While Maugham adopts a notable density of Wildean themes, structures, and casting, the critique of marriage in *The Constant Wife* is distinctively from a female rather than male point of view. John Middleton, unlike Sir Robert, is isolated in the play, located in a female and domestic world in which his profession of surgery largely functions as a transparent alibi for escape from home into the arms of his female lover/"patient" and reiterated "operations." His profession is hardly taken seriously, whereas Constance's decision to work and its economic outcome prove crucial to her liberation. In comparison, Wilde's dazzling *An Ideal Husband* might be said to privilege the male public sphere of politics and government, with the consequent flattening of the domestic sphere and its female denizens—from the routed femme fatale to the corralled Lady Chiltern to the romantically disempowered Mabel.[46]

In 1895, Wilde's self-conscious writing of masculinity—in all its variety and complexity—was relatively rare for its time and seems laudable; his address to the topical woman question in this society comedy is characteristically attentive and witty. But it is also, as comparison with Maugham's much later drama shows, very much of its period. Despite the radical notes it strikes, unexpectedly (for Wilde) it nonetheless endorses conventional marriage and subordinated women —certainly in the marriage of the Chilterns, if more ambiguously in that of the Gorings.[47] Joseph Bristow makes a good case for incorporation into Wilde's "intention" of this gap between the play's ending and "the crisis it has opened up": it is part of Wilde's "critique of a culture" that wants clear meaning: "For it is . . . the evident intention of each of Wilde's Society comedies," he argues, "not to present the audience with ideal endings. Marriage, in particular is the institution that fails most visibly in this respect."[48] But Bristow also accepts that however fresh Wilde's rewriting of Society comedy may be, it is not always or necessarily "transgressive."[49]

Thus, a complex trail that leads from Wilde's *An Ideal Husband* to Maugham's *The Constant Wife*, and the relationship between these two plays (as well as with *Mr. and Mrs. Daventry* and *Penelope*) may be used to tease out meanings of them all. What the argument of *An Ideal Husband* does, ultimately and predominantly, is to clear space for male autonomy—autonomy for secrets of state, secrets of politicians, and secrets of male sexual activity. In the course of the play, it makes the larger case for the "fallen," the imperfect men *and* women in the domestic and public spheres, a case unevenly endorsed at its end. *An Ideal Husband* leaves the responsibility for tackling the implications of Wilde's transgressive evenhandedness to others, such as Maugham to tackle the implications of that transgressive evenhandedness. Through its rich gestation, Maugham's 1926 play takes up many of the opportunities of Wilde's legacy. In *The Constant Wife*, Maugham's discerning readings and refashioning of a particular clutch of Wilde's dramas and ideas match that of fellow modernists such as T. S. Eliot and Ezra Pound, who similarly redeploy texts of their predecessors in their writing, seeking to build new work on selective and fabricated traditions.

Notes

1. Richard Cave, "Wilde's Plays: Some Lines of Influence," in *The Cambridge Companion to Oscar Wilde*, ed. Peter Raby (Cambridge: Cambridge University Press, 1997), 229.

2. Anthony Curtis, introduction to W. Somerset Maugham, *Plays: One*, Methuen Drama (London: Random House, 1997), xv.

3. See Curtis, introduction to Maugham, *Plays: One*, xvii.

4. Curtis, introduction to Maugham, *Plays: One*, xxviii.

5. I am grateful to Professor Linda K. Hughes, Texas Christian University, for drawing Kelly's portrait to my attention.

6. See, for example, Lyn Pykett, "What's 'New' about the 'New Woman'? Another Look at the Representation of the New Woman in Victorian Periodicals," *Australasian Victorian Studies Journal* 6 (2000): 102–12. Pykett reviews and contextualizes arguments about attribution of the phrase and the dating of the term "New Woman."

7. Peter Raby, "Wilde's Comedies of Society," in Raby, *Cambridge Companion*, 158.

8. Alan Sinfield, "'Effeminacy' and 'Femininity': Sexual Politics in Wilde's Comedies," *Modern Drama* 37 (1994): 41.

9. The Chiltern Hundreds is a procedural device that allows members of Parliament to resign from the House of Commons by standing for electoral constituencies that have no duties or electorate.

10. Various accounts of the marriage and its aftermath had been published by the 1920s. See Robert H. Sherard, *The Story of an Unhappy Friendship* (London: Hermes Press, 1917), 174 (Sherard's book first appeared in 1902); and Arthur Ransome, *Oscar Wilde: A Critical Study* (London: Martin Secker, 1912), 80–81. Additionally, Maugham, as an aware young man of twenty (one of whose homosexual friends fled to the Continent in response to the Wilde trials), was alert to Wilde and his position as early as 1895. According to Samuel J. Rogal, Maugham "closely followed the proceedings." Rogal, *A William Somerset Maugham Encyclopaedia* (Westport, CT: Greenwood, 1997), 309.

11. Maugham, *The Constant Wife*, in *Plays: One* (London: Random House, 1997), 276; further page references appear in parentheses.

12. St. John Ervine, "At the Play—*The Constant Wife*," *Observer*, 8 May 1927, 15.

13. Regenia Gagnier, *Idylls of the Marketplace: Oscar Wilde and the Victorian Public* (Stanford, CA: Stanford University Press, 1986), 131.

14. Sinfield, "'Effeminacy' and 'Femininity,'" 49.

15. Richard Dellamora, "Oscar Wilde, Social Purity, and *An Ideal Husband*," *Modern Drama* 37 (1994): 126.

16. In an appendix to his New Mermaids edition of *An Ideal Husband*, Russell Jackson includes a discarded exchange of dialogue that makes the possibility of Gertrude's flirtation with Goring evident (*Two Society Comedies:* A Woman of No Importance *and* An Ideal Husband, ed. Ian Small and Russell Jackson [London: Ernest Benn, 1983], 293). For earlier versions of Gertrude's sexual temptation, see Sos Eltis, *Revising Wilde: Society and Subversion in the Plays of Oscar Wilde*

(Oxford: Oxford University Press, 1996), 144. Jackson notes that in other respects, the decadence of earlier versions is toned down in the published form of the play, which was performed in 1895 but not published until 1899. See Jackson, "The Importance of Being Earnest," in Raby, *Cambridge Companion*, 167. In comparison with Maugham's later play, however, the suppression of the plot of the betrayal of Sir Robert by his friend and his spouse does endorse the power of male friendship and of the marriage ties in Wilde's play. *An Ideal Husband* barely manages to remain an exception to the general truth of Joseph Bristow's observation about the world of Wilde's plays: "Everywhere we look married life inhibits the kind of friendship that promises to harmonise the soul and body." Bristow, "'A Complex Multiform Creature': Wilde's Sexual Identities," in Raby, *Cambridge Companion*, 215.

17. Jackson notes that by the time Wilde wrote *An Ideal Husband*, he had experienced sexual blackmail, which is here represented as political ("Importance of Being Earnest," 168). This displacement and the coupling of Baron Arnheim with "the old Greek" in the play support Jackson's reading that the Baron Arnheim–Sir Robert relationship is a version of the corruption of a youth by an older man that we see in *The Picture of Dorian Gray* in the characters of Lord Henry Wotton and Dorian Gray. These same-sex relationships in turn are a reversal of the Platonic ideal in which an older man loves and educates a younger ephebe. While the link between Baron Arnheim and Sir Robert is textually explicit in *An Ideal Husband*, unlike the other Society plays, Arnheim never materializes but remains outside the action in the present. Unlike Lord Henry in Wilde's novel, Baron Arnheim is stowed in the furthest reaches of the past: he is safely dead, represented only in Robert's memory and Mrs. Cheveley's intervention. This appears to be a strategic absence and very wise retrospectively, given the unfolding circumstances of 1895, which resulted in Wilde's imprisonment in May that year.

18. The cigarette case also has a Wildean analogue, in the first act of *The Importance of Being Earnest* (see *CW*, 6:11). I am indebted to Joseph Bristow for this point.

19. Just as *The Constant Wife* opens with a choric discussion of Constance Middleton's marriage in her absence, so too does Wilde's first act provide a stream of dialogue about marriage in the remarks of the married aristocratic women such as Lady Markby, Mrs. Marchmont, and Lady Basildon (see, for example, *CW*, 5:29). Early in act 1, Mrs. Cheveley sets the scene: "Oh, I don't care about the London season! It is too matrimonial. People are either hunting for husbands, or hiding from them" (*CW*, 5:18). For a discussion of the relation of Wilde's drama to late-Victorian debates about public and private life, see Kerry Powell, *Oscar Wilde and the Theatre of the 1890s* (Cambridge: Cambridge University Press, 1990).

20. Jerusha McCormack observes that the title of *An Ideal Husband* is an ironic reversal of the recent Parnell scandal, in which Parnell's personal life toppled his public political status. The location of Wilde's play about sins in and against the public sphere in the domestic drawing room, in which the stability of marriage rather than government is purportedly the primary consideration, is suggested by the title. McCormack, "The Wilde Irishman: Oscar as Aesthete and Anarchist," in *Wilde the Irishman*, ed. Jerusha McCormack (New Haven, CT: Yale University Press, 1998), 89–90. I am arguing that the title and the feminized domestic location of Wilde's comedy are in considerable tension with events in the male public sphere, which ultimately dictate the outcome of the marriage drama. But I agree that it is also true that the domestic setting permits a full discussion of the politics of the family and marriage.

21. Richard Dellamora (in "Oscar Wilde") locates "social purity" as a prime target of *An Ideal Husband;* he sets this preoccupation in relation to other works by Wilde, notably "The Soul of Man under Socialism" (1891).

22. Sarah Grand (Frances Elizabeth McFall), *The Heavenly Twins* (London: Heinemann, 1893). The British Library has an additional three-volume reprinting from 1893, advertised as the "Fourth Thousand"; by 1894, Heinemann had published a single-volume edition in Britain. An edition attributed to Madame Sarah Grand appeared in the United States in 1893.

23. Although there were women advocates of free union in the 1890s (such as Mona Caird, Olive Schreiner, and Annie Besant), most women involved in feminist campaigns preferred not to risk undermining their particular cause—whether it be the vote, higher education for women, or social work—through violation of the hegemonic notion of feminine purity. Dellamora observes that women like Gertrude Chiltern were "forced to exert influence as *public* proponents of *private* or domestic values. In these circumstances, the purity of women in the private sphere functioned as a necessary condition of their public efficacy" ("Oscar Wilde," 126–27). For further discussion about this issue of feminists and sexuality, see Lucy Bland, *Banishing the Beast: English Feminism and Sexual Morality, 1885–1914* (Harmondsworth, UK: Penguin, 1995), esp. 151–56.

24. John Stokes, "Wilde Interpretations," in *Oscar Wilde: Myths, Miracles and Imitations* (Cambridge: Cambridge University Press, 1996), 162.

25. Jackson notes that in 1892 the Women's Liberal Association supported the campaign for women's suffrage; in doing so, they opposed Gladstone, who did not support the 1892 campaign or bill (Small and Jackson, *Two Society Comedies*, 187).

26. See Gagnier's astute comment on the gendered fortunes of Sir Robert and Mrs. Cheveley: "Whereas women were wrong to go to any lengths for money and power, politicians were right to do so" (*Idylls of the Marketplace*, 130).

27. Ella D'Arcy (1851–1939) was one of the New Women writers who were contemporary with Wilde; at the time, her short stories were appearing in the quarterly *Yellow Book* (1894–97), where she was assistant literary editor. An 1890s quarterly published initially by Elkin Mathews and John Lane and sumptuously illustrated in its first year by Aubrey Beardsley (who served as art editor), the *Yellow Book* severed its connection with Beardsley once Wilde went on trial in 1895 because of fears that the public associated Beardsley with Wilde and thus with the quarterly, although it had never published anything by Wilde.

28. For more on these matters, see Margaret Diane Stetz, "The Bi-social Oscar Wilde and 'Modern' Women," *Nineteenth-Century Literature* 55 (2001): 515–37. In this context, Wilde's 1887–89 editorship of the *Woman's World*—a journal aimed at politically aware women—is significant.

29. Reviews of the play at its opening clearly identified Lady Chiltern as a Puritan, as may be seen in the *Daily Telegraph*, written in the persona of a male reviewer: "Lady Chiltern is a very dragon of virtue. Her Puritanism passes all belief" (unsigned review, "Mr Oscar Wilde's New Play at the Haymarket," *Daily Telegraph*, 4 January 1895, 3). The *Sketch*'s Monocle likens her to "a petticoat Torvald Helmer," "heartless" and "dull" (Monocle [Edward Fordham Spence], "An Opinion of 'An Ideal Husband,'" *Sketch*, 9 January 1895, 496). In our own time, Joel Kaplan suggests that Wilde's object of critique is earnestness (Kaplan, "Wilde on the Stage," in Raby, *Cambridge Companion*, 258). I agree, but I view this as a choice between kinds of feminism, rather than between feminism and earnestness. Kaplan implies this, citing several "stage Puritans" in Wilde's plays, all of whom are women. By the 1914 production of the play, the alliance with purity among feminists had become less widespread, and Kaplan reports that the play was met by derision in the theater and in the press (in *Votes for Women*, a suffrage weekly). Even in 1895, it had been parodied in *Punch* by Ada Leverson soon after its opening (though these *Punch* parodies were published on 12 and 19 January 1895, not on 23 May as Kaplan states). See [Ada Leverson,] "Overheard Fragment of a Dialogue," *Punch*, 12 January 1895, 24, and "A Penny Plain—but Oscar Coloured (An Entertainment Antagonistic to Amusement)," *Punch*, 19 January 1895, 36.

Laurel Brake

30. Shaw's polemical drama *Mrs. Warren's Profession*, which focuses on the clash between a wealthy woman brothel-keeper and her Cambridge-educated New Woman daughter, was written in 1893 and published in 1898 but was not licensed for performance in public until 1925.

31. The New York City production of November 1926 starred Ethel Barrymore as Constance and ran for three hundred performances, while the London production at the Strand Theatre, beginning 6 April 1927, lasted for only seventy performances.

32. The *Athenæum* reviewer of *Penelope* names two playwrights whose work was allegedly influential on Maugham's play: Victorien Sardou (in *Divorçons* [1880]) and Oscar Wilde (whose Bunbury, in *The Importance of Being Earnest*, is the fictional friend who serves as a model for Mrs. Mack, Dickie's fictional and convenient patient). [F. G. Bettany,] review of *Penelope*, by Somerset Maugham, *Athenaeum*, 16 January 1909, 83.

33. Other differences between *Penelope* and *The Constant Wife* include the staged opening of the earlier play, which is manipulated by Penelope rather than by her visitors. Although she is absent at first (as in *The Constant Wife*), after her delayed and dramatic entry Penelope reveals her husband's infidelity to the others and announces that she wants a divorce; this contrasts with the comic device in *The Constant Wife* of Constance's visitors trying to tell her. Similarities between the two plays include the occupation of the erring husband in medicine, which echoes Maugham's education as a medic, and the departure of the Penelope figure for the Continent with her lover at the end of the action. The origin of the late play in the earlier is further suggested by the name of Constance and John Middleton's daughter, Helen, who, because she is at boarding school, never dramatically materializes but nevertheless invokes Helen of Troy, in whose name the Trojan Wars were fought. In the later redaction of *Penelope*, Helen seals its origins as she carries the trace of its Homeric reference from *An Ideal Husband*.

34. *Man and Wife*, a discarded early title of Maugham's play, echoes the generic irony that Joyce achieved by invoking Homer directly in the title of his novel about twentieth-century Dublin life.

35. For an explanation of Wilde's multiple sales of the scenario to raise money, see Frank Harris, *Mr. and Mrs. Daventry*, ed. H. Montgomery Hyde (London: Richards Press 1956), 11–12, 21; and *The Complete Letters of Oscar Wilde*, ed. Merlin Holland and Rupert Hart-Davis (London: Fourth Estate, 2000), 1189n3, 1211–12. See also the introduction to the present volume.

36. The review in the *Athenaeum* begins, "With the persistent reports that assign Mr. Frank Harris a share only, and that the minor, in the play with which Mrs. Campbell resumes possession of the Royalty we are nowise concerned. Two backs may well have been needed to sustain the burden of responsibility for the most daring and naturalistic production of the modern English stage" ([J. Knight,] review of *Mr. and Mrs. Daventry*, by Frank Harris, *Athenaeum*, 3 November 1900, 587). A month later, in Wilde's terse obituary in the *Athenaeum*, another reference to his putative authorship was included in its reference to "the four or more [dramatic] pieces which he wrote" (Drama: Obituaries, *Athenaeum*, 8 December 1900, 768). Following this production, Mrs. Patrick Campbell interestingly persisted in producing a string of "daring and naturalistic" plays at the Royalty; these include Arthur Wing Pinero's *The Notorious Mrs. Ebbsmith* (1895) and *The Second Mrs. Tanqueray* (1893) (Drama: Obituaries, *Athenaeum*, 8 December 1900, 768). That this policy may reflect the favorable economics of notoriety is suggested by T. H. Bell, Harris's emissary to Wilde at the time. He reported that "Mrs. Pat" made Harris's play "more risqué than . . . intended" to lengthen its run and that Harris was thus able "to get out of his immediate [monetary] trouble" (T. H. Bell, "Oscar Wilde's Unwritten Play," *Bookman* [New York] (April and May 1930): 148–49). The *Telegraph* obliged by reporting, "It is a play of sordid, very sordid, intrigue" ("Royalty Theatre: 'Mr. and Mrs. Daventry,'" *Daily Telegraph*, 26 October 1900, 8ff).

The *Athenaeum* signaled to its readers the play's attractions by making the following lament in the 3 November 1900 review: "There is no character with the slightest claim to our respect" (587).

Besides the reviewers, other contemporaries attested to the rumors. Bell wrote, "It was rumored widely at the time that it was Wilde's play and its first night was well attended" ("Oscar Wilde's Unwritten Play," 148). Harris bitterly noted the rumors in an appendix dedicated to the story of the writing of *Mr. and Mrs. Daventry:* "Nine people out of ten believed that Oscar had written the play and that I had merely lent my name to the production in order to enable him, as a bankrupt, to receive the money from it. Even men of letters [such as George Moore] deceived themselves in this way." Harris, *Oscar Wilde: His Life and Confessions,* 2 vols. (New York: privately published, 1916), 2:589.

37. See Robert Calder, *Willie: The Life of W. Somerset Maugham* (London: Heinemann, 1989), 37–44. Maugham's London flat mate from 1897 was Adey Walter Payne, whose father was a music-hall impresario. The young men had met in Heidelberg in the early 1890s, when Maugham had begun to write plays. By 1894, Maugham was translating Ibsen's *Ghosts* into German, to learn the structure of the language. In January 1895, Maugham attended the disastrous first night of Henry James's *Guy Domville,* the failure of which provided the opening for the production of *The Importance of Being Earnest* in George Alexander's St. James's Theatre in mid-February. Given the young Maugham's interest in the theater as an aspiring playwright and Payne's theatrical connections, Maugham's attendance at such a production as Harris's play in 1900 is likely, especially since it played for over a hundred performances. He may have also seen the original production of *An Ideal Husband.*

38. Although *A Man of Honour* had been produced in the Imperial Theatre in February 1903, it was a standard Stage Society production of two or three performances, on a Sunday evening and Monday matinee, after which it closed. See Ted Morgan, *Somerset Maugham* (London: Jonathan Cape, 1980), 99–101.

39. Quoted by Hyde in Harris, *Mr. and Mrs. Daventry,* 9.

40. Katharine Worth compares the scenes between Lady Chiltern and Mrs. Cheveley to those between Hedda and Thea Elvsted. Worth, *Oscar Wilde* (Basingstoke, UK: Macmillan, 1983), 130–31. Worth also points to the similarity between the use of the past in Ibsen's *Pillars of Society* (which Wilde saw in 1889) and its similar power over the present in *An Ideal Husband.*

41. Wilde to George Alexander, *Complete Letters,* 600. The collection's editors, Holland and Hart-Davis, suggest that this letter dates from August 1894.

42. Harris, *Mr. and Mrs. Daventry,* 11n2. Karl Beckson contests this premise vehemently: nowhere "in his extant letters or in his MSS, does Wilde ever mention the titles." Beckson, "*Mr and Mrs Daventry* or *Constance,*" in Beckson, *The Oscar Wilde Encyclopedia* (New York: AMS Press, 1998), 225.

43. Wilde, *Constance,* in *Les œuvres libres,* ed. Guillot de Saix and Henri de Briel, 101 (October 1954): 201–302.

44. See the anonymous contemporary reviewer who made the following complaint in the *Times:* "If there had been any emotion whatever in the play, some one might have had the pleasure of being shocked, but it is hard even to be shocked by a bowl of goldfish swimming coldly but in an elaborate pattern, after one another's decorative tails." Unsigned review of *The Constant Wife,* by W. Somerset Maugham, *Times,* 7 April 1927, 14b.

45. According to Cyril Connolly, the other great influence on Maugham that dates from this year is his discovery of the East. Connolly, "Somerset Maugham," *Sunday Times,* 19 December 1965.

46. Sos Eltis reads this as a strength of the play (*Revising Wilde*, 133–35), and John Stokes notes that in 1992 Peter Hall's emphasis on the public sphere as the primary source of the melodrama made his production "all the more realistic" (Stokes, "Wilde Interpretations," 162).

47. In the last lines of act 4, there is a play on words with reference to the marriage of Mabel and Arthur, on the distinction between Arthur as an "ideal" husband, which Mabel rejects, and her insistence that she will be a "real" wife. But the inflection of the latter, situated as it is in a breathless paroxysm of romantic deference and enthusiasm—"All I want is to be ... to be ... oh! A real wife to him" (lines 548–49) somewhat weakens its promise of a liberated marriage in this younger generation. That the tone of this exchange is largely determined by its position at the end of the play, adjacent to the even more exaggeratedly romantic curtain line of Lady Chiltern, is highly probable and is at distinct odds with the rebarbative Mabel in the body of the text (and, indeed, with Arthur's pleasure in her wit). However, Dellamora reads Mabel and Goring more strongly as "the hero and heroine of the play" and goes on to explore whether both of them may be bisexual and the marriage doomed ("Oscar Wilde," 129, 132).

Many critics comment on the end of Lady Chiltern, to insist on irony (Gagnier, *Idylls;* Eltis, *Revising Wilde;* and Raby, "Wilde's Comedies," 143–60) and the gap Wilde constructs between Society and his critique of it. Others read it as earnest: Kaplan suggests that Wilde misjudged the strength of feminism in the period and privileged his critique of earnestness instead ("Wilde on the Stage," 258). Richard Cave links her compromise with the necessity for pragmatism evident in the colonial context of Ireland in which Wilde wrote the play: the vicissitudes of private life are sacrificed for the appearance of a "stable united front" to "face the public," while "[t]he conventions stand revealed as a kind of subtly sophisticated censorship" ("Wilde's Plays," 223).

48. Joseph Bristow, "'Dowdies and Dandies': Oscar Wilde's Refashioning of Society Comedy," *Modern Drama* 37 (1994): 56, 62.

49. Bristow, "Dowdies and Dandies," 67.

Transcripts and Truth

Writing the Trials of Oscar Wilde

LESLIE J. MORAN

> That gentleman [H. Montgomery Hyde] relies for his facts upon a transcript of the shorthand notes and for his comments upon letters and other writings extending over many years.
>
> —The Rt. Hon. Sir Travers Humphreys (1948)

> When the verdict and sentence were announced the prostitutes danced in the streets around the Old Bailey. . . . The truth had been exposed.
>
> —Sir John Mortimer (2003)

> Court scenes grip in "Oscar Wilde" film.
>
> —Film correspondent, *Daily Telegraph* (1960)

THESE THREE EPIGRAPHS share the common belief that we can know the facts of the proceedings of the criminal trials involving Oscar Wilde, which began on 3 April 1895 and resulted seven weeks later in his imprisonment for two years with hard labor in solitary confinement. Moreover, these comments share the assumption that the three trials provide us with indisputable facts about the life of Oscar Wilde. The first two epigraphs come from a particular genre of Wilde scholarship dedicated to the trials, purporting to provide verbatim accounts of the proceedings. This is a well-established genre of writing older than (and certainly as durable as) posthumous biographical and literary-critical scholarship about Wilde's life and work.[1] The observation by Sir Travers Humphreys is taken from his 1948 foreword to the book *The Trials of Oscar Wilde*, composed by H. Montgomery Hyde.[2] Ed Cohen describes Hyde's volume as the canonical and "de facto official" account of the criminal trials involving Wilde.[3] Humphreys, at the time of writing, was the last surviving lawyer who took part as a barrister in all three of the court cases involving Wilde. Sir Travers's comment endorses the main claim associated with Hyde's transcription: it tells the truth of the trials. "Shorthand" is central to this particular claim. It is presented as a benign technology that seeks simultaneously to capture the event of each trial and, by way of subsequent transcription, make the full details of the event accessible to a general reader. "Facts" therefore remain distinct from "fictions" and from "comments" (perhaps a hybrid, part fact and part fiction) in this telling of the trials.

The second quotation, written some fifty years later, is taken from the foreword to the most recent book within this genre of verbatim accounts: Merlin Holland's *Irish Peacock and Scarlet Marquess: The Real Trial of Oscar Wilde* (2003).[4] Holland's volume is limited to the first of the criminal trials, in which Oscar Wilde, using a charge of criminal libel, brought criminal proceedings against the Marquess of Queensberry. Holland ups the epistemological ante offering the truth of Wilde's libel suit: "[F]or the first time," the publisher declares on the book jacket, we have "the true record, without distortions." The foreword to Holland's transcript is again by a lawyer, another eminent barrister, Sir John Mortimer QC, also a well-known author perhaps most famous in Britain for his *Rumpole of the Bailey* novels and scripts.[5] Mortimer, like Humphreys before him, takes the opportunity to rehearse the truth claims that are central to Holland's book. Mortimer's comment suggests that the facts of the event of the legal process tell not only the "truth" of that process but also the "facts" and "truth" of the incidents that were the basis of the criminal proceedings.

The third quotation is a headline taken from an anonymous film review of *Oscar Wilde* (1960), directed by Gregory Ratoff and starring Robert Morley in the leading role. This was the first of two films of the life of Oscar Wilde, both of which were released almost simultaneously in 1960. The second film, *The Trials of Oscar Wilde*, was directed by Ken Hughes, with Peter Finch as the main protagonist.[6] At the heart of both films is a courtroom drama based on Hyde's book. The re-viewer's remarks accentuate a common theme that runs throughout the reception of these films: commentators repeatedly stress the cinematic significance of the trial scenes, which dominate both of these works. The *Manchester Guardian*, for example, explained that these scenes made *The Trials of Oscar Wilde* "a drama not of fiction but of detailed truth."[7] Another reviewer observed that "[w]ith the trial scenes the whole film comes suddenly to life."[8] Such notices clearly share the epistemological concerns that link the representations of the trials to truth, but they take us in another direction as well. They draw attention to the way in which the courtroom exchanges have special import in the context of other genres of writing, whether in the form of life writing or literary-critical analysis and other modes of representation, from the printed text to visual representations such as film. Both of these films from 1960 thus disclose that the trials literature has been plundered as a rich resource, providing facts that offer to tell the truth of not only Wilde's encounters with the law but also the wider facts of his life, his conversations, his character, his philosophy, and his oratorical and literary skills.

Such epistemological claims are most obviously associated with the four volumes that comprise the tradition of the Wilde trials literature. Chronologically speaking, the first of these is the anonymous *The Trial of Oscar Wilde from the Shorthand Reports,* which was published in Paris in 1906 by Charles Carrington: a bookseller, best known for his lists in clandestine erotic fiction, had permission from Wilde's literary estate to publish authorized editions of the Irish author's works.[9] The 1906 volume is the most concise account purporting to be a verbatim record. Its shorthand reports deal only with the two proceedings in which Wilde, after his libel suit against the Marquess of Queensberry failed, was prosecuted by the state, leading to his eventual conviction for the offense of gross indecency. This account was also a private publication (on handmade paper) with a limited circulation (five hundred copies), which suggests that it was aimed at an exclusive collector's market at a time when Wilde's reputation remained sullied by the adverse publicity surrounding the trials and his subsequent imprisonment.

The second work at the heart of the trials tradition is Christopher Sclater Millard's 1912 *Oscar Wilde: Three Times Tried,* which is described in the preface as "a complete and accurate account of this long and complicated case."[10] Initially published anonymously and later attributed to Millard (a gifted researcher who wrote several significant works on Wilde as Stuart Mason), this is the first supposedly complete account produced for popular consumption.[11] The third work, as I mention above, is Hyde's *Trials of Oscar Wilde,* first published in 1948 and revised in 1962 (with the second edition reprinted in 1973).[12] Finally, the most recent transcript of Wilde's courtroom experience, confined this time to the first of the criminal proceedings, is Holland's *Irish Peacock and Scarlet Marquess.*

My interest in studying the nature and persistence of the epistemological claims associated with the Oscar Wilde trials literature was in part inspired by Ed Cohen's important 1993 study, *Talk on the Wilde Side.* Cohen makes an iconoclastic intervention into our understanding of and engagement with the literature on the Wilde trials. In an intellectual journey to uncover and analyze the social and cultural forces at work in Wilde's criminalization, as recorded in the transcripts of the shorthand writers' record of the trials, Cohen questions the validity of the trials literature in general and of Hyde's "canonical" and "de facto 'official version'" in particular. Early in his discussion, Cohen arrives at the startling conclusion that if these transcripts did exist, he could find no evidence of them. Further, he realized, after exchanging correspondence with Hyde, that such transcripts were not the source of Hyde's verbatim accounts. In 1985, Hyde informed Cohen, "I did not use any transcripts of the trials in my book and in fact relied on press reports in addition to *Oscar Wilde: Three Times Tried* published anonymously by Stuart Mason (Christopher Millard)" (Cohen, *Talk on the Wilde Side,* 4). In Cohen's book, this excerpt from Hyde's letter is followed by what appears to be a summary of a further point contained in the correspondence that pertains to Millard's volume: namely, that *Oscar Wilde: Three Times Tried* was also "based on press reports and personal reminiscences" (*Talk on the Wilde Side,* 4). As a consequence, Cohen largely leaves behind Hyde's book and the trials literature about Wilde to explore a range of 1895 newspaper reports of the proceedings, which take on the status of key source material for his searing social and cultural analysis. Cohen's intervention has not resulted in the wholesale abandonment of the belief that Hyde's popular volume contained facts and the truth. Moreover, Hyde's account is still used as a source of fact and referenced in subsequent life writing and critical scholarship.[13]

The publication of Holland's *Irish Peacock and Scarlet Marquess* added another twist to the tradition of writing the truth of the trials. This volume breathes new life into the epistemological claims of truth and facts associated with previous verbatim accounts. Holland's volume is presented as "the original courtroom transcript" based on the notes of several shorthand writers (xi). *Irish Peacock and the Scarlet Marquess,* he explains, offers "for the first time . . . the true record, without the distortions of previous accounts" (front blurb). This event has also made an impact on life writing about Wilde. Neil McKenna's 2003 sexual biography, *The Secret Life of Oscar Wilde,* refers to Holland's publication as a source of information about Wilde's "immensely rich and complicated sexual life between 1892 and 1895."[14] Despite Cohen's critique, this longstanding genealogy of verbatim accounts would appear to be very much alive and kicking.

However valuable Cohen's iconoclastic approach to the trials literature, he seems not to have considered some evidence about the nature of Hyde's trials text. A forensic analysis of Hyde's trials text (as well as two earlier texts of the trials) appears in the reported judgment of the English High Court relating to court proceedings, which began in April 1960. The report of the court's decision, not published until 1969, contains a fascinating analysis of the key trial books and offers us a further understanding of their origins and methods of production.[15] The forensic analysis of Hyde's canonical text that took place in the case of *Warwick Film Productions Ltd. v. Eisinger and Others*[16] involved discussion of earlier transcripts that claimed to record the truth of the trials. The facts found in these various verbatim accounts of the trials, however, have had mixed fortunes in the intervening years, as various techniques were applied to fabricate the epistemological claims associated with them.[17]

The Trial of "The Trials . . ."

In the opening months of 1960, media reports began to appear of an "all out scramble" and "battle" between two simultaneous film productions of the life of Oscar Wilde: *Oscar Wilde* was in production at the Walton-on-Thames studios, while *The Trials of Oscar Wilde* was in production barely twenty miles away at Elstree.[18] The race was on to reap the rewards of being the first film on screen. In April 1960, Warwick Film Productions, the production company behind the film *The Trials of Oscar Wilde,* petitioned the High Court in London to influence the outcome of that race. The defendants were the scriptwriter (Jo Eisinger), director (Gregory Ratoff), production company (Vantage Films), and distributor (20th Century Fox) of the film *Oscar Wilde.* The legal proceedings were based on a claim by Warwick Films that Warwick owned the copyright in the "verbatim accounts" of both Hyde and Millard and that the film *Oscar Wilde* was in breach of that right. Warwick Films sought an interlocutory injunction to stop the premiere of that film.[19] On 3 May 1960, the London *Evening Standard* reported that in court proceedings a preliminary undertaking had been given by Vantage Films not to show or export the Ratoff film. The full interlocutory hearing came before the court on 16 May.[20] The attempt to obtain the injunction failed. Ratoff's *Oscar Wilde* premiered first, just five days before its competitor, *The Trials of Oscar Wilde*. Seven years passed before the copyright argument (and with it the forensic analysis of the trials literature) was fully aired. As trial court judge Justice Plowman noted, in the wake of the unsuccessful interlocutory application the plaintiffs "seem to have lost any enthusiasm they ever had for bringing their action to trial" (*Warwick Film Productions Ltd. v. Eisinger,* 512 e). Central to Warwick's legal action were Hyde's and Millard's books. Warwick claimed that the script of the defendants, in its account of the trials, violated Warwick's rights of copyright in these two texts.

The scriptwriter, Eisinger, is the central figure in these legal proceedings. He developed his interest in making a film about Oscar Wilde after seeing the stage play *Oscar Wilde,* written by Leslie Stokes and Sewell Stokes, starring Robert Morley in the title role in the 1938 New York production.[21] A distinctive feature of this drama was its use of extracts from accounts of the three criminal trials involving Wilde. The play drew upon Millard's book, although, as Justice Plowman noted, "Eisinger not only made no direct use of 'Three Times Tried,' but he had never even heard of it" (*Warwick Film Productions Ltd. v. Eisinger,* 525 c–d). Drawing inspiration from the stage production, Eisinger planned to develop a film that would not only make extensive use of the trial scenes in the drama but also use Hyde's verbatim account as a key source of information. Early discussions about the making of such a film, with 20th Century Fox in the United States, came to a halt on the basis that the censorship code (often known as the Hays Code) would make the film difficult to produce and distribute. Eisinger then pursued his project in Britain with several individuals, including the director Ken Hughes. When these discussions broke down (in large part because of Eisinger's failure to write the script), Eisinger went on to develop and realize his project, *Oscar Wilde,* with Gregory Ratoff, Vantage Films, and 20th Century Fox. Working with Warwick Film Productions, which obtained rights to Hyde's text, Hughes (together with producer Irving Allen) wrote the script and subsequently directed *The Trials of Oscar Wilde.*

Warwick Film Productions' copyright claim was based on an infringement of Warwick's alleged exclusive rights to Hyde's text and rights to Millard's text that flowed from Hyde's use of that earlier transcription.[22] Eisinger's defense invoked the epistemological attributes associated with these verbatim accounts. He argued that there was no breach of copyright, because he had only made use of reports of the actual trial events, counsels' speeches, the words of the judge, and Wilde's answers. He had relied on the statements by Travers Humphreys in Humphreys's 1948 foreword to Hyde's book about the factual nature of the courtroom encounters and on Hyde's assertions, such as the one found in the last sentence of Hyde's introduction to the first edition: "Now let the records of the trials speak for themselves" (Hyde, 101, quoted in *Warwick Film Productions Ltd. v. Eisinger*, 525 e).[23] As the trial judge explained, "It never occurred [to Eisinger] that a person who frankly stated that he merely reproduced contemporary verbatim reports of a public trial could claim copyright in such material" (*Warwick Film Productions Ltd. v. Eisinger*, 525 e–f). The epistemological claims associated with the trials literature were thus placed at the heart of the dispute.

In establishing Warwick's rights in Hyde's text and in rejecting the production company's claim to have interests in Millard's one, the court undertook a forensic examination of Millard's *Oscar Wilde: Three Times Tried* and, to a lesser degree, the earlier *Trial of Oscar Wilde from the Shorthand Reports*. So what were the court's findings? In preparation for his consideration of Millard's transcript, Justice Plowman briefly considered the nature of the 1906 book. This volume, he concluded, contains only extracts from the two criminal proceedings brought by the state against Wilde and is not a report of the trials in book form. His attention then turned to Millard's transcript.[24] First, he noted the style of the work, which is written as a day-to-day account of the legal proceedings, with additional comments and descriptive passages. He then considered the source of the information in *Oscar Wilde: Three Times Tried*. To begin with, he commented that the transcript appeared to have been written by someone with "inside information" (*Warwick Film Productions Ltd. v. Eisinger*, 516). Anticipating Hyde's comments to Cohen, Justice Plowman concluded that "some of the passages are based on newspaper accounts" (516). But he continued, "[I]t would have been impossible to assemble from those [newspaper] reports the record of the trials which is found in 'Three Times Tried'" (516). He asserted that "[t]he author of the book was . . . plainly working on a transcript of a shorthand note of the pro-

Leslie J. Moran

ceedings; whose is unknown" (517). This is a point that he reiterates in the penultimate paragraph of his judgment when drawing attention to the absence of a claim of interest in the copyright of the transcript. Millard's account of the trials is described by the judge as a "source-book for subsequent studies in the same field," specifically for Hyde's *Trials of Oscar Wilde* (517).

Perhaps the most surprising aspect of this judicial exploration of Millard's *Oscar Wilde: Three Times Tried* is the judge's comments about the existence of a transcript of the Wilde trials. Justice Plowman uses Hyde's evidence to the court in support of his judgment that Millard must have used a transcript. The report of Hyde's evidence to the court suggests that Hyde presented a rather different story about Millard's volume and the transcripts to the court than the one that he offered Cohen.

The court's conclusion that Millard's work could be viewed as a copyright text—that is, seen as a literary work—offers further forensic insights into the nature of his verbatim account of the trials (*Warwick Film Productions Ltd. v. Eisinger*, 516). The court decided that Millard's book was not a straightforward reproduction of a verbatim account. The court also observed that the size of *Oscar Wilde: Three Times Tried* was far too small to contain every word spoken during fourteen days of court proceedings; there was evidence of a drastic process of selection. Furthermore, in the court's eyes the volume had a particular slant because it appeared to be a partial account, written by someone "sympathetic to Oscar Wilde" (516 a–b).

The judge's analysis of Hyde's book followed from this observation. Hyde, the court ascertained, had "substantially copied" Millard's account (524 g). At the same time, Justice Plowman concluded that Hyde had engaged in "a good deal of editing": "Certain portions of his account printed in square brackets were his own contribution, and he added material, omitted material, made verbal alterations, rearranged material, transposed material and abbreviated material. . . . Hyde frequently put into oratio recta [direct speech] speeches which are reported in 'Three Times Tried' in oratio obliqua [indirect speech]" (525 a–b). The pleadings included a "Schedule of Textual Alterations," which reported eighty-eight examples of Hyde's editorial interventions. Another document that formed part of the pleadings and was referred to in the judgment, "Table C," set out the parts of Hyde's book that were not derived from Millard's text (529 e–g). These additions, interventions, and rearrangements (which amounted in legal terms to a collocation evidencing the expenditure of sufficient labor and skill) were central to the court's reasoning that Hyde's text of the trials was a literary work and, as such, capable of protection under copyright.

Subsequent to establishing copyright in Hyde's *Trials of Oscar Wilde*, the court had to decide whether Eisinger's use of this volume was in breach of that copyright. Extracts from Eisinger's examination-in-chief, reproduced in Justice Plowman's judgment, give an insight into Eisinger's use of Hyde's book and the assumptions that informed his selection of text. Eisinger admitted that in producing his script, he had taken those parts that purported to be the verbatim accounts of the trials from Hyde's volume. He also consulted other sources. He explained, "I went to whatever source I could find where the trial reports were printed, and had no inhibitions about using that. . . . I found many works and each work repeated the other; and I never heard anybody screaming that, 'This belongs to me'" (527 e). Eisinger's belief that the selected verbatim accounts were facts relies on not only the explicit assertions made by Humphreys and Hyde but also the frequency with which these exchanges were faithfully reproduced in other texts, which in turn (re)presented the facts of courtroom interactions.[25] Ultimately, the nature of the items copied as well as the limited extent of the copying in relation to Hyde's volume as a whole led the court to determine that Eisinger was not in breach of copyright.

The forensic analysis found in the reported decision of *Warwick Film Productions Ltd. v. Eisinger* offers us a mixed message about the nature of the verbatim accounts found in both Millard's *Oscar Wilde: Three Times Tried* and Hyde's *Trials of Oscar Wilde*. On the one hand, the forensic analysis offers some evidence against Cohen's challenge to the truthfulness of these accounts. Justice Plowman does not specify which transcripts might have been used in Millard's version of the trials, but his observations offer judicial weight to the findings that transcripts were indeed a source of information about the trials. In this regard, *Warwick Film Productions Ltd. v. Eisinger* adds some support to the tradition of verbatim accounts and the possibility of a true record of the trials. On the other hand, Justice Plowman's forensic analysis also supports Cohen's iconoclastic intervention, providing some detailed evidence that these verbatim texts are fabrications and, more specifically, partial accounts. The events reported therein are edited and composite fabrications of the proceedings informed by the imagination and produced through a creative process, seeking to portray a particular version of what happened.

Leslie J. Moran

Making the Facts of the Trials

Some of the facts under this regime of creative fabrication have an essential life, and their form and substance can be followed as they move from one text to another. The first of these is Wilde's famous speech from the witness box on "the Love that dare not speak its name," taken from the second trial, as it passes from the 1906 volume to Millard's book and then to Hyde's transcriptions. In the 1906 reports that Carrington published, the speech is reported in the following terms:

> Witness.—Lord Alfred explained that the word "shame" was used in the sense of modesty, i.e. to feel shame or not to feel shame.
>
> Mr. Gill.—"You can, perhaps, understand that such verses as these would not be acceptable to the reader with an ordinarily balanced mind?"
>
> Witness.—"I am not prepared to say. It appears to me to be a question of taste, temperament and individuality. I should say that one man's poetry is another man's poison!" (Loud laughter.)
>
> Mr. Gill.—"I daresay! There is another sonnet. What construction can be put on the line, 'I am the love that dare not speak its name'?"
>
> Witness.—"I think the writer's meaning is quite unambiguous. The love he alluded to was that between an elder and younger man, as between David and Jonathan; such love as Plato made the basis of his philosophy; such as was sung in the sonnets of Shakespeare and Michael Angelo; that deep spiritual affection that was as pure as it was perfect. It pervaded great works of art like those of Michael Angelo and Shakespeare. Such as 'passeth the love of woman.' It was beautiful, it was pure, it was noble, it was intellectual—this love of an elder man with his experience of life, and the younger with all the joy and hope of life before him."
>
> The witness made this speech with great emphasis and some signs of emotion, and there came from the gallery, at its conclusion, a medley of applause and hisses, which his lordship at once ordered to be suppressed. (*Trials of Oscar Wilde from the Shorthand Reports*, 59)

By comparison, in Millard's *Oscar Wilde: Three Times Tried*, the record of the incident is significantly different. In the following excerpt, the portions of the extract in italics highlight additions to the facts of the speech:

> Mr. Gill: Your view, Mr. Wilde, is that the "shame" mentioned there is that shame which is a sense of modesty.

WITNESS: [T]hat was the explanation given to me by the person who wrote it. The sonnet seemed to me obscure.

During 1893 and 1894 you were a good deal in the company of Lord Alfred Douglas?—Oh yes.

Did he read that poem to you?—yes.

The next poem is described as "Two Loves." [I]t contains these lines:—

> *Sweet youth,*
> *Tell me why, sad and sighing, dost thou rove*
> *These pleasant realms? I pray thee tell me sooth,*
> *What is thy name? He said, "My name is Love."*
> *Then straight the first did turn himself to me,*
> *And cried, "He lieth, for his name is Shame.*
> *But I am Love, and I was wont to be*
> *Alone in this fair garden, till he came*
> *Unmasked by night; I am true Love, I fill*
> *The hearts of boy and girl with mutual flame."*
> *Then sighing said the other, "Have thy will,*
> *I am the Love that dare not speak its name."*

Was that poem explained to you?—I think that is clear.

There is no question as to what it means?—Most certainly not.

Is it not clear that the love described relates to natural love and unnatural love?—No.

What is the "Love that dare not speak its name"?

—The *"Love that dare not speak its name" in this century* is such a great affection of an elder for a younger man as *there was* between David and Jonathan, such as Plato made the very basis of his philosophy, and *such as you find* in the sonnets of *Michelangelo and Shakespeare. It is* that deep spiritual affection that *is* as pure as it *is* perfect. It *dictated* and pervades great works of art like those of *Shakespeare and Michael Angelo, and those two letters of mine, such as they are. It is in this century to be understood, so much misunderstood that it may be described as the "Love that dare not speak its name," and on account of it I am placed where I am now.* It *is* beautiful, it *is* fine, it *is the noblest form of affection. There is nothing unnatural about it.* It is intellectual, *and it repeatedly exists* between an elder and a younger man, *when an elder man has intellect, and the younger man has all* the joy, hope and glamour of life before him. *That it should be so the world does not understand. The world mocks at it and sometimes puts one in the pillory for it.* (270–72)

Leslie J. Moran

Millard's contextual commentary continues:

> Wilde's words created a sensation in court. As he stopped speaking there was loud applause, mingled with some hisses, in the public gallery of the court. Mr. Justice Charles at once said: "If there is the slightest manifestation of feeling I shall have the court cleared. There must be complete silence preserved." The speech of Wilde was declared by some to be "the finest speech of an accused man since that of Paul of Agrippa." It thrilled everyone in the court. Mr. Robert Buchanan considered it "marvellous." (272)

The contrast between the two versions of this famous speech and the interactions that immediately precede and follow it point to some interesting differences between the verbatim accounts published in the 1906 volume and in Millard's book. With regard to Wilde's speech, the longer version found in Millard's edition might be explained by reference to the idea of truth as a progression and, correspondingly, truth as a movement from recognition of limitations to the provision of a fuller and a more complete account of the proceedings. Grammatical differences and changes in tense might also be read as evidence of accuracy, particularly with regard to the speech of someone as literary as Wilde. Millard also offers more description of the interaction and responses in the courtroom.

These differences raise a question about the ethics of transcription and the editorial function. Did the editor of the 1906 volume omit parts of an extant text and Millard return the transcript to its full glory? Did Millard improve or embellish the transcript (whose veracity if not existence might be in question) with additional evidence—for example, from eyewitness accounts or media reports? There is also a curious difference in the layout of the courtroom exchanges that we see in the 1906 edition and those that appear in Millard's book. The 1906 account formalizes the exchanges by way of clear attribution of the exchanges, whereas in Millard's *Oscar Wilde: Three Times Tried* the speakers are less formally designated. Is this an editorial decision to reject a fashioning of the exchanges according to a transcript style of speech (one that is authentic) according to the different requirements of a written text for a wider, popular audience?

As might be expected in the wake of Justice Plowman's conclusion that Hyde's *Trials of Oscar Wilde* copied much of Millard's *Oscar Wilde: Three Times Tried*, it is not surprising that Hyde's account of this courtroom interaction is similar to Millard's version of the events. But there are also differences. The same court-room exchanges said to have been recorded by Hyde follow Millard's text:

> Mr. Gill: Your view, Mr. Wilde, is that the "shame" mentioned there is that shame which is a sense of modesty.
>
> Witness: That was the explanation given to me by the person who wrote it. The sonnet seemed to me obscure.
>
> During 1893 and 1894 you were a good deal in the company of Lord Alfred Douglas?—Oh yes. (200)

Hyde's version of events then takes a different turn from Millard's with the addition of the following exchange between the counsel for the prosecution, Sir Charles Gill, and Wilde:

> "You can perhaps understand that such verses as these would not be acceptable to THE READER WITH AN ORDINARY BALANCED MIND?
>
> "I am not prepared to say," Wilde answered. "It appears to me to be a question of taste, temperament, and individuality. I should say that one man's poetry is another man's poison!"
>
> "I daresay!" commented Gill dryly, when the laughter had subsided. (200)

Hyde's version then returns to Millard's account of the facts: "The next poem . . ." (200).

How are we to make sense of Hyde's additions? Hyde's additional encounter repeats an exchange found in the 1906 text but missing from Millard's, possibly ignored, maybe edited out by Millard. Hyde also resorts to a different set of poetic conventions in his representation of the facts, no longer presented according to the requirements of a dramatic script: it now appears in a prose style, a narrative with more description of the emotional dynamics of the courtroom event that provides a clearer guide to the reader's appropriate emotional response to the facts. This example of the transforming facts of Wilde's response and the courtroom interactions surrounding it might reflect the oft-repeated claim that successive versions of the trials offer a more complete and more accurate text. Such an impression, however, is not always sustained in the transmission of facts from an earlier to a later text.

My second example is taken from an extract of the cross-examination of Wilde on the meaning of phrases in a letter he wrote to Lord Alfred Douglas.

Leslie J. Moran

First, let me quote the 1906 version:

> Mr. Gill.—"I wish to call your attention to the style of your correspondence with Lord A. Douglas."
>
> Witness.—"I am ready. I am never ashamed of the style of any of my writings."
>
> Mr. Gill.—"You are fortunate—or shall I say shameless? I refer to passages in two letters in particular."
>
> Witness.—"Kindly quote them."
>
> Mr. Gill.—"In letter number one. You used this expression: 'Your slim gilt soul,' and you refer to Lord Alfred's 'rose-leaf lips.'"
>
> Witness.—"The letter is really a sort of prose sonnet in answer to an acknowledgement of one I had received from Lord Alfred."
>
> Mr. Gill.—"Do you think that an ordinarily constituted being would address such expressions to a younger man?"
>
> Witness.—"I am not, happily, I think an ordinarily constituted being."
>
> Mr. Gill.—"It is agreeable to be able to agree with you Mr. Wilde." (Laughter)
>
> Witness.—"There is, I assure you, nothing in either letter of which I need to be ashamed." (59–60)

The sections of Millard's text dealing with the same events read as follows (italics indicate additions):

> Mr. Gill then read the letters written by Oscar Wilde to Lord Alfred Douglas. They had been produced and read in the Queensberry case. The first contained references to the "slim gilt soul" and the "red rose-leaf lips" *and the second contained the words, "You are the divine thing I want," and described Lord Alfred Douglas's letter as being "delightful, red and yellow wine to me."*
> Mr. Gill sought to apply Wilde's definition of this misunderstood love to these two letters. Wilde answered: There is nothing in that of which I am ashamed. It is full of deep affection. The first letter was more of a prose poem, and the second more of a literary answer to a sonnet he had sent me. (273)

Here Millard resorts to summary and paraphrase in contrast to the style of the 1906 edition, which seems to take the form of a verbatim record of the cross-examination. Millard's editorial decision appears to undercut the claims made in his preface that his text is "a complete and accurate account of this long and complicated case" (iii). The project of truth now appears to turn from one of progression by way of addition to one of contraction. Meanwhile, Hyde reverts to the style of reportage found in the 1906 volume. He also makes an addition, a fact that appears in Millard's account—one that is evident in the italicized passage above—which, as Justice Plowman noted, puts into "oratio recta" speeches that Millard reported in "oratio obliqua."

The final fact that I wish to analyze appears in another exchange taken from the second trial. The 1906 version of the exchange reads as follows:

> Mr. GRAIN.—"Do you remember being introduced to an elderly man in the City?"
>
> WITNESS.—"No."
>
> Mr. GRAIN.—"Did you take him to your room, permit him to commit sodomy with and upon you, rob him of his pocket book and threaten him with exposure if he complained?"
>
> WITNESS.—"I. No." (38)

Here is Millard's version of the exchange:

> Do you remember being introduced to an elderly man in the city?—No.
>
> Did you take him to your room and rob him of his pocket book?—No. (232)

In light of Millard's declaration that his project was driven by a desire to be accurate and, more particularly, by an objective to counteract distortion (he decries "the mud of the moralists" and the "vague fog of obscenity" [vii]), it is somewhat surprising that the references to sodomy have been edited out of Millard's version of events. Thus, his avowed goal of moving toward a more accurate account of the various trials needs to be treated with some caution. Various factors might inform the progression toward truth evidenced in Millard's circumlocution. As noted in Millard's contract with the reader set out in his preface, he declares that while the details of the proceedings are as full as possible, he nonetheless conveys them with due "discretion" (20). Truth, this remark clearly indicates, is never simple or straightforward, because it is mediated by way of civility.[26]

A factor influencing the more explicit (and accurate) account offered in the 1906 volume might lie in the idea that this text was produced for limited circulation. It was also produced in France, where different obscenity laws and a different sensibility of the civility of his transcript might have been at work. Indeed,

Hyde makes reference to the impact of obscenity law on projects dedicated to revealing the truth. The 1948 edition of his volume, Hyde explains, was written under the shadow of the law of obscenity and thus subject to his own acts of censorship. Subsequent to the passage of the Obscene Publications Act of 1958, the 1962 edition of his book (republished in 1973) was enlarged. In that new edition, he observes that he was able to reproduce some portions of the evidence verbatim "which discretion obliged me to paraphrase in the earlier edition" (21). Perhaps for Millard, the truth represented in this extract was produced under the shadow of his perception of the obscenity laws operating at the time. The absence of the exchange reported in the 1906 text from Hyde's version of the verbatim accounts, however, suggests that some other factors were informing Hyde's record of the truth. A common denominator linking each of these different versions of the courtroom encounters is that at the time of their publication, all of them purported to be statements of fact—just as all of them purported to be the truth.

Truth and the Imagination: From Facts to . . .

The facts of the trials also have another existence in the context of other genres of writing, whether in life writing or critical literary analysis and in other modes of representation from the printed text to visual representations such as film. The trials literature has been plundered as a rich resource, providing details that offer to tell the truth of not only Wilde's encounters with the law but also wider information about his life, his conversations, his character, his philosophy, his oratorical and literary skills. What happens to facts in this setting?

I want to return at this point to the reported judgment in the case of *Warwick Film Productions Ltd. v. Eisinger.* During the course of the forensic examination, Eisinger informed the court how he made additions to the verbatim extracts and then put them together: "I did not follow the continuity of the actual trial record. Some scenes were taken. I say 'scenes,' I mean some actual portions of the actual trial I took out of context, either ahead [of] or behind their actual point of development" (526).[27] He went on to comment that once he had compiled his notebook from the various texts, a further reshaping took place: "I then created many passages in the trials, which actually never took place in the trials—passages between Sir Edward Carson and Oscar Wilde. I did not falsify, but I dramatized the prevailing attitudes between Carson and Wilde by creating passages" (527).

Later in the process, as a result of conversations with Robert Morley, who had played Wilde in the Stokeses' stage play *Oscar Wilde*, Eisinger made further changes to the trial scenes to "enhance the dramatic value of the script" (528 b–c).

The facts of the trials have therefore been manipulated and mediated by a whole series of interventions that heighten their effect. Whereas reviewers of the two 1960 films about Wilde's life singled out the way in which the facts of the trial scenes resulted in making the visual representations and the story more generally "a drama not of fiction but of detailed truth,"[28] Eisinger's description of the scriptwriting process does not support the maintenance of a clear boundary between fact and fiction in that context. But this is not a particularly startling revelation in relation to biographical projects. Critical scholarship on life writing (in particular, biography) frequently comments, as does Richard Holmes, on the idea that in that setting the boundary between fact and fiction is "controversial and perilous."[29] But this need to establish and maintain the boundary seems to be more urgent in the context of those projects, such as the texts dedicated to writing the truth of the trials, that depend upon their separation. How do these texts approach the project of making and maintaining the fact/fiction boundary?

Epistemological Framing: Making Facts, Making Truth

The claims of truth and fact associated with the trial texts from the 1906 edition to Holland's 2003 volume literally and metaphorically frame each publication. They appear, as I have observed, in the titles of each work, in the preface, foreword, and introduction, and in the front and back blurbs. The truth of the 1906 transcription, for example, appears in the title's reference to the shorthand reports. Holland makes the same move in the rather suspect proclamation that the book reports the "real trial" of Oscar Wilde.[30] In the case of the 1906 book, the veracity of the incidents reported is reinforced in the declaration that the work is not an authored work but an "edited" one. This is a device also used by other authors, including Hyde (who describes himself as an "editor").[31] These features reveal that a common theme throughout this literature is the sharp distinction that each work makes between facts and fictions.

In Charles Grolleau's preface to the 1906 edition, the facts are "impartially" set up against prejudice—moral, aesthetic, and religious—that has informed representations of Wilde's behavior in general and his criminalization in particular (*Trial of Oscar Wilde from the Shorthand Reports*, iii). Millard, like the editor of

1906 volume, offers the facts of the trials to expose bias and distortion, "clearing the man's figure from the filthy web of lies which has entangled it" (*Oscar Wilde: Three Times Tried*, vii–viii). Millard's volume provides evidence of two other techniques of truth: first, the citation of other, earlier texts, and second, the practice of distinguishing one from the other. In this way, he represents truth as a movement and a process of revelation, from a partial to a "full and complete" account of the trials. The cited reports of the trials are various. These range from the unofficial reports found in the mass media to the report of the proceedings found in Central Criminal Court Sessions Papers of April, May, and June 1895.[32] The former are distinguished as the source of the filthy web of lies that corrupt the truth. The Session Papers, Millard explains, while they profess to give the whole proceedings, fail to provide such an account. These particular reports of the trials "occupy only a few lines each, not a single word of evidence being included" (iv).

Using the same techniques, Hyde also cites and distinguishes these impoverished official accounts, but he attributes their silence to the censorious and prudish response of officials. Details of this kind were not included in *The Trials of Oscar Wilde*, because such information was reported as "unfit for publication" (20).[33] In *Oscar Wilde: Three Times Tried*, Millard similarly cites the 1906 volume only to distinguish it on the basis that it is not only an abridged report of the trials but also an account that is "untrustworthy and misleading" (iv).[34] Millard offers his own text, *Three Times Tried*, as "a complete and accurate account of this long and complicated case" (iv). In this tradition, Hyde cites Millard and gives due recognition in *The Trials of Oscar Wilde* to the pioneering nature of Millard's volume on the trials because it is the "first full length and impartial account of the proceedings" (20). Hyde then proceeds to distinguish Millard's text from his own account of the trials. Millard's work, Hyde observes, did not give a verbatim account of the proceedings. Neither did it provide the "necessary" background that would enable the evidence to be "correctly appreciated" (20). Holland also makes good use of these techniques. His distinctive contribution is in his treatment of Hyde's account of the trials. Having cited and distinguished Millard's text from his own verbatim account, Holland states that one of the problems with Hyde's *Trials of Oscar Wilde* is that it was corrupted by the limits of Millard's *Oscar Wilde: Three Times Tried*. Hyde, Holland contends, further compounded this problem by adding new layers of error by way of additions to the text based on "newspapers . . . and imaginative reconstructions" that involve artificially rendering indirect into direct speech (*Irish Peacock and Scarlet Marquess*, xl).

Citing and distinguishing texts is a practice of truth that I, as a legal scholar, am only too familiar with because it is an epistemological strategy beloved by lawyers trained in the methods associated with the English common law tradition. The truth and error of the law emerge by way of citation of earlier sources and by techniques that enable a judge to distinguish different (prior) statements of the truth of law. These techniques situate the project of verbatim accounts as one of a process of revelation, exposing previous inadequacies and limits, revealing a hidden truth, rather than existing as a project that resorts to the political imagination to fabricate a new representation of the events.

Before we leave behind these particular techniques of truth, we should remember that within this juridical approach to truth, new breath may also enter those earlier, previously distinguished and dismissed texts in the service of truth. The epistemological traditions and techniques associated with English common law locate the truth of law in the past, beyond living memory, "time immemorial."[35] This time out of mind protects law from the corrupting forces of temporal and spatial contexts that might produce a multiplicity of truths about the meaning of law. Hyde offers us an example of the technique of breathing truth into a previously dismissed text in his reference to *The Trial of Oscar Wilde from the Shorthand Reports*. In sharp contrast to Millard, Hyde cites the 1906 book as a source that is more authentic than Millard's. This 1906 volume, Hyde maintains, is an earlier and more authentic source of "evidence verbatim" that Hyde uses to "correct" parts of the proceedings that Millard paraphrased.

The blurb is another lively platform for making epistemological claims. For example, the front blurb of a 1956 U.S. edition of Hyde's *Trials of Oscar Wilde* describes the work as "the first complete account of all three sensational trials Oscar Wilde underwent. It includes the complete transcriptions of all three trials —with Wilde's witticisms competing with legal terminology" (see Cohen, *Talk*, 3, 5). Similar claims are made in the back blurb. Likewise, the blurb on the 1973 Dover edition of Hyde's work explains that the volume "draws on previous accounts, documents, correspondence, (some previously unpublished) and personal conversations with persons involved. Lengthy portions of the actual transcript are included." The appearance of the reference to the transcripts here is surprising, as it is subsequent to the litigation, described above, which cast a considerable shadow over such claims. The front blurb to Holland's account makes similar assertions about the truth of the text that follows.

A different technique to establish truth appears in the front blurb of the 1962 edition of Hyde's book. Hyde explains that the original publication of his book of the trials was published as part of a series titled Notable British Trials, founded in 1905 by Harry Hodge. Hyde explains, "As Managing Director of William Hodge & Co. Ltd, Publishers and Shorthand Writers, Hodge had a vast knowledge of both the Scottish courts and criminology—he was himself an expert shorthand writer—and this is reflected in his careful selection of editors and his insistence on the accurate reporting of trials for The Notable British Trials Series."[36] Here the text of the Wilde trials is inserted into a series of similar texts, which thus echo its epistemological claims. These credentials are also rehearsed in the statement of integrity and skills, Hyde's vast knowledge and expertise as a shorthand writer, all of which is in turn associated with the managing director who founded, selected, and originally published the volumes in the series.

The credentials of others (specifically, other authors) are to be found in those works that resort to a foreword written by a third party. The truth of the volume is not only rehearsed in the substance of the foreword but also generated by association with the background and status of the third party who writes it. In Hyde's account, as we have seen, this imprimatur is provided by Sir Travers Humphreys, whose authenticity and status are connoted by the fact that he was the last surviving lawyer who participated in the trials and whose integrity is suggested by his then status as a respected judge and member of the Privy Council.

The final technique of truth making to which I want to refer here can be illustrated by reference to Holland's volume—specifically, to the technology of shorthand and transcription that is capable of producing and translating the verbatim accounts into a format for popular consumption.[37] As Holland notes, the process of transcription raises some doubts about the veracity of the final product. Evidence of this problem is to be found on the surface of these documents, in the unevenness of the handwriting, which appears to make the transcript more of a patchwork of different contributions. In the end, Holland reads this uneven textual surface not as proof of the limits of shorthand to capture the event but as evidence that several shorthand writers were united in a common task of bringing a benign technology to bear upon the events, to capture that event, and to produce a transcript that speaks the truth with a single voice (*Irish Peacock and Scarlet Marquess,* xi).

Should, however, Holland's claim lead the reader toward the belief that *Irish Peacock and Scarlet Marquess* shows no mark of intervention beyond the mechanical process of turning shorthand into a printed text, then disappointment will follow. Holland offers a series of caveats, which suggest that the process of turning the verbatim accounts from transcript to book was a more invasive process. Holland accounts for his interventions in the following terms: "The text has been laid out as a play with proper names for ease of reading, though in the [manuscript] the 'characters' are generally designated 'Q' or 'A.' Punctuation has been added and regularised throughout to make sense of some excessively long unpunctuated sentences. Misspelled names have been altered according to official records. And where the sense of the [manuscript] has been obscure, a consensus of opinion has been taken from Millard, Hyde and the newspaper reports, and the fact noted" (xli). These remarks disclose that the truth of the content of the transcripts is not fully apparent on the surface of the transcript but requires (and is an effect of) various interventions. Holland resorts to a style of presentation that stages the event. Furthermore, facts appear to require a degree of correction or embellishment with some grammatical intervention, standardization of spelling, and certain clarifications, additions, and corrections, which are made in part with the aid of Hyde's account of the trial.

The Fact/Fiction Divide

The controversial and perilous blurring of the fact/fiction divide identified above in relation to biographical writing is a characteristic of all of the works that purport to be verbatim accounts authenticated by reference to shorthand writers' notes. In some respects, Holland's volume is the most problematic and controversial of these works. In Holland's book, the division between facts and fiction, between truth and works of the imagination, appears to be most neatly and completely separated. As I mention earlier, Justice Plowman drew attention to the impact of the imagination in relation to Millard's *Oscar Wilde: Three Times Tried* in his reference to the fact that it told of Wilde's encounters with the law from a very particular perspective. Likewise, we can read Hyde's comment that the objective in producing his book of the trials was to represent the trials "in their proper perspective" as an indication that his political imagination played a key role in the fabrication of the truth of the court proceedings (*Trials of Oscar Wilde*, 20). Discovery of the transcripts—albeit only of those of the first of the three trials—might suggest that the division between facts and fictions has at last been restored. I would, however, stress that Holland's description of his interventions during the course of transforming a shorthand transcript into a published volume (and the display of the techniques of truth making that surround the body of the text of the transcripts, no matter how apparently benign) shows that this boundary remains blurred, controversial, and perilous. Telling the truth of the real trials of Oscar Wilde is, and is likely to remain, a project closely associated with the imagination.

What sense are we to make of these repeated claims of truth? One answer is that they are poetic conventions of various genres of writing associated with empirical social science and subgenres of life writing, such as "true crime" or "courtroom drama." In other words, the facts provide an epistemological platform for the generation of the truth of the many fictions of Oscar Wilde—both criminal and otherwise.

Notes

1. The earliest example of this genre of writing takes the form of an anonymous pamphlet published in April 1895: *Just Out, Complete: The Life of Oscar Wilde as Prosecutor and Prisoner* (London: n.p., 1895). The second text dedicated to the trials is the pseudonymic I. Playfair, *Gentle Criticisms on British Justice* (London: n.p., 1895). It is made up of ten chapters: I. Introduction; II. General Conduct of the Authorities; III. Some Light on the Origin of the Recent Case of *Regina v. Wilde;* IV. A Little Light on Some Sources of the Evidence re *Regina v. Wilde;* V. Motives of the Prosecution, or a Little Light on a very Dark Place; VI. Methods of the Prosecution; VII. The Letter—Counsels' Arguments; VIII. The Judges' Summing Up; IX. The Latter Continued—Reasonable Arguments; and X. Lord Alfred Douglas's Poems. John Stokes discusses this document in detail in *Oscar Wilde, Myths, Miracles, and Imitations* (Cambridge: Cambridge University Press, 1996), 39–64. Stokes identifies "I. Playfair" as James H. Wilson.

Merlin Holland suggests that the first book of the trials, based on newspaper reports, was *Der Fall Wilde und das Problem der Homosexualität* (Leipzig: Max Spohr, 1896), which passed into several editions. See Holland, ed., *Irish Peacock and Scarlet Marquess: The Real Trial of Oscar Wilde* (London: Fourth Estate, 2003), xxxix; further page references appear in parentheses.

2. H. Montgomery Hyde, *The Trials of Oscar Wilde,* 2nd ed. (1962; repr., New York: Dover, 1973); all page references to this edition appear in parentheses. The Dover edition reprints the 1962 second edition published by Penguin Books. The first edition of Hyde's book is *The Trials of Oscar Wilde,* Notable Trials (London: William Hodge, 1948). There are significant differences between the first and second editions of Hyde's text.

3. Ed Cohen, *Talk on the Wilde Side: Toward a Genealogy of a Discourse on Male Sexualities* (New York: Routledge, 1993), 3, cited in the text as *Talk on the Wilde Side;* further page references appear in parentheses.

4. The U.S. edition of Holland's book has a different title: *The Real Trial of Oscar Wilde: The First Uncensored Transcript of the Trial of Oscar Wilde vs. John Douglas, Marquess of Queensberry,*

1895 (New York: Fourth Estate, 2003). Several aspects of Holland's account of the "real trial" remain open to question. First, he does not clarify the origins of the shorthand reports on which he bases his transcription. Neither does he attribute the transcription of shorthand into ordinary prose to anyone. Moreover, the provenance of the shorthand transcription of the trial remains obscure. In public presentations about his book, Holland remarked that when he was given the opportunity to examine and then publish the shorthand record of the first trial, he agreed to keep the name of the owner of this document confidential.

5. Mortimer's television play, *Rumpole of the Bailey*, first appeared in the British Broadcasting Company's series *Play for Today* in 1975. The success of this drama led to two series of television plays about this character, together with a sequence of novels, which remain popular to this day.

6. There seems to have been almost universal critical acclaim for Ken Hughes's *Trials of Oscar Wilde* and withering criticism of Ratoff's *Oscar Wilde*. For an analysis of the reviews, see Leslie J. Moran, "On Realism and the Law Film: The Case of Oscar Wilde," in *Law's Moving Image*, ed. Leslie J. Moran, Emma Sandon, Elena Loizidou, and Ian Christie (London: Glasshouse Press, 2004), 77–94. Hughes's film was released as *The Man with the Green Carnation* in the United States.

7. Unsigned review of *The Trials of Oscar Wilde*, directed by Ken Hughes, *Manchester Guardian*, 22 May 1960.

8. Elizabeth Frank, "After the Epigrams Wilde Comes Alive," *News Chronicle*, 20 May 1960. Frank's comments relate to Ratoff's *Oscar Wilde*.

9. Anonymous, *The Trial of Oscar Wilde from the Shorthand Reports* (Paris: Charles Carrington, 1906). This edition contains a preface by one of Wilde's most important French translators, Charles Grolleau; Grolleau's preface first appeared in French in Wilde, *Intentions*, trans. Hughes Rebell (Paris: Charles Carrington, 1906). For some background on this 1906 volume on the trial, see Patrick Pollard, "Wilde and the French," *English* 53 (2004): 19. For Carrington, see Peter Mendes, *Clandestine Erotic Fiction in English, 1800–1930: A Bibliographical Study* (Aldershot, UK: Scolar Press, 1993), 32–39.

10. Stuart Mason [Christopher Sclater Millard], *Oscar Wilde: Three Times Tried*, Famous Old Bailey Trials of the XIX Century (London: Ferrestone Press, 1912), iii; further page references appear in parentheses.

11. Hyde reports that the wider circulation of Millard's book was initially threatened when the Times Book Club refused to circulate the book among its readers (*Trials of Oscar Wilde*, 1962 edition, 20). Under the pseudonym Stuart Mason, Millard published several other works about Wilde, including *Oscar Wilde: Art and Morality—A Defence of "The Picture of Dorian Gray"* (London: J. Jacobs, 1908), *Oscar Wilde: Art and Morality*, 2nd ed. (London: Frank Palmer, 1912), and *Bibliography of Oscar Wilde* (London: T. Werner Laurie, 1914). The last of Hyde's numerous books to be published during his lifetime was *Christopher Sclater Millard (Stuart Mason): Bibliographer and Antiquarian Book Dealer* (New York: Global Academic Publishers, 1989).

12. Holland suggests that the first edition of Hyde's account of the trials was intended not for the general reader but for lawyers and "a 'specialist' market." Holland, "Biography and the Art of Lying," in *The Cambridge Companion to Oscar Wilde*, ed. Peter Raby (Cambridge: Cambridge University Press, 1997), 5.

13. Hyde wrote a biography of Wilde, more than half of which is dedicated to the trials and their aftermath. Hyde, *Oscar Wilde: A Biography* (London: Farrar, Straus and Giroux, 1975). He also included extracts from his version of the trials in Hyde, *Lord Alfred Douglas: A Biography* (London: Methuen, 1984). An example of post-Cohen scholarship that persists in using Hyde's accounts is Michael Foldy, *The Trials of Oscar Wilde: Deviance, Morality and Late Victorian Society* (New Haven, CT: Yale University Press, 1997). While acknowledging the impact of Cohen's exposé

of Hyde's canonical account, Foldy nevertheless returns to that account "as a 'reliable' resource" (x, xii).

14. Neil McKenna, *The Secret Life of Oscar Wilde* (London: Century, 2003), xvi–xvii. McKenna also refers to other "recently discovered" transcripts of interviews with witnesses who reported having sexual relations with Oscar Wilde, although he does not specify these sources.

15. Inquiries at the National Archive at Kew, London, and the Royal Courts of Justice in the Strand suggest that none of the court papers relating to this litigation survive.

16. *Warwick Film Productions Ltd. v. Eisinger and Others* [1969], 1 Chancery 508, cited in the text as *Warwick Film Productions Ltd. v. Eisinger;* further page and section references appear in parentheses.

17. For a useful and engaging critical analysis of the problems associated with the use of any official reports of criminal proceedings involving sexual relations between men, see Gordon Brent Ingram, "Returning to the Scene of the Crime: Uses of Trial Dossiers on Consensual Male Homosexual Urban Research with Examples from Twentieth-Century British Columbia," *GLQ* 10, no. 1 (2003): 77.

18. Edward Goring, "The Wilde Fight Warms Up," *News Chronicle,* 16 April 1960, and [anonymous,] "Battle of Oscars," *Daily Herald,* 8 April 1960.

19. Goring, in "The Wilde Fight Warms up," reports that the two films were scheduled to have their premiere on the same night, 25 May 1960.

20. An interlocutory hearing does not hear the full legal argument but merely establishes that an issue of substance exists. The injunction is to maintain the status quo on a temporary basis, until the full dispute can be heard and resolved.

21. The Stokes brothers' *Oscar Wilde* premiered at the Gate Theatre Studio, London, in 1936, with Robert Morley in the title role. The production was transferred to the Fulton Theatre, New York City, in 1938. In the *Observer,* leading theater critic Harold Hobson observed of the London production that "the play is little but a précis of notorious facts which seem to emphasise the sordid at the expense of the significant." The Stokeses' play was revived in London in 1938 and 1948 and in Los Angeles in 1977. For details of the production history of the play in London and New York City, see Robert Tanitch, *Oscar Wilde on Stage and Screen* (London: Methuen, 1999), 20–24. See also chapter 10 in the present volume.

22. Counsel for Vantage, Sir Andrew Clark, noted that Warwick's first attempt to obtain copyright in the Millard version of the trials was rather late in the day, on 6 April 1960, just before proceedings began. Clark described this as "an 11th hour and 59th minute" to secure rights in that book. Quoted in "Film Makers' Rusty Swords," *Daily Telegraph,* 15 May 1960.

23. The sentence is missing from the 1962 and 1973 editions of the trials. In the later editions, the introduction that appeared in the 1948 edition has been replaced by three sections, entitled "Preface," "Background," and "The Prelude."

24. For the discussion of Millard's *Oscar Wilde: Three Times Tried,* see *Warwick Film Productions Ltd. v. Eisinger,* 515–17.

25. The veracity of the trial interaction is also a factor in the defense counsel's argument that copyright could not subsist in parts of a text where raw material had been merely copied.

26. For an examination of the relationship between civility and censorship, see Leslie J. Moran, "Dangerous Words and Dead Letters: Encounters with Law and 'The Love That Dares to Speak Its Name,'" *Liverpool Law Review* 24 (2002): 1–13.

27. For an analysis of the stories told in these two films, see Margaret D. Stetz, "Oscar Wilde at the Movies: British Sexual Politics and the *Green Carnation* (1960)," *Biography* 23 (2000): 90–107.

28. Unsigned review, *Manchester Guardian,* 21 May 1960.

29. Richard Holmes, "The Proper Study?" in *Mapping Lives: The Uses of Biography,* ed. Peter France and William St Clair (Oxford: Oxford University Press, 2002), 16.

30. This is a questionable title because it misrepresents the nature of the proceedings reported in the volume. Contrary to what is suggested by the title, Wilde was not on trial. The marquess was the defendant in these proceedings, while Wilde had the role normally occupied by the state in criminal proceedings, that of prosecutor. A similar point might be made of Millard's volume, which suggests that Wilde was "three times tried" although the author was tried by the state on only two occasions.

31. Hyde appears as editor in both the 1948 and 1962 editions of his book of the trials. The descriptor is missing from the 1973 Dover reprint.

32. The only official report of the trials of Lord Queensberry and Oscar Wilde is to be found in Central Criminal Court Sessions Papers 122, parts 726–28: 531, 582, and 625. Copies of the official report of the trials could be obtained from any law bookseller.

33. In Hyde's text, the quotation is referenced (footnote 1) as "Sessions Papers cxxi, 531–32."

34. In his comprehensive bibliography of Wilde, Millard again repeats his condemnation of the 1906 edition's 106-page account of the trial as "inaccurate and incomplete" (*Bibliography of Oscar Wilde,* 580).

35. On this point, see Peter Goodrich, *Languages of Law: From Logics of Memory to Nomadic Masks* (London: Weidenfeld Publications, 1990).

36. Here Hyde offers an argument in support of the truth of Millard's text, only to undermine it a few pages later.

37. Hyde also explains the truth of his text by alluding to the citation of other "authentic sources" (21–22). Such sources include conversations with five persons who were present for part or all of the proceedings—Sir Travers Humphreys, junior counsel for Wilde; Lord Alfred Douglas; Sir Max Beerbohm; Sir Seymour Hicks; and Sir Albion Richardson—and communications with others who knew Wilde personally (Sir Arthur Quiller-Couch, W. B. Yeats, and Richard Le Gallienne). Moreover, Hyde draws attention to access to state documents (Home Office and Prison Commissioners papers) relating to the Wilde proceedings that were previously unavailable. The authenticity of these materials is referenced by way of the citation of the original text of *De Profundis* and Wilde's letters. See Wilde, *The Letters of Oscar Wilde,* ed. Rupert Hart-Davis (London: Rupert Hart-Davis, 1962).

The Artist as Protagonist

Wilde on Stage

FRANCESCA COPPA

Bosie, relax: you're a winner, and I am a star.

—Rufus Wainwright, "In with the Ladies" (2005)

OSCAR WILDE appears in two different guises in E. M. Forster's *Maurice*, the novel of male homosexual love that Forster composed in 1913 but felt unable to publish during his lifetime. (Forster's narrative appeared posthumously, a year after his death, in 1971.) Wilde is named overtly in the novel as the eponym of Maurice Hall's psychological problem ("I'm an unspeakable of the Oscar Wilde sort"), but he also appears more covertly in the figure of Lord Risley, who stands in for a half century's worth of Wilde-inspired, Oxbridge-educated dandies and queer fish ("I am a child of light," Risley says).[1] Risley makes exaggerated gestures and speaks with "unmanly superlatives"; he is described as being always "at play, but seriously" (33). Believing that Risley can help him, Maurice pursues Risley back to his college rooms. There he finds not Risley but the handsome, masculine Clive Durham, and the intense Greek-infused love affair that follows therefore occurs as the result of Risley's influence; Risley is the star that has led Maurice to Clive. Risley remains a reliable star for Maurice to steer by. Later, when Clive has outgrown his undergraduate homosexuality, Maurice tries to turn to women and takes a lady-friend to a concert. But Risley is at the concert, too, and instantly reignites Maurice's homosexual feelings by informing him that Tchaikovsky fell in love with his nephew, sending Maurice racing first for a biography and subsequently for a boy.

But the Wildean dandy serves a different function in the 1987 Merchant-Ivory film *Maurice*. If Forster sees Risley as a guiding star, then the film takes Risley's star for a bad omen and turns his story into a cautionary tale for the protagonists. The film extends Risley's story beyond Forster's narrative and into the familiar terrain of Wilde's life history, entirely inventing a subplot wherein Risley goes to a working-class tavern, flirts with some soldiers, and offers them money for sex. He is arrested, and we are shown Clive's quiet terror as he reads the sensational headline: "Viscount Risley arrested on immorality charge." The film then treats us to a number of images familiar from the Wilde trials: a row of bewigged barristers, a court packed with spectators, Lord Risley standing in the dock. Clive attends the trial in disguise and is present when Risley is sentenced to six months' imprisonment with hard labor. The terms of condemnation are familiar: "The defendant is a man of breeding who, rather than setting an example, has regrettably attempted the corruption of his social inferiors. He is a man of considerable learning who has taken advantage of the gullibility and the baser passions of his intellectual inferiors." The film even adds Risley's name to Maurice's associative self-diagnosis: "I'm like Lord Risley," he says. "I'm an unspeakable of the Oscar Wilde sort."

The Forster and Merchant-Ivory versions of *Maurice* give us two Lord Risleys, which is to say, two reflections of Oscar Wilde. But they are very different, and the difference is only made starker by the fact that they are supposed to be the same character in the same work. The rewriting of Lord Risley between 1913 and 1987 demonstrates the rapid evolution of ideas about male homosexuality in general and the received significance of Oscar Wilde's life in particular. Forster's novel gives us a world in which a certain kind of Hellenistic homosexuality is fairly widespread but will be outgrown by many of its most ardent advocates; Forster is explicit about Clive's change of sexuality being internal and, in fact, states that "Clive did not give in to the life spirit without a struggle" and that he "tried to think himself back into the old state" by avoiding women and going to Greece (120). But by the 1980s, the filmmakers could only read Clive's change as the repression of his fixed and authentic sexual nature, and they find a reason for

Francesca Coppa

that repression in the Wilde trials. Thus, Forster's Edwardian view of Wilde as a brightly shining but distant star gives way to the suffering martyr of the gay rights movement. The subtle distinctions of the novel, whose characters illustrate a great variety of homosexual identities, theories, and practices (Risley is not Clive is not Maurice is not Alec Scudder—the gamekeeper with whom Maurice ultimately disappears into a pastoral "greenwood"), are collapsed to build sympathy for a single, albeit nobly intentioned, argument: namely, that homosexuals en masse have been oppressed and that a few courageous men have defied and survived that oppression. In his study *Cultural Politics—Queer Reading*, Alan Sinfield defines what he terms "faultline" stories: that is, stories that address "contested aspects of our ideological formation."[2] Throughout the twentieth century, Wilde stood at the center of a veritable earthquake, and representations of him were affected by the rocks that slipped and slid beneath his feet.

Early Stage Representations: Stokes, MacLiammóir, Gay, Bentley

The many years that elapsed between the composition of Forster's novel and the release of Merchant-Ivory's film make the case of *Maurice* particularly striking, but in fact, all representations of Wilde tell you more about the artist's time than about Wilde's. Wilde is arguably more famous as a dramatic character than as a dramatist; there are more plays featuring Wilde than he wrote. Wilde began his life as a fictional character early in his career, agreeing to become the real-life cognate of the fictional aesthetic poet Reginald Bunthorne in Gilbert and Sullivan's *Patience* (1881); other early Wildean characters include Esmé Amarinth in Robert Hichens's novel *The Green Carnation* (1894) and Wilde's Lord Henry Wotton in *The Picture of Dorian Gray* (1890, revised 1891). For several years after Wilde's arrest, imprisonment, and death, the formal depiction of his persona was certainly non grata, though his distinctive personality and mode of self-presentation filtered rapidly through the culture and formed the basis of the early-twentieth-century gay stereotype.[3]

Continental Europe and the United States offered the earliest dramatic embodiments of Wilde. Between the 1910s and the early 1930s, his fascinating persona took center stage in at least four plays. The first was a Dutch tragedy by Adolphe Engers dating from the 1910s. Carl Sternheim's *Oskar Wilde: Sein Drama* followed in 1924. In 1928, American author Lester Cohen published his eponymous play about the writer, and the well-known publisher Flammarion issued

Maurice Rostand's *Le procès d'Oscar Wilde* in 1934. Yet by far the most influential of this growing stable of dramas dedicated to elaborating Wilde's life was the first British stage treatment: Leslie Stokes and Sewell Stokes's *Oscar Wilde* (1936). The Stokeses' play lays out the template that many later biographical dramas would follow: a first act that shows Oscar living dangerously; the courtroom drama leading to his conviction as a second-act climax; and a third act of drunkenness and decline. In hindsight, it is surprising how overt the play is about Wilde's homosexuality, giving Wilde an entourage of two effeminate men: Louis Dijon, who, being French, apparently takes Wilde's behavior as a matter of course; and Eustace, an Englishman who admits to using rouge and was one of the many crowding the boat-trains out of London when Wilde was arrested at the Cadogan Hotel on 5 April 1895 (together, we are told, these two fictional characters "fold sheets with the proficiency of chambermaids").[4] Then again, perhaps the overt depiction of homosexuality is not surprising: in 1936, a play about Oscar Wilde would have been one of the few places where such representation could legitimately and openly occur.

According to Alfred Douglas, who contributed a preface to the published version, the Stokeses' play succeeded in arousing "great sympathy for a man whom I consider to have been cruelly and unjustly treated and whose brilliant genius, if he had not been condemned by an ungrateful country to prison and resulting early death, would have enriched the English stage with many more masterful pieces of dramatic art" (11). Wilde, having by this time become the icon for queerness, is psychoanalyzed as an early-twentieth-century gay stereotype and consequently depicted as a man whose desire for beautiful boys comes from a deep and secret pain. This reading is bolstered by Wilde's heartfelt recitation of his prose poem "The Artist" (1894), in which an artist fashions "*[t]he Pleasure that abideth for a Moment*" from bronze stolen from the tomb of "*[t]he Sorrow that endureth For Ever*" (*CW*, 7:203). The response of Charlie Parker, the Royal Artillery gunner who later testified to committing indecencies with Wilde at the Savoy Hotel, to Wilde's performance is apt: "Were you ever a play-actor?" (55).[5] Despite the play's attempt to engender sympathy for Wilde, poetic justice demands that he be punished, so the third act shows us a Wilde in greatly reduced circumstances: drunk, dissolute, and slyly cadging money from friends and strangers alike. Nevertheless, the Stokes brothers take pains to show Wilde as sexually unrepentant and still in the grip of a great romantic passion—not with "Bosie" (the nickname by which Douglas was known) but with a beautiful young soldier to whom Wilde gives his heart's desire: a nickel-plated bicycle.

While the Stokeses' drama thus concretizes the now-familiar characterization of Wilde as tragic hero ("Who's looking tragic now?" Charlie Parker plaintively asks [55]), it also does something extremely unusual for Wilde bio-dramas: it characterizes Bosie as a faithful friend. The play is strikingly kind to Douglas, not only citing and admiring both his poetry and his wit but also showing his continued loyalty and devotion to Wilde throughout the trials and after.[6] The play goes so far as to end with Wilde's tearful "Thank you, Bosie. Thank you" (150). While it might be easy to dismiss this merely as the authors' pragmatic flattery of the litigious, still-living lord, contemporary scholars are making many of these same arguments. Both Neil McKenna, in *The Secret Life of Oscar Wilde* (2003), and Caspar Wintermans, in his 1999 biography of Bosie, support several of the play's key assertions, particularly that Bosie was strongly pressured to stay away from Wilde after his release from prison, that sexual jealousy was one of the motives driving those enforcing the Wilde-Bosie separation, and that Bosie (despite claims to the contrary) did in fact give Wilde money after he came into his legacy ("Bosie's chequebook," Wintermans tells us, "happily establishes" the fact).[7] They also agree that Bosie's poetry is ripe for reappraisal; Wintermans includes in his biography a large appendix of Bosie's annotated poems in service of that purpose.

Such was the dislike of Alfred Douglas during the century, however, that the very suggestion seems to raise the hackles of critics. Novelist Jane Stevenson, reviewing Wintermans's book under the headline "Self-Pity, Doggerel and Beastliness," in London's conservative *Daily Telegraph,* snorts that Bosie's poetry "jangl[es] with the trisyllabic semi-precious stones and vegetation common in 'aesthetic' verse."[8] A sentence or two later, Stevenson reveals that her problem with the poems is more political than aesthetic, since his works strike her as objectionable because of "the desire they show for the consumption of boys as commodities." Her approach seems to me to hold Bosie responsible for the sins of all aesthetic—which is to say, *gay*—writing. The late nineteenth and early twentieth centuries saw the development of a modern gay literary tradition that extends from French symbolism to British aestheticism through Wilde, then through Ronald Firbank and Jean Genet in the 1920s and 1930s and up to Joe Orton during the 1960s. Its aesthetic values not only the jangling jewels and polysyllabic vegetation that Stevenson complains about but also the sensual description of a variety of swirling colors, textures, and fabrics; it is a literary style that celebrates semantic excess. Moreover, I am not sure what separates the commodified desire that Stevenson finds in Bosie's work from the expression of homosexual desire full stop. Stevenson's observation that "the romanticised perception of juvenile beauty in his verse fudges the reality of power and money in these relationships" seems an odd accusation; certainly, history is littered with oppressed gay men who indulged in the oppressive practices of prostitution and sexual tourism. But Bosie seems to be held particularly (and unusually) responsible for it—even though he is a poet whose fame rests on his memorable formulation of homosexual silence. It was Bosie, as every devotee of Wilde is sure to know, who gave voice to "the Love that dare not speak its name."[9]

Leslie Stokes and Sewell Stokes's play, with its dissolute Oscar and benevolent Bosie, remained the definitive stage presentation of Wilde for twenty years, eventually becoming the basis of the 1960 film starring Robert Morley, which Leslie J. Moran discusses in the present volume (chapter 9). After this flurry of activity in the 1930s, there would be no new stage portrait of Wilde until the 1960s, triggered at least partly by the theatrical excitement generated by the post-1956 playwrights. Theater in the 1960s, as any history of the period reveals, managed to be a site of both hip subversion and nationalistic tradition, celebrating working-class and other historically marginalized voices while simultaneously defining itself as part of a second Elizabethan age. This was a perfect time for Wilde to make a comeback, as he was both a scandalous outsider and the ultimate insider. The author of the greatest society comedy in the English language was also a figure who could speak to and for the sexually and politically insubordinate world that emerged after the Suez Crisis of 1956 and, soon after, the publication of the 1957 Wolfenden Report (which recommended the decriminalization of male homosexuality in Britain).

The Importance of Being Oscar (performed in 1960 and published three years later), a one-man performance piece by Micheál MacLiammóir, perfectly captures this moment. It is a hybrid piece in many ways, not least of which is the easy mixing of storytelling and quotation as MacLiammóir slips between narrating and impersonating Wilde. The performance also profitably investigates the border between English and Irish drama, positioning Wilde at the point of intersection. As founder of the Gate Theatre in Dublin, whose mission was to explore Irish drama beyond the worlds of the cottage or the tenement, MacLiammóir was known for his attempt to connect Irish drama to the larger modern dramatic

Francesca Coppa

tradition of Europe, not only by bringing European plays to Dublin but also by reinforcing the Irishness of canonical dramatists such as George Bernard Shaw and Samuel Beckett. Culturally, MacLiammóir was in many respects Wilde's opposite number; as Paul Taylor noted in 1997 in the London *Independent,* "where Wilde was an Irishman who refashioned himself as a London sophisticate, 'MacLiammóir' was the invented name of Alfred Willmor of Willesden whose cultural remaking was in the opposite direction."[10]

Regardless of the authenticity of his pedigree as an Irishman, MacLiammóir became a potent symbol of the Irish stage. His performance of Wilde thus represents the first real reconceptualization of Wilde as an Irishman, anticipating the wave of postcolonial Wilde studies by about thirty years.[11] In the play's opening moments, MacLiammóir explores another paradox, depicting Wilde as both an ordinary and an extraordinary Irishman:

> Well, he was bound to attract attention. And this made him exquisitely happy: to pass unnoticed anywhere would have seemed to him a most ostentatious form of obscurity. As he said himself in later years, "I have no wish to pose as being ordinary, great Heaven!"
>
> Indeed the one ordinary thing Oscar Wilde seems to have done in his life was to have fled away from his native Ireland as soon as he possibly could. This, of course, was pretty ordinary in every sense of the word, because for one thing, you see, everybody was doing it. Oh yes, I assure you, in those days every young Irish man, particularly if he had any literary or imaginative talent or ambition, seems to have left the unfortunate country as soon as he had had his first shave, and for once Oscar Wilde was no exception to the Irish rule.[12]

By protesting too much ("Oh yes, I assure you, in those days"), MacLiammóir argues both that the situation for Irish artists is different and that it is still the same. Wilde is thus posited as a forerunner to the new cultural intelligentsia then taking over London, many of whose members hailed from the previously ignored areas of northern England, Ireland, Wales, and Scotland. MacLiammóir insists on Wilde as an Irish humorist who married an Irish girl and could drink anyone under the table but insinuates that Wilde developed a "curious new note" in his personality after years of London success (25). Still, MacLiammóir does not regard this curious new note as bad or corrupting, taking pains, in fact, to note that if "you were the sort of person who did approve of that sort of thing, you said it was 'deliciously, deciduously exotic,' and you tossed your head, gazed at the ceiling, and breathed through your nose" (27). It was quite daring for MacLiammóir, himself homosexual and affected in the manner of Wilde, to admit not only that there were those who approved of "that sort of thing" but also that "people haven't changed a bit really" (27). More important, *The Importance of Being Oscar* portrays Wilde as a likeable charmer and a literary genius even after conceding the "curious" note in his works; in fact, MacLiammóir allows Wilde to be funny even after prison, citing "the incurably blithe spirit of his humor" (56). Bosie is given evenhanded treatment, too. MacLiammóir takes pains to distinguish him from "the strange and sinister" Dorian Gray and instead describes him as "a considerable poet" (37). Later, MacLiammóir notes that Wilde and Bosie were "forced" to part after Wilde's release from prison by "circumstances both sordid and tragic" (68), thus resisting the later melodramatic narratives of abandonment or betrayal.

The Importance of Being Oscar was the dominant stage portrayal of Wilde until MacLiammóir's death in 1978; by then, however, another one-man show was on the boards, this time written by screen and television writer John Gay. *Diversions and Delights*, which premiered in San Francisco in 1977, gives us a Wilde perfectly pitched to the "Me Generation." Starring Vincent Price, the play is set in a Parisian concert hall in 1899 (two years after the Irish writer's release from jail) and imagines the impecunious Wilde, now exiled in France, returning to his career as a lecturer. The play delivers on its upbeat title; the majority of the show consists of thematically linked "bits," in the matter of standup comedy. Wilde gives us five minutes on America, five minutes on romance, five minutes on art, on morality, on actors. Most of this material is Wilde's own, skillfully linked into patter; even Wilde's repeated calls for more absinthe (which he drank during his postprison days in Paris), together with assurances that "he offends indiscriminately," sound like comedy club banter.[13] Some jokes are stolen from Wilde's four society comedies. The second act, for instance, opens with Wilde claiming that he was just playing piano, not accurately but with wonderful expression. And new jokes are coaxed out of familiar material; in the 1982 Westwood Playhouse audio recording of the play, Vincent Price got one of the evening's biggest laughs with "To this day, I vividly recall the first American I met, a customs agent. He wanted to know *what I had to declare*." (Wilde is reputed to have said to customs officials when he disembarked from the S.S. *Arizona* at the start of his year-long American lecture tour, "I have nothing to declare except my genius.")[14] Price's significant pause at that point, presumably accompanied by a suggestive facial gesture, elicits an explosive laugh from the audience, who are in on a joke that Wilde could not have made at the time: that he had considerably more to declare, had he been able to speak with perfect candor.

Wilde's postprison suffering serves primarily to enhance his stature as a comedian; as in the best stand-up tradition of American humor (for example, Lenny Bruce and Richard Pryor), there is an element of soothsaying, or even shamanism. Wilde's outcast status empowers him to tell the truth, and many of Wilde's truths are sexual ones. *Diversions and Delights* frames Wilde as a sexual revolutionary, and his exhortations to give in to temptation found a very different reception in 1970s San Francisco than in 1890s London. Like the Stokeses' *Oscar Wilde*, *Diversions and Delights* alludes to Wilde's prose poem "The Artist," but in Gay's version, the artist's ability to fashion "*[t]he Pleasure that abideth for a Moment*" is a sign of radical sexual possibilities. Whereas Leslie Stokes and Sewell Stokes use the poem to locate the source of Wilde's pleasure in pain, Gay focuses on the production of pleasure as an end in itself. There is no particular sexual agenda advocated here, either—no particular sexual politics other than polymorphous pleasure. "What is the difference between one form of sexual indulgence and another?" this Wilde asks his audience.

If John Gay casts Wilde as the godfather of the sexual revolution, then Bosie Douglas is its dark underbelly, depicted as callow, selfish, and unworthy: a kind of nineteenth-century Mr. Goodbar. Far from being praised as "a considerable poet," Bosie is denied credit even for his most famous line; when Wilde speaks in glowing terms about "the Love that dares not speak its name," he says only "that's what they called it." Bosie here loses his role as romantic lead and becomes the villain of the story, responsible because "his hatred of his father was greater than his love of me." Wilde declares that his love for Bosie "has long since expired," but Wilde's passion for passion itself lives on.

If *Diversions and Delights* functions as a general call to hedonism in the wake of the culture wars, then Eric Bentley's *Lord Alfred's Lover* (1981) may be the first of the Wilde bio-plays to be framed in terms of postdecriminalization gay history (that is, after the 1967 Sexual Offences Act, which, after a decade-long delay, followed the recommendations of the Wolfenden Report). Perhaps for that reason, the play is highly sympathetic toward Bosie, whom Bentley uses to frame the action, which is structured as the elderly Alfred Douglas's confession to a Catholic priest. (In 1911 Douglas converted to Catholicism. His conversion formed part of a much larger pattern of aesthetes and Decadents who turned to Rome.)

This device also has the advantage of allowing Bentley to set the play in 1945 (the year of Douglas's death), which allows him to evoke World War II as a backdrop. In his preface to the play, Bentley confesses his outrage at the repeated Victorian assertion that "there is no worse crime than that with which the prisoners are charged," to which he adds, "Not the crimes of Nero, one asks oneself, the crime of Judas? Would these judges have spoken differently had they lived to know the crimes of a Hitler or a Stalin?"[15] Bentley juxtaposes the elderly Douglas's 1945 context ("They said on the wireless that Hitler only has weeks to live") with a Victorian judge intoning the following words of wisdom: "People who can do these things must be dead to all sense of shame. That you, Oscar Wilde, have been at the center of a circle of extensive corruption of the most hideous kind among young men, it is impossible to doubt" (20).[16] In the harsh light of twentieth-century history, is Wilde's corruption really the *most* hideous kind? The effect is a jolting sense of perspective.

In *Lord Alfred's Lover*, Bosie is presented as a man who has sought the love of several fathers: his biological father, the Marquess of Queensberry, whom Wilde sued for libel; Wilde, sixteen years Douglas's senior; and the Catholic priest, his religious father. But the play also anticipates more-recent scholarship by showing Bosie, not Wilde, to be the political figure. It is Bosie who is the devoted "Uranian" (the term that in 1970 Timothy d'Arch Smith influentially used to define boy-loving poetry of late-Victorian homophile writers),[17] while Bentley's Wilde does not even know the word.[18] And it is Bosie who sees in Wilde the leader of a new movement in history. "You *are* that movement," he proclaims (56). Bosie also asks Wilde if he's "ready for the next step":

> OSCAR: What *is* the next step?
>
> BOSIE: When some distinguished Uranian comes right out with it—says, Yes, he is, and he's not ashamed of it either.
>
> OSCAR: A little letter to *The Times*. "You all believe I'm practicing hideous unmentionable vices, the worst offenses in the statute book, the most monstrous of sins against nature. I am. Join me Saturday at combined orgy and black mass. Your loving sister, Oscar Wilde."
>
> BOSIE: Don't you think the day will come?
>
> OSCAR: The Kingdom of Sod is not at hand! And you can keep your old cross and the rusty nails for somebody other than yours truly!
>
> BOSIE: I expect the world of you.
>
> OSCAR: Don't expect a Uranian world of me. I'm only a part-time Uranian! (57)

Francesca Coppa

Of course, a Uranian world is—ultimately, implicitly—exactly what Wilde gives Bosie, though not within his lifetime. In *Diversions and Delights,* Gay's Wilde laments that "[t]he only flaw in the perfect symbolism of the gospel story is that Jesus was betrayed by Judas the foreigner when he should have been betrayed by John the beloved disciple."[19] With his reference to the "old cross and the rusty nails," Bentley also compares Wilde to Jesus, but his Jesus is a lot more Hellenic; Bentley suggests that Wilde, like a good Greek lover, dies trying to live up to the ideal self that exists in the imagination of his beloved: he is, truly, Lord Alfred's lover. In the dock, Wilde delivers his speech on "the love that dare not speak its name," after "looking across at Bosie, after a careful pause" (76). Moreover, Bentley gives additional force to that speech by insisting that the love between Oscar and Bosie was entirely (instead of just mostly) sexless. Oscar and Bosie are thus framed as kindred spirits, and, indeed, there is real biographical evidence to suggest that what Bosie found primarily attractive about Oscar, at least at first, was his willingness, as an established older man, to help younger men deal with blackmail and other sexual troubles. Considering that Bosie had had several friends, as well as his beloved older brother, commit suicide as a result of looming homosexual scandals, he must have genuinely appreciated Wilde's willingness to help and would have seen it as an act of sexual-political solidarity.[20]

The fact that the Uranian movement fails in *Lord Alfred's Lover* is merely a sign of the historical times and not a judgment on Wilde's choices or Bosie's politics. Rather, Bosie is made sympathetic to a post-Stonewall audience by making manifest his dream of a day when people can be "out" about their sexuality. Similarly, Wilde is made to anticipate the argument that eventually carried the day vis-à-vis the British decriminalization of homosexuality: "I shall not be pursued down into the underworld: such things are not done. Lest others more important than I be exposed" (71). As Jeffrey Weeks observes, the Wolfenden Report made this very argument: "What was proposed was that offences which were difficult to discover and troublesome (and politically embarrassing) to prosecute should be removed from the statute book."[21] But these viewpoints and strategies were ahead of their time. Interestingly, Bentley frames Wilde, rather than Bosie, as the betrayer of homosexual ideals. Wilde, on the one hand, recants his erotomania while in prison (though, as the elderly Douglas points out, Wilde lived long enough to recant his recantation).[22] Douglas, on the other hand, is condemned to the closet for almost fifty years in the wake of Wilde's death, though Bentley benevolently lets him confess himself to the audience and be absolved: "I was 'so.'

I still am 'so' inside. Oh, dear! The thing that didn't happen was . . . repentance. Switched to this other life—just—never—repented" (120). Oscar closes the play with a similarly unrepentant declaration of gay pride: "[U]nsaved, unregenerate, impenitent, shame-less! Declining to be shamed by a shameful world" (124).

Later Stage Representations: Eagleton, Kaufman, Stoppard, Hare

Soon after the character of Wilde is introduced in *Lord Alfred's Lover,* Bentley has him tell the story of Robert Louis Stevenson's *Strange Case of Dr. Jekyll and Mr. Hyde* (1886) to his two young sons, Cyril and Vyvyan, in the manner of the fairy stories he devised for them in *The Happy Prince and Other Tales* (1888). Wilde's version reverses not only the characters' titles but also their morals:

> OSCAR: *(slowly, thinking it out as he speaks)* The Strange Case of Mr. Jekyll and Dr. Hyde. Once upon a time, there was a man named Dr. Hyde. He was nice. He was nice looking, and he had a nice time. So the princes of the world hated him, and the chief prince commissioned a biography of Dr. Hyde which would be forbidding enough to act as a warning. The biographer linked niceness with wicked temptations. A nice time amounted to nothing more nor less than giving way to these temptations. So in the biography, Dr. Hyde lost his looks and became rather a fright. (25)

Like many of the important arguments and themes of *Lord Alfred's Lover,* this joke against biographers is directed more to the play's contemporary audience than to young Cyril and Vyvyan. By 1981, Wilde's life had been chronicled by a host of biographers: Robert Harborough Sherard, Robbie Ross, Frank Harris, Hesketh Pearson, and H. Montgomery Hyde, with another yet to come—Richard Ellmann, with his *Oscar Wilde* (1987). Ellmann's biography, by far the most substantial to have appeared to that date, triggered a new wave of interest in Wilde that swelled with the 1995 anniversary of the trials and the centenary of his death in 2000.

The post-Ellmann wave of plays seems to be marked by a particular awareness that the story of Wilde has perhaps been told a time or two (or ten) before. This self-consciousness marks them as meta-plays: they do not simply tell Wilde's story but tell the story of telling Wilde's story, or the story of how others have told it. Recent plays have had to situate themselves vis-à-vis this wealth of scholarly, historical, and dramatic material; they have had to find moments not yet staged, interpretations not yet made. For this reason, the later plays tend toward bravura displays of virtuosity, the very well-wornness of the material perhaps serving as a theatrical challenge to the bold and the brave.

Saint Oscar (1989) by Terry Eagleton is a case in point. In his foreword, Eagleton describes his astonishment at how "Wilde's work prefigures the insights of contemporary cultural theory," and his play—a Brechtian series of nonrealist scenes and songs—can be seen to view the Wilde story through an impressive number of theoretical lenses.[23] Eagleton's primary lens is postcolonial, focusing on Wilde's subjected cultural position as an Irishman (as Eagleton admits, he wrote the play after discovering that hardly any of his students realized that Wilde was Irish). But lest we get too comfortable with that analysis, Eagleton undercuts it by interrogating the various class positions, not only mocking Wilde as a creature of privilege—"I was a socially disadvantaged child: public school, Trinity College, Dublin, Magdalen College Oxford" (8)—but also giving voice to the working-class boys whom Wilde and his circle routinely exploited. In the Brechtian "Song of the Rent Boys," Eagleton examines the economics of prostitution without sentimentality or judgment:

> If you can't get a job
> Find yourself a nob
> And nick his wallet while he lies a-snoring.
> If you need a sugar-daddy
> Find a big softhearted Paddy
> The work is skilled though sometimes rather boring. (37)

Eagleton rereads Wilde's radical sexuality from the perspective of class politics, and he finds that there is nothing particularly radical about the sexual exploitation of working-class youths by upper-class men. As the character of the socialist Richard Wallace observes to Wilde, "[t]he noble lords are all libertine ruffians at heart; you just give it a radical twist" (27). Eagleton extends this critique in a feminist direction by engendering sympathy for Wilde's spouse, Constance, drawing our attention to the fact that during late 1894 and 1895 (when Wilde was embroiled in the ongoing drama of his love affair with Bosie and his escalating battle with Queensberry), she was alone and in pain from the spinal injury that would eventually kill her. Eagleton also stages a complex queer context of jubilation and self-hatred. He creates one of the stage's most noxious Bosies—nasty, shallow, selfish, backbiting—and has Wilde spit at him, "You bitch. You rotten little queer" (53). I can only believe that this line is meant to make us think about the ways in which homophobia is—and is not—dispelled in the Wilde mythos. The characterization of Douglas as a "rotten little queer" often seems to draw the lightning of hate away from Wilde for those who wish to canonize him: we can like him because we have displaced all our residual homophobia and hateful labels onto Bosie (who is particularly susceptible to the big three: *childish, promiscuous, proselytizing*).

One of the cleverest exchanges in *Saint Oscar* ties several of these theoretical strands together:

> CARSON: You are a bugger, Mr. Wilde, are you not?
>
> WILDE: Not at all, sir; I am Irish. There are no buggers in Ireland; the Church would not allow it. We are a God-fearing people, pious to a fault; we even dance chastely, arms pinned to sides. We are also one of the most sexually prolific nations in the world. Simple arithmetic will indicate that Irish sodomites must be unusually thin on the ground, otherwise whence all those great hordes of children? We are, moreover, a people characterized by what I might venture to call a dialectal habit of thought—the unity of opposites. Unlike the English, we tend to believe that one thing is true, but also its antithesis. It is not that we are illogical, merely economical. A belief in the unity of opposites is quite incompatible with any form of homoeroticism. (35)

This passage not only deconstructs both Irish and queer identity (and positions them, alongside national identity, as a kind of performance) but also actively deconstructs itself. Wilde sets up a series of opposites (bugger versus Irish, god-fearing versus sexual, homosexual versus procreative) and then happily explains to us that all of these oppositions are easily collapsed: the Irish, we are told, unify their opposites all the time. But this outcome undermines the entire point of Wilde's previous argument, which depended on drawing a distinction between those oppositional categories (not a bugger, but Irish) as mutually exclusive. Eagleton's hilarious punch line to this Derridean nightmare—that the unity of *opposites* is not *homo*erotic—is pure showing off.

If Eagleton surveys the various critical approaches to Wilde, then Moisés Kaufman ambitiously reviews the whole range of historical writings on the Irish writer. While *Saint Oscar* is overtly Brechtian with its songs, direct address to the audience, and deliberate flattening of character, *Gross Indecency: The Three Trials of Oscar Wilde* (1997) can best be categorized as documentary theater. Others before him recognized that the Wilde trials make great theater, but it was Kaufman's idea to embody all of the evidence: to present the vast multiplicity and diversity of viewpoints in all their glory. Kaufman's play thus stages a cacophony of opinions and voices; it is a human collage.

This documentary format not only allows for a great number of biographical and cultural voices to be heard but also enables those voices to be contextualized —both literally, with footnotes, and more figuratively, by juxtaposing various opinions. The result is a kind of theatrical hyperspace, where to allude to a piece of biographical evidence is to bring that evidence, living and breathing, before us:

> NARRATOR 4. From *Oscar Wilde* by Frank Harris:
>
> HARRIS: At the Cadogan Hotel, an angry mob had gathered in the street. Inside, Wilde sat as if glued to his chair, and drank hock and seltzer steadily in almost unbroken silence.
>
> QUEENSBERRY: If the country allows you to leave, all the better for the country!
>
> NARRATOR 2. From a note sent to the Cadogan Hotel:
>
> QUEENSBERRY: But if you take my son with you, I will follow you wherever you go and shoot you.
>
> NARRATOR 2. Oscar's wife on hearing of the court's decision said:
>
> CONSTANCE WILDE. *(Crying.)* I hope Oscar is going away abroad!
>
> WILDE. I shall stay and do my sentence whatever that may be.
>
> HARRIS. He then lapsed into inaction.
>
> DOUGLAS. Oscar, I will go to the House of Lords to talk to my cousin. I'll see if he can use his influence to prevent a prosecution. *(He kisses Oscar and exits.)*
>
> WILDE. With what a crash this fell.[24]

This passage, which occurs near the climactic end of the first act, shows Kaufman weaving together stories from people who were not sharing the same time or space. Obviously, neither Constance nor Queensberry was at the Cadogan Hotel with Wilde; less obviously, neither was Frank Harris.[25] On the one hand, this method may allow us a fuller picture than we would otherwise have, but on the other, it also contains a paradox: the evidence presented is not only contextualized but also radically decontextualized. Kaufman has already sifted, selected, and weighted the historical record, and now everything said in the theater has the force of a living human being behind it. Ultimately, everything said about Wilde in *Gross Indecency*—no matter how contradictory or implausible—is presented as true: a state of theatrical affairs that Wilde himself might well have loved. Still, there is a feeling of playing fast and loose with the facts, and the play's staged epilogue ranges from the incomplete ("After his release from prison, Wilde left for France where he lived under an assumed name in exile and poverty for the rest of his life") to the inaccurate ("After Wilde's death Lord Alfred Douglas became a Catholic, married, and had two children") (80).[26]

Gross Indecency was only the first of a series of late-1990s plays about Wilde: the big guns had yet to be drawn. So astounded were the reviewers that both Tom Stoppard and David Hare had taken on Wilde that they tended to review these authors' plays together or with deliberate reference to each other. Of the two dramas, Stoppard's *Invention of Love* (1997) seems to have better survived the comparison, though this may well be because, ironically enough, there is much less Wilde in it. Stoppard's play is about the contemporary (and closeted) English poet A. E. Housman, and Wilde serves primarily as Housman's dramatic foil, albeit a mostly absent one. But the fact that Wilde barely appears in the play does not stop him from dominating it. The trick is actually the same one that Stoppard played in *Rosencrantz and Guildenstern Are Dead* (1966); there, too, Stoppard got theatrical mileage from suggesting that the real action was happening elsewhere. There, the drama was Hamlet's; here, the offstage action is Wilde's. While the play chronicles Housman's scholarly obsessions and romantic disappointments, it does so in the evoked context of Wilde's life, in which love was considerably less academic.

The Invention of Love is concerned with both the corruption of morals and the corruption of text, and it relates these ideas through the figure of Housman, the classics scholar whose great reputation rests not on his scholarly research but on *A Shropshire Lad,* the volume of poetry he published anonymously in 1896. (Housman may well have arranged for a copy of this work, which contains some quietly coded homoerotic poems, to be sent to Wilde in jail.)[27] The corruption shared by morality and textuality amounts to far more than a pun, though Stoppard does not mind punning, and in fact introduces the intersection of these two corruptions with a letter asserting man's duty to "stamp out unnatural mice."[28] But Housman has devoted his life to, and channeled his passion into, fixing the corruptions of Classical text that conceal the homoerotic truths of the past from modern eyes. Housman is also keen to render those truths in honest and beautiful English translations, this being a political statement at a time when references to unnatural vice were routinely excised: "In the translation of Tibullus in my College library, the *he* loved by the poet is turned into a *she:* and then when you come to the bit where his 'she' goes off with somebody's wife, the translator is equal to the crisis—he leaves it out" (40). This bowdlerization of literature and history is a form of corruption worse than any unnatural vice, but Stoppard suggests that Housman pursues textual truth at least in part because he is unable to partake in the "corruption" of morality that is homosexuality in the age of Wilde. In this way, Housman is the reverse image of Wilde, his contemporary at Oxford and himself a fine classicist; unlike Wilde, who claimed to have put his genius into his life, poor Housman has put his genius into his unrewarding scholarly work. Our view of Housman—the man who longs for but never gets the young athlete he adores (the strapping Moses Jackson)—is colored by our knowledge of Wilde and the hedonistic fun we know he is having somewhere in the wings.

Stoppard contrives to make reference to Wilde at every possible point in the narrative, though the man in the flesh is rarely seen. Wilde's absence, however, merely contributes to his legend; he seems to know everyone and to be doing everything, as if he were living the lives of three or four ordinary people at once. John Ruskin makes offhand reference to "an Irish exquisite, a great slab of a youth with white hands and long poetical hair" (15); Moses Jackson finds himself baffled by a fellow in velvet knickerbockers who told him his left leg was a poem (18); Benjamin Jowett, Master of Balliol, in a hilarious tirade, somehow mistakes the mousy Housman for his more provocative contemporary: "If you can rid yourself of your levity and your cynicism, and find another way to dissimulate your Irish provincialism than by making affected remarks about your blue china and going about in plum-coloured velvet breeches, which you don't, and cut your hair—you're not him at all, are you?" (22). In this reference, as in the others, Wilde is not named; the pleasure comes in our immediate recognition of his profile, as distinctive as a fingerprint. In *The Invention of Love,* Wilde haunts Housman's life, standing as a constant reminder of everything he is not doing, everything he does not have: Wilde is the prince, and Housman only the messenger. When Wilde is arrested, Housman writes a bitterly sympathetic poem, and we are told that Robbie Ross read Housman's Shropshire poems to Wilde in prison, which informed Wilde's own poem *The Ballad of Reading Gaol* (1898). In reality, the two men never met, but Stoppard orchestrates a dramatic climax in which Wilde and Housman meet after death, on the occasion of the Queen's Diamond Jubilee.

It is a masterful buildup. By the time Wilde appears, we have heard so much about him that we are longing to see him, the way we might long to see any other larger-than-life celebrity. When the scholar and the artist meet, the result is just what you would expect: Housman is polite and buttoned-up, while Wilde has huge emotions and breaks down frequently. Housman offers sympathy for the unfairness of Wilde's trials, but Wilde scorns it: "Better a fallen rocket," he retorts, "than never a burst of light" (96).[29] But Stoppard also draws comparisons between the two men as poets who immortalized the men they loved and suffered for them. Wilde goes so far as to claim that he did not simply immortalize Bosie but invented him: "[Bosie] is spoiled, vindictive, utterly selfish and not very talented, but these are merely the facts. The truth is he was Hyacinth when Apollo loved him, he is ivory and gold, from his red rose-leaf lips comes music that fills me with joy, he is the only one who understands me. . . . We would never love anybody if we could see past our invention. Bosie is my creation, my poem" (95).[30] Here, again, Bosie's character is sacrificed on the pyre of Wilde's artistry: he has to be awful so that Wilde can make something wonderful of him. But this invention of Bosie has its parallel in Housman's own poetry, which, Wilde assures him, is "all that will still matter" (97). Ultimately, Stoppard's Wilde and Housman are united by suffering, just as Hamlet and Rosencrantz and Guildenstern are made equal in death. If Wilde's life was a grand tragedy and Housman's life a quiet one, then the end of the play finds them occupying the same pagan afterlife, waiting for the boatman Charon to take them down the river Styx.

Though very different in form, David Hare's *Judas Kiss* (1998) presents a similarly cosmic idea of love. Here, too, Bosie must be seen to be patently unworthy so that we can appreciate the beauty and purity of Wilde's love for him. Untainted by anything like a proximate cause, Wilde's love is perfect because it is as unconditional as God's love. Hare's play takes place in two acts: the first, subtitled "Deciding to Stay," occurs at the Cadogan Hotel on the afternoon of Wilde's arrest; the second, subtitled "Deciding to Leave," is set at the end of Wilde and Bosie's time together in Naples after Wilde's release from prison. In both scenes, Wilde is caught between two opposite but equally petty forces: Robbie Ross, who seems to want to save him, and Bosie, who seems to want to destroy him. The view of Bosie this implies is a familiar one (Eagleton's "rotten little queer," in fact), but it provides new perspective on Ross. Reputedly Wilde's first homosexual lover (perhaps during 1887 when Ross stayed as a paying guest at the Wilde family home in Tite Street, Chelsea), Ross remained a devoted friend and was at Wilde's side at the time of his death. Subsequently, he became Wilde's literary executor, helping to clear the debts that accumulated around the estate in 1906. If *The Judas Kiss* has a new idea vis-à-vis the Wilde story, then it is that Wilde was brought low as much by the supposed goodness of his friends (Ross, Constance) as by the betrayals of his enemies (Bosie, Queensberry).

In the first act, Wilde is torn between Robbie, who wants him to flee to Paris, and Bosie, who wants him to stay in England and fight. While the argument between Wilde and Bosie is familiar from the biographies, the argument between Wilde and Robbie is not. When Robbie tries to play hardball to get Wilde on the last train, Wilde chastises him: "Please allow us all to live our own lives."[31] Later, when Robbie rails against Bosie and insists that Wilde really must flee, Wilde quietly notes that the fatal human passion, "the source of all sin on this earth," is "the gratuitous pleasure of giving others advice" (49). Ross's advice to Wilde does not take into account Wilde's fiercely independent nature, his desire to control his own life and not be driven out. Ross also underestimates the extent to which Wilde values his love for Bosie, even if Bosie does not value it: "It is what I have left. It is what remains to me. All else has now been taken away" (49). When Bosie returns to the hotel, it is only to tell Wilde that his friends have advised him not to be present at the arrest, but in the religious language evoked by the play's title, this abandonment only makes Wilde's love—and his sacrifice— more beautiful and sacred.

In the second act, Wilde is again torn between Ross's controlling "helpfulness" and Bosie's complete self-centeredness. Ross, who is committed to reconciling Wilde and Constance, comes to Naples, where Wilde and Bosie are sharing a villa. Again, what should be kindness on Ross's part is, in fact, cruelty: Robbie has once more come to play hardball with Wilde, this time to insist that either he leave Bosie or Constance will cut him off without a penny. Wilde's quietly outraged response to this tyrannical act of "benevolence" is at the heart of Hare's play: "I am not just to live, but I must also live in a way of which you approve?" (82). A few minutes later, Wilde elaborates:

> WILDE: I have taken my punishment. Was that not enough? Was that not
> what was asked of me? Have I not suffered? Have I not endured? But
> no, the rules are now to be changed. I have done my term, but now new

obligations are to be imposed. No longer is punishment enough. The moral of my punishment must be stuffed down my throat. I must choke on it.

He is so savage that Ross is stopped, hesitant to ask the next question.

Ross: Do you really see no difference . . . Oscar, do you see no difference between those who put you in prison and those who now seek to help you?

WILDE: Oh, yes. Once I was punished from simple malice. Now I am punished in the interests of moral example. (87–88)

When Wilde refuses to give in to Robbie's demands, Robbie says, with all apparent reluctance, that he must dispatch a message to Constance, who will cut off Wilde's funds. Of course, to maximize the dramatic irony, Bosie arrives and reveals that he is leaving Wilde because of his mother's threat to cut off *his* funds. Wilde has thus made a noble decision that was not reciprocated; again, Bosie has shown himself to be a shallow and unworthy person. But Wilde does not mind. As in Stoppard's *Invention of Love,* here Wilde treats his love for Bosie as his own artistic creation, something truer than the truth and realer than the real: "Love is not the illusion. Life is" (95). Hare's drama ends with the eponymous Judas kiss. Wilde commands the kiss from Bosie as Jesus commanded Lazarus, saying, "Come towards me. Walk" (113). After Bosie's fateful kiss, Hare again has Wilde rue the artistic flaw of the Gospels: that Jesus is betrayed by Judas and not John.

The Judas Kiss successfully makes the point that both Ross and Bosie—though they seem opposed and opposite—think of love (wrongly and callously) as a rational and practical exchange, a kind of quid pro quo. But to advance this argument, Hare has to finesse numerous facts, particularly where Bosie is concerned. For instance, most biographers agree that Bosie spent the time while Wilde was ensconced in the Cadogan frantically running around town trying to find someone—anyone—who could help Wilde; similarly, they also agree that Wilde and Douglas lived together in Posilippo, Italy, in relative happiness until their relatives determined that they be separated. Faced with serious financial pressure from both sides, Oscar and Bosie reluctantly agreed not to live together, but both met whenever possible. Ellmann cites a letter that Bosie wrote to his mother around this time, in which he asked her how he was supposed to tell Wilde

I cannot come and live with you now. I lived with you before and stayed with you and lived *on* you, but that was when you were rich, famous, honored and at the summit of your position as an artist, now I am very sorry of course, but you are ruined, you have no money, you have hardly any friends, you have been in prison (chiefly, I admit, on my account and through my fault), you are an ex-convict, it will do me a great deal of harm to be seen about with you, and besides, my mother naturally objects to it very strongly, and so I'm afraid I must leave you to get on as best you can by yourself. (*Oscar Wilde*, 554)

The awful and selfish behavior that the real Bosie Douglas decries is imputed to him by Hare in *The Judas Kiss* without any irony whatsoever. Hare also has Bosie both deny his homosexuality ("I am not disposed, as you are, to love my own sex" [102]) and chide Oscar for being too cowardly to admit his own sexuality in open court ("You could have defended Greek love" [101]). While, admittedly, Douglas lived long enough that he did, over the years, hold all of these contradictory positions and more, it is difficult to imagine anyone but a psychopath holding them simultaneously, as Hare has him do.

Both Hare's and Stoppard's hostile characterizations of Bosie, in conjunction with their attribution of an almost unearthly love to Wilde, has understandably led to a certain skepticism about the biographical representations in *The Invention of Love* and *The Judas Kiss*. Oscar and Bosie seem not so much men as literary metaphors, and problematic metaphors at that: like the gay equivalent of the Madonna-whore complex—perhaps what we might call "the saint and the sinner." Neither Stoppard nor Hare has a particular history of writing gay characters or being interested in gay issues,[32] and so there is a sense that Oscar and Bosie are placeholders for something else: the tragic overreacher and his *homme fatale*, the Christ-like lover and his betrayer. But they also present very extreme (and problematic) modes of gay sexuality: the effeminate martyr-artist (though to be fair, Wilde himself is responsible for concretizing the image of Christ as martyr-artist) and the cold, calculating bitch.

Metatheater: Bartlett

Neil Bartlett's *In Extremis* (2000) is perhaps the most metatheatrical of the recent bio-plays and, consequently, the least concerned with factual truth. The play was "spun from a single historical fact": Oscar Wilde's consultation with a Society palm reader called Mrs. Robinson a week before his trial.[33] Bartlett's two-character piece is structured so as to pit one kind of professional liar against another: the dramatist versus the spiritualist, the man of the theater versus the fortune-teller. Both of these characters know how to spin a tale that meets the needs and desires of their target audience. *In Extremis* is therefore not about facts but about the stories we need to tell one another and the stories we need to hear.

The palmist Mrs. Robinson, speaking from beyond the grave, tells the story of how the famous Wilde came to see her: he wanted to know what would happen to him if he did not flee England. "What I wanted to say was: I'm sorry. I'm so, so sorry," she confesses, but instead she tells him what he wants to hear: "I see a triumph. A very great triumph" (50). Wilde is relieved, his thoughts immediately flying to Bosie, and he walks home with eyes full of tears, "for I knew I was safe" (51). But Mrs. Robinson's reading of Wilde was a misreading. Or was it? For, as Mrs. Robinson says to the audience, "I told him I saw a great triumph. Well, was I lying?" (52).

Perhaps by 2000, this was the only kind of play left to do about Wilde, one in which we admit that our interpretations of his biography are as self-interested as those of a fortune-teller. Mrs. Robinson has a stable of obvious truths that she trots out during her readings—"You are swayed by the opinions of others more than you would like," "You are not always sincere with those you love," "You have not yet achieved all that you once hoped to" (31)—because she knows that these are things that we all feel, that we all fear. Wilde asks Mrs. Robinson to read his palm, to interpret his life, "desperate for her to tell me what to do. Longing for a paid fool to speak to me and say kind words" (35). But Mrs. Robinson is no fool: she knows that the secrets her clients most long to hear "are ones that they already know" (47).

So perhaps the lesson of *In Extremis* is that we come to see Wilde on stage hoping to have our own fortunes told. Or perhaps, for the moment, Wilde has declared everything he had to declare: in the wake of the various commemorative anniversaries and celebrations, even the most devoted follower of Wilde would be forgiven for sympathizing with David Benedict's plea in the *Independent*, an article titled "Kindly Leave the Theatre: Oscar Wilde Was Indeed a Literary Great and Cruelly Treated, But Let's Give the Story a Rest, Eh?"[34] Still, we have not yet had an Oscar Wilde for the post-post Stonewall, *Queer as Folk* generation, and today's well-heeled metrosexuals might well take Bosie rather than Oscar as their patron saint. Gay singer-songwriter Rufus Wainwright perhaps comes closest in his 2005 bonus track "In with the Ladies," in which he reimagines Oscar Wilde as a jaded Hollywood mogul ("Get me new faces, new faces, I'm tired of the old ones") and Bosie Douglas as fresh meat ("Little Lord Bosie, cut from the daisy chain").[35] This Wilde cruises down Sunset Boulevard in his Mustang and seduces Bosie with confidence and promises of fame: "Bosie, relax: you're a winner, and I am a star." It is a plausible enough interpretation: the artist with connections, the beautiful young wannabe. Just as every generation is said to have its Hamlet, so too might every generation come to have its definitive Oscar Wilde.

Notes

1. E. M. Forster, *Maurice* (New York: W. W. Norton, 1971), 159, 33; further page references appear in parentheses.

2. Alan Sinfield, *Cultural Politics—Queer Reading* (Philadelphia: University of Pennsylvania Press, 1994), 3.

3. For a detailed discussion of Wilde's influence on the creation of twentieth-century gay stereotypes, see Alan Sinfield, *The Wilde Century: Effeminacy, Oscar Wilde, and the Queer Moment* (London: Cassell, 1994).

4. Leslie and Sewell Stokes, *Oscar Wilde* (New York: Random House, 1938), 121; further page references to this edition appear in parentheses.

5. During the first trial, when he failed in his suit against the Marquess of Queensberry for criminal libel, Wilde was cross-examined by Edward Carson about Parker: "'Was he a literary character?' Carson quipped. 'Oh, no!' Wilde replied.... Culture was not his strong point. He was not an artist." H. Montgomery Hyde, *The Trials of Oscar Wilde*, 2nd ed. (1962; repr., New York: Dover, 1973), 126.

6. Douglas's public attitude toward Wilde oscillated between devotion and hostility during the forty-five years after the Irish writer's death. Although he remained publicly loyal to Wilde's memory (publishing a fine sonnet in memory of Wilde, "The Dead Poet," in the *Academy* in 1907), his attitude changed radically after he discovered that Wilde's literary executor, Robert Ross, had released the complete text of the work that Ross named *De Profundis.* This 55,000-word work, which takes the form of a letter from Wilde to Douglas, was completed during Wilde's final months in Reading Gaol. Parts of this long document make recriminatory observations about Douglas's behavior. In 1905, Ross published a tactfully abridged version of *De Profundis* that omitted references to Douglas. In 1912, however, when Douglas discovered that Ross had released the complete document to Arthur Ransome (whose informative monograph, *Oscar Wilde: A Critical Study* [1912], refers to Wilde's negative perspective on Douglas), Douglas sued for criminal libel. Exhibiting his deepened hostility toward Ross, Douglas put his name on a work purporting to be a memoir, *Oscar Wilde and Myself* (1914), which was written mainly by T.W.H. Crosland, who harbored an intense dislike of Wilde. Later, Douglas continued his tirade against Ross with *The Rossiad* (1916), a verse satire. In 1929, eleven years after Ross's death, Douglas published a more positive account of Wilde in his *Autobiography.* By 1940, in *Oscar Wilde: A Summing Up,* he confirmed his support toward Wilde but disavowed his own homosexual past. For more information on Douglas's changing attitude toward Wilde, see Karl Beckson, *The Oscar Wilde Encyclopedia* (New York: AMS, 1998), 75–80, and the introduction to the present volume.

7. Caspar Wintermans, *Alfred Douglas: A Poet's Life and His Finest Work* (London: Peter Owen, 2007), 19. Wintermans's biography first appeared in Dutch in 1999.

8. Jane Stevenson, "Self-Pity, Doggerel and Beastliness," *Daily Telegraph*, 5 May 2007, 26; further quotations also appear on this page.

9. Alfred Douglas, "Two Loves," in John Francis Bloxam's magazine *The Chameleon* (1894); the poem is reprinted in Brian Reade, ed., *Sexual Heretics: Male Homosexuality in English Literature from 1850 to 1900* (London: Routledge and Kegan Paul, 1970), 162. During the second trial, prosecutor Charles Gill quoted Douglas's poem and asked "What is the 'Love that dare not speak its name'?" Gill's query prompted Wilde's famous defense of "such a great affection of an elder for a younger man as there was between David and Jonathan, such as Plato made the very basis of his philosophy, and such as you find in the sonnets of Michelangelo and Shakespeare." Hyde, *Trials of Oscar Wilde*, 201.

10. Paul Taylor, "Oscar Nominated," *Independent*, 20 March 1997, 19.

11. See, for example, Davis Coakley, *Oscar Wilde: The Importance of Being Irish* (Dublin: Town House, 1994); Jerusha McCormack, ed., *Wilde the Irishman* (New Haven, CT: Yale University Press, 1998); and Richard Pine, *The Thief of Reason: Oscar Wilde and Modern Ireland* (Dublin: Gill and Macmillan, 1995).

12. Micheál MacLiammóir, *The Importance of Being Oscar* (Gerrards Cross: Colin Smythe, 1995), 16; further page references appear in parentheses.

13. John Gay, *Diversions and Delights*, performed by Vincent Price, Westwood Playhouse, Los Angeles, 1982. MP3 available at http://voices-in-the-dark.anagkh.net/ (accessed 15 June 2007); my transcription.

14. This anecdote is recorded in Richard Ellmann, *Oscar Wilde* (New York: Random House, 1988), 160; further page reference appears in parentheses.

15. Eric Bentley, *Lord Alfred's Lover* (Toronto: Personal Library, 1981), 9; further page references appear in parentheses.

16. Bentley's lines are adapted from a transcript of Mr. Justice Wills's summing-up at the end of the third trial on 25 May 1895. Hyde, *Trials of Oscar Wilde*, 272.

17. Timothy d'Arch Smith employs the term "Uranian," which he derived from nineteenth-century Austrian writer Karl Heinrich Ulrichs's path-breaking studies of the "Urning" (that is, the man-loving man), in his study of boy-loving poetry written by men in the late-Victorian and early-twentieth-century period: *Love in Earnest: Some Notes on the Lives and Writings of English "Uranian" Poets from 1889 to 1930* (London: Routledge and Kegan Paul, 1970). The English use of the term "Uranian" has its origins in John Addington Symonds's homophile study *A Problem in Modern Ethics* (privately published, 1891), which was circulated in an edition of one hundred copies; in French, the word was used in sexological studies, such as Marc André Raffalovich, *Uranisme et unisexualité: Étude sur différentes manifestations de l'instinct sexuel* (Paris: Masson, 1896), which condemns Wilde's sexual profligacy.

18. Wilde did in fact know the word. In February 1898, he informed Robert Ross, "To have altered my life would have been to have admitted that Uranian love is ignoble." Wilde, *Complete Letters*, ed. Merlin Holland and Rupert Hart-Davis (London: Fourth Estate, 2000), 1019.

19. Wilde's story about Judas versus John has its origins in Frank Harris's *Oscar Wilde: His Life and Confessions* and is picked up and adapted by both John Gay and David Hare. In fact, Frank Harris claims the idea as his own and quotes Wilde quoting *him*: "Do you remember once telling me that the only flaw you could find in the perfect symbolism of the gospel story was that Jesus was betrayed by Judas, the foreigner from Kerioth, when he should have been betrayed by John, the beloved disciple; for it is only those we love who can betray us? Frank, how true, how

tragically true that is! It is those we love who betray us with a kiss." Harris, *Oscar Wilde: His Life and Confessions*, 2 vols. (New York: privately published, 1918), 2:526.

20. There has been speculation that Douglas's older brother, Francis (Viscount Drumlanrig), took his life in October 1894 from fear of exposure of his intimate relationship with the then foreign secretary, the Earl of Rosebery.

21. Jeffrey Weeks, *Coming Out: Homosexual Politics in Great Britain from the Nineteenth Century to the Present* (London: Quartet Books, 1977), 166.

22. In his 2 July 1896 petition to the home secretary for reading materials during his final ten months in Reading Gaol, Wilde declares that during "the three years preceding his arrest . . . he was suffering from the most horrible form of erotomania" (*Complete Letters*, 657).

23. Terry Eagleton, *Saint Oscar* (Derry: Field Day, 1989), vii; further page references appear in parentheses.

24. Moisés Kaufman, *Gross Indecency: The Three Trials of Oscar Wilde* (New York: Dramatists Play Service, 1999), 47–48; further page reference appears in parentheses.

25. Harris's sensationalizing biography, which sold well when first published in 1916, is notoriously unreliable. Harris misleads his readers, for example, by suggesting that he was present at the Old Bailey when Wilde was sent down on 25 May 1895. He does not, however, presume to have been at the Cadogan Hotel when Wilde was arrested. See Harris, *Oscar Wilde: His Life and Confessions*, 1:238.

26. Douglas married poet Olive Custance in 1902, had a son (Raymond Douglas) later that year, and converted to Roman Catholicism nine years later. Douglas and his spouse separated in 1913, though they spent time together in the 1920s.

27. There is conflicting information about the date when Wilde read Housman's *Shropshire Lad*. Housman, in 1928, claimed that Robert Ross, during one of his visits to Reading Gaol, discovered that Wilde had learned some of Housman's poems by heart (Wilde, *Complete Letters*, 923). Housman's poems "IX" and "XLVII" echo in Wilde's *Ballad of Reading Gaol* (1898).

28. Tom Stoppard, *The Invention of Love* (New York: Grove Press, 1997), 25; further page references appear in parentheses.

29. In this line, Stoppard would appear to be making an ironic allusion to Wilde's 1888 fairy tale "The Remarkable Rocket."

30. This speech adapts and revises Wilde's memorable phrasing in a love letter he wrote to Douglas in January 1893: "My Own Boy: Your sonnet is quite lovely, and it is a marvel that those red rose-leaf lips of yours should have been made no less for music of song than for madness of kisses. Your slim gilt soul walks between passion and poetry. I know Hyacinthus, whom Apollo loved so madly, was you in Greek days" (*Complete Letters*, 544). This letter was stolen by blackmailers, fell into the hands of Queensberry's henchmen, and was quoted in court by Queensberry's defense (Edward Clarke) as compromising evidence of Wilde's sexual preference. Hyde, *Trials of Oscar Wilde*, 101, 115.

31. David Hare, *The Judas Kiss* (New York: Grove Press, 1998), 43; further page references appear in parentheses.

32. "Even perfectly reasonable chaps like Tom Stoppard and David Hare spotted Wilde anniversaries and popped the playwright on stage. . . . And while I have nothing against either playwright, the almost total absence of homosexuals in their previous works does cast their espousal of Wilde in an odd light. (And I know that Hare created a gay vicar in his masterpiece *Racing Demon* but that merely proves both the rule and my point.)" David Benedict, "Kindly

Leave the Theatre: Oscar Wilde Was Indeed a Literary Great and Cruelly Treated, But Let's Give the Story a Rest, Eh?" *Independent*, 21 July 1999, 11.

33. Neil Bartlett, *In Extremis* (London: Oberon, 2000), 7; further page references appear in parentheses.

34. Benedict, "Kindly Leave the Theatre."

35. Rufus Wainwright, "In with the Ladies," bonus track on the UK release of his album *Want* (New York and London: Polydor, 2005).

Wilde Lives

Derek Jarman and the Queer Eighties

MATT COOK

IN WILL SELF's novel *Dorian* (2002), the eponymous hero takes perverse delight in transmitting the HIV virus to as many as possible while himself remaining both youthful and healthy. Self deploys the structures, characters, and themes of Oscar Wilde's novel, *The Picture of Dorian Gray* (1890, revised 1891), to give a particularly nihilistic account of gay London in the late 1980s and early 1990s. He weaves selfishness, deceit, malicious infection, and a decadent hedonism into his fictional account of the early years of the AIDS crisis. It is a clever, gripping, and deeply disturbing novel, written in a social and cultural context very different from the one in which the novel is set. By the time Will Self was writing, combination therapy had given new hope to many people living with HIV and AIDS, and sex and relations between men had gained a new (though certainly not universal) acceptability. In Britain, virulent homophobia and the intense collective anger of the gay community had abated by many degrees. In this changed context, it was possible for accounts of the AIDS crisis to be less polarized and for Wilde's life and work to be deployed somewhat differently in relation to it.[1]

Such an observation begs the question of how Wilde was being used in the 1980s and early 1990s—prior to this partial recession in homophobic rhetoric.

The diaries of one of the most well-known, controversial, and vocal AIDS activists of the period—the filmmaker, artist, set designer, writer, and gardener Derek Jarman—provide us with a partial answer. The ways Wilde was written in and out of Jarman's story of himself, his art, and his politics demonstrate what it was about this period that made certain appropriations of Wilde possible and others much more problematic.

Contexts

Wilde, an omnipresent and controversial cultural figure throughout the twentieth century, achieved particular prominence in the 1980s and 1990s with an unprecedented outpouring of writing about him.[2] This phenomenon often went beyond the need to justify or deride the dead playwright or to replay his story as the classic tale of "gay doom."[3] Instead, it frequently explored Wilde's significance in terms of identity and sexual subjectivity.[4] Both Wilde and Wildean strategies were increasingly seen as ways of thinking about the constitution and malleability of homosexual identity in the 1880s and 1890s and also as a means of self-invention, affirmation, and endurance in the present. This perspective on Wilde owed much to the postmodern and poststructuralist debates of the 1980s and after about the fluidity of subjectivity and the instability of supposedly essential identity categories—debates that clearly also informed Jarman's work.[5] Wilde himself grappled with the idea that the self might be (in Chris Waters's words) "something one creates or makes up," and he explored the power of shifting perceptions and contexts on subjectivity.[6] This was part of his particular appeal in the late twentieth century to scholars researching discourses of homosexuality and to queer activists who were keen, as Waters observes, "to celebrate new modes of performative selfhood that owe[d] little to earlier conceptions of an innate homosexual condition—an innate condition which could all too easily be labelled sick or perverse."[7] This theorizing of identity came in part through the emerging fields of gender studies and lesbian and gay studies in which we started to explore deconstructively the coordinates of masculinity and femininity and of gay, homosexual, and queer sexualities. This project involved not only reclaiming the gay past and gay forebears—the gay lineage that had likewise been important to Wilde and his contemporaries—but also thinking about how we might use and deploy that history and those figures. In this intellectual environment, it became increasingly apparent that Wilde did not have to mean one thing, and thus a space opened up to claim his life and works in different and complex ways.

The second key context for Jarman was the advent of HIV and AIDS and, in Britain, the rise of the New Right and the quest for some illusory Victorian values. In his diaries, Jarman records not only his own uncertain health but also the many deaths of lovers, friends, and acquaintances. For him, it was a time of intense anger and grief. Clause 28 of the Local Government Act of 1988, meanwhile, outlawed the so-called promotion of homosexuality by local authorities. Three years later, the Criminal Justice Bill extended the law in relation to soliciting by gay men. While the gay press reported an apparent increase in homophobic attacks and action against gay men and gay venues by the police, several of the mainstream newspapers reveled in damning and inaccurate coverage of the new "gay plague."[8] Jarman received death threats in the mid-1980s, and when his films *Jubilee* (1976) and *Sebastiane* (1978) appeared on Channel 4 television in 1986, the moral crusader Mary Whitehouse launched a campaign against him. Meanwhile, Winston Churchill, MP (grandson of the wartime leader), attempted, unsuccessfully, to extend censorship legislation.[9]

Many gay men in the 1980s and the early 1990s found in Wilde and his generation a muffled echo of their own concerns and experiences. Such felt resonances are at least partly attributable to changes to the law in the late nineteenth century, a perceived increase in legal action against male-male sexual activity at this time,[10] and coincident attempts to legitimize such activity on the part of men such as John Addington Symonds, Edward Carpenter, Henry Havelock Ellis, and, of course, Oscar Wilde. This perception that the two fin de siècles resonated with each other does not imply that in the intervening period gay men did not experience similar feelings of marginalization and a profound desire for self and community expression. George Ives, an early campaigner for homosexual law reform, testifies to experiencing both of these things acutely in the first half of the twentieth century. But when Mary Whitehouse and the National Listeners and Viewers Association and Margaret Thatcher and her government turned precisely on the visibility, vocal presence, and radicalism of gay men in the 1980s, Wilde's fame and flamboyance, his notoriety and disobedience, became academically, politically, and personally compelling for many gay men.

One of the most brilliant evocations of Wilde during the 1980s—one that draws together rigorous research, autobiography and a fervent queer politics— was Neil Bartlett's *Who Was That Man? A Present for Mr. Oscar Wilde* (1988): a book that helps to elucidate the complexities of Jarman's engagement with Wilde in the same period. Bartlett sees precisely the need for self-invention and self-contemplation as a gay man, particularly one under fire: "I subject my story of my own life as a gay man to constant scrutiny," he writes; "we all do, because we're making it up as we go along."[11] Bartlett draws on some of the words, histories, flowers, faces, and possessions that Wilde gathered together and uses them to orientate himself in London a century later. They give him a sense of difference, belonging, and purpose, and he starts to see Wilde "as the beginning of my story"; until then, he writes, "like a lot of men . . . I'd seen America and the 1970s as the start of everything" (xx–xxi).

Wilde was "the beginning of" but certainly not the whole story. For what Bartlett also touches on—and what is particularly significant when we look at Jarman—is ambivalence about Wilde's legacy. This ambivalence does not relate to the aesthete/athlete or effeminate/masculine binaries (as it often had before)[12] but rather to Wilde's omnipresence for gay men in the twentieth century. In two letters addressed to Wilde toward the end of *Who Was That Man?* Bartlett expresses his mixed feelings about the shadow that the subject of his book has cast. In the first letter, he dedicates his work and research to Wilde, as a lover might. "Darling, it's all for you," he writes, as he describes purchasing flowers from the Burlington Arcade, traveling to Paris and placing them on Wilde's grave "out of real love and respect" (211). "Oscar you fat bitch," the second letter begins: "[L]ast night I dreamed . . . you were there in the bed, big and fat, like I've been told you were, lying in bed smoking and taking up the room. . . . I noticed that I didn't recognize the smell or the brand of your cigarettes. . . . I realized that I had no idea what your voice would sound like" (212). Again, Bartlett's voice is intimate, but Wilde here is both profoundly unknowable and also domineering, preventing the later writer from finding his own voice. "You old queen," Bartlett concludes, "you've got your hand on my face. I can't talk now" (213). By both embracing and rejecting Wilde, Bartlett demonstrates vividly and movingly how the Irish writer could be used within, but was also not of, his 1980s London and the particular crises and pleasures of that decade.

Jarman and Wilde

Although Jarman's engagement with Wilde is much less direct than Bartlett's, we get a similar sense in his diaries. Wilde is woven into but also excluded from the

Matt Cook

filmmaker's story of himself; the queer past is grasped for the present with ambivalence. Jarman was an obsessive diarist and note keeper, especially after he received his HIV diagnosis on 22 December 1986. He took his diary everywhere,[13] and he found writing cathartic and personally sustaining. He also wrote explicitly for a wider audience, however, and his journals were published as *Modern Nature*, covering the period 1989–90, and *Smiling in Slow Motion*, which were edited and published posthumously by Jarman's partner Keith Collins and cover the final period 1990–94. Tara Brabazan observes that in these works, and in his other extensive writing, Jarman showed "an extraordinary ability to articulate his social subjectivity."[14] This was an ability and project that he shared with Bartlett and many other gay men writing urgently in the first fifteen years of the AIDS pandemic.[15] All of these men, including Jarman, were acutely aware of their social and cultural positioning and the need to assert and insist on their presence and—what felt especially crucial at this time—their difference.

Jarman certainly had a sense of Wilde's significance to his own struggle. Wilde figures in the predictable canon of "forebears who validated [Jarman's] existence"; Jarman took part in direct action protests outside Bow Street police station, London, where Wilde was first taken after his arrest; and he wrote letters in support of a commemorative statue for Wilde, finally unveiled in 1998.[16] Jarman was also friendly with Wilde experts Neil Bartlett and Neil McKenna (Wilde's latest biographer and a key player in the statue campaign), and in his last year he conceived a film version of *The Picture of Dorian Gray* at the latter's suggestion.[17] Jarman was also defensive of Wilde and his legacy and voiced anger with Richard Ellmann's biography for "neutering" him,[18] for not foregrounding relations between men as central to his creativity and his life—as McKenna was later to do in *The Secret Life of Oscar Wilde* (2003). Such considerations were pivotal in the intellectual, political, and cultural contexts of the 1980s. As Jeffrey Weeks reminds us, at this time the personal and the intimate were determinedly political.[19] Part of what Jarman achieved by using the diary form was to place his desires and relations with other men at the center of his art. He could not accept an analysis of Wilde that did not suggest something similar.

Some of these details about his interest in Wilde are mentioned in passing in the diaries, as are references to the purchase of a copy of *De Profundis* and to Jarman's panic at receiving an invitation to direct the Richard Strauss opera of Wilde's *Salomé* at Lyons.[20] There is also an anecdote about Wilde boasting to André Gide about one of his lovers being a murderer, something Jarman boasts about, too.[21] But elsewhere, mention of Wilde is relatively sparse, and though the playwright was apparently referred to by Jarman when he first came out (to theologian Roger Jones), he is significantly not included in Jarman's various published accounts of this event.[22] There again seems to be some discomfort with the weight of Wilde's legacy. Jarman rails, for example, against the routinely provocative British newspaper columnist Julie Burchill: "[S]he said she preferred homosexuals limp-wristed and dragged up in velveteen like Oscar, and hated the new faggots with their political agendas and macho styles" (*Modern Nature*, 232). Was the image of Oscar as a "pansy" "pinned to us?" he wrote in *Modern Nature* (30). Yet patterns of writing and reinvention in Jarman's diaries echo the ways in which Wilde began to frame the possibility of sexual difference at the end of the nineteenth century. Jarman's writing marshals similar structures of thought and feeling. Wilde thus becomes part of the "creative self portraiture" in which Jarman was engaged. This term—"creative self portraiture"—was first used by William E. Buckler to characterize Wilde's own project in his prison manuscript, which posthumously became *De Profundis*.[23] It usefully characterizes the endeavors of both men.

We can find these connections on a number of levels, not least in the frames of cultural reference that they share. Richard A. Kaye observes the significance of Saint Sebastian for Wilde (chapter 4 in the present volume), a saint whom Jarman depicted controversially in one of his early feature-length films (*Sebastiane*). The idealized Hellenic male appears in *The Picture of Dorian Gray* and in Jarman's extended description of a chiseled Adonis in a sex club in London's Leicester Square.[24] Similarly, Wilde's "Portrait of Mr. W.H." (1889) resonates with Jarman's conjuring with Shakespeare's sonnets in his film *The Angelic Conversation* (1985), which is a poetic evocation of love between two men. But beyond these immediate homologies, the two men manipulated the interwoven concepts of time and space in similar ways to forge a clear sense of their sexual dissidence.

Time and the Beautiful Present

The aesthetic movement of the late nineteenth century famously validated the beautiful moment. "Art," Oxford don Walter Pater wrote in his *Studies in the History of the Renaissance* (1873), "comes to you proposing frankly to give nothing but the highest quality to your moments as they pass, and simply for those

Matt Cook

moments' sake."[25] This was an ethos enthusiastically endorsed and explored by Wilde in his work, and in jail he was still writing that "in Art one is only concerned with what a particular thing is at a particular moment to oneself."[26] These ideas, Regenia Gagnier argues, "resisted the Victorian values of utility, rationality, scientific factuality, and technological progress."[27] They refuse the civilizing march into the future, which was allied with a temporal progression, and time is instead opened out for an alternative aesthetic and a validation of the sensory in the moment. Wilde plays with alternative temporalities most obviously in *The Picture of Dorian Gray,* in which Dorian famously sidesteps the conventional chronology of the aging process. Dorian also conjures other times and spaces in his rooms through his Renaissance hangings, exotic collections, and wild concerts, not for what they tell him of that past and those places but for what they add to the sensual intensity of the present—and Wilde is insistent that the novel is set in the present and represents present dangers and possibilities.[28] What Wilde was doing in a coded way was linking sexual dissidence with temporal subversion and with a valuation of the sensual moment rather than a progressive life story. Jarman plays with time in similar ways in his diaries as a means of responding to the crises in health and homophobia that he faced very directly in the 1980s.

That Jarman chose to write about himself in a diary and chose to use diary extracts and a diaristic structure in his two autobiographies—*Dancing Ledge* (1984) and *At Your Own Risk* (1991)—is significant for the way in which he wanted to present himself and his relationship to time. Jarman's diaries draw us into individual days rather than forming a chronological story of a life. He inserts memories, histories, Classical and Renaissance mythology, and nostalgia for the 1960s and 1970s, apparently randomly. He starts his daily record wherever he wants, then returns to and reinvents pivotal events. His coming out, for example, is rendered differently in *Dancing Ledge, Modern Nature,* and *At Your Own Risk,* as is his earliest sexual experience (*Modern Nature,* 30). Jarman's biographer Tony Peake observes acutely that Jarman, like Wilde, was "a deft mythologiser of his own life."[29]

Jarman sees no virtue in constructing a true history and chronology. Indeed, he sees neither as possible, keying in again to poststructuralist debate, which so informed queer theory. Although he lists his gay forebears and figures himself as part of a queer artistic lineage, he envisages this ancestry circling him in the present rather than preceding him. He uses the past and these figures unapologetically in and for that present in ways that resonate not only with Bartlett but also with Wilde—in *The Picture of Dorian Gray* and, in court, Wilde's celebrated justification of "the Love that dare not speak its name."[30] In the words of Jim Ellis, Jarman "fucks with the dead and speaks to the living" at a moment when the constitution of a defiant identity felt especially critical.[31]

Once diagnosed with the HIV virus, Jarman describes beginning to exist in a different temporal framework. Having the virus, he says, gives "finality to every gesture" (*Smiling in Slow Motion,* 34). Time is thus limited, and the impulse—which the diaries capture vividly—is to focus on a vibrant present rather than an unknown and compromised future. Psychologically and practically, the virus and his ensuing illness foist this alternative time frame on him—he has no choice. But as a means of countering this imperative, Jarman pursues different ways of self-consciously understanding or visualizing time. His diaries allow for an accumulation of detail, memory, and experience and allow him to exist on the cutting edge of time, marking an insistent presence in that moment. Even when he was desperately ill in the hospital, the diaries witness that existence and the struggle it involved:

> March 21 1992: Could not get up. Burning eyes. Face. Sad.
> March 22nd: Should I give up?
> March 23rd: I'm still here.[32]

If keeping the diaries was a means of personal endurance, then publishing them was a defiant gesture to those who had written him off. They provide evidence of a life fully lived in the here and now—a life marked by voracious artistic productivity. They were also a means of taking control of his legacy in the face of an illness that had been stigmatized in virulently homophobic ways. Wilde professes a similar impulse in *De Profundis,* having had the charge of "gross indecency" pinned to him. He wants to remind the neglectful Alfred Douglas of what he has been through as he served time, but he also has his eye on future readers: "[S]ome day," he writes, "the truth will have to be known—not necessarily in my lifetime . . . but I am not prepared to sit in the grotesque pillory they put me into, for all time."[33] Jarman's diaries form a similar counternarrative, and he and Wilde deploy supposedly intimate genres—the diary and the (love?) letter[34]—to redeem and redefine themselves and their artistry for the future.

If Wilde's and Jarman's respective writings enable them to mark an insistent present in the supposed oblivion of the jail or the hospital and to provide a personal corrective to the domineering record, then their toying with time also allows for an escape of sorts. In 1987, soon after receiving his HIV diagnosis, Jarman bought Prospect Cottage on a desolate stretch of the Kent coast and began to create a garden there against the extraordinary backdrop of the Dungeness nuclear power station. "The gardener," he wrote on 7 March 1989, "digs in another time, without past or future, beginning or end, a time that does not cleave the day with rush hours, lunch breaks or the last bus home. As you walk in the garden you pass into another time—the moment of entering can never be remembered. Around you the landscape lies transfigured. Here is the Amen beyond the prayer" (*Modern Nature*, 30). The rhythm of the garden and its seasons begin to overlay the daily rhythm of the diary,[35] and the convergence of memory, history, and daily events are supplemented by plant folklore, which adds a mythological timeframe. Jarman, Daniel O'Quin argues, is trying to "situate queer identity in a condition of timelessness," rupturing monumental narrative history and allowing other voices and experiences into his account and into his life.[36]

There is an echo here not only of *The Picture of Dorian Gray* but also of the intersecting temporalities of *De Profundis*. Wilde marks his time in prison—how much he has served, how much to go—and also provides an incredibly detailed and precise chronology of his friendship with Douglas: "one morning in the early October of '92"; "three months later, in June"; "I refer to your conduct to me from 10th–13th October, 1894"; "at eleven o'clock you came into my room" (*Complete Letters*, 687, 692, 696, 698). But this precision is framed by a more timeless sense of the mythological, of the biblical, and of the ancient world and—perhaps most strikingly if we read *De Profundis* alongside Jarman's diaries—by the fantasized embrace of a redemptive nature and her rhythms, of a bigger sense of time not marked out in minutes and hours.

Both Jarman and Wilde work with parallel temporalities and refuse to be railroaded into conventional narrative as they give their respective accounts of their lives and careers. For Jarman, this impulse does not merely relate to academic debate in the 1980s about the nature and constraints of history and narrative and about the possibilities of self-constitution. It harks back to the way Wilde experimented with time in *The Picture of Dorian Gray* and how, in prison, he pondered his existence beyond the law.

Space and Flowers

I have suggested already that both Wilde and Jarman communicate a sense of exclusion and that both of them look to nature to an extent to make amends. Echoing the biblical account of Christ's ordeal, Wilde writes movingly of his ejection from London: "[T]hree times have I been tried. The first time I left the box to be arrested, the second time to be led back to the House of Detention, the third time to pass into a prison for two years. Society, as we have constituted it, will have no place for me, has none to offer; but Nature, whose sweet rains fall on unjust and just alike, will have clefts in the rocks where I may hide, and secret valleys in whose silence I may weep undisturbed" (*Complete Letters*, 777–78). There is a similar trajectory in Jarman's diary. He repeatedly refers to himself being excluded in the 1980s rather as he describes being thrust into an alternative time frame by the HIV virus. He talks of being a refugee, of being exiled, of existing in no man's land, of being thrown out of the garden. But he pledges defiantly that before he finishes he will "celebrate our corner of Paradise, the part of the garden the Lord forgot to mention" (*Modern Nature*, 23). This metaphorical garden gains material substance at Prospect Cottage, and in the diary there is a palpable sense of relief when he retreats there.

There is nothing especially new about imagining a separate space to escape to or through which to conjure an alternative social structure. Utopias have a long history, and so does the appeal to nature and pastoral. But Wilde and Jarman do not merely provide two further examples of an appeal in extremis to an archetypical nature; something rather more complex and more deeply aesthetic (in the fin-de-siècle sense of the word) is going on. Theirs is not simply the bucolic English world that Martin Wiener argues lies at the heart of ideas of Englishness, a world used by John Addington Symonds, Edward Carpenter, and E. M. Forster to legitimize their queer desires and to show continuity with the natural as it enfolds them.[37] What Wilde and Jarman do instead is reinvent space and nature so that the escape is highly individualized and far from generic—indeed, it is not only an escape but also a powerful further affirmation of difference.

I have argued elsewhere that Wilde explored the shifting meanings of space, of space being aligned with the individual perspective and co-opted for an alternative lifestyle and set of values. Perception, physical context, and subjectivity become interdependent, with a change or conscious manipulation in one prompting the others to re-form. Thus, he claimed in his dialogue piece "The Decay of Lying"

Matt Cook

(1889, revised 1891) that a Japanese effect could be achieved in Piccadilly simply by steeping oneself in *Japonisme* at home (*CW*, 8:48). It is a kind of magical re-creation that allows the public spaces of the city to become private, colonized to the interior vision of the subject—an ethos that runs powerfully through *The Picture of Dorian Gray* and the ways in which the protagonist engages with London.[38] It is no different with nature. In "The Decay of Lying," Wilde's main speaker, Vivian, observes, "[W]hat is nature? Nature is no great mother who has borne us. She is our creation. It is in our brain that she quickens to life" (*CW*, 8:42). In Wilde's supposed personal use of the green carnation and in the languor of Basil Hallward's garden in the opening pages of *The Picture of Dorian Gray*, flowers and nature become malleable: they are literally and perceptually molded to the individual and his (invariably his) perspective and purpose.[39] In *De Profundis*, the redemptive nature he imagines an escape to is specifically responsive to his needs,[40] and the gardens he looks forward to seeing on leaving prison are constituted to be continuous with and also to evoke his desires. The latter are sensually rich and have the same kind of heady exoticism as Hallward's garden, described in terms that echo Enobarbus's famous speech on Cleopatra's seduction of Antony in Shakespeare's play—one of Wilde's favorite passages.[41] Desire, seduction, and epic love are thus drawn together in his imagined postprison retreat into sumptuous nature. "I tremble with pleasure," he writes, "when I think that on the very day of my leaving prison both the laburnum and the lilac will be blooming in the gardens, and that I shall see the wind stir into restless beauty the swaying gold of the one, and make the other toss the place purple of its plumes so that all the air will be Arabia for me. . . . I know that for me, to whom flowers are part of desire, there are tears waiting in the petals of the rose" (*Complete Letters*, 777).

Writing almost a century later, Jarman uses similar imaginative structures to create and re-create his world in his diaries. While his father would attack "anything that became too luxurious" in their family garden, he took inspiration from his Uncle Teddy, who preferred "to push horticulture to its tropical extreme" (*Modern Nature*, 28). He remembers being given a bunch of arum lilies as a boy: "I worshipped those arums," he says; they were "a symbol of my obsession with flowers: glossy, exotic, *fin de siècle*. Dad, I know would have preferred a brace of pistols" (*Modern Nature*, 28). Just as Bartlett seized on the exuberant floristry associated with Wilde, J.-K. Huysmans, and the fin de siècle in *Who Was That Man?* so too does Jarman attest to their symbolic significance. In his garden and his love of exotic flowers and their associations, he finds, like the others, a resonance with his desires, a kind of emotional fecundity and a means of memorialization.

Although the gardens and spaces of nature that Wilde imagines in *De Profundis* are largely symbolic and metaphorical, the ones in Jarman's world have material existence. He takes the reader first to Hampstead Heath in North London, a part of which is a well-known cruising ground. Although Jarman acknowledges that the heath sometimes drew both queer-bashers and the police (*Modern Nature,* 83), he also conjures it as a permissive, magical, and transformative space in his diary. As he enters it, he says, he crosses "the invisible border [where] your heart beats faster and the world seems a better place" (*Modern Nature,* 84). Jarman relishes the insistent queer colonization of the area. He loves its difference—the sex, the fleeting conversations, the shared unspoken knowledge, and the sense of community, however tenuous: "In the dark for one brief moment age, class, wealth, all the barriers of class, are down. An illusion you say, I know but a sweet one" (*Modern Nature,* 84). On the heath, Jarman can, in Andrew Moor's words, celebrate the "nocturnal homosexual subculture as one of magical potential,"[42] linking to Jarman's keen interest in Renaissance alchemy and magic[43] (and, I would add, Wilde's aesthetic transformations). Framed in this way, nature is both malleable and multiple, and it allows Jarman to reconnect with Eden: "[T]he alfresco fuck," he writes, "is the original fuck. . . . [S]ex on the heath is an idyll pre-fall" (*Modern Nature,* 84).

There was serious debate about whether to include these sections about Hampstead Heath in the published diary, not only because of wider sensibilities[44] but also perhaps to keep the place obscure, a place to go Bunburying,[45] and so maintain what Oliver S. Buckton describes as "the potent erotic and aesthetic pleasures of secrecy itself."[46] But Jarman went ahead in publishing these passages, and I think this decision was partly because the heath represented the opportunity to insist on the continued erotic pleasures of gay life in the age of AIDS and also to attest to a putative cultural, sexual, and subjective distinctiveness beyond the orthodoxies of what Jarman angrily refers to as "heterosoc" (*At Your Own Risk,* 69). Wilde's redemptive nature is less defiant but is no less expressive of distance and difference from "Society as we have constituted it" (Wilde, *Complete Letters,* 777–78).

This sense of difference becomes even more pronounced in Jarman's diaries as he describes his visits to and work on his garden at Prospect Cottage. He plants the garden in inhospitable ground—indeed, he at first believed it would be an

Matt Cook

impossibility ("the shingles preclude a garden," he wrote sadly in an unpublished section of his diary).[47] What results in the stark landscape of Dungeness is thus all the more remarkable. He worked found objects into the beds and among the flowers to make circles—prehistoric, magical—stretching out from his home; there is no boundary to show where it begins and ends. O'Quin describes it as "a sacred sodomitical space,"[48] gathering memories of other gardens, other men, and what Jarman describes as his "frosted generation" into a unique and modern nature. Jarman writes in another unpublished diary section, "We must fight fears that threaten our garden, for make no mistake, ours is the garden of the poets, of William Shakespeare's sonnets, of Marlowe, of Plato and Wilde, all those who worked and suffered to keep it watered."[49] O'Quin shows how Jarman in his diary evokes Eden, Gethsemane, the decadent Borghese gardens, and the nearby Sissinghurst of Vita Sackville-West to construct the garden at Prospect as a shadow Eden. In this way, it gains its own sanctity; there, on 22 September 1991, Jarman was indeed canonized as "saint Derek of Dungeness of the Order of the Celluloid Nights" by the London chapter of the Sisters of Perpetual Indulgence. The canonization was continuous with his sense of the importance of retaining and building a distinctive queer sense of the mythological and sacred in the drive to preserve a sense of self, community, and belonging.

In *De Profundis*, Wilde describes reading the Gospels in ancient Greek in prison, and he likens this return to the Greek to be like "going into a garden of lilies out of some narrow and dark house" (*Complete Letters*, 748). Wilde here cogently brings together an ancient script, his biblical scholarship, and a redemptive opening out of space. He returns repeatedly to such gardens, and these become part of his production and understanding of the sacred: the production of an aestheticized Christ and of himself as Christ-like. These sacred figures and gardens take him, as they later took Jarman, beyond the march of time and into a redemptive and affirmative—rather than a censorious—space.

Wilde, Jarman, and "The Return of Affect"

Both Wilde and Jarman—middle-class, highly and classically educated, Londoners for much of their lives, and also artists in the public eye—drew on remarkably similar icons and images and spatial and temporal strategies to create structures of survival and endurance—in other words, to etch out a presence and a distinctiveness for the outlaw and for vilified desires and behavior.[50] Their skill was not in simply refusing a domineering culture but in co-opting and reinflecting hegemonic forms and structures to insist on their own place in a symbolic and sacred order.[51] Flowers, gardens, diaries, letters, art, theology, history—these were all for Jarman and Wilde a means of cleaving space and time, of exploring another way of doing things and (in Jarman's words) of "writing of sad times as a witness" (*At Your Own Risk,* 119).

"Steps forward," Jarman wrote in his diary on 26 July 1991, "came by the example of our lives, one David Hockney in 1960 was worth more than the 1967 act [which legalized sex between two civilian males over twenty-one years of age in private] and did more to change lives. The aim is to open up discourse and with it broaden our horizons; that can't be legislated for" (*Smiling in Slow Motion,* 43). It is a statement that feels very much of its artistic, cultural, and theoretical moment, and this idea of utilizing cultural resources or opening them out for self-constitution in part accounts for the changing ways in which Wilde was being marshaled to a sense of queer identity and an urgent radicalism. This radicalism, as Bartlett points out, is one that Wilde did not, could not, share in the same way,[52] but that does not prevent him from being commandeered for the purpose by Bartlett, McKenna, Jarman, and others in their work and protests.

What I am trying to pinpoint here is something both more and less than Wilde's influence on later gay artists. The idea of influence suggests a direct and acknowledged effect, yet Jarman mentions Wilde less than other artists and writers such as David Hockney, Pier Paolo Pasolini, Andy Warhol, Carlo Ginsburg, and William Burroughs. The word *influence* also rather misses or neglects the frisson of empathy and connection, those resonant bonds between contemporaries and figures across time that are often unformalized by conventional ties and are often unseen by the historian and critic. Such bonds are nevertheless pivotal to the way in which we think about ourselves and others and are the kinds of connection with the past that Edmund White pinpoints beautifully in his comment on the cover of *Who Was That Man?* Bartlett, White says, "has grabbed history by the throat and made bitter love to it." There is a similar sense of a profound affective relationship with the past in Jarman's description of holding hands in grief in his garden with dead friends (his personal history) and, further, with "the forgotten generations . . . who died so silently . . . quietly protesting their innocence" (*Modern Nature,* 69). To acknowledge such "bitter love making" and such hand holding is to begin to key into the complex range of emotion in male-male relations, which, as David M. Halperin suggests, takes the history of (homo)sexuality beyond being an analysis only of sex and sexual relations.[53]

I am not trying to suggest some sort of essentialist gay aesthetic here, any more than I am trying to collapse the experiences of two very different men, but I am contemplating how time, memory, and heritage can work in the way we think about identity and subjectivity. Although a fairly uniform image of homosexuality was pedaled in the press in the later 1980s, Jarman saw multiple points of difference within his so-called community at that time. He was stunned by statistics that suggested that 50 percent of gay men might vote again for Thatcher, and he was appalled at the actor Ian McKellen's accepting a knighthood alongside the homophobic police chief James Anderton.[54] Many gay men were uninterested in Wilde—he comes up only sporadically in the testimonies gathered in the Hall-Carpenter oral history project in the 1980s and early 1990s—and were equally sanguine about Jarman. Many others were too immersed (for Jarman's own liking) in a consumerist gay culture. Jarman certainly had comrades and deep friendships in the present and was very much part of his artistic generation. But he also looked to the past for emotional, artistic, and political sustenance. His work, to use David van Leer's words (writing in a different context), "challenges our everyday vocabulary of sameness" while also opening out the "terms for [expressing and experiencing] difference" that can be found across time and between eras.[55] We begin to conceptualize, then, what Barbara H. Rosenwein describes as "emotional communities" not only in a series of different contexts in the present but also with the past:[56] in other words, with the personal past (as Jarman does in his memorialization of his lost friends) and with other histories—of Edward II, Shakespeare, the Renaissance, Wilde and the Victorian fin de siècle—all of which carried for him an intense emotional freight.

Halperin makes a compelling argument about the use of emotion in the making and utilization of the queer past. He suggests that emotion enabled and limited understandings of that past. Grief and anger—felt and expressed intensely by Jarman—gave urgency to the reclamation of the queer past but also narrowed the kinds of history that felt useful or even possible. Other emotions, and other emotive connections with the past, were not so politically acceptable, argues Halperin: "Bad gay emotions . ... included narcissism, shame, self-loathing, passivity, sentimentality, cowardice."[57] Unlike grief and anger, these emotions seemed to express weakness rather than a sense of collective devastation: "[T]hey even in the 1980s implied pathology, the lingering effects of oppression from which we had insufficiently liberated ourselves" (Halperin, *Among Men*, 4). Thus while George Rousseau argues that the history of depression is crucial to understanding the queer past and figures in that past,[58] this was not a history that was seen as expedient to explore in the 1980s. It was certainly not a history that Jarman engaged with in his exploration of history and literature or in the manners in which he described himself. The depths of Jarman's despair emerge more fully in Peake's biography and in the unpublished diaries than in anything Jarman chose to publish.

Will Self, who wrote *Dorian* just ten years after Jarman died, constructs an account of the 1980s that is fired by different emotional imperatives, and he deploys Wilde in more nihilistic, less redemptive ways than I have suggested Jarman did. Contextualizing uses of Wilde not only in their social and cultural moment but also for their emotional import (the need to affirm and to endure, for example) might thus help us to grasp more fully the richness of what Wilde provided for a century of gay men. Meanwhile, looking at 1980s and 1990s appropriations of Wilde and the fin de siècle might give us different kinds of access into gay men's lives and provide fresh perspectives on the tangled intersection of emotion and subjectivity at particular moments in the past.

Notes

I am extremely grateful to Chris Waters for his comments on an early draft of this chapter.

1. Had it appeared during these crisis years, Will Self's novel would surely have been greeted with a measure of outrage from gay and AIDS groups similar to that exhibited toward Rupert Haselden's similarly fatalistic "Gay Abandon" piece for the London *Guardian,* published on 7 September 1991, 11.

2. For a sensitive account of the different approaches to Wilde in the twentieth century—and this upsurge of interest in the 1980s—see the final chapter of John Sloan, *Authors in Context: Oscar Wilde* (Oxford: Oxford University Press, 2003), 168–82.

3. Leslie J. Moran, "'Oscar Wilde': Law, Memory and the Proper Name," in *Legal Queries: Lesbian, Gay and Transgender Legal Studies,* ed. Leslie J. Moran, Daniel Monk, and Sarah Beresford (London: Cassell, 1998), 16. See also Lisa Duggan, "Theory in Practice: The Theory Wars or, Who's Afraid of Judith Butler?" *Journal of Women's History* 10 (1998): 16.

4. See, for example, Ed Cohen, *Talk on the Wilde Side: Towards a Genealogy of a Discourse on Male Sexualities* (London: Routledge, 1993); Jonathan Dollimore, *Sexual Dissidence: Augustine to Wilde, Freud to Foucault* (Oxford: Clarendon, 1991); Alan Sinfield, *The Wilde Century: Effeminacy, Oscar Wilde, and the Queer Moment* (London: Cassell, 1994); and Joseph Bristow, *Effeminate England: Homoerotic Writing after 1885* (New York: Columbia University Press, 1995).

5. Michel Foucault, Judith Butler, and Eve Kosofsky Sedgwick are indicative of, and were particularly influential in, this fresh exploration of personal reinvention and the performance of the

self. See especially Michel Foucault, *Foucault Live: Interviews, 1966–1984* (New York: Columbia University Press, 1989) and *The History of Sexuality,* vol. 1, *An Introduction,* trans. Robert Hurley (Harmondsworth: Penguin, 1990); Eve Kosofsky Sedgwick, *Epistemology of the Closet* (Berkeley: University of California Press, 1990); and Judith Butler, *Gender Trouble: Feminism and the Subversion of Identity* (London: Routledge, 1990) and *Bodies that Matter: On the Discursive Limits of Sex* (London: Routledge, 1993).

6. Chris Waters, "From Wilde to Wildeblood: Effeminacy, Extravagance, and the Making of the Modern Homosexual," unpublished paper delivered at the annual meeting of the North American Conference on British Studies, Chicago, 18 October 1996. I am very grateful to Professor Waters for loaning me a copy of this paper.

7. Waters, "From Wilde to Wildeblood."

8. For accounts of this period see, for example, Simon Shepherd and Mick Wallis, eds., *Coming on Strong: Gay Politics and Culture* (London: Unwin and Hyman, 1989); Simon Watney, *Pornography, AIDS and the Media* (London: Cassell, 1989); Jeffrey Weeks, *Sex, Politics and Society: The Regulation of Sexuality since 1800,* 2nd ed. (Harlow, UK: Longman, 1989), 292–300.

9. Tony Peake, *Derek Jarman* (London: Abacus, 2001), 357.

10. Although this has been the perception, more-recent historians have demonstrated that there was in fact often a reticence to arrest and prosecute during that period, and the legal changes were more pragmatic than has previously been suggested. See H. G. Cocks, *Nameless Offences: Homosexual Desire in the 19th Century* (London: I. B. Tauris, 2003); Matt Cook, *London and the Culture of Homosexuality, 1885–1914* (Cambridge: Cambridge University Press, 2003); and Sean Brady, *Masculinity and Male Homosexuality in Britain, 1861–1913* (Basingstoke, UK: Palgrave Macmillan, 2005).

11. Neil Bartlett, *Who Was That Man? A Present for Mr. Oscar Wilde* (London: Serpent's Tale, 1988), 30; further page references appear in parentheses.

12. See Joseph Bristow, *Effeminate England: Homoerotic Writing after 1885* (New York: Columbia University Press, 1995), 19–20.

13. Peake, *Derek Jarman,* 563n47.

14. Tara Brabazan, "At Your Own Risk: Derek Jarman and the (Semiotic) Death of a Film-Maker," *Social Semiotics* 3 (1993): 183.

15. There was an outpouring of autobiographical writing, film, and, famously, quilt making as AIDS-related illnesses took their toll. This work frequently not only interrogated the particular and individual challenges presented by HIV and AIDS but also meditated on the social positioning of those with the virus and of gay men more generally. See, for example, Oscar Moore, *PWA: Looking AIDS in the Face* (London: Picador, 1996); Paul Monnette, *Borrowed Time* (London: Collins Harvill, 1988); and David Wajnorowicz, *Close to the Knives: A Memoir of Disintegration* (London: Serpent's Tale, 1992).

16. Neil McKenna, *The Secret Life of Oscar Wilde* (London: Century, 2003), 506.

17. Peake, *Derek Jarman,* 473, 563n51.

18. Derek Jarman, *At Your Own Risk: A Saint's Testimony* (London: Vintage, 1992), 82; further page references appear in parentheses.

19. Weeks, *Sex, Politics and Society,* 283.

20. Derek Jarman, *Smiling in Slow Motion,* ed. Keith Collins (London: Century, 2000), 54; and Jarman, *Modern Nature* (London: Vintage, 1991), 78; further page references to both sources appear in parentheses.

21. Jarman, *Smiling in Slow Motion,* 93.

22. See Derek Jarman, *Dancing Ledge* (London: Quartet, 1991), 60; Jarman, *Modern Nature,* 195; Jarman, *At Your Own Risk,* 41. See also Matt Cook, "'Words Written without Any Stopping': Derek Jarman's Written Work," in *Derek Jarman: A Portrait,* ed. Roger Wollen (London: Thames and Hudson, 1996), 106; and Peake, *Derek Jarman,* 87.

23. William E. Buckler, "Oscar Wilde's Aesthetic of the Self: Self Realization in *De Profundis,*" *Biography* 12 (1989): 96.

24. Jarman, *Dancing Ledge,* 244–46. For the fuller unpublished version, see Peake, *Derek Jarman,* 282.

25. Walter Pater, conclusion to *The Renaissance: Studies in Art and Literature,* ed. Adam Phillips (Oxford: Oxford University Press, 1986), 153.

26. Wilde to Alfred Douglas, in *The Complete Letters of Oscar Wilde,* ed. Merlin Holland and Rupert Hart-Davis (London: Fourth Estate, 2000), 732. Holland and Hart-Davis note that this letter (pages 683–780 in their edition, cited in the text as *Complete Letters*) was written between January and March 1897. In 1905, Robert Ross published part of this document as *De Profundis*— the title by which it has been known ever since.

27. Regenia Gagnier, *Idylls of the Market Place: Oscar Wilde and the Victorian Public* (Stanford: Stanford University Press, 1986), 138. See also Linda Gertner Zatlin, *Beardsley, Japonisme, and the Perversion of the Victorian Ideal* (Cambridge: Cambridge University Press, 1997), 154.

28. For an extended discussion of these issues in relation to *The Picture of Dorian Gray* see Matt Cook, *London and the Culture of Homosexuality,* chapter 5.

29. Peake, *Derek Jarman,* 535. Peake also observes Jarman's repeated reworking of his account of an early sexual experience (31–32).

30. The famous phrase "The Love that dare not speak its name" first appeared in Alfred Douglas's poem "Two Loves," in John Francis Bloxam's magazine, *The Chameleon* (1894); the poem is reprinted in Brian Reade, ed., *Sexual Heretics: Male Homosexuality in English Literature from 1850 to 1900* (London: Routledge and Kegan Paul, 1970), 162.

31. Jim Ellis, "Queer Period: Derek Jarman's Renaissance," in *Out Takes: Essays on Queer Theory and Film,* ed. Ellis Hanson (Durham, NC: Duke University Press, 1999), 290.

32. Jarman, *Smiling in Slow Motion,* 324.

33. Wilde to Robert Ross, 1 April 1897, in *Complete Letters,* 780.

34. The question mark here is important. As Ian Small argues, there is considerable generic uncertainty about *De Profundis.* See Small, "Love Letter, Spiritual Autobiography or Prison Writing? Identity and Value in *De Profundis,*" in *Wilde Writings: Contextual Conditions,* ed. Joseph Bristow (Toronto: University of Toronto Press, 2003), 86–101.

35. See, for example, Jarman, *Modern Nature,* 273.

36. Daniel O'Quin, "Gardening, History and the Escape from Time: Derek Jarman's *Modern Nature,*" *October* 89 (1999): 116.

37. Martin Wiener, *English Culture and the Decline of the Industrial Spirit* (Cambridge: Cambridge University Press, 1981), 49. See also Raymond Williams, *The Country and the City* (London: Chatto and Windus, 1973), 248; Simon Schama, *Landscape and Memory* (London: HarperCollins, 1995), 181–84; and Glen Cavaliero, *The Rural Tradition in the English Novel, 1900–1939* (London: Macmillan, 1977), 3–8. On Symonds's, Carpenter's, and Forster's use of the pastoral, see Cook, *London and the Culture of Homosexuality,* 122–42.

38. Cook, *London and the Culture of Homosexuality,* 103–16.

39. The green carnation, Karl Beckson argues, has been mythologized in relation to Wilde, and there is some doubt about whether and how often he wore one and also about how firmly

it was linked specifically to homosexuality, as opposed to aestheticism and decadence more broadly. See Beckson, *The Oscar Wilde Encyclopedia* (New York: AMS Press, 1998), 122–24.

40. Wilde writes, for example, "She will hang the night with stars so that I may walk abroad in the darkness without stumbling, and send the wind over my footprints so that none may track me to my hurt" (*Complete Letters*, 778).

41. From *Antony and Cleopatra:*

> The barge she sat in, like a burnished throne,
> Burned on the water: the poop was beaten gold;
> Purple the sails and so perfumed that
> The winds were lovesick with them; the oars were silver,
> Which to the tune of flutes kept stroke and made
> The water which they beat to follow faster,
> As amorous of their strokes

William Shakespeare, *Antony and Cleopatra*, ed. John Wilders, *Arden Shakespeare* (London: Routledge, 1995), act 2, scene 2, 139–41. On Wilde's fondness for this passage, see *The Picture of Dorian Gray*, ed. Joseph Bristow, vol. 3 of *The Complete Works of Oscar Wilde* (Oxford: Oxford University Press, 2005), 393–94.

42. Andrew Moor, "Spirit and Matter: Romantic Mythologies in Derek Jarman's *Blue*," in *Territories of Desire in Queer Cinema*, ed. David Alderson and Linda Anderson (Manchester: Manchester University Press, 2000), 58.

43. See Ellis, "Queer Period," 293.

44. Peake, *Derek Jarman*, 463 and 488.

45. In Wilde's 1895 society comedy *The Importance of Being Earnest*, Algernon informs his pal Jack, "I have invented an invaluable permanent invalid called Bunbury, in order that I may be able to go down into the country whenever I choose. . . . If it wasn't for Bunbury's extraordinary bad health, for instance, I wouldn't be able to dine with you at Willis's tonight" (*CW*, 6:19–20). To some readers, Bunbury serves as an alias that provides Algernon with an excuse to enjoy otherwise prohibited (homo)sexual pleasures.

46. Oliver S. Buckton, *Secret Selves: Confession and Same-Sex Desire in Victorian Autobiography* (Chapel Hill: University of North Carolina Press, 1998), 15.

47. Quoted in Peake, *Derek Jarman*, 401.

48. O'Quin, "Gardening," 115.

49. Quoted in Peake, *Derek Jarman*, 380.

50. The phrase in the subheading for this section is taken from the title of David M. Halperin's "Among Men: History, Sexuality and Return of Affect," in *Love, Sex, Intimacy and Friendship between Men, 1550–1800*, ed. Katherine O'Donnell and Michael O'Rourke (Basingstoke: Palgrave, 2003), 1–12.

51. For more on this topic, see Cook, "Words Written."

52. Bartlett, *Who Was That Man?* xxii.

53. See Halperin, "Among Men." See also Alan Bray, *The Friend* (Chicago: University of Chicago Press, 2003).

54. See Peake, *Derek Jarman*, 464–65.

55. David Van Leer, *The Queering of America: Gay Culture in Straight Society* (New York: Routledge, 1995), 7.

56. Barbara H. Rosenwein, "Worrying about Emotions in History," *American Historical Review* 107 (2002): 842.

57. Halperin, "Among Men," 4.

58. George Rousseau, "'Homoplatonic, Homodepressed, Homomorbid': Some Further Genealogies of Same-Sex Attraction in Western Civilization," in *Love, Sex, Intimacy and Friendship between Men, 1550–1800,* ed. Katherine O'Donnell and Michael O'Rourke (Basingstoke, UK: Palgrave, 2003), 12–53.

Matt Cook

Oscar Goes to Hollywood

*Wilde, Sexuality, and the Gaze
of Contemporary Cinema*

OLIVER S. BUCKTON

IN HIS RECENT BIOGRAPHY of Oscar Wilde, Neil McKenna argues that, despite Wilde's status as an icon of homosexuality, his sexual life has frequently been misrepresented by biographers. According to McKenna, "most accounts of Oscar's life present him as predominantly heterosexual, a man whose later love of men was at best some sort of aberration, a temporary madness and, at worst, a slow-growing cancer, a terrible sexual addiction which slowly destroyed his mind and his body."[1] Wilde contributed to this perception of his homosexuality as a disease by writing to the British home secretary from Reading Gaol in July 1896 that his "offences are forms of sexual madness and are recognized as such not merely by modern pathological science but by much modern legislation" and adding that "during the entire time [the three years preceding his arrest] he was suffering from the most horrible form of erotomania, which made him forget his wife and children, his high social position in London and Paris, his European distinction as an artist, the honour of his name and family, his very humanity itself, and left him the helpless prey of the most revolting passions."[2] Despite the important pragmatic motives for this self-lacerating language—Wilde was petitioning for early release from prison—it has surely contributed to the reading of Wilde's homosexuality as an "aberration," a tragic straying from the heterosexual path on which he had been traveling.

This issue of Wilde's sexuality and its complex effect on his writing has been pivotal to the construction of Wilde as a central figure of fin-de-siècle decadence and hence to Wilde's legacy in the twentieth and twenty-first centuries. As an enduring figure in popular culture, Wilde's image has been determined by his relation to discourses of hetero- and homosexuality and the unstable relation between them. Wilde has been kept alive as a vital cultural figure by the numerous stage productions of his plays, the vast amount of scholarship on his life and work, and his iconic status in queer culture. From the outset, moreover, Wilde's "identity" as homosexual has been based on visual representation. Research on the media coverage of Wilde's trials and imprisonment has shown that his construction as a modern sexual criminal was founded on the use of Wilde as spectacle and was designed to highlight the visible legibility of his perversion. In modern culture, cinema is the medium through which popular perceptions of Wilde have been constructed and mediated for a mass audience. There have, of course, been numerous films focusing on Wilde and his work. Albert Lewin's adaptation of *The Picture of Dorian Gray* (1945) significantly diminished the homosexual references in the novel by assigning Dorian a female love object in the person of painter Basil Hallward's "niece." The adaptation of *The Importance of Being Earnest* helmed by British director Anthony Asquith (1952) was effectively a filmed version of the London stage production with which it shared several cast members. A decade later, two films were released that focused on Wilde's trials: *The Trials of Oscar Wilde,* aka *The Man with the Green Carnation* (directed by Ken Hughes, 1960), starring Peter Finch in the title role; and *Oscar Wilde* (directed by Gregory Ratoff, 1960), starring Robert Morley as the main protagonist.[3]

There have been more recent representations of Oscar Wilde in *Wilde* (directed by Brian Gilbert, 1997) and *The Importance of Being Earnest* (directed by Oliver Parker, 2002), which reflect the construction of Wilde as spectacle in contemporary cinema. To what extent do these recent representations of Wilde in film reinforce the cultural perception of Wilde as a predominantly heterosexual artist led astray by the "dangerous" temptation of homosexuality? Given the changes in legal and social attitudes toward homosexuality since Wilde's conviction, can Wilde's same-sex desire be at once recognized and affirmed by the gaze of contemporary cinema?[4] Examination of the film *Wilde*—which is based on Richard Ellmann's 1987 biography—and the recent film version of *Earnest* (which

Oliver S. Buckton

follows Oliver Parker's earlier adaptation of *An Ideal Husband* [1999]) suggests that there is an uneasy and at times covert collusion between the gaze of the modern cinema and the panoptic, punitive gaze of Victorian law and society that sought to imprison Wilde within the grid of sexual perversion.

The Birth of the Queer Author

As those who are familiar with Wilde's life and with the history of late-Victorian sexualities know, something changed dramatically in the year of 1895. The opening night of *The Importance of Being Earnest,* on 14 February that year, represents the crowning achievement of Wilde's career as a dramatist and, arguably, of late-Victorian theater. Yet in the course of a few weeks, Wilde would become embroiled in a scandal that would end his career and land him in prison. After receiving the insulting visiting-card from the Marquess of Queensberry—a card that, ironically, would accuse Wilde of a kind of "acting" by "posing as somdomite" [*sic*]—Wilde began libel proceedings against him. In April 1895, Wilde was charged with criminal acts and by the end of May would be convicted of "gross indecency" (under the Criminal Law Amendment Act of 1885) and sentenced to two years in prison with hard labor. This sentence, which brought to an abrupt end Wilde's domination of the Victorian stage—his two plays, *Earnest* and *An Ideal Husband,* were both enjoying successful runs in the West End at the time of his arrest—also radically disrupted Wilde's making of sentences, transforming his writing generically from the public stage to the private letter, culminating in the 1897 letter to Lord Alfred Douglas that became known, following its partial publication in 1905, as *De Profundis* (from the depths).

Wilde's conviction for gross indecency in 1895 produced another, unintended effect. It created the figure of the modern homosexual, the figure that for Michel Foucault became a "species" that displaced the "temporary aberration" of the sodomite. Born out of multiple, conflicting representations and identifications —the aesthete, the dandy, the decadent, the pervert—the homosexual was at once a product of legal prohibition, sexual dissidence, individual style, and popular representation.[5] As Joseph Bristow argues, "Wilde was indisputably a pathological figure.... But this *image* of the perverted homosexual—when both words gained their pathological inflections—only emerged once the trials had run their course."[6] Moreover, as Alan Sinfield has argued, Wilde's conviction for "gross indecency" brought ineluctable sexual significance to a range of signifying practices such as "effeminacy" that "might be attached to any deviant perspective"; yet "there is no reason to suppose that Wilde either envisaged or would have wanted, a distinctively queer identity."[7]

As Ed Cohen has argued, Wilde's arrest and trials were accompanied by and reported in a series of graphic representations in newspapers that "designated Wilde as a kind of sexual actor without explicitly referring to the specificity of his sexual acts, and thereby crystallized a new constellation of sexual meanings predicated upon 'personality' and not practices."[8] Cohen observes that the visual images of Wilde served to contrast him with the norm of masculine sexuality, citing a report in the *Star* that described Wilde's "old pose with arms folded on the dock front . . . his hands limply crossed and drooping or clasped around his brown suede gloves."[9] In the courtroom, Wilde was the focus of the public gaze and played to the crowd with his defense of "the Love that dare not speak its name" and spirited banter with Edward Carson, the prosecuting counsel.[10]

Yet even when Wilde was removed from the public stage and held in prison, the exploitation of him as a spectacle had not ended, and he was not safe from the gaze of a hostile public. In his earlier public appearances—such as his curtain call on stage following the opening night of *Lady Windermere's Fan* (1892) in which he congratulated the audience "on the *great* success of your performance, which persuades me that you think *almost* as highly of the play as I do myself"[11]— or at times in court, Wilde was in control of his persona, defined by his witty speeches. Following his imprisonment, by contrast, Wilde was compelled to enact a degraded role that had been constructed for him. As he writes Douglas from prison, "Twice in my public appearances at the Bankruptcy Court, twice again in my public transferences from one prison to another, have I been shown under conditions of unspeakable humiliation to the gaze and mockery of men" (*Complete Letters*, 727). Wilde narrates one of these traumatic accounts of public exposure later in the letter to Douglas, in a passage that emerges like a repressed visual memory, a nightmarish illustration of the point that "[w]e are clowns whose hearts are broken" (756):

> On November 13th 1895 I was brought down here from London. From two o'clock till half-past two on that day I had to stand on the centre platform of Clapham Junction in convict dress and handcuffed, for the world to look at. I had been taken out of the Hospital Ward without a moment's notice being given to me. Of all possible objects I was the most grotesque. When people

Oliver S. Buckton

saw me they laughed. Each train as it came up swelled the audience. Nothing could exceed their amusement. That was of course before they knew who I was. As soon as they had been informed, they laughed still more. For half an hour I stood there in the grey November rain surrounded by a jeering mob. For a year after that was done to me I wept every day at the same hour and for the same space of time. (*Complete Letters*, 756–57)

This passage is significant for the construction of Wilde as an object for the "amusement" of an "audience." In this regard, it is relevant for the cultural production of Wilde as spectacle in the cinematic apparatus. First, the public reaction to the spectacle is not initially determined by, or even connected to, Wilde's homosexuality. Rather, it is produced by the "grotesque" appearance of the prisoner "in convict dress and handcuffed." In a sense, the subsequent recognition of Wilde by the mob makes no difference, as they merely "laughed still more." Intriguingly, the revelation of Wilde's identity as sexual criminal provokes not hostile actions or violence but further laughter: rather, one might say that the form taken by public hostility is that of laughter, the malevolence of the public amusement being reflected in the phrase "a jeering mob." Wilde's reference to the crowd's discovery of "who I was" is ambivalent, for he recognizes that his identity as a famous author is ruined and that he is now labeled as sexual pervert and criminal. The removal of Wilde's name from the London theaters was symptomatic of the view that "Oscar and everything that he represented must be done away with," and his past-tense reference to "who I *was*" (emphasis added) suggests that he viewed himself as having become coterminous with the homosexual, as the homosexual image becomes a fixed position in a representational system of sexual difference.[12] The key to Wilde's anguish is his exposure to the public gaze, as he later wrote to the home secretary, describing himself in the third person: "The ordeal he underwent in being brought in convict dress and handcuffed by a mid-day train from Clapham Junction to Reading was so utterly distressing, from the mental no less than the emotional point of view, that he feels quite unable to undergo any similar exhibition to public gaze" (*Complete Letters*, 803). Wilde's recognition that he has become a kind of "exhibition," an object intended for display before the "public gaze," presents him as a kind of cautionary figure on the stage (of which the train platform is an example) whose function is both to amuse and to warn the audience. At the moment when Wilde's career as a playwright comes to an end, therefore, his new identity as a sexual criminal begins.

Wilde's conviction, and the use made of his writings in the trials, illustrates the sense of deep personal history and reference that helps to define what Roland Barthes calls "The Author" who "when believed in, is always conceived of as the past of his own book. . . . The Author is thought to nourish the book, which is to say that he exists before it, thinks, suffers, lives for it."[13] Paradoxically, the very practice of "reading" Wilde's life through his works that established him as author also resulted in his "death" as author. As Barthes explains, "The *explanation* of a work is always sought in the man or woman who produced it, as if it were always in the end, through the more or less transparent allegory of the fiction, the voice of a single person, the *author* 'confiding' in us" (143; original emphasis). One detects in Barthes's words an echo of Wilde's character Basil Hallward, from *The Picture of Dorian Gray* (1890, revised 1891): "I will not bare my soul to their shallow, prying eyes. My heart shall never be put under their microscope. . . . An artist should create beautiful things, but should put nothing of his own life into them. We live in an age when men treat art as if it were meant to be a form of autobiography" (*CW*, 12:17–18). Basil's objection to scrutiny of his art by the public also anticipates Wilde's agonized self-consciousness under the gaze of the crowd. Yet the strategy of reading Wilde's art as autobiography, of scrutinizing his life—specifically, his sexuality—for the explanation of his work, did not consolidate his role as author but brought about its destruction, his "removal," described by Barthes as "the Author diminishing like a figurine at the far end of the literary stage" (145). The death of Wilde as author is coterminous with his banishment from the stage—both the London theater and the literary stage more broadly.

Wilde on Screen

Even as Wilde's career as a playwright was ending, the stage was on the brink of being superseded by a new form of spectacle for public entertainment. According to Stephen Heath, "Something changes between 22 March and 28 December 1895. Between the scientific and industrial presentation (the first Lumière demonstration of the cinématographe . . .) and the start of commercial exploitation (the first public performance in the Grand Café), the screen is fixed in what will come to be its definitive place. The spectators are no longer set on either side of a translucent screen but have been assigned their position in front of the image which unrolls before them—*cinema* begins."[14] This "fixing" both of the screen

Oliver S. Buckton

and of the position of the spectators who watch it brought to an end the golden era of theatrical representation, in that the cinema "cuts off the spectator from production, from performance" (9). The apparently limitless representational possibilities of the cinematic apparatus provide its chief advantage over the stage production, for "where the stage has 'wings,' fixed limits, the screen . . . is said to be lacking in any frame, to know only the implied continuation of the reality of the image" (11). If, as Barthes argues, "the birth of the reader must be at the cost of the death of the author"(148), then, equally, the death of theater may be said to result from the birth of the cinema, with "the public screened from production, fixed in the image" (*Questions of Cinema,* 9).

Wilde's rebirth on the cinematic screen has been a reincarnation (or "afterlife") that tends to eviscerate Wilde's status as author while reproducing him as spectacle for popular consumption. This reinvention of Wilde as the object of the cinematic gaze is closely tied to construction of him as a spectacle during the trials and, in this way, is implicated in the punitive definition of Wilde as sexual Other. Significantly, the representation of Wilde's homosexuality in this cinematic rebirth is paradoxical. On the one hand, Wilde is foregrounded as a heterosexual who has fallen victim to the temptations of same-sex desire. On the other hand, the traces of homoeroticism are deleted from the film versions of Wilde's plays, indicating that the work is primarily heterosexual in focus. The connective link between Wilde and his work that had been used to incriminate him—in Barthes's terms, "the claim to decipher a text" in a way that is "tyrannically centered on the author, his person, his life, his tastes, his passions" (143)—is dissolved in the attempt to salvage Wilde's life and work for consumption by the popular gaze of contemporary cinema.

A hundred years after Wilde's release from prison in 1897, Wilde's career and downfall would again become the subject of cinematic spectacle, with the release of *Wilde,* the powerful film based on Richard Ellmann's 1987 biography, directed by Brian Gilbert (who had previously directed *Tom and Viv,* another adaptation of a famous literary love life) and produced by Marc Samuelson and Peter Samuelson. A Samuelson Production, sold to Sony Classics in the United States and to the British Broadcasting Corporation, Sky and Polygram in the United Kingdom, *Wilde* attracted generally favorable critical reviews. Especially praised was the performance of British actor Stephen Fry in the title role: as Alexander Walker wrote in London's *Evening Standard,* "Fry's presence is monumental . . . a credible combination of physical strength and moral weakness, he is recognizably a man of the period and carries total conviction."[15] Meanwhile, Steve Grant wrote in London's well-known events listing magazine, *Time Out*, "If anybody was born to play Oscar Wilde, it must have been Stephen Fry. . . . As Wilde, descending from would-be doting father to follower of his own 'nature' and finally ruined and disgraced martyr on the tree of English hypocrisy, Fry is utterly convincing."[16] The film presented the first feature-length cinematic treatment of Wilde's life in almost forty years; its release was soon followed by cinematic adaptations of Wilde's final two plays, *An Ideal Husband* (1999) and *The Importance of Being Earnest* (2002), both directed by Oliver Parker. Within a few short years, then, Oscar Wilde—who had been largely absent from the big screen for a generation—was catapulted to cinematic prominence.[17]

This recent renewal of cinematic attention to—and, by extension, popular interest in—Wilde and his work is of cultural and ideological significance, for these recent films are by no means minor or small-scale productions: they feature some of the leading artistic and creative talents of the English-speaking world, including Stephen Fry, Julian Mitchell (screenwriter), Brian Gilbert (director), Marc and Peter Samuelson (producers), Rupert Everett, Cate Blanchett, Colin Firth, Jude Law, Judi Dench, Tom Wilkinson, and Vanessa Redgrave. While obviously not produced as blockbusters, these films are clearly designed for and marketed to a popular, mainstream audience and have achieved respectable results at the box office. As the producer of *Wilde* states, "[F]or its budget and within its context the film has been enormously successful."[18] Taken together, the films provide evidence of the ongoing fascination with Wilde as a historical figure, especially with the scandal surrounding his 1895 conviction for "gross indecency," as it was legally termed at the time. Certain cultural forces—perhaps most significantly an increased tolerance for and media representation of homosexuality—are of course influential in this resurgence of attention to Wilde. In the runaway success of American cable shows such as *Queer as Folk* and *Queer Eye for the Straight Guy*, we have examples of the new visibility of queer culture and style in the popular media: a visibility, however, that arguably reinforces as many stereotypes as it challenges.

Given the frankness with which *Wilde* represents the homosexual activity of Oscar and others, a climate of relative tolerance for homosexuality was certainly a condition of its production and release, at least by a major company such as Sony Pictures. Even so, producer Marc Samuelson has addressed the difficulty of raising the finances, based on the script: "I'm absolutely sure that a number

Oliver S. Buckton

of people couldn't get their heads around the subject matter, who felt somehow that this was distasteful or found it difficult. . . . [I]t went beyond any simple question of commerciality or the quality of the screenplay."[19] There are other cultural indicators of increased popular interest in Wilde: the steady stream of biographies, one recent example of which (Neil McKenna's *Secret Life of Oscar Wilde*) offers new arguments for the centrality of sexuality to Wilde's life; new editions of his works (such as Joseph Bristow's definitive Oxford variorum edition of *The Picture of Dorian Gray*); and a new edition of his *Complete Letters*, published in 2000. Yet cinema has a popular reach and cultural impact that is unmatched by any of these publishing ventures, and as such it is at once more reflective of and influential on current cultural trends and popular attitudes to Wilde. Hence, I explore the representations of Wilde and his works from a specific perspective: the ways in which these films adapt, modify, and challenge the myths and stereotypes of Oscar Wilde, as they have evolved in the century since his death. Obviously, Wilde's scandalous sexuality is a central part of this myth—his name became synonymous with the homosexual for the first part of the twentieth century, as reflected in E. M. Forster's *Maurice* (written in 1913–14 but not published until 1971), in which the title character, wracked by guilt over his homosexuality, describes himself as "an unspeakable of the Oscar Wilde sort."[20]

In the cultural context, the myth of Wilde might be summed up, at the risk of oversimplification, that he was first and foremost a homosexual, who happened also to be a writer of plays.[21] In terms of literary production, Wilde's prominence as a dramatist has long overshadowed his achievements in other genres, such as the critical essay and the short story. As Josephine M. Guy and Ian Small observe, "[I]t is no accident that it is Wilde's later works, particularly the Society Comedies . . . which have received the closest scrutiny from critics interested in his writing career."[22] They identify "the usual reading of Wilde's life as a writer" as consisting of "two distinct stages": the first one of "relative failure . . . the second as a short five-year burst of success" (15).

Other components of the popular myth of Wilde include Wilde the "wit" (evidenced by volumes of Wildean wit available in the bookstores) and Wilde the "aesthete" and "dandy"—complete with images of shoulder-length hair, green carnations, velvet jacket, and knee-length breeches. Ellen Moers has traced the evolution of Wilde's dress from the Oxford undergraduate's "tiny bowler hats . . . bright tweeds and loud checks patterned uniformly over coat, trousers and waistcoats" to the full regalia of the "Professor of Aesthetics": "the knee breeches, drooping lily, flowing green tie, velvet coat, and wide, turned-down collar."[23] Yet as Moers observes, Wilde's costume became more conservative with his rise to prominence in the 1890s: "when the success of his plays brought him a wide and deserved fame . . . Wilde's dress became coldly and formally correct. He was content to express his individuality . . . with a single detail: a green boutonniere, a bright red waistcoat or a turquoise and diamond stud" (299).

Though such aspects of the popular representation of Wilde relate to fashion in the sartorial sense, I am examining how cinematic representation might *fashion* Wilde in the sense of "make, create, form, mould" (*OED*) his image and work. I consider this process as a "re-making" insofar as it alters or challenges perceptions or portrayals of Wilde that have become widespread and dominant. I would note, however, that the transforming connotation is already present within an earlier sense of the word *fashion*, meaning "change the fashion of; modify, transform" (*OED*). Crucially, all of these characteristics of Wilde and the myth they help to produce are attributed to his sexual identity. That is, all of the signs of Wilde's departure from Victorian middle-class masculine norms are condensed into a single all-embracing claim: that Wilde was a homosexual and therefore inevitably (yet also inscrutably) at odds with his society.

The majority of my discussion focuses on *Wilde,* although I shall be referring at less length to *Earnest.* Ultimately, neither of these films contests the highlighting of the latter years of Wilde's career; indeed, they reinforce the popular perception of Wilde as the successful dramatist who sprung into being in 1892 and came crashing down in 1895, overlooking ways in which Wilde's most famous plays drew on and recycled elements from his earlier, less renowned work. This emphasis is particularly significant in *Wilde,* because it is established generically as a biographical film that claims to narrate the story of Wilde's entire career.

Wilde

With its opening scene, *Wilde* declares its departure from popular stereotypes about Wilde, especially concerning his effeminacy, urbane wit, and aesthetic milieu. A viewer who had purchased a ticket to watch *Wilde* and arrived at the cinema during this scene might suspect that she had entered the wrong theater. In this scene, a posse of men on horseback ride across a mountainous, craggy landscape identified as "Leadville, Colorado 1882." They are watched by several men in the hills, one of whom shouts to a group gathered near a settlement of huts and tents, "He's coming." There follows a shot of a party approaching on horse-back, the central member of which dismounts and is welcomed to the Matchless Silver Mines (fig. 29). This man is then introduced to the large group of miners as "Oscar Wilde." This visit to Colorado formed part of Oscar Wilde's year-long lecture tour of the United States, in which he promulgated the values of aestheticism. Wilde is dressed elegantly, as the familiar dandy from London and Oxford, but appears in this unfamiliar context more like a flamboyant cowboy than a well-dressed man of letters. Wilde is then lowered by a winch system into the silver mine, with a troubled expression on his face as he looks up to the sky (fig. 30). This descent directly foreshadows his plunge into the dark world of imprisonment after his trials, where he would again be confined with men who were manual laborers; deprived of light and space; and removed from his famil-iar, comfortable world. The scene is paralleled in reverse by a later one in which Wilde is led upstairs from the cells before his sentencing and conviction, then led through a hostile waiting crowd.

Generically, the opening scene evokes the Western—the popular imaginary of the Wild (not Wilde) West—with its upbeat soundtrack of sweeping strings, its Panavision-esque landscapes of the Rocky Mountains, and its group of riding cowboys. This generic code is confirmed by the whooping and the gunshots that greet Wilde's arrival, as though he were the hero (Wilde Bill?) come to protect the community against the "bad guys." After he has been lowered into the mine, Wilde addresses a group of miners, lecturing them in this subterranean setting on the Italian Renaissance silversmith Benvenuto Cellini, as though they were Oxford undergraduates or polite members of London Society: here the nature of Wilde's interests—arts and crafts and Renaissance history (he refers to Cellini as "a Renaissance man")—conforms more to his image as cultured aesthete. But the question posed by one of the young miners when informed that Cellini is dead—"Who shot him?"—returns us to the Western's familiar conventions of fast shooting and vigilante violence. The jarring between such conventions and Wilde's cultured aestheticism makes the moment humorously effective.

Part of the impact of this opening is its discrepancy with what Hans Robert Jauss has influentially called the "horizon of expectations" surrounding a cultural figure such as Wilde.[24] The Western is a conventionally masculine genre, featuring tough heroes, violence, clear-cut moral oppositions, and aggressive physical action in the great outdoors. Wilde, by contrast, is typically associated with the arts, urban and intellectual centers (Oxford and London), moral ambiguity, interior/domestic

Figure 29. Wilde on horseback at the Matchless Silver Mines, Colorado. From *Wilde* (dir. Brian Gilbert, 1997). Courtesy of Sony Pictures Classics.

Figure 30. Wilde being lowered into Colorado silver mine. From *Wilde* (dir. Brian Gilbert, 1997). Courtesy of Sony Pictures Classics.

spaces, and femininity. The man's world of the Wild West does not seem an obvious context for the editor of the *Woman's World*.[25] Yet this is part of the manipulation of genre by which the film refashions Wilde, presenting him in unfamiliar or contradictory contexts, invoking conventions that suggest an aggressive, indeed violent masculinity, while also showcasing Wilde's cultivated aestheticism and hinting at his same-sex desire. Hence, the presence of Wilde in this context refashions the genre of the Western, unmasking its thinly veiled homoeroticism, displaying the ease with which aggression and violence blend into masculine desire and erotic tension.[26] Wilde is clearly impressed with the physical beauty of the young miners (is there a play on "minors," given Wilde's later sexual association with young men?) who greet him (he says, "I thought I was descending into hell, but with these angel faces to greet me, I must be in paradise"); he then gazes longingly at the young, handsome, bare-chested miner who fills his cup with whisky. Yet the same young man into whose eyes Wilde gazes then asks, "Who shot him?" The film suggests, at this early stage, a link between male beauty and fatality that will dominate the narrative.

Although the opening of *Wilde* homoeroticizes the Western, it also masculinizes the aesthete. The scene reminds us that Oscar Wilde was a physically imposing (six feet, four inches tall), heavily built man who looks most formidable on horseback. Moreover, these images prepare us for a later scene in which Wilde, incensed by the Marquess of Queensberry's bullying intrusion into his home, confronts his antagonist verbally, then marches up to Queensberry and breaks the marquess's (implicitly phallic) staff in two: a gesture of physical self-assertion that explicitly challenges the popular image of a passive, effeminate Wilde. The Western opening also reminds us that Wilde was indeed—or would become—an outlaw, defined as a criminal for his sexual persona, occupying the margins (or frontier) of civilization, and destroyed by a system of justice no less brutal than the vigilante violence of the cowboy. The film's skillful play with generic convention and its defiance of expectations—even the Beardsley-esque titles and graphics during the credit sequence seem to jar with the Wild West landscape—raise provocative and timely questions about the ways in which Wilde has been constructed by previous representations of him.[27] In doing so, the film makes a serious point: Wilde was always outside respectable English society. In this sense, he did belong in the Wild West, where social (and perhaps sexual) transgressions were more tolerated, where masculine desire was expressed more openly and freely than in the drawing rooms of Victorian society. Yet this circumvention of expectations is short-lived, as *Wilde* soon shifts its action to the more familiar milieu of late-Victorian London. The larger part of the narrative is devoted to Wilde's literary career, with a pronounced emphasis on his work as a dramatist.

The opening of the film is captioned with the date "1882"; within twenty-three minutes of the film, the narrative has already reached the opening of Wilde's first society comedy, *Lady Windermere's Fan*, which brings us to 1892. This structure means that the first thirty-eight years of Wilde's life, including the first eleven years of his literary career—if one dates that from the publication of his first substantial book, *Poems* (1881)—is covered in a comparatively short amount of screen time. Because the film runs for 117 minutes (just short of two hours), that leaves 94 minutes, or 80 percent, of the screen time for the final eight years of Wilde's life. Wilde's publications prior to his first major dramatic success (*Lady Windermere's Fan*) are referred to only fleetingly, if at all. There is no reference to the publication of *Poems* or the controversy over his gift of the book to the Oxford Union (which rejected the gift, claiming that the poems were derivative). His fairy tales are deftly interwoven into the film by scenes of Wilde reading them to his sons, with several voice-overs of Wilde (Fry) reading the fairy tale "The Selfish Giant" (1888), but the effect of this is partly to ascribe selfishness to Wilde. *The Picture of Dorian Gray,* even though it is Wilde's most significant prose work, is dispatched by way of a brief conversation between Wilde's wife and his mother; the former worries that "hardly anyone will speak to us any more" following the publication of the controversial novel (which aroused hostility in the press), while the latter rhapsodizes about the narrative's beauty and brilliance. The interpretation is clear: Wilde was a dramatist, and all his other works led up to this period of success with the dramatic form (as Lady Wilde states, "It'll be a great success. Oscar was made for the stage").

Yet if his other nondramatic writings are marginalized by *Wilde*, it would be more accurate to say that Wilde's entire literary career serves as a backstory to the film's chief dramatic focus: Wilde's complex relationships with Lord Alfred Douglas (nicknamed Bosie) and Douglas's father, the Marquess of Queensberry, and the trials that resulted from those relationships. Interestingly, the two previous biopics on Wilde, from 1960, both focused explicitly on the trials and conviction (one, in fact, was called *The Trials of Oscar Wilde*). The 1997 film, with its more inclusive title and its proclaimed basis in Ellmann's biography of Wilde, gestures toward a more complete or balanced portrayal of Wilde's life and work: the theatrical trailer included with the *Wilde* DVD announces that "his story

Oliver S. Buckton

has never been fully told until now" and describes the film as "the first definitive film about the extraordinary life of Oscar Wilde." Yet the film's emphasis on Bosie and the trials registers a significant (cultural) fact: the scandalous relationship and spectacular trials of Wilde for "gross indecency" remain the most compelling incidents in Wilde's life—compelling, that is, for biographer, filmmaker, and audience. Indeed, Wilde's ever-changing yet somehow always scandalous status as "homosexual"—whether as predator, victim, or martyr—is the (unspoken) reason why the film was made at all. The cultural mythology of Wilde as aesthete-homosexual—or, perhaps, that compelling mix of upper-class decadence, effeminacy, and homosexuality traced by Joseph Bristow in *Effeminate England* and Alan Sinfield in *The Wilde Century*—makes the emphasis on Wilde's final catastrophe irresistible from a storytelling point of view. So naturalized has this version of Wilde's life become (the trajectory from struggle to success to scandal) that even versions setting out to revise or challenge it end up reinforcing it. Thus, the cinematic telling of Wilde's life story is in fact always a retelling, a dramatization of a story that everyone knows already because it is part of the mythology of Wilde. The casting of a famous (in Britain) gay actor as Wilde only serves to confirm the natural status of this version, representing Wilde as always already homosexual. The director Brian Gilbert states, "Of course, the Wilde story is an incredible . . . a terrible tragedy. It's a story, on a simple level, of appalling injustice. It's a kind of injustice we've perhaps been much more aware of in the last thirty years with the rise of gay rights, but it has always been there for people of conscience." Gilbert adds, "He's had such a big impact on the way he's regarded, and there's the encrustations of myth. . . . It's part of our job to get behind the propaganda and strip away the myth." Yet Gilbert's remark occludes how film is also a technology of mythmaking, and *Wilde* reinforces and creates as many myths about Wilde as it "strips away."[28]

Hence, even in a film that represents the scene of Wilde's first homosexual affair as his seduction by teenage Robbie Ross in the Wilde home—a scene that functions as a narrative turning point, and inscribes a "before" and "after" to the homosexual coming-to-terms—Wilde can only be portrayed as always having been homosexual. The film—or perhaps the audience—is unable to imagine that Wilde *became* a homosexual, either by choice or circumstance, or that this becoming involved no invalidation of his heterosexual relationships. The essentialized view of homosexuality—as an identity defined by, and exclusively focused on, same-sex attraction or relationships—that emerged only during or after the Wilde trials (and is perhaps their most enduring effect) is portrayed as having always been present in Wilde, from the opening scene where he flirts with and gazes admiringly at the miners to the scene where Ross seduces him.

However, this assumption of Wilde having been always already homosexual renders certain aspects of the film problematic as narrative: the film clearly establishes a sequence of young, attractive men in Wilde's life, which culminates in his consuming and fatal passion for Bosie. This sequence begins with Ross's seduction of Wilde (the irony is that Ross is a friend of Wilde's wife, Constance); continues with working-class poet John Gray, whom Wilde meets at an exhibition and who provides the inspiration for Dorian Gray; and culminates with Bosie, who is presented as an incarnation of Wilde's ideal of male beauty. But this sequence of love-objects is not so clear-cut: in a scene *prior* to his affair with Ross, Wilde is hailing a cab outside a London store when he is accosted by one of the renters—a very well-dressed young male prostitute—who suggestively asks him, "Looking for someone?"[29] The camera dwells on Wilde's longing yet anxious look, then follows him as he seems to panic and abruptly walks away to find his cab. This question, "Looking for someone?" suggests that Wilde is indeed in search of visual pleasure, that he has a particular fantasy of male beauty in mind that is not satisfied and will not be until he "finds" this "someone": the scene thus prefigures his encounter with Bosie. Yet the scene strains credulity. How is it that the Wilde who is so at ease with half-naked miners in Colorado that he refers to them as "angels" and lets his gaze fall admiringly on the exposed torso of one would be so flummoxed by a proposal from an elegantly dressed male renter that he would flee? Either Wilde was always aware of his homosexuality or he was not. If he was, then the narrative trajectory of discovery (Wilde refers to it as "relief" in the scene with Ross) does not make sense. If he was not, then the opening-scene familiarity with half-naked men is incoherent. The film seems to want to tell two parallel yet conflicting stories: first, that Wilde was always homosexual and knew it, but needed encouragement to act on his desire; and second, that Wilde was unaware of his homosexuality until seduced by Ross, that he became homosexual through a variety of influences and predispositions. The combination of these narratives reflects a contradiction resulting from unresolved tension between essentialist and constructionist conceptions of homosexuality.

Presumably to add complexity to our understanding of Wilde's sexuality, the film's editing sutures the coexistence of Wilde's married/domestic life and his homosexual encounters and relationships. As Stephen Fry, who plays Wilde,

Oliver S. Buckton

comments, "one of the strengths of the film, I think, is the love that Wilde palpably shows for Constance and for his children . . . one of the greatest heartbreaks of the episode was that he never saw his children again."[30] Certainly, *Wilde* portrays its protagonist as moving almost seamlessly between his lovers and his family. In one striking transition, the scene in which Wilde is seduced by Robert Ross has the sound bridge of babies crying, which leads into a scene of Wilde parting from his wife and crying children, making his excuses ("I'll be dining late at the Asquiths"), and then to another scene of Wilde making passionate love with Ross. The juxtaposition suggests either that Wilde was bisexual, marrying and fathering children and living the life of a family man while also (concurrently) exploring his homosexuality, or that marriage and family were merely covers for a primary homosexuality that was always there, a reading that suggests "Bunburying" (the practice in *Earnest* whereby an alibi is used to excuse one from unwanted commitments). Here a dinner party is used to excuse Wilde from domestic duties in the same manner as Algy uses "Bunbury" to escape dining with his aunt; but in *Wilde,* this turns out to be a screen for his homosexual activity. The editing thus reveals the sexual transgression implied by "Bunburying," one that enables a secret life of sexual adventure. Whereas Algy may or may not have used "Bunbury" as a cover for a secret homosexual life, the film leaves no doubt that Wilde did so.[31]

In later scenes, Wilde's sexuality becomes inseparable from the representation of his trials and conviction for "gross indecency." Yet might the film's visualization of Wilde's trials and imprisonment, and the destruction of his personality (as well as his career) that it entailed, represent a continuation or repetition of that punishment? For Foucault, the modern prison emerges as a powerful institution within what he terms "disciplinary" society: powerful precisely for its capacity to extend carceral "discipline" beyond the confines of the prison. The foundation of the modern prison, and the basis of its disciplinary regime, for Foucault, is the "compulsory visibility" it enforces.[32] Inmates are always watched, their separation into "cells" both a precaution against possible resistance (no communication) and part of the individualization that takes place in prison by means of the "disciplines": the orders of knowledge (such as medicine, psychiatry, and so forth) that both classify and investigate the individual inmate, constructing him or her as a "case." Both as objects of the gaze (under the regime of Panopticism) and as objects of expertise (under the discourses of power-knowledge), prison inmates are exposed to ongoing scrutiny and control, from which there is no escape. This model of "discipline" is designed to continue beyond the prison walls, as the success of the system of Panopticism is the extent to which the prisoner internalizes the discipline and the regime of surveillance. In a powerful scene, we see how Wilde has internalized prison discipline, anticipating a scrutiny of his table-setting that is no longer taking place, illustrating the purpose of prison to instill "time-tables, compulsory movements, regular activities, solitary meditation, work in common, silence, application, respect, good habits"(*Discipline and Punish*, 128). Under this regime, "visibility is a trap" in that the surveillance, the constant visual access to and scrutiny of the prisoners, is a key part of the system of control (*Discipline and Punish*, 200).

Lee Edelman has explored the implications of this "compulsory visibility" for the emergence of the modern homosexual. In Wilde's case, of course, the prison regime of surveillance and labor coincided with his construction as homosexual —or "pervert"—in the public domain. In other words, Wilde's punishment consisted of being branded as a sexual criminal, then subjected to a constant hostile gaze from which that sexual identification became inseparable. One might argue, then, that the gaze was a form of branding, a public punishment that took control of Wilde's identity and constructed him as an object of knowledge (the scene in *De Profundis* in which he is exposed to public ridicule on the platform of Clapham Junction would illustrate this hostile gaze). Wilde's conviction and imprisonment thus forms part of what Edelman terms "this imperative to produce 'homosexual difference' as an object of cognitive and perceptual scrutiny": it is only insofar as he can be made "legible" as homosexual that Wilde can be punished and classified.[33] In Edelman's view, the "liberationist" practice of "coming out"—or, more problematic still, of "outing"—can accede to a demand that homosexuality be "visible" or "legible," a demand that has its origins as part of a punitive regime. Edelman points to "the homophobic insistence upon the social importance of codifying and registering sexual identities" that is very much part of the "disciplinary project" or model outlined by Foucault (*Homographesis*, 4). Registering the "versions of the graphic inscriptions of homosexuality," the gay body becomes marked by its sexuality in a way that conforms to cultural demands of legibility (*Homographesis*, 7). Thus, by constructing "the gay body as text" (*Homographesis*, 6) a homophobic culture confirms its ability to "read" sexual difference as indelibly marked on that body, as an "alien" signifying practice that identifies the body as requiring surveillance and control. Edelman is interested in the way that this construction of homosexual "difference" impinges

Oliver S. Buckton

on the sexual field as a whole, for "once sexuality may be read and interpreted in light of homosexuality, all sexuality is subject to a hermeneutics of suspicion" (*Homographesis*, 7). For Edelman, the construction of "'homosexual difference' as a determinate entity rather than as an unstable differential relation" (*Homographesis*, 3) is a perilous one, authorizing a regime of sexual surveillance and social policing that is homophobic in its effects.

Of course, the film *Wilde* cannot be said to "out" its subject or reveal to its audience anything new in its identification of Wilde as a homosexual.[34] If there is any "fact" about Wilde that the film audience can be presumed to have known, then it is that he was a homosexual. Yet the film, by visualizing Wilde as both a homosexual and a prisoner, reinforces the constructions of the homosexual's body as both visibly recognizable and criminalized, and marked with indelible signs of difference. At the same time as this representation confirms the cultural understanding of homosexuality as a criminal identity, it also reveals the construction of homosexual identity as a kind of prison from which Wilde—who (reluctantly) comes to recognize his desire as part of his nature—tried to escape in vain.

Another way to approach this question is to consider whether the gaze that consumes the spectacle of *Wilde* might be assimilated with the gaze that monitors the prisoner and/or the gaze that identifies and scrutinizes and punishes the homosexual body for signs of its difference. To what extent is the audience complicit with the policing of sexual "difference" in which Wilde was a key figure? I explore this question by examining several scenes from the film in which the gaze of the spectator *of* the film converges with that of spectators *in* the film. To be sure, these are gazes that have very different effects and implications. But they move toward the construction of Wilde as an object defined by his sexuality. These are also points at which the narrative of the film—the telling of Wilde's life story—is arrested and displaced by an aesthetically self-conscious framing of Wilde as subject.

Cinema, as Stephen Heath has argued, operates in a tension between narrative and framing within a signifying practice. Arguing that the spectator adopts a "relation of vision" to the screen, Heath states that the terms of this relation are "those of a *memory*, the constant movement of retention of the individual as subject, framed and narrated" (*Questions of Cinema*, 10; original emphasis). The cinematic image operates as a tension between a "lack" and a "memory" or "retention" of an absent subject. On the one hand, "[i]n its process, its framings, its cuts, its intermittences, the film ceaselessly poses an absence, a lack, which is ceaselessly bound up in and into the relation of the subject, is, as it were, ceaselessly recaptured *for* the film" (*Questions of Cinema,* 13; original emphasis). On the other hand, "from machine to film with its own tie procedures, cinema develops as the apparatus of a formidable memory, the tracing of a subject" (*Questions of Cinema,* 14). Clearly, the visual image of Wilde on the screen cannot disguise the absence or "lack" of the actual person of Oscar Wilde. This absence is indeed emphasized by the narrative of the film, with its ceaseless movement, "its cuts and intermittences." The "framings" of Wilde, which approach or imitate pictorial representation, tend to arrest or decelerate the narrative and create the effect of a presence—of a "memory" that seems to retain Wilde as "subject."[35]

The first scene I discuss is where Wilde appears on stage at the end of the opening night of *Lady Windermere's Fan.* Here Wilde is the object of an admiring gaze, following the success of his play; he is also part of the performance, an actor on the stage who commands the audience's attention as a speaking subject. It is in this respect a scene in which Wilde is in complete command of his audience, speaking back to it with assurance, even arrogance (the cigarette Wilde is smoking adds to this effect). Wilde occupies the position of the subject of the film-as-narrative, achieving mastery of his craft and his audience, attracting admiration from friends and theatergoers, and launching his dramatic career (and hence the film itself) into a new phase. At the same time, he is framed as an object of visual pleasure, with his impeccably dandyish appearance and beautifully tailored suit, as well as his witty speech (fig. 31).[36] Hence he combines the masculine and feminine roles in the film text, a transgression that might be termed a cinematic bisexuality. As Bristow remarks, "[T]he late Victorian dandy . . . is always potentially like a woman, especially where his narcissistic attention to dress is concerned."[37] Bristow also points to the sexual transgression implied by the dandyish "performance": "[I]t is this feminine aspect of the dandy that at times . . . avails him as a figure of homosexual definition in Wilde's writings" and, moreover, "dandiacal femininity, and thus effeminacy, often rivals women for social attention and admiration."

The companion scene to this is where Wilde is called onto stage following the successful opening of *Earnest.* Within the narrative arc of Wilde's career—*Earnest* being the play of Wilde's that enjoyed the most positive critical reception and has since become his most famous work—one might expect an intensification of the effects of the earlier scene. In one respect this is true: the audience ap-

Oliver S. Buckton

Figure 31. Wilde speaks to the audience, while smoking a cigarette, at the end of the premiere of *Lady Windermere's Fan.* From *Wilde* (dir. Brian Gilbert, 1997). Courtesy of Sony Pictures Classics.

plauds more rapturously than before, highlighting the play's success. Yet there are two key differences that underscore Wilde's loss of control. The first is his apparent reluctance to go on stage and face the audience, in contrast to his earlier eagerness to do so. Rather than suggesting false modesty, the hesitancy intimates Wilde's sense of the audience or crowd as a potentially hostile force.[38] The second key difference is that Wilde remains silent on stage; indeed, he is silenced by the unceasing applause of the crowd. He is framed from above, diminishing his stature, and his repeated bows suggest subjection rather than confidence. The effect of the scene is that Wilde is mastered by his audience, rather than controlling them. In contrast to the earlier scene, Wilde offers no witty speech but remains relatively static on the stage, stripped of his role as speaking subject and participant in the performance. Wilde is framed as though already on trial, a prisoner in the dock; and the scene, as a framing, prepares us for the courtroom sequences that follow.

There are two companion scenes from the courtroom sequence that I will here compare as framings of Wilde, with implications for the visual construction of him as a sexualized object. By his presence in the dock, Wilde is already in the process of being fixed as a sign of sexual difference: he has, in a visual as well as a legal and judicial sense, been arrested, his sexuality has passed from an "unstable differential relation" in which his marriage coexists with his same-sex relationships to a "determinate entity," in Edelman's phrase, in which all of Wilde's texts and utterances are imbued with homosexual significance. Required by the court to justify and defend—or alternatively to refute—his own texts' representations of "unnatural" desires, Wilde becomes inescapably textualized by this process. In one scene, Wilde is asked to explain the meaning of "the Love that dare not speak its name," and he does so with reference to "such a great affection of an elder for a younger man as there was between David and Jonathan, such as Plato made the very basis of his philosophy, and such as you find in the sonnets of Michelangelo and Shakespeare. . . . The world mocks at it, and sometimes puts one in the pillory for it." Adducing the Classical origins of such "affection," Wilde here reclaims his status as a man of culture and speaking subject, holding an audience captive with his eloquence and producing "a spontaneous outburst of applause from the public gallery, mingled with some hisses." In framing Wilde's performance, the film constructs continuity between the theater and the courtroom, as the court in effect becomes an extension of the stage on which Wilde captivates the public attention. It is as though Wilde has written the script, so deftly does he absorb the line of questioning into his own discourse of desire ("a deep spiritual affection that is as pure as it is perfect").[39]

Wilde's dramatic control of the courtroom is short-lived, however, as the testimony of numerous male prostitutes who received gifts from Wilde in exchange for sex creates too great a gulf between Wilde's idealized definition of same-sex affection and his actual sexual practices. Under the punitive gaze of the court and legal system, the interrogation presents too formidable a challenge to Wilde's self-image as a Greek lover, and it appropriates him for a discourse of modern perversion. Following his conviction, Wilde is shown subjected to a gaze of incomparably hostile effect, representing in visual terms what Bristow calls "the abuse that Wilde experienced from each and every quarter of English society in 1895."[40] Framed by the crowd as he is led away from court (fig. 32), Wilde is again reduced to silence, but this time by the jeers and abuse of the spectators (the scene also echoes the cheers that greet his arrival in the film's opening scene). His construction as a sexual outcast now complete, Wilde is utterly controlled by the reactions of others, who are empowered by the legal system to dismiss him from the stage of society as a pervert. Although, as Bristow argues, "Wilde knew

Oliver S. Buckton

Figure 32. Wilde being led out of the courtroom. From *Wilde* (dir. Brian Gilbert, 1997).
Courtesy of Sony Pictures Classics.

only too well how the institutions of power in England sought to regulate sexual acts" (16), this knowledge did not translate into power for Wilde. Rather, Wilde is compelled to "confront hostile forces that are indeed impending" and that Wilde anticipated "in plays, novels, and poems" (*Effeminate England,* 20). Two nonverbal—indeed, theatrical—gestures stand out in this scene: the first when a member of the crowd spits in his face, the ultimate signal of contempt; the second when Robbie Ross appears in the crowd and silently raises his hat as Wilde walks by, a countering gesture of respect in which the court's power is contested.

One effect of the renewed public interest in Wilde's life and work generated by *Wilde* may be seen in the adaptation of two of his plays for the cinema. *An Ideal Husband* (1999) and *Earnest* (2002), both directed by Oliver Parker, have brought Wildean drama back into the mainstream cinema. It is perhaps appropriate that it should be the two plays whose success in the West End was terminated by Wilde's arrest that were chosen for adaptation: this choice reinforces the association that I have been exploring between Wilde's stagecraft and his homosexuality, as well as the link between the social construction of Wilde's identity as homosexual and his public role of dramatist. Because of constraints of space, I focus the remainder of this chapter on *Earnest.*

The Importance of Being Earnest

Notwithstanding my discussion of the film *Wilde,* the refashioning of Wilde in contemporary cinema does not uniformly emphasize sexual transgressions in his life and his works. The recent film version of *Earnest* significantly diminishes both the homoerotic overtones of Wilde's play and its suggestion of cross-class relationships. That it does so without making major changes to the script—indeed, while restoring a scene of Wilde's that is often omitted from stage productions—may indicate the power of cinema to remake literary texts into mass cultural products with very different ideological effects. The film removes traces of the connection between the Jack/Algy and Wilde/Bosie relationships that for some readers have suggested that the play alludes covertly to Wilde's homosexual life in the 1890s.[41] The film removes these traces—by, for example, converting Algy into the older of the two men, as well as inserting flashback scenes in which Algy, as a young boy, looks into the pram in which Miss Prism has placed the baby Jack/Ernest. Given Wilde's description of the "Love that dare not speak its name" as occurring between "an elder and a younger man," this change of ages cannot but be significant. This change breaks the symmetry between Jack's earlier pretense of having a younger brother called Ernest and his subsequent discovery that Algernon is in fact his younger sibling: "Algy's elder brother! Then I have a brother after all. I knew I had a brother! I always said I had a brother!" The change is also significant because it modifies the older/younger man relationship that scandalized the Victorian public in Wilde's trials: for while Jack remains the more active character, he has become the younger man. Jack's joke at the end of Wilde's play—"Algy, you young scoundrel, you will have to treat me with more respect in the future"—which reminds us of his status as the older brother, is deleted in the film, the emphasis shifting to the younger brother's search for an elusive identity (*CW,* 6:181).

The most relevant of the film's changes can be seen in the opening act of the play, in which Jack's intimacy with Algy and their shared secret of a double life are developed. The opening scene of the film represents one of its most significant departures from the text of the play: the scene is at night in Victorian London, and a man elegantly attired in formal evening dress is being pursued through the streets by men who appear to be policemen. Knowing of Wilde's scandalous conviction for homosexuality—a key component of the Wilde myth promulgated by *Wilde*—the viewer might anticipate that this character is being pursued

Oliver S. Buckton

Figure 33. Algernon Moncrieff pursued by the law. From *The Importance of Being Earnest* (dir. Oliver Parker, 2002). Courtesy of Miramax Films.

for his sexual transgressions. This man (Algy, as it turns out), however, is being pursued by the law not for sexual offenses, as Wilde was, but for nonpayment of his dining bills (fig. 33). Like the opening of *Wilde*, the opening of *Earnest* plays with our expectations about the Wilde myth, subverting it with a narrative invention that substitutes the relatively innocuous crime of unpaid debts for gross indecency and rescues the film from a potentially scandalous (and noncommercial) theme.

In Wilde's play, the opening dialogue concerning the "private cigarette case" and the secret practice of "Bunburying" takes place in the privacy of Algernon's flat in Half-Moon Street: an appropriately discreet and intimate space for the discussion between the play's two central male characters, with "their life of unnamed pleasures."[42] The revelation that each man has been pursuing a secret existence, using a different fictional persona to further his subterfuge, has dramatic impact because of their withdrawal from society in the seclusion of a bachelor apartment. Only the presence of Lane, the reticent servant, reminds us of the possibility of social judgment, and Lane's reply to Algy's opening question whether he heard what Algy was playing on the piano—"I didn't think it polite to listen, sir" (*CW*, 6:1)—assures us of his complete discretion. Jack's assertion that "it is a very ungentlemanly thing to read a private cigarette case" (*CW*, 6:12) has ironic force because the context of his words is itself private. His apparent fear of incrimination is reflected by the secret surroundings of their discussion.

The film, by contrast, sets the dialogue between Jack and Algy in a cabaret/ nightclub, a blatantly public space in which Algy and Jack have a chance meeting. The camera depicts Algy cheering at the exposed petticoats of the showgirls, and—following Jack's admission that he has come to London for "pleasure, pleasure!"—we see two young women glancing with interest at the men, creating a visual link between Jack's stated motive of pleasure and the sexual pursuit of women.

The ensuing conversation between the two men takes place in the presence of a crowd in the lounge area, members of which respond at key moments to the discourse, and significantly the two men are surrounded by attentive women who laugh at some of their remarks: a context that again emphasizes the heterosexuality of the men and dilutes the homoerotic frissons of their dialogue. Far from being a secret, Algy's and Jack's double life as "Bunburyists" seems to be common knowledge, and they are comfortable with such public familiarity with their private lives. Whereas Jack's motives to "come up to town" are left unspecified in the play (*CW*, 6:7), the film identifies this motive as the company of women. Rather than suggesting unnamed, perhaps unspeakable pleasures (of the kind Wilde and Douglas were enjoying at Alfred Taylor's brothel), the practice of "Bunburying" is identified visually with the typical womanizing of the Victorian man-about-town.[43] In its embrace of heterosexuality, the film omits Algy's misogamist line, "If ever I get married I'll certainly try to forget the fact," as well as his ambiguous assertion that "if you ever get married, which seems to me extremely problematic, you will be very glad to know Bunbury" (*CW*, 6:8, 22).

The focus of this scene is the cigarette case that Algy has found, the inscription in which he quizzes Jack about. This object was an important piece of evidence used to incriminate Wilde, and its criminal implications are suggested by the "large reward" that Jack proposed to offer for it, and that Algy wishes he would offer, when Algy says, "I happen to be more than usually hard up" (*CW*, 6:11).[44] The case from which the film's Algy offers a cigarette to Jack in the club is, of course, Jack's missing possession, as in the play; but rather than being a private object passing between the two men—revealing one man's secrets to the other— this case is publicly displayed and discussed during the club scene. In an inter-

Oliver S. Buckton

Figure 34. Algernon Moncrieff and Jack Worthing smoking cigarettes. From *The Importance of Being Earnest* (dir. Oliver Parker, 2002). Courtesy of Miramax Films.

esting piece of mise-en-scène, both Algy and Jack are smoking cigarettes taken from the case, each of which is lit by a young woman (whose presence in the club is never explained). The cigarette is here portrayed as a token of heterosexual interest and flirtation rather than a sign of illicit homoerotic desire (fig. 34). The cigarette's scandalous connotations—registered when Wilde shocked the audience at the opening of *Lady Windermere's Fan* by smoking during his curtain-call speech—are minimized in the film.[45] For rather than functioning as a metaphor for cross-class mixing and homoerotic intimacy, it is used to introduce the theme of heterosexual desire. In the film, therefore, Wilde's comedy is thus well on the way to its refashioning as a heterosexual comedy of errors rather than a social satire suggestive of same-sex desire and erotic duplicity.[46]

The dramatic impact of Jack and Algy's conversation in the opening scene of the play, with its coded references to homoerotic desire, is further diminished in the film through the fragmented dialogue, thus splitting it between several locations. The dialogue begins in the club, and it continues in the street later that evening, where Jack explains that he has pretended to have a younger brother to escape to London. When Algy charges Jack with being an "advanced Bunburyist," however, the street scene is interrupted by debt collectors again pursuing Algy. There follows a scene between Cecily and Miss Prism at the Manor House (which opens act 2 of *Earnest*), and the explanation of Bunburying is deferred until the next scene, in which Jack visits Algy for tea. Hence, the cumulative impact of Algy and Jack's private discourse—in which an apparently innocent object, a "private cigarette case," leads to the unraveling of an entire alibi for a double life—is lost.

The scenes featuring Algy's pursuit by the police serve another function in terms of the film's refashioning of Wilde's play. They anticipate a later scene at the Manor House in which Algy—masquerading as Ernest to woo Cecily—is threatened with arrest for debt by solicitor Mr. Gribsby. These debts, under the name "Ernest," have of course been run up by Jack under his pseudonym. The scene adds to the confusion of identities and illustrates Jack's fraternal concern when he agrees to pay Ernest's debts.[47] By including the Gribsby episode, therefore, the 2002 film identifies itself with the four-act version, a significant refashioning of the play given the influence of film adaptations on audiences and readers, as well as future productions. Moreover, the film's addition of scenes of Algy's pursuit by the police integrates the Gribsby episode more fully into the structure of the play, by establishing the young men's extravagant and profligate lifestyle. The two central male characters are shown as avid consumers: we witness Algy and Jack as men-about-town, enjoying the extravagant pleasures of upper-class gentlemen, yet we also observe them as they refuse to pay their bills and are pursued by the law. Economic irresponsibility rather than sexual transgression therefore emerges as the besetting vice of the men in the film. Moreover, only while Algy is playing the role of Ernest is the physical intimacy between the men suggested, as they attempt to appear to the company as brothers. In one scene, a mirroring effect is created as the two men, in close physical proximity, argue over who should claim the name of Ernest (fig. 35).

Again, one can read the influence of *De Profundis* into the film treatments of Wilde, as Wilde portrays Bosie as his dark double, repeatedly bemoaning Bosie's expensive tastes, Bosie's unbounded consumption, and the ruinous consequences to Wilde of having to pay for all their pleasures (Wilde apparently forgets that he too consumed these articles).[48] This film adaptation of *Earnest* therefore reflects some of Wilde's most pressing concerns at the time of its composition, situating its characters on the brink of financial ruin. Yet its insistence on bla-

Oliver S. Buckton

Figure 35. Algernon Moncrieff and Jack Worthing mirror each other. From *The Importance of Being Earnest* (dir. Oliver Parker, 2002). Courtesy of Miramax Films.

zoning the heterosexual interests of the central characters again incarcerates the transgressive pleasures of Wilde's dramatic exploration of "the Love that dare not speak its name."

Wilde's Afterlife

The renewal of cinematic interest in Wilde's life and work has helped to maintain and extend Wilde's legacy into the twenty-first century. Particularly in the case of *Wilde*, recent film treatments of the author have contested certain myths and stereotypes about Wilde concerning his effeminacy, his lack of interest in heterosexuality, and the confinement of his activity to an urban, aesthetic milieu. The adaptations of two of Wilde's society comedies, *An Ideal Husband* and *The Importance of Being Earnest*, have arguably introduced Wilde's dramatic work to a new audience of filmgoers and may generate new readers of his oeuvre. Yet despite their play with generic conventions and challenge to certain aspects of the horizon of expectations surrounding Wilde, the films I have discussed eventually reach somewhat conservative conclusions. In the case of *Wilde,* Oscar is constructed (biographically) as always already homosexual, a man whose sexuality was a matter of his essential nature and for which he was (therefore) unjustly punished. Yet by subjecting Wilde to the gaze of the cinema, the film replays the strategic choice to identify and classify Wilde exclusively in terms of his sexuality, making his erotic difference an object of visual knowledge and spectacle. In the case of *Earnest,* the subversive homoerotic significations of the play, which Wilde skillfully encoded in witty dialogue, are all but erased by the assertion of the protagonists' active heterosexuality and extravagance. The inclusion of the Gribsby episode is less significant as a choice of textual variants than as a further screen for the play's sexual dissidence, as the film presents profligacy and philandering as the dangerous vices. Despite the earnest promise of Hollywood to rescue Oscar from misprision, the cultural conventionality of its offerings is closer to the words of Miss Prism in *Earnest:* "The good ended happily, and the bad unhappily. That is what Fiction means."

Notes

1. Neil McKenna, *The Secret Life of Oscar Wilde: An Intimate Biography* (New York: Basic Books, 2005), xi. One might wonder what McKenna means by "most accounts of Oscar's life." Richard Ellmann's 1987 biography *Oscar Wilde* (New York: Knopf, 1987), which has (for better or worse) become established as the definitive account of Wilde's life, suggests that Wilde was always already homosexual. Indeed, McKenna's claim that "little has been written about Oscar's sexuality and his sexual behavior" (xi) seems bizarre, given the recent outpouring of work on just this subject.

2. Oscar Wilde, *The Complete Letters,* ed. Merlin Holland and Rupert Hart-Davis (New York: Henry Holt, 2000), 656, 657; further page references appear in parentheses.

3. For a detailed discussion of these two films and the role of the trial transcripts in their representations of Oscar Wilde, see chapter 9 of the present volume.

4. In Britain, the most significant legal change came with the Sexual Offences Act (1967), which partly decriminalized male homosexual activity between consenting adults over the age of twenty-one.

5. Michel Foucault, *The History of Sexuality,* vol. 1, *An Introduction* (New York: Vintage, 1980), 43.

6. Joseph Bristow, *Effeminate England: Homoerotic Writing after 1885* (New York: Columbia University Press, 1995), 18 (emphasis added).

7. Alan Sinfield, *The Wilde Century: Effeminacy, Oscar Wilde and the Queer Moment* (New York: Columbia University Press, 1994), 78, 18.

8. Ed Cohen, *Talk on the Wilde Side: Toward a Genealogy of a Discourse on Male Sexualities* (New York: Routledge, 1993), 131.

9. Quoted in Cohen, *Talk on the Wilde Side,* 141.

10. See Wilde to Lord Alfred Douglas, in *Complete Letters,* 703. Holland and Hart-Davis date this letter as January–March 1897. This letter is the text of the work that was known from 1905 onward as *De Profundis.*

11. Quoted in Bristow, *Effeminate England,* 29.

12. McKenna, *Secret Life of Oscar Wilde,* 382.

13. Roland Barthes, "The Death of the Author," *Image Music Text,* essays selected and translated by Stephen Heath (New York: Hill and Wang, 1977), 145; further page references appear in parentheses.

14. Stephen Heath, *Questions of Cinema* (London: Macmillan, 1981), 1 (original emphasis); further page references appear in parentheses.

15. *Wilde* Web site, http://www.oscarwilde.com.

16. Quoted in John Pym, ed., *Time Out Film Guide,* 8th ed. (Harmondsworth: Penguin, 2000), 1167.

17. For a discussion of how the two 1960 films about Wilde reflect a growing cinematic fascination with Wilde as a courtroom spectacle, see chapter 9 in the present volume. The contemporary movie industry in some ways resembles the literary culture of Wilde's period, as Josephine M. Guy and Ian Small describe it: "Wilde's writing and publishing practices also confirm the suspicion that the late nineteenth-century literary market was ruthlessly competitive and commercial, and that professional writers who need to earn a living with their pen were in no place to resist or even contest those values." Guy and Small, *Oscar Wilde's Profession: Writing and the Culture Industry in the Late Nineteenth Century* (Oxford: Oxford University Press, 2000), 10.

18. Marc Samuelson, in "Still Wild about Wilde," included in Special Features, *Wilde,* directed by Brian Gilbert, DVD Special Edition, Sony Pictures Classics, 1997.

19. Samuelson, "Still Wild about Wilde."

20. E. M. Forster, *Maurice* (New York: Norton, 1971), 159.

21. In this regard, it continues a penchant for the notorious lives and scandalous deaths of British gay playwrights that we saw a decade earlier with *Prick Up Your Ears,* the 1987 Stephen Frears film (based on John Lahr's biography of Joe Orton), which dwelt on the tragic (and ultimately fatal) relationship of Orton and his lover Kenneth Halliwell. In both cases, the playwright's scandalous homosexuality provides the "subject" of the film, with its (inevitable) culmination in tragedy.

22. Guy and Small, *Oscar Wilde's Profession,* 14; further page reference appears in parentheses.

23. Ellen Moers, *The Dandy: Brummell to Beerbohm* (Lincoln: University of Nebraska Press, 1978), 295; further page reference appears in parentheses.

24. Hans Robert Jauss, "Literary History as a Challenge to Literary Theory," *The Norton Anthology of Theory and Criticism,* ed. Vincent B. Leitch (New York: Norton, 2001), 1556. Jauss writes that "the horizon of expectations of a work allows one to determine its artistic character by the kind and the degree of its influence on a presupposed audience" (1550–64). Interestingly, Jauss remarks that the "disparity between the given horizon of expectations and the appearance of a new work" may result in "a 'change of horizons' through negation of familiar experiences" (1556).

25. Wilde served as the editor of this largely feminist journal, 1887–89.

26. For a recent cinematic deconstruction of the homosexual dimension of the cowboy and the American West, I would cite Ang Lee's 2005 *Brokeback Mountain,* adapted from Annie Proulx's story of the same name.

27. Aubrey Beardsley (1872–1898) was an influential late-Victorian illustrator and writer whose work became significant in the Decadent Movement. Among Beardsley's most famous

work are his illustrations for the first English edition of Wilde's play *Salome* (London: Elkin Mathews and John Lane, 1894).

28. My transcription of comments that appear in "Still Wild about Wilde." With regard to the narrative structure of *Wilde,* Gilbert's comments are interesting because they allege its simplicity: "I was happy to return to a fairly simple, straightforward, let's say, telling of the story, given that the complexities of the material are sufficient" ("Still Wild about Wilde").

29. Costume designer Nic Ede identified this scene as his favorite from the film, because all of the costumes and details were "period" ("Still Wild about Wilde").

30. Stephen Fry, "Still Wild about Wilde."

31. For a persuasive argument for the homosexual and sodomitic valence of "Bunburying," see Christopher Craft, "Alias Bunbury: Desire and Termination in *The Importance of Being Earnest*," *Representations* 31 (1990): 19–46.

32. Michel Foucault, *Discipline and Punish: The Birth of the Prison,* trans. Alan Sheridan (New York: Vintage, 1979), 187 (Foucault's study first appeared in French in 1975); further page references appear in parentheses.

33. Lee Edelman, *Homographesis: Essays in Gay Literary and Cultural Theory* (New York: Routledge, 1994), 4; further page references appear in parentheses.

34. Brian Gilbert stated that his intention, somewhat paradoxically, was "not to make sexuality the focus, but it is a very important part of the story" ("Still Wild about Wilde").

35. Heath points to the correlation between the "frame" in pictorial representation and the "frame" as a unit of film, the single transparent image that, projected at a certain speed, produces the illusion of movement. Yet, Heath argues, "film destroys the ordinary laws of pictorial composition because of its moving human figures which capture attention against all else" (*Questions of Cinema,* 10). Nevertheless, at certain key points in the film, Wilde is "framed" in a way that does invite reflection and allows the spectator to contemplate his or her own relation to the image.

36. For the spectator of the film, Wilde is, moreover, an object of visual pleasure, in Laura Mulvey's terms, in that at this moment of triumph he occupies a heroic position with which the spectator would like to identify. Mulvey points out that the spectator seeks identification with an idealized representation on the screen, a character who is able to influence the course of the action and drives the narrative. Such characters, for Mulvey, are usually male and provide a point of identification for the male and female spectator—but the latter must identify "against herself." Yet in other regards, Wilde occupies the position ascribed to the female figure, an object of visual pleasure that tends to arrest the progress of the narrative, providing a point of stasis in which the desirable object may be the focus of the spectator's gaze. In other words, the tension between narrative and framing that produces cinema is recoded by Mulvey in terms of gender, with the male character chiefly driving the narrative, while the female is framed as an object of visual pleasure. See Laura Mulvey, *Visual and Other Pleasures* (Bloomington: Indiana University Press, 1989), especially chapter 3, "Visual Pleasure and Narrative Cinema" (14–26).

37. Bristow, *Effeminate England,* 40; the later quotation appears on the same page.

38. The hostile potential of the audience is indicated by the earlier scenes of the sequence, portraying Queensberry's thwarted attempt to enter the St James's Theatre and cause a scandal by hurling vegetables at the actors.

39. The quotation of "[t]he Love that dare not speak its name" is from Lord Alfred Douglas's poem "Two Loves," in Karl Beckson, ed., *Aesthetes and Decadents of the 1890s: An Anthology of British Poetry and Prose* (Chicago: Academy Editions, 1981), 82. In the film, Wilde (Fry) reads the lines from a transcript of the trials; compare H. Montgomery Hyde, *The Trials of Oscar Wilde,* 2nd ed. (1962; repr., New York: Dover, 1973), 201.

40. Bristow, *Effeminate England,* 23; further page references appear in parentheses.

41. Brian Gilbert, the director of *Wilde,* comments that "for all its zany, brittle comedy, *Earnest* is really quite autobiographical" ("Still Wild about Wilde").

42. Bristow, *Effeminate England,* 30.

43. Bristow remarks on the "wider anxieties about the social and moral standards set by the theater as a whole" and notes that "the musical-halls had gained greatest notoriety in the mid-1890s for allowing an undesirable traffic between respectable and unrespectable types" (*Effeminate England,* 30). This notoriety, however, would primarily be ascribed to the presence of female prostitutes.

44. The *Oxford English Dictionary* (*OED*) defines *hard up* as "in want, esp. of money." However, a colloquial meaning of *hard-up* is "tobacco from cigarette-ends, etc.," which would continue the cigarette theme, that is, Algy is too impoverished to buy his own cigarettes.

45. For an interesting discussion of the cigarette's significance in Wilde's *Dorian Gray* and on the opening night of *Lady Windermere's Fan,* see Bristow, *Effeminate England,* 29–30.

46. As Bristow remarks, "Timothy d'Arch Smith has pointed out how 'earnest' served as a codeword for homosexual among the 'Uranian' poets who belonged to the subculture in which Wilde moved" (*Effeminate England,* 28). Bristow argues that in *Earnest,* Wilde was seeking "a form that could articulate, as legitimately as possible, same-sex desire" (28).

47. The so-called Gribsby episode has an interesting publishing history. It was included in the original four-act version of *Earnest* submitted by Wilde to George Alexander at the St. James's Theatre. When Leonard Smithers published *Earnest* in 1899, the three-act version—without the Gribsby episode—was the one that was chosen and formed the basis for most editions and productions in the twentieth century. The 1952 film version, directed by Anthony Asquith, follows the three-act version and does not contain the Gribsby episode. However, in 1987, an edition of the four-act version was published. Moreover, a 1989 edition of *The Complete Works of Oscar Wilde* contains the four-act version, justified by Vyvyan Holland on the grounds that "it seems a pity that George Alexander should have a permanent influence on the play." *The Complete Works of Oscar Wilde,* ed. Vyvyan Holland (New York: HarperCollins, 1989), 13.

48. See, for example, Wilde to Alfred Douglas, [January–March 1897,] *Complete Letters,* 688 (published by Ross as *De Profundis*).

Select Bibliography

Ackroyd, Peter. *The Last Testament of Oscar Wilde.* New York: Harper and Row, 1983.

Bartlett, Neil. *In Extremis.* London: Oberon, 2000.

———. *Who Was That Man? A Present for Mr. Oscar Wilde.* London: Serpent's Tail, 1988.

Beckson, Karl, ed. *Oscar Wilde: The Critical Heritage.* London: Routledge and Kegan Paul, 1970.

———. *The Oscar Wilde Encyclopedia.* New York: AMS Press, 1998.

Bentley, Eric. *Lord Alfred's Lover.* Toronto: Personal Library, 1981.

Borland, Maureen. *Wilde's Devoted Friend: A Life of Robert Ross, 1869–1918.* Oxford: Lennard, 1990.

Bristow, Joseph. *Effeminate England: Homoerotic Writing after 1885.* New York: Columbia University Press, 1995.

———, ed. *Wilde Writings: Contextual Conditions.* Toronto: University of Toronto Press, 2003.

Cahun, Claude. *Écrits.* Edited by François Leperlier. Paris: Jean Michel Place, 2002.

Cohen, Ed. *Talk on the Wilde Side: Toward a Genealogy of a Discourse on Male Sexualities.* New York: Routledge, 1993.

Cook, Matt. *London and the Culture of Homosexuality, 1885–1914.* Cambridge: Cambridge University Press, 2003.

Davray, Henry-D. *Oscar Wilde: Là tragédie finale—suivi de épisodes et souvenirs et des apocryphes.* Paris: Mercure de France, 1928.

Dollimore, Jonathan. *Sexual Dissidence: Augustine to Wilde, Freud to Foucault.* Oxford, UK: Clarendon Press, 1991.

Douglas, Alfred. *Autobiography.* London: Martin Secker, 1931.

———. *Oscar Wilde: A Summing-Up.* London: Duckworth, 1940.

———. *Oscar Wilde and Myself.* London: John Long, 1914.

———. "Une introduction à mes poèmes, avec quelques considérations sur l'affaire Oscar Wilde." *La revue blanche,* 1 June 1896, 484–90.

———. *Without Apology.* London: Martin Secker, 1938.

Dowling, Linda. *Hellenism and Homosexuality in Victorian Oxford.* Ithaca, NY: Cornell University Press, 1994.

Downie, Louise, ed. *Don't Kiss Me: The Art of Claude Cahun and Marcel Moore.* London: Tate Publishing, in association with the Jersey Heritage Trust, 2006.

Eagleton, Terry. *Saint Oscar.* Derry, UK: Field Day, 1989.

Edwards, Louis. *Oscar Wilde Discovers America.* New York: Scribner, 2003.

Ellmann, Richard. *Oscar Wilde.* London: Hamish Hamilton, 1987; New York: Knopf, 1988.

Eltis, Sos. *Revising Wilde: Society and Subversion in the Plays of Oscar Wilde.* Oxford, UK: Clarendon Press, 1996.

Foldy, Michael. *The Trials of Oscar Wilde: Deviance, Morality and Late Victorian Society.* New Haven, CT: Yale University Press, 1997.

Fryer, Jonathan. *André and Oscar: Gide, Wilde, and the Gay Art of Living.* London: Constable, 1997.

———. *Robbie Ross: Oscar Wilde's Devoted Friend.* New York: Carroll and Graf, 2000.

Gagnier, Regenia. *Idylls of the Marketplace: Oscar Wilde and the Victorian Public.* Stanford: Stanford University Press, 1986.

Gaines, Jane. *Contested Culture: The Image, the Voice, and the Law.* Chapel Hill: University of North Carolina Press, 1991.

Gide, André. *Oscar Wilde: A Study.* Translated by Stuart Mason [Christopher Sclater Millard]. Oxford, UK: Holywell Press, 1905.

Guy, Josephine M, and Ian Small. *Oscar Wilde's Profession: Writing and the Culture Industry in the Late Nineteenth Century.* Oxford: Oxford University Press, 2000.

Hare, David. *The Judas Kiss.* New York: Grove Press, 1998.

Harris, Frank. *Mr. and Mrs. Daventry: A Play in Four Acts, Based on a Scenario by Oscar Wilde.* London: Richards Press, 1956.

Hoare, Philip. *Oscar Wilde's Last Stand: Decadence, Conspiracy, and the Most Outrageous Trial of the Century.* London: Duckworth, 1997.

Holland, Merlin. *Coffee with Oscar Wilde.* London: Duncan Baird, 2007.

———, ed. *Irish Peacock and Scarlet Marquess: The Real Trial of Oscar Wilde.* London: Fourth Estate, 2003.

———. *The Wilde Album.* London: Fourth Estate, 1997.

Housman, Laurence. *Echo de Paris: A Study from Life.* London: Jonathan Cape, 1923.

Hyde, H. Montgomery. *Christopher Sclater Millard: Bibliographer and Antiquarian Book Dealer.* New York: Global Academic, 1990.

———. *The Trials of Oscar Wilde.* Second edition. New York: Penguin, 1962.

Jarman, Derek. *At Your Own Risk: A Saint's Testimony.* London: Vintage, 1992.

———. *Dancing Ledge.* London: Quartet, 1991.

———. *Modern Nature.* London: Vintage, 1991.

———. *Smiling in Slow Motion.* Edited by Keith Collins. London: Century, 2000.

Kaufman, Moisés. *Gross Indecency: The Three Trials of Oscar Wilde.* New York: Dramatists Play Service, 1999.

Kettle, Michael. *Salome's Last Veil: The Libel Case of the Century.* London: Hart-Davis, MacGibbon, and Granada, 1977.

Kingston, Angela. *Oscar Wilde as a Character in Fiction.* New York: Palgrave Macmillan, 2007.

Kohlmayer, Rainer. *Oscar Wilde in Deutschland und Österreich.* Tübingen: Max Niemeyer, 1996.

Lemonnier, Léon. *La vie d'Oscar Wilde.* Paris: Éditions de la Nouvelle Revue Critique, 1931.

Lewis, Lloyd, and Henry Justin Smith. *Oscar Wilde Discovers America.* New York: Harcourt, Brace, 1936.

Lounsbery, G. Constant. *The Picture of Dorian Gray: A Play.* London: Simpkin, Marshall, 1913.

MacLiammóir, Micheál. *The Importance of Being Oscar.* Gerrards Cross, UK: Colin Smythe, 1995.

Mahaffey, Vicki. *States of Desire: Wilde, Yeats, Joyce and the Irish Experiment.* Oxford: Oxford University Press, 1998.

Mahon, Derek. *The Yellow Book.* Oldcastle, Ireland: Gallery Press, 1997.

Marowitz, Charles. *Wilde West.* New York: Dramatists Play Service, 1988.

Mason, Stuart [Christopher Sclater Millard]. *Bibliography of Oscar Wilde.* London: T. Werner Laurie, 1914.

————. *Oscar Wilde: Art and Morality—A Defence of* The Picture of Dorian Gray. London: J. Jacobs, 1908.

————. *Oscar Wilde: Three Times Tried.* Famous Old Bailey Trials of the XIX Century. London: Ferrestone Press, 1912.

McCormack, Jerusha, ed. *Wilde the Irishman.* New Haven, CT: Yale University Press, 1998.

McKenna, Neil. *The Secret Life of Oscar Wilde.* London: Century, 2003.

Meyerfeld, Max. "Oscar Wilde in Deutschland." *Das litterarische Echo* 5 (1903): 458–62.

Mikhail, E. H., ed. *Oscar Wilde: Interviews and Recollections.* 2 volumes. Basingstoke: Macmillan, 1979.

Mirbeau, Octave. *Diary of a Chambermaid.* Translated by Anonymous. New York: Harper Perennial, 2006.

————. *Sebastien Roch.* Translated by Nicoletta Simborowski. London: Dedalus, 2000.

Nelson, James G. *The Early Nineties: A View from the Bodley Head.* Cambridge, MA: Harvard University Press, 1971.

————. *Publisher to the Decadents: Leonard Smithers in the Careers of Beardsley, Wilde, Dowson.* University Park: Pennsylvania State University Press, 2000.

Page, Norman. *An Oscar Wilde Chronology.* Basingstoke, UK: Macmillan, 1991.

Pennington, Michael. *An Angel for a Martyr: Jacob Epstein's Tomb for Oscar Wilde.* Reading, UK: Whiteknights Press, 1987.

Powell, Kerry. *Oscar Wilde and the Theatre of the 1890s.* Cambridge: Cambridge University Press, 1990.

Proust, Marcel. *Sodom and Gomorrah.* Translated by John Sturrock. New York: Penguin, 2002.

Raby, Peter, ed. *The Cambridge Companion to Oscar Wilde.* Cambridge: Cambridge University Press, 1997.

Reed, Jeremy. *Dorian.* London: Peter Owen, 1997.

Ricketts, Charles. *Oscar Wilde: Recollections.* London: Nonesuch Press, 1932.

Roden, Frederick S., ed. *Palgrave Advances in Oscar Wilde Studies.* Basingstoke, UK: Palgrave, 2004.

Ross, Margery, ed. *Robert Ross, Friend of Friends: Letters to Robert Ross, Art Critic and Writer, Together with Extracts from His Published Articles.* London: Jonathan Cape, 1952.

Sako, Tomako, and Lionel Lambourne, eds. *The Wilde Years: Oscar Wilde and the Art of His Time.* London: Barbican Center and Philip Wilson Publishers, 2000.

Satterthwaite, Walter. *Wilde West.* London: HarperCollins, 1992.

Savage, Jon. *Teenage: The Creation of Youth Culture.* London: Chatto and Windus, 2007.

Schroeder, Horst. *Additions and Corrections to Richard Ellmann's* Oscar Wilde. Second edition. Braunschweig: Privately printed, 2002.

Self, Will. *Dorian.* London: Viking, 2002.

Sherard, Robert Harborough. *Bernard Shaw, Frank Harris, and Oscar Wilde.* London: T. Werner Laurie, 1937.

————. *The Life of Oscar Wilde.* London: T. Werner Laurie, 1906.

————. *Oscar Wilde: The Story of an Unhappy Friendship.* London: Hermes, 1902.

————. *The Real Oscar Wilde.* London: T. Werner Laurie, 1915.

Sinfield, Alan. *Cultural Politics—Queer Reading.* Philadelphia: University of Pennsylvania Press, 1994.

————. *The Wilde Century: Effeminacy, Oscar Wilde, and the Queer Moment.* London: Cassell, 1994.

Smith, Hester Travers. *Psychic Messages from Oscar Wilde.* London: T. Werner Laurie, 1924.

Stetz, Margaret D. "The Bi-Social Oscar Wilde and 'Modern' Women." *Nineteenth-Century Literature* 55 (2001): 515–37.

———. "Oscar Wilde at the Movies: British Sexual Politics and *The Green Carnation.*" *Biography* 23 (2000): 90–107.

Stokes, John. *Oscar Wilde: Myths, Miracles, and Imitations.* Cambridge: Cambridge University Press, 1996.

Stokes, Leslie, and Sewell Stokes, *Oscar Wilde.* New York: Random House, 1938.

Stoppard, Tom. *The Invention of Love.* New York: Grove Press, 1997.

Stuart-Young, J. M. *The Antinomian: An Elegiac Poem and a Prose Trifle—In Memory of Sebastian Melmoth.* London: Hermes Press, 1909.

———. *Osrac the Self-Sufficient and Other Poems, with a Memoir of the Late Oscar Wilde.* London: Hermes Press, 1905.

———. *Out of Hours: Poems, Lyrics, and Sonnets.* London: Arthur Stockwell, 1909.

Tainitch, Robert Tainitch. *Oscar Wilde on Stage and Screen.* London: Methuen, 1999.

Tydeman, William, and Steven Price. *Wilde: Salome.* Cambridge: Cambridge University Press, 1996.

Viereck, George Sylvester. "Is Oscar Wilde Living or Dead?" *Critic* (New York), July 1905, 87–89.

Von Hofmannsthal, Hugo. "Sebastian Melmoth." *Selected Prose.* Translated by Mary Hottinger and Tania and James Stern. New York: Pantheon Books, 1952.

Weeks, Jeffrey. *Coming Out: Homosexual Politics in Great Britain from the Nineteenth Century to the Present.* Second edition. London: Quartet Books, 1990.

Wilde, Oscar. *Collected Works.* Edited by Robert Ross. 14 volumes. London: Methuen, 1908.

———. *The Complete Letters of Oscar Wilde.* Edited by Merlin Holland and Rupert Hart-Davis. London: Fourth Estate, 2000.

———. *Criticism: Historical Criticism, Intentions, The Soul of Man.* Edited by Josephine M. Guy. The Complete Works of Oscar Wilde. Oxford: Oxford University Press, 2007.

———. *De Profundis: "Epistola: In Carcere et Vinculis."* Edited by Ian Small. The Complete Works of Oscar Wilde. Oxford: Oxford University Press, 2005.

———. *Letters.* Edited by Rupert Hart-Davis. London: Rupert Hart-Davis, 1962.

———. *Oscar Wilde's Oxford Notebooks: A Portrait of a Mind in the Making.* Edited by Philip E. Smith II and Michael S. Helfand. Oxford: Oxford University Press, 1989.

———. *The Picture of Dorian Gray.* Edited by Joseph Bristow. The Complete Works of Oscar Wilde. Oxford: Oxford University Press, 2005.

———. *Poems and Poems in Prose.* Edited by Karl Beckson and Bobby Fong. The Complete Works of Oscar Wilde. Oxford: Oxford University Press, 2000.

———. *The Portrait of Mr. W.H. as Written by Oscar Wilde Sometime after the Publication of His Essay, of the Same Title, and Now First Printed from the Original Enlarged Manuscript which for Twenty-Six Years Has Been Lost to the World.* New York: Mitchell Kennerley, 1921.

———. *Salome.* Translated by Alfred Douglas. 1894; facsimile reprint, New York: Dover, 1967.

———. *The Soul of Man under Socialism and Selected Critical Prose.* Edited by Linda Dowling. Harmondsworth, UK: Penguin, 2002.

Wintermans, Caspar. *Alfred Douglas: A Poet's Life and His Finest Work.* London: Peter Owen, 2007.

Woodcock, George. *The Paradox of Oscar Wilde.* London: T. V. Boardman, 1949.

Contributors

Laurel Brake is professor emerita at Birkbeck, University of London, and director of the Nineteenth-Century Serials Edition (http://www.ncse.ac.uk). Her books include *Subjugated Knowledges* (Basingstoke, UK: Macmillan, 1994) and *Print in Transition* (Basingstoke, UK: Palgrave, 2001), both on the Victorian press, and *Walter Pater* (Plymouth, UK: Northcote House, 1994). Her research interests lie in gender and nineteenth-century print culture, especially the press, the history of the book, and Walter Pater. She is currently co-editing, with Marysa Demoor, *Dictionary of Nineteenth-Century Journalism* (Gent and London: Academia and British Library, 2008). A biography of Walter Pater is to follow. Recent articles include "Vernon Lee and the Pater Circle" and "Maga, the Shilling Monthlies, and the New Journalism."

Joseph Bristow is a professor of English at the University of California, Los Angeles, where he edited the journal *Nineteenth-Century Literature* from 1997 to 2007. His recent books include *Wilde Writings: Contextual Conditions* (University of Toronto Press, 2003) and *The Fin-de-Siècle Poem: English Literary Culture and the 1890s* (Ohio University Press, 2005). He has edited both the Oxford English Texts edition and the World's Classics edition of Wilde's *Picture of Dorian Gray* (Oxford University Press, 2005 and 2006). He is also series editor of Palgrave Studies in Nineteenth-Century Writing and Culture.

Oliver S. Buckton is a professor of English at Florida Atlantic University, Boca Raton, where he teaches Victorian literature, critical theory, and film. He is the author of *Cruising with Robert Louis Stevenson: Travel, Narrative, and the Colonial Body* (Ohio University Press, 2007) and *Secret Selves: Confession and Same-Sex Desire in Victorian Autobiography* (University of North Carolina Press, 1998) and has published essays on Charles Dickens, John Henry Newman, Oscar Wilde, and Olive Schreiner. His chapter in this volume is part of a larger project on the diverse representations of Oscar Wilde in popular culture.

Matt Cook is a senior lecturer in history at Birkbeck College, University of London. He is the author of *London and the Culture of Homosexuality, 1885–1914* (Cambridge University Press, 2003) and editor of *A Gay History of Britain: Love and Sex between Men since the Middle Ages* (Greenwood World Publishing, 2007).

Francesca Coppa is an associate professor of English and the director of film studies at Muhlenberg College, Pennsylvania, where she teaches twentieth-century dramatic literature, sexuality theory, and performance studies. She is the editor of Joe Orton's early works as well as a collection of critical essays on his plays, and she has written numerous articles on Oscar Wilde, including the chapter on performance in Frederick S. Roden, ed., *Palgrave Advances in Oscar Wilde Studies* (Palgrave Macmillan, 2004).

Erin Williams Hyman held a Mellon postdoctoral fellowship in the Society for the Humanities at Cornell University in 2006–7. Her articles on fin-de-siècle topics such as the New Woman novel, French symbolist art criticism, and anarchism in avant-garde theater have appeared in the journals *ELT, French Forum,* and *Comparatist.* She is currently working on a book project entitled "Terror and the Failure of Words: Anarchism, Symbolist Aesthetics, and the Landscape of Modernity."

Yvonne Ivory is an assistant professor of German and comparative literature at the University of South Carolina, Columbia. Her research interests revolve around the history of sexuality, with her most recent project, "The Homosexual Revival of Renaissance Style," examining how late-nineteenth-century British and German sexual dissidents deployed redemptory discourses of Renaissance self-fashioning. Her publications include articles on Oscar Wilde's reception of the Italian Renaissance and Stefan George's rejection of Paterian aestheticism.

Richard A. Kaye is an associate professor of English at Hunter College and the Graduate Center of the City University of New York. He is the author of *The Flirt's Tragedy: Desire without End in Victorian and Edwardian Fiction* (University Press of Virginia, 2002) and *"Voluptuous Immobility": St. Sebastian and the Decadent Imagination* (Columbia University Press, forthcoming). His essays have appeared in *Victorian Literature and Culture, Modernism/Modernity, Studies in English Literature, Modern Fiction Studies, College Literature,* and *Arizona Quarterly.* His essay on late-Victorian sexual theory appears in Gail Marshall, ed., *The Cambridge Companion to the Fin de Siècle* (Cambridge University Press, 2007).

Lucy McDiarmid is the Marie Frazee-Baldassarre Professor of English at Montclair State University. Her most recent book is *The Irish Art of Controversy* (Cornell University Press and Lilliput Press, 2005). In 2005–6 she was a fellow of the Cullman Center for Scholars and Writers at the New York Public Library. She is also a former Guggenheim fellow. Her other books include *Auden's Apologies for Poetry* (Princeton University Press, 1990) and *Saving Civilization: Yeats, Eliot and Auden between the Wars* (Cambridge University Press, 1984); she coedited *Lady Gregory: Selected Writings* (Penguin, 1995) and *High and Low Moderns: Literature and Culture 1889–1939* (Oxford University Press, 1996). She has also been visiting professor of English at Princeton University, Segal Visiting Professor of Irish Literature at Northwestern University, and the first Cloud Visiting Professor of English at the College of William and Mary.

Leslie J. Moran is a professor of law at Birkbeck College, University of London. He has published widely in areas relating to sexuality and law, including *Sexuality Identity and Law* (Ashgate, 2006), *Sexuality and the Politics of Violence and Safety* (written with Beverley Skeggs; Routledge, 2004), *Legal Queeries: Lesbian, Gay, and Transgender Legal Studies* (New York: Continuum, 1998), *Legal Perversions* (a special edition of *Social and Legal Studies,* 1997), and *The Homosexual(ity) of Law* (Routledge, 1996). He has also published work on hate crime (as in *Critical Reflections on Hate Crime,* a 2001 special edition of *Law and Critique*) and in the area of law and culture. He jointly edited *Law's Moving Image* (Routledge Cavendish, 2004), which focuses on law and film. His current research is on the sexual diversity of the judiciary, which includes a study of judicial biography and an analysis of representations of the judiciary in film and television. He also continues his inquiries into the law of Oscar Wilde.

Daniel A. Novak is an assistant professor of English at Louisiana State University. His study *Realism, Photography, and Nineteenth-Century Fiction* was published by Cambridge University Press in 2008. He is currently working on a book manuscript focusing on the beginning of Wilde studies as a field, as well as a book on Victorian literature on the Cagots —an ethnic group of unknown origin, unclear history, and ambiguous race found in France and Spain.

Lizzie Thynne is a filmmaker and senior lecturer in media and film at Sussex University, England. She has published on practice as research, women's employment in television, and queer representation. She has made award-winning films for television and gallery exhibition; she completed a documentary about Claude Cahun and Marcel Moore, *Playing a Part,* in 2004.

Julie Townsend is an associate professor of interdisciplinary humanities in the Johnston Center for Integrative Studies at the University of Redlands, California. Her article "Synaesthetics: Symbolism, Dance, and the Failure of Metaphor" appeared in the *Yale Journal of Criticism* in 2005, and she is currently preparing a book-length manuscript on the figure of the dancer in French literature.

Index